Heaven on Earth

Heaven on Earth

Reimagining Time and
Eternity in Nineteenth-Century
British Evangelicalism

Martin Spence

Foreword by
David W. Bebbington

PICKWICK Publications • Eugene, Oregon

HEAVEN ON EARTH
Reimagining Time and Eternity in Nineteenth-Century British Evangelicalism

Copyright © 2015 Martin Spence. All rights reserved. Except for brief quotations in critical publications or reviews, no part of this book may be reproduced in any manner without prior written permission from the publisher. Write: Permissions. Wipf and Stock Publishers, 199 W. 8th Ave., Suite 3, Eugene, OR 97401.

Pickwick Publications
An Imprint of Wipf and Stock Publishers
199 W. 8th Ave., Suite 3
Eugene, OR 97401

www.wipfandstock.com

ISBN 13: 978-1-62032-259-8

Cataloguing-in-Publication Data

Spence, Martin

Heaven on earth : reimagining time and eternity in nineteenth-century British evangelicalism / Martin Spence, with a foreword by David W. Bebbington

xvi + 308 p. ; 23 cm. Includes bibliographical references.

ISBN 13: 978-1-62032-259-8

1. Eschatology—History of doctrines—19th century. 2. Millennium (Eschatology). I. Bebbington, D. W. (David William), 1949–. II. Title.

BT891 S724 2015

Manufactured in the U.S.A.

To Molly, with great affection.

Table of Contents

Foreword by David W. Bebbington | ix
Acknowledgements | xiii
Abbreviations | xv

Introduction | 1
1 Evangelicalism's Eternal Vision | 9
2 Eschatology and the Evangelical Imagination | 31
3 The Romance of History | 74
4 The Renewal of Time and Space | 100
5 Premillennialism and "The Age of Incarnation" | 146
6 Prophecy and Policy | 204
7 The Afterlife of Mid-Nineteenth-Century Evangelical Eschatology | 250

Bibliography | 269
Index | 299

Foreword

"Premillennialism," according to David Brown, "is no barren speculation—useless though true, and innocuous though false." Brown, the most capable critic of premillennial teaching in the mid-nineteenth century, was recognizing its power. This form of prophetic theorizing, he went on, virtually constructs "a whole world of its own."[1] What might seem to subsequent generations an obscurantist preoccupation was in the mid-nineteenth century an enormously influential way of thinking that colored all the opinions of its advocates and molded their priorities for action. Premillennialists upheld the view that the second coming of Christ was to be expected before a millennium of peace and prosperity on earth. The specific form of premillennialism that was dominant in the early Victorian years has been labelled "historicist" because it held that the book of Revelation predicted the historical events of the Christian era. Historicist premillennialism is the subject of this book.

The phenomenon is diagnosed as an expression of Romanticism in religion. The early nineteenth century was marked by the spread of views associated with the Romantic revolution in values that challenged the intellectual hegemony of the Enlightenment. The blending of Romantic taste with Evangelicalism generated historicist premillennialism. Evangelicals swayed by the Enlightenment had commonly adopted a postmillennial view of the future. The second coming, on this view, would not take place until after the millennium. Postmillennialists looked soberly at the course of world events, supposing the Almighty operated by regular methods, so that nothing unusual, nothing beyond the bounds of "enlightened Christian sagacity," was to be expected in the near future. But others, touched by the Romantic temper, were inspired (Brown wrote) by "the force of intuitive perception" so that when they encountered the historicist premillennial

---

1. David Brown, *Christ's Second Coming: Will It Be Premillennial?* 3rd edn (Edinburgh: Johnstone & Hunter, 1853), 8.

perspective "they *feel*—they *know* it to be true."[2] Such ardent souls took a passionate interest in time, looking around them for confirmation of their paradigm. They became dedicated students of prophecy.

The historicists should not, however, be confused with futurist premillennialists. Futurists, so-called because they believed that the bulk of scriptural prophecies were to be fulfilled in the future, existed in the early Victorian period, but at the time in much smaller numbers. Their chief exponent, J. N. Darby, invented the system of dispensationalism that the historicists rejected. But in later years dispensationalists were to outpace their rivals and their scheme became immensely influential among Fundamentalists. It is a central contention here that historians have previously underestimated the difference between historicists and dispensationalists, so attributing something of the backward-looking, world-rejecting stance of Darby's followers to the mid-nineteenth-century premillennialists. Far from being arch-conservatives, the historicists held broad views showing affinities with those of contemporary liberal theologians, actually looking at the prospects of the world with as much optimism as their secular contemporaries who embraced the idea of progress. Historicist premillennialists were part of the theological and intellectual mainstream.

One among their number was Lord Shaftesbury. This Evangelical peer has often been celebrated for his leadership of the campaign for the restriction of factory working hours and for his championship of other measures of social reform. There has appeared to be a conundrum in that a man who wanted to make the world a better place was also somebody who dismissed the world. This book resolves the problem. As a historicist premillennialist, Shaftesbury accepted the importance of the incarnation and so appreciated the needs of the human body. He was therefore committed to the improvement of the physical environment. These beliefs, far from clashing, formed a coherent whole. Others in the school of thought joined Shaftesbury in taking organized action to improve the human lot, believing more than their Evangelical predecessors in the influence of the environment over human behavior. His contemporaries, in fact, anticipated some of the policies of a later social gospel generation, showing distinctively progressive characteristics.

Martin Spence has identified a hole at the center of studies of the Evangelical movement. Nobody before him has made a sustained

2. Ibid., 10.

academic investigation of historicist premillennialism. He has absorbed a body of literature that has been almost entirely neglected by historians. Engaging with previous commentators on the period, he shows persuasively that his subjects were scholarly rather than populist and aligned with their contemporaries in Victorian society rather than perennially pitted against them. He demonstrates that Evangelicalism changed over time, embracing in the middle of the nineteenth century an estimate of the future that has much in common with views of twenty-first-century Evangelical commentators such as N. T. Wright who see eschatological fulfilment as earthly rather than heavenly. Martin has not only seen a hole: he has filled it.

David W. Bebbington

University of Stirling, July 2014

Acknowledgments

THE INITIAL RESEARCH UPON which this book was based was funded by the Arts and Humanities Research Council of Great Britain. I am grateful for the liberating luxury of fully-funded graduate studies, and I acknowledge the contribution of the United Kingdom taxpayer in endowing funding for the humanities. A research grant, provided by the Scouloudi Foundation in association with the Institute of Historical Research, enabled me to complete some further research into avenues of enquiry that had emerged since I first completed my doctoral work. A publication grant, also provided by the Scouloudi Foundation in association with the Institute of Historical Research, provided help toward the costs associated with bringing the manuscript into a published form. I am indebted to my current institution, Cornerstone University, Grand Rapids, Michigan, for providing some additional funding. I have benefitted also from the institutional and human capital of numerous libraries, particularly the Bodleian Library, Oxford, the British Library, and the National Library of Scotland.

As this is the preface to my first published book I wish to place on record my gratitude to those who have encourage my creativity, curiosity, and critical thinking. In particular, I would like to acknowledge my high school history teachers, Mike Foley, Trevor McVeigh, and Dudley Whittaker. In particular, Dudley's willingness to drive a minibus to the Suffolk County Records Office each Tuesday afternoon, alongside his other job as Head Teacher of a High School, whet my appetite for archival research. I am grateful also to Marie Spillett, who specialized in mordant observation and personal academic encouragement.

At Corpus Christi College, Oxford, Brian Harrison gave me the first taste of scholarly conversation as he probed my conclusions within the confines of the admission interview. As I describe in the introduction, he also set this research in motion. During my time at Corpus, I was unfailingly encouraged by John Watts, whose first year tutorials on the politics of late medieval England opened my eyes to the richness of language and the complexities of image making in a way that continues to shape my approach to probing the very different terrain of modern religious communities. Jay Sexton proved to be a reliable guide and advocate. I am grateful to Sarah Williams for inviting me into the world of modern religious history. My D.Phil. supervisor, Jane Garnett, provided calm, reassuring, detailed, and reliable guidance throughout the lonely days of research. Mark Smith was an equitable friend and conversation partner, as well as a generous doctoral examiner. My external doctoral examiner, David Bebbington, has been for me, as for many others in this field of the history of Evangelicalism, a model scholar and mentor. His stores of knowledge, unremitting attention to detail, and incisive critique are marks of his deep and abiding concern both for the importance of Evangelical history, and for those individuals who make it their topic of study.

Friends and colleagues have proved invaluable conversation partners, sharpening my thoughts and opening new avenues of enquiry, and listening to my ramblings on many disparate topics. I am particularly indebted in this regard to Benjamin Fischer and Paul Baxter, as well as to my father-in-law, Paul R. House.

Finally, I acknowledge the unfailing love and support of my immediate family. I am grateful for my parents, Colin and Jeanette, who nurtured in me a sense of inquisitiveness, a concern for justice, and a spirit of empathy, and who provided the loving and stable home in which to grow personally and academically. I am, most of all, profoundly honored and blessed to be married to Molly, who has endured, encouraged, critiqued, and inspired this project—and, more importantly, its author—for the ten years that we have known each other. My life, work, and faith are richer and stronger for her steadfast friendship and love. During the preparation of this book, I have been privileged to share with her the joy and adventure of becoming the parents of our son, Caleb—God's amazing gift of new creation.

Abbreviations

CIS	*Christian Influence Society*
CLM	*Christian Lady's Magazine*
CMR	*Churchman's Monthly Review*
CO	*Christian Observer*
ECA	*Early Closing Association*
LDOS	*Lord's Day Observance Society*
LSPCJ	*London Society for the Promotion of Christianity Among the Jews*
MDA	*Metropolitan Drapers' Association*
QJP	*Quarterly Journal of Prophecy*
SICLC	*Society for Improving the Condition of the Labouring Classes*

Introduction

OVER THE PAST TWENTY years a subtle shift has occurred in the tectonics of Evangelical Protestantism. Reacting against a belief that Christian salvation means "going to heaven when you die," theological revisionists have instead stressed God's purposes for the renewal of the entire created order. The phenomenon can be observed in the writings of British Anglican theologian N. T. Wright. In books such as *Surprised by Hope*, Wright has argued that the Christian hope is not life after death in an ethereal heaven, but life *after* life after death, on a revitalized earth. Wright is the most prominent example of a more general theological re-envisioning, noticeable enough to have become the cover story of *Time* magazine in April 2012.[1] In this new theological vision, heaven will be a place on earth.

Although this eschatological reappraisal is probably still not the majority opinion among average churchgoers, such changes are percolating slowly into the mainstream.[2] My current academic institution, an American Christian liberal arts college originally founded in the 1940s as a Baptist Bible College in the Fundamentalist tradition, had until the 1990s asked faculty to subscribe to a belief that Christians would be raptured away from earth at the second coming of Christ. When I joined the faculty in 2012, however, I was asked to sign a recently revised confessional statement that endorsed "God's plan to . . . renew creation" and championed "the redemption of all things at Christ's return."[3] I was also

---

1. Meacham, "Heaven Can't Wait."

2. The non-earthly view of heaven is also still prevalent and highly popular, as evidenced by best-selling books such as Don Piper, *90 Minutes in Heaven* (2004) and Todd Burpo, *Heaven is for Real: Little Boy's Astounding Story of His Trip to Heaven and Back* (2010).

3. "Our Confession," Cornerstone University, Grand Rapids, MI. (May, 2011), accessed May 23, 2014, http://www.cornerstone.edu/our-confession.

pleased to find that I had two colleagues whose research focused on new creation eschatology.[4]

Future generations may contend that the underlying reason for our theological transmutations was a religious version of the late twentieth-century environmental movement—we have been longing for our carbon to be offset by God's eternal Earth Day—or perhaps a transmuted version of the socio-economic culture of the 1970s and 1980s that has encouraged us to cling on to the material world for all eternity, a kind of Thatcherite "right to buy" policy for our previously rented terrestrial council house. A proper judgment on our own generation will not be made for several decades, but historians should possess enough self-awareness of their social context and its potential to shape them within the continual flux of historical contingencies to be able to disclose to readers possible biases. Therefore I must admit that, as a participant-observer within the North Atlantic Protestant Evangelical community, who has himself been shaped by the current emphases within this community, I warm to at least some of the central themes of the protagonists whom I discuss, even if many of the materials with which they constructed their eschatological cathedrals appear archaic and obsolete.

While I am going to present a story of individuals with whom I share certain dispositions, it is also important to note that I did not set out looking to the historical record in order to find individuals to act as the star witnesses to my own theological convictions. Indeed, at the start of this research process I was completely unaware of the existence of this particular theological tradition in Victorian Britain. I was not alone in my ignorance. The novelty of this book is to present to the historical community a hitherto unexplored and often completely misunderstood aspect of nineteenth-century Evangelicalism.

The nursery that germinated the research upon which this book is based was an undergraduate dissertation under the guidance of Prof. Brian Harrison at Corpus Christi College, Oxford. Prof. Harrison invited me to write about Victorian Sabbatarianism, a topic that he had studied from a social and political perspective. As I studied the primary literature of the nineteenth-century Sabbath question I noted two things. First, I perceived that there was a whole raft of poetical and lyrical justifications

---

4. John Duff has researched the seventeenth-century Puritan vision of the renewal of the created order. Duff, "A Knot Worth Unloosing." Michael Wittmer has written about the popular theology of heaven and the new earth. Michael Wittmer, *Heaven is a Place on Earth*.

for "keeping Sunday special" that had not been registered by the majority of historians, probably due in part to the mid-twentieth-century predilection for interpreting religious belief as the conduit for some prior social or economic disposition. The sources dripped with romantically-tinged images of the way in which Sunday bridged the gap between time and eternity, offering stasis and rest in a rapidly changing world.

Second, I realized that, although Sabbatarianism was rooted in a specific scriptural injunction (the Fourth Commandment), the Victorian Sunday observance movement did not arise simply from a "puritanical" or legalistic form of biblical fidelity. Instead, it expressed a concern to adjust and renew the structures of corporate time. Viewing Sabbatarianism in this light, it appeared to me bound to another campaign of the era with which several Evangelicals were involved: the factory reform movement, sometimes called the Ten Hours Movement. This campaign aimed to restrict the number of hours an individual could legally work in factories. Both Sabbatarianism and the factory reform movements were in turn connected with other campaigns for early closing of business that emerged in the late 1840s and early 1850s. Was it mere coincidence that these movements focusing on the reform of public time occurred around the same moment and enjoyed support from at least a subsection of the Evangelical community? And how were these attempts at temporal restructuring related to the simultaneous Evangelical concern with time in its largest dimension, namely, the interest in prophecy and apocalypse that also pulsed through Evangelicalism in the middle decades of the nineteenth century?

The undergraduate dissertation left most of these questions suspended in mid-air. After an interim, writing a master's thesis about the work of Billy Graham in 1950s Britain, I resurrected the question of Victorian Evangelicals and their apprehension of time at the start of my doctoral studies, under the direction of Dr. E. J. Garnett at Wadham College, Oxford. I began by reading Jerome Buckley's classic *The Triumph of Time*, which presents a compelling argument that the nineteenth-century literary world was haunted by the spectral presence of temporality. Reflecting upon his boyhood, Alfred, Lord Tennyson remembered lying in bed, broad awake, hearing "time flowing in the middle of the night, / And all things creeping to a day of doom," while, with similar melancholy, Thomas Carlyle observed that "Saturn, or Chronos, or what we call TIME, devours all his Children: only by incessant Running, by incessant

Working may you (for some threescore-and-ten years) escape him: and you too he devours at last."[5]

As I moved on to explore some of the sociological and anthropological investigations of time, I began to realize that a clear definition of the word "time," is highly *elusive,* and the phenomenon that the word is intended to signify is reckoned by many scholars to be highly *illusive.* Thinkers over many centuries have used the term to refer to the experience of some restless force working against us, or to the more technical measurement and allocation of the units of work and leisure, or, even more broadly, to all sub-lunar activity bound by cause and effect, change and decay, rest and motion. In some discourses "time" is studied at the level of subatomic physical structure, in others it is approached from the plane of worldviews, religion, and mythology.[6] Entire interdisciplinary academic projects, such as that led by Julius Thomas Fraser (1923–2010), have been devoted to the study of time.[7] Fraser's introduction to one of these compendiums of time study captures the multivalent nature of the subject:

> Time conjoins the ideas of life and purpose; it links the individual to the astronomical universe; it forms the substratum of the great continuities of civilization; magic, religion, the sciences and the arts; and it subsumes certain paradigms of tension, such as free will and determinism, contingency and necessity, being and becoming, permanence and change.[8]

Reading this kind of heady prose, I came to suspect that "time" was merely a synonym for "human existence." I found others agreed with this conclusion. In one of the most accessible introductions to the topic, anthropologist Alfred Gell notes that "we feel time as a quasi-substantive dynamic force pulsing through the world because we have to *work* to stay abreast of it; but this work we put into changing *ourselves,* ditching our old belief-inscriptions and installing new ones. Time is not the least dynamic; it is we, on the contrary, who are."[9]

And yet the concept of time still seemed to have explanatory purchase, as long as its multi-dimensional meaning was acknowledged.

---

5. Buckley, *Triumph of Time,* 3–4.

6. See, for example, Whitrow, "Reflections on the History and Concept of Time"; Brandon, "Deification of Time."

7. Fraser, "Backward Glance," xviii.

8. Fraser, "Study of Time," 480.

9. Gell, *Anthropology of Time,* 173.

Indeed, the way in which "time" could be interpreted by humans as both an external phenomenon acting upon us, and yet also simply a poetic, even mythological, description of the human condition—of being born, living, remembering, anticipating, and dying—seemed to prove a conceptual advantage as my research moved into reading the primary sources of the nineteenth-century Evangelical prophetical movement. In these texts, which are the foundation for the research on which this book is based, I found an eschatological vision not only triggered by the Victorian awareness of the pulse of time, but one that also placed the entire temporal order—meaning physical life on earth, marked by progress, growth, and development—squarely center-stage in its vision for the future of the world.

The use of the word "time" to refer to mean "temporal" life—basically, life as we know it, bounded by the constraints of sequential existence within a geographical locale—is, of course, given depth in Christian and classical philosophical discourse by an implicit contrast with its binary opposite: eternity. In this constructed dichotomy, "time" means human, physical, successive, developmental, organic existence. "Eternity" is everything opposite: the unchanging, permanent, spiritual, essential dimension of God's immortal existence and therefore, in many dimensions of Christian understanding, also the state within which all Christians will live after they quit the earth. The term "eternity" has therefore also been used as an imprecise synonym for "heaven," meaning the realm of God and the often presumed destiny of Christian believers—the place in which Christian salvation is actualized after death. "Heaven"/"earth," "eternity"/"time": I use these terms in this book in their broadest possible sense without pretense to any technical philosophical distinction. This is not a study of the overt philosophy of "time" so much as it is an attempt at using these broad categories to pry open the imaginative theology of a group of Victorian Evangelical Protestants.

This book is about time and eternity at several levels. In particular, it is about a significant shift in the thought and practice of nineteenth-century British Protestant Evangelicalism that has been almost completely unrecognized by historians of the movement. Evangelicalism is often presented as an intensely anti-worldly movement, which emphasized the necessity of renouncing the temporal sphere so that one's "soul" could gain "eternal life" in a non-terrestrial "heaven." This book will present evidence to show that a significant number of influential Victorian Evangelicals, including Edward Bickersteth (1786–1850), Gerard Noel (1782–1851),

John Cumming (1807–81), Thomas Rawson Birks (1810–83), and Charlotte Elizabeth Tonna (1790–1846), were animated by a hope not for the salvation of the "soul" in a spiritual "heaven," but rather for the resurrection of the body on a renewed, physical earth. In fact, these individuals often criticized an Evangelical spirituality that drove a wedge between "this life" and "the life to come," or between "time" and "eternity." Like today's Evangelical revisionists, they also hoped for heaven on earth.

Many of these women and men, mostly members of the national churches of Great Britain and Ireland, were "premillennialists." This means that they believed in the imminent return of Christ followed by the inauguration of a one thousand-year reign of righteousness on earth. Nineteenth-century premillennialism has almost uniformly been characterized as a "world-denying" and "pessimistic" outlook. This book significantly revises this view, particularly in regard to the eschatological tradition called "historicist premillennialism."[10] I will argue that this brand of end-times speculation was a radical, optimistic, and often liberalizing creed, which transformed the thinking of these individuals away from older Evangelical assumptions about the gulf separating God and humanity, about the dissimilarity of time and eternity, and about the divide between "flesh" and "spirit." Historicist premillennialism encouraged speculations in keeping with the type of theological ideas that historian Boyd Hilton has argued characterized a late Victorian "age of incarnation." Such revisionary impulses included a softening of the doctrine of hell, a high view of the human body, an interest in temporal development and progress, a focus on the humanity of Christ, and a robust view of the created order. In short, nineteenth-century historicist premillennialism represented a highly positive re-assessment of the temporal-spatial sphere.

The book will also highlight the way in which a number of these Evangelicals became involved in campaigns to improve public health and working conditions, initiatives that aimed to improve the temporal order. Such activity showed that Evangelicals in the mid-nineteenth century were moving away from a tendency to link poverty with individual sin, and toward a more progressive view of the environmental causes of social and spiritual deprivation. While historians have often struggled to explain why premillennialists like the Earl of Shaftesbury[11] committed

---

10. A full explanation of this unfortunately cumbersome term will be given in chapter 2.

11. Antony Ashley Cooper, Lord Ashley, (1801–85) succeeded as seventh Earl of Shaftesbury in 1851. He is therefore referred to as Ashley up until 1850 while he still

themselves to such ameliorative social reform projects, the book argues that both theology and action were moving in tandem toward a more positive assessment of the temporal-spatial sphere as a place for authentic Christian activity.

The insistent theme of my argument will be that, despite these individuals' ostensibly eccentric apocalypticism, the basic drift of their thought and action was perfectly in keeping with broader, mainstream trends in nineteenth-century society and culture. Socially, these Evangelicals were products of the interest in time, history, movement, and development triggered by industrial and urban change. They posited a restless, moving, temporally-involved God. Their view of the world to come was one where time, motion, discovery, and invention continued to be the basic reality of existence. Intellectually, they were romantics, longing for the unification and coalescence of the temporal and eternal. They delighted in poetic speculations about the world that was soon to dawn. They believed, just like English romantic poets, that the divine was found in and through the physical world, not simply beyond it. Theologically, their interest in the coming kingdom of God on earth aligned them with the growing number of so-called "broad church" theologians who were increasingly arguing that God's salvation would be worked out in the temporal-spatial sphere.

Because the temporal-spatial optimism of mid-century Evangelicalism was couched in apocalyptic symbols, historians have often been distracted from perceiving the essential similarity between Victorian premillennialism and broader developments in nineteenth-century religious and intellectual thought concerning the importance of history, the material world, and the immanence of God within time and space. A central burden of this book is to prove that nineteenth-century Evangelicalism, even when at its supposedly most gloomy and reactionary, was much more firmly in the mainstream of Victorian intellectual and theological life than has been previously imagined. I hope that the evidence presented in this book should encourage the work of deconstructing the false ecclesiastical demarcations bequeathed to us by nineteenth-century commentators. Religious ideas, even ones that strike modern commentators as off-beat and outmoded, are always part of a complex web of social, cultural, theological, and linguistic realities. By taking seriously the artifacts of popular theology rather than relying on *a priori* presuppositions

---

sat as MP in the House of Commons, and as Shaftesbury from 1851 onwards, when he took his seat in the House of Lords.

about the content and meaning of certain theological beliefs, these synergies emerge with greater clarity.

Although this is primarily a work of religious history, the book also speaks to those currents within the contemporary Evangelical movement that emphasize the new creation, the priority of social justice, and the possibility that salvation may be broader than some Evangelical teaching has traditionally allowed. These viewpoints, such as that recently proposed by Rob Bell in his controversial bestseller, *Love Wins* (2011), have alarmed some within the Evangelical community with their radical iconoclasm. It is intriguing to discover that these sometimes startlingly modern views on eschatology existed in the nineteenth century within a theological framework (premillennialism) that today is associated with the outmoded Evangelical/Fundamentalist package from which contemporary revisionist Evangelicals like Bell seek to break. That Evangelicals had already gone down some of these "new" paths of theological speculation nearly two centuries ago should serve to temper the *avant-garde* pride with which some writers and Christian leaders announce their allegedly new startling discoveries. It should also calm the panic of those who fear that the latest trendy book to hit the Christian bookstores proves that Evangelical Protestantism has been unexpectedly injected with a new lethal heresy. These ongoing discussions about our common future are indeed profound and vital; it is essential that we ground them in a proper understanding of the past.

1
Evangelicalism's Eternal Vision

> Time, like an ever-rolling stream,
> bears all its sons away;
> they fly, forgotten, as a dream
> dies at the opening day.
>
> —ISAAC WATTS (1674–1748)

The Evangelical Enterprise

THE MODERN EVANGELICAL MOVEMENT sprang from a series of interlinked religious revivals within eighteenth-century British and North American Protestant Christianity. The preaching, prayer, and worship of eighteenth-century Evangelicals reignited the central doctrines propounded by the sixteenth-century Protestant reformers: justification by grace alone, obtained through faith alone, authorized by Scripture alone.[1] Into this Reformation fabric were woven three new strands.[2]

First, Evangelicals adopted the accent of Pietism, a renewal movement within late seventeenth-century German Lutheranism that proposed that "real faith" was a matter of a pervasive experience of God rather than bald creedal affirmations about his nature. British and American Evangelicals absorbed the temperament of this movement

---

1. For introductions to the eighteenth-century Evangelical revival, see Noll, *Rise of Evangelicalism*; Ward, *Protestant Evangelical Awakening*; Kidd, *Great Awakening*; Ditchfield, *Evangelical Revival*; Sweeney, *American Evangelical Story*.

2. Douglas A. Sweeney argues that Evangelicalism can be defined as "Reformation Christianity with an eighteenth-century twist." Sweeney, *American Evangelical Story*, 24.

through literature and personal contacts.[3] Evangelicals claimed that correct doctrine *about* Christ should be supplemented by a deep experience *of* Christ that would transform the emotional center—"the heart"—of the individual.[4] "If religion be necessary at all it must be a religion of the heart," wrote nineteenth-century Congregational minister Alexander Fletcher (1787–1860) in characteristic fashion.[5] The entry point into this "vital" Christian experience was described by Evangelicals as "the new birth," defined by the Evangelical pioneer and founder of Methodism, John Wesley (1703–91), as "that great change which God works in the soul when he brings it into life when he raises it from the death of sin to the life of righteousness."[6] This conversion translated the individual from the realm of formal assent to orthodox doctrine into a sphere of dynamic and joyful Christian experience. "We must distinguish between real and vital Christianity and what constitutes a merely nominal adherence to its external ordinances," explained nineteenth-century Anglican Evangelical Daniel Wilson (1778–1858).[7]

The second eighteenth-century "twist" on classical Protestantism was the enlightenment-inspired claim that one could know truths about the nature of reality—in this case about God and salvation—through individual sense perceptions. This belief owed much to the epistemological theories popularized by thinkers such as John Locke (1632–1704) and Scottish "Common Sense" philosophers. Evangelicals presumed that one could feel confident and assured of the reality of salvation because of a personal encounter with the divine.[8] This mindset led to a robust and confident faith that appealed to personal testimony, particularly to narratives of conversion, in order to prove the redemptive power of Christ.[9] As Welsh Evangelical Howell Harris (1714–73) described his own

---

3. Pietism is the name given to the movement particularly associated with Lutheran leaders Philip Spener (1635–1705) and August Francke (1663–1727). Multifarious in its expressions, the movement broadly stressed repentance, conversion, and the fellowship of all believers. Noll, *Rise of Evangelicalism*, 54–5.

4. Walsh, "Origins of the Evangelical Revival," 132–62, esp. 148–53.

5. Fletcher, "Inward Religion," 290.

6. Wesley, "Sermon XLV: The New Birth," 66.

7. Wilson, *Evidences for Christianity*, 2:239.

8. Bebbington, *Evangelicalism in Modern Britain*, 48–55; Bebbington, "Revival and Enlightenment"; Noll, *Rise of Evangelicalism*, 150–51.

9. Bebbington, *Evangelicalism in Modern Britain*, 5–10; Bebbington, *Evangelical Conversion*.

Evangelical conversion: "I knew that I was His child, and that He loved me and heard me."[10] This new epistemological disposition also heightened Evangelical confidence in the Bible as a clear and lucid revelation of God, the meaning of which was plain and accessible to any individual who approached it with confidence in its divine origin.[11]

Finally, eighteenth-century Evangelicalism was characterized by a commitment to dynamic and expansive missionary strategies. This impulse was also derived from the Pietist movement, in particular from the Moravians, a lay community that traced its roots back to the followers of Jan Hus (c.1369–1415) in late fifteenth-century Bohemia. Fired by the Pietist conviction that the joy of an experiential relationship with Jesus Christ ought to encourage individuals to share their faith with others, Moravians established religious communities, orphanages, and evangelistic enterprises across Europe and the Americas. Their example was widely emulated among eighteenth-century British and North American revivalists, not least by John Wesley, whose own experience of having his "heart... strangely warmed" owed much to his encounter with Moravian Christians. From field preaching to the foundation of international mission societies, Evangelicals poured time, energy, and money into enterprises of proclamation and persuasion. These agencies aimed for both individual conversion and societal regeneration.[12]

Evangelicalism did not create a single new church or international religious order. Instead it seeped into the veins of North Atlantic Protestantism, creating and reforming the structures, priorities, and tone of multiple Christian communities. In some cases Evangelical renewal stimulated the creation of new ecclesiastical groupings, such as the Methodists in the eighteenth century or the Plymouth Brethren in the nineteenth century. In other instances, Evangelicalism helped generate distinct groupings within historic denominations, such as the "Evangelical Party" in the Anglican churches of England and Ireland and the Presbyterian Church of Scotland. On occasions, Evangelical impulses fractured churches, as evidenced by the mass exit of Evangelicals from the Church of Scotland in 1843 to create the Free Church of Scotland. At other times, though, Evangelicalism was a force for unity and consolidation, as exemplified by the foundation of the interdenominational British Evangelical Alliance in 1846.

---

10. H. Harris, *Brief Account of the Life of Howell Harris*, 15.
11. Bebbington, *Evangelicalism in Modern Britain*, 12–14.
12. Ward, *Protestant Evangelical Awakening*, 116–59.

The diversity inherent in the movement meant that there was no single way of being Evangelical; there was neither membership nor formal confession. However, the diffusion of Evangelical energy across multiple institutions in several continents was guarded from atomization by the imaginative ability of Evangelicals to perceive unity and solidarity despite their obvious ecclesiastical and theological divergences. "Evangelicalism" is thus more than a convenient label that historians have attached to a certain way of being Protestant; it describes the reflexivity possessed by certain Christians about their own identity. Evangelicals have not only shared certain beliefs or performed certain activities, they have also always been *conscious* of "being part of a complicated fellowship and infrastructure of trans-denominational Evangelical organizations."[13] Utilizing the assumptions and techniques of the eighteenth-century marketplace, most notably a relentless exploitation of print media,[14] Evangelicals established a conversational community that encouraged participants to narrate their personal and local spiritual experiences, and in turn, to authenticate others' religious experiences as valid and significant works of God.[15] This multi-national, multi-denominational "Evangelical" community can be described as one of the eighteenth century's several new "imagined communities."[16]

By the conclusion of the Napoleonic Wars in 1815, Evangelical Christianity had become a visible part of British culture. William Gladstone believed that one-eighth, or around 1500, of all Anglican clergy were "Evangelical" by 1836. The *Eclectic Review* thought the true figure was twice that number.[17] It has also been suggested that Evangelical parishes in

---

13. Marsden, "Introduction," xiv. For this reason I have chosen to capitalize the word "Evangelical" throughout this work. In doing so I follow the observation of Doug Sweeney that "Evangelicals . . . are [not] the only ones to whom the term evangelical applies." Sweeney, *American Evangelical Story*, 24. This issue is further discussed in my "Unravelling."

14. On Evangelicalism and the "eighteenth-century marketplace," see Lambert, *Pedlar in Divinity*, 11–94. On Evangelicals and publishing, see O'Brien, "Eighteenth-Century Publishing Networks"; O'Brien, "Transatlantic Community of Saints."

15. Coffey, "Puritanism, Evangelicalism, and the Evangelical Protestant Tradition," 275–76.

16. The phrase was used by Benedict Anderson to describe the birth of national communal identity in Anderson, *Imagined Communities*. The applicability of the concept of "imagining" to Evangelicalism, at least in eighteenth-century America—although, by extension, also for other sectors of the movement—is demonstrated by Lambert, *Inventing the Great Awakening*.

17. Smyth, "Evangelical Movement in Perspective"; 164; Rennie, "Evangelicalism

the Church of England attracted a far larger attendance than others, based on a sampling of the 1851 Religious Census.[18] Meanwhile, a large majority of Protestant Nonconformists, who formed around 47 percent of the total churchgoing population in 1851, could be classed as Evangelical.[19]

By the early nineteenth century Evangelicalism was no longer associated with field preachers and risible "enthusiasts." It had become the stated creed of numerous prominent politicians, bankers, civil servants, authors, and leaders of the national churches.[20] Most notable among these was the small think-tank and lobby group dubbed the "Clapham Sect." Its most famous member was the anti-slavery, pro-morality campaigner, William Wilberforce (1759–1833). Through mission societies, tract publishers, religious journals, moral and social reform campaigns, and countless sermons and other printed devotional material, Evangelicalism established itself as a popular and even fashionable religious disposition. The pervasiveness of the movement on the eve of Queen Victoria assuming the British throne has led some historians to suggest that Evangelicalism single-handedly infused Victorian society with its earnest sobriety and moral fervor.[21]

Evangelical commitment to mission and moral reformation was the dynamic behind the formation of huge national voluntary societies and myriad local associations, each convened to support the call of Christ to make disciples of the British nation, and of all nations. British Evangelicals campaigned against slavery, protested against public "vice," tried to halt Sabbath desecration, and participated in movements that aimed to reform factories, housing, and education. "Ours is the age of societies," wrote Sir James Stephen of the Evangelical movement in 1844. "For the redress of every oppression that is done under the sun, there is a public meeting. For the cure of every sorrow by which our land or our race can be visited, there are patrons, vice-presidents and secretaries. For the

and English Public Life," 7.

18. Bebbington, *Evangelicalism in Modern Britain*, 108.

19. Watts, *Dissenters*, 2:2–3, 23, 27.

20. The term "enthusiast" was commonly used to describe Evangelical Christians, often, although not always, in a derogatory sense. For a contemporary discussion, see Nospmis [pseud.]. "On Enthusiasm." *Evangelical Magazine* 4 (June 1796), 234–37.

21. Ian Bradley contends that "Evangelicalism, more than any other single influence, was responsible for giving the Victorians their notorious seriousness and high-mindedness." Bradley, *Call to Seriousness*, 18. For similar sentiments, see Meacham, "Evangelical Inheritance," 89, and Vidler, *Church in an Age of Revolution*, 49.

diffusion of every blessing of which mankind can partake in common, there is a committee."[22]

All of this activity was the outworking of the central Evangelical conviction, expressed, for example, by the Evangelical Anglican minister and apologist Thomas Scott (1746–1821), as "real faith must and will prove itself by its fruits."[23] It was these "fruits" of salvation, contended Evangelicals, that distinguished authentic believers from those nominal Christians whose actions proved their profession of faith was a matter only of external conformity or even hypocritical sham. This focus upon activity and endeavor gave Evangelicals an intense concern to use their time wisely and to devote their energies indefatigably to the work of communicating the gospel.[24] As the late eighteenth-century Anglican Evangelical author, Hannah More (1745–1833), put it: "Action is the life of virtue, and the world is the theatre of action."[25]

However, although Evangelicals almost single-handedly pioneered modern voluntary activity in the public sphere, scholars have been quick to remind us that they had a decidedly traditional motivation: they wanted to save souls from hell. Despite the activist bent of the movement, Evangelicals have been characterized as having possessed little hope of improving the world. Instead, they prioritized the inculcation of godliness in individuals and nations so that, when this world passed away, every one might be prepared to stand upright before the judgment seat of God. As Kenneth Inglis concluded, in a sentence that exemplifies historiographical consensus on this point, for the nineteenth-century Evangelical "the duty of a Christian was to reject the world, not to sanctify it."[26]

In such a conceptual universe, the notions of earth and heaven—or, as they were often called in Evangelical shorthand, "time" and "eternity"—were often presented as polar opposites. "The main purpose of our living here is to prepare for eternity," wrote anti-slavery campaigner Thomas Fowell Buxton (1786–1845). "It matters little how we fare in

---

22. Stephen, *Essays in Ecclesiastical Biography*, 584.

23. Bebbington, *Evangelicalism in Modern Britain*, 64.

24. For example, Christopher Tolley, *Domestic Biography*, paints a picture of the "evangelical obsession with redeeming the time" (165), particularly manifested through scrupulous self-examination in dairies and letter-writing of four major families associated with the Clapham Sect.

25. More, *Thoughts*, 69.

26. Inglis, *Churches and the Working Classes*, 304; cf. Rosman, *Evangelicals and Culture*, 246.

this world providing a better awaits for us."[27] That an individual whose reforming zeal helped destroy slave-holding in the British Empire articulated such "other-worldly" sentiments underscores the purchase of the Evangelical insouciance to the temporal sphere. Evangelicals have often appeared anti-worldly, anti-materialistic, and congenitally disabled from expressing a positive view about life on earth. "What folly is that with such care about the body which is dying, the world which is perishing before our eyes, time which is perpetually disappearing, we should little care about that eternal state in which we are to live for ever, when this dream is over!" wrote John Venn (1750–1833), one of the founders of the Anglican Church Missionary Society.[28] For Evangelicals such as Venn, earthly existence was insubstantial and fleeting; life was but a dream.

In the next chapter I am going to initiate an argument that will attempt to nuance this depiction of Victorian Evangelical attitudes toward material, temporal-spatial existence. However, before proceeding to make this revisionist case, it is necessary to concede ground to where the older interpretation of Evangelicalism is correct. After all, talk of "shifts" and "reconfigurations" of the Evangelical discourse only make sense if we are aware of a well-delineated position with which these new attitudes can be contrasted. Because there has never been a systematic examination of this topic it is necessary to outline briefly the features of the very real Evangelical tendency to dichotomize between time and eternity, a tendency that may be understood as having been comprised of an interlocking web of at least five layers of assumptions and theological predilections.

Time and Eternity: The Evangelistic Imperative

Language that drew contrasts between time and eternity was, first and foremost, an evangelistic cry. It was bound to the heart of the Evangelical passion for announcing the good news of salvation in Jesus Christ. The use of dichotomous terminology urged the turning aside from all that might distract one from the essential priority of seeking forgiveness in the cross of Christ. The call to prepare oneself for eternity was a call to be put right with God because it was in eternity that one would face the consequences of decisions made during one's time on earth. The image of the enduring nature of eternity and the inverse image of the fleetingness

27. Buxton, *Memoirs*, 273.
28. Venn, *Sermons*, 1:225.

of time was meant to awaken people to the momentousness of the choice facing them. The renowned Scottish Evangelical Presbyterian Thomas Chalmers (1780–1847) explained that, when faced with an individual languishing in spiritual torpor,

> we would ring into our patient's ears the message of death, which every body knows, but few know with application. We would try to awaken his inner man, by the tidings of its immortality, which all profess to have faith in, while scarcely any human being lives under the power of it.[29]

Such a missionary strategy would not have been considered effective had Evangelicals themselves not been haunted by their own mortality. In an era where the average life expectancy was just forty-two years, death (and thus divine judgment or reward) was an ever-present reality.[30] As Chalmers put it: "[There is not] a living man who does not know, that the march of our actual generation is but one vast progressive movement to the grave."[31]

One strategy for coping with the all-pervasiveness of death—a strategy favored, no doubt, by Evangelical ministers faced with the need to provide pastoral comfort to the bereaved—was to view death not as a threat but rather as the gateway into promised eternal life. "To Christian pilgrims what is death?" pondered John Venn. He answered his own question with the comforting statement that "it is the end of their toilsome journey. They have arrived at home: they have reached their Father's house, and are received like children long expected and greatly desired."[32] Death was thus an object of Evangelical hope. If sinners should be warned of the dangers of dying and entering eternity without Christ, the corollary was that believers could be consoled with the hope of dying as a Christian. The believer thus "looks to the day of death as the day of release, of escape, and of joy," wrote a contributor to the *Christian Observer*, a monthly periodical that served as the *de facto* magisterium of Anglican Evangelicalism in the early nineteenth century.[33] The natural consequence of such language was that many parts of Evangelicalism

---

29. Chalmers, "Introductory Essay," xiii.

30. Life expectancy in England and Wales in 1841 was around forty. Lindert, "Unequal Living Standards," 361–63.

31. Chalmers, "Introductory Essay," x.

32. Venn, *Sermons*, 1:349.

33. "Family Sermons No. CCLXIII." *Christian Observer*, 1st ser., 29 (1829), 747.

exhibited a persistent description of Christian salvation as liberation from the earth and the body. This produced a pervasive discursive inflexion that suggested that the core of divinely-endorsed reality was to be found only after one had departed from the earth. "Death has loosed thee, as from a prison!" exclaimed the *Evangelical Magazine* to a hypothetically-deceased believer.[34]

Time and Eternity: The Ethical Imperative

The urgency of preparing individuals' souls for their eternal destiny meant that Evangelicals desired to remind people constantly that eternity outweighed all other temporal considerations. The world, with its pleasures and pains, was a distraction from this most essential decision. In this, the second layer of discourse about time and eternity, Evangelicals specifically rejected "worldliness" and warned against entanglement with vain and decadent pursuits of ambition and pleasure. In sounding this alarm Evangelicals were making an ethical rather than an evangelistic point. Of course, the future destiny of individuals was always prominent in the Evangelical mind, because debauched behavior was indicative of rebellion against God. Nevertheless, the typical Evangelical warning against "worldliness" was concerned more with chiding nominal or backsliding Christians about hypocrisy and lukewarm faith than it was with convincing the unbeliever of his or her unregenerate state. Evangelical fear of embroilment with temporal distractions was thus directed inward to nurture piety rather than outward to inspire conversion.[35] John Venn expressed this aspect of Evangelical concern when he wrote:

> This is then the ground and foundation of a Christian's deadness to the world: he is deeply impressed with a sense of the supreme importance of eternal objects, and acts upon that conviction: the course of his life is ordered in such a manner as shall not prevent his attention to the great concern of the soul. The employment of his leisure hours, the choice of his company, his very diversions are so regulated, that in the pursuit of the one thing needful he is at least never impeded by them.[36]

34. "Death, a Departure." *Evangelical Magazine* 4 (1796), 233.
35. Rosman, *Evangelicals and Culture*, 69.
36. Venn, *Sermons* 2:346.

This campaign against worldliness was the product of two converging streams in eighteenth- and early nineteenth-century Evangelicalism. First, the search for holiness and complete sanctification associated with John Wesley and the Methodist movement bequeathed a powerful tradition of serious-minded disciplined living to all who were influenced by the Methodist revival. Second, the concern to promote godly behavior in individuals and communities particularly associated with Evangelical Anglicans and Presbyterians, such as the members of the Clapham Sect, encouraged a concern with public morality and public decency, which was mobilized particularly against the perceived societal decadence of the Hanoverian era.[37] Institutions such as the Society for the Suppression of Vice (founded 1802) embodied this strong ethical dimension within the Evangelical movement.

Evangelicals had a varied menu of specific activities that were believed to be morally dubious and "worldly," including reading novels, theater attendance, and concert going, as well as the more obvious activities of card playing, drinking, and gambling. Of course there was some variation between Evangelicals concerning permitted and prohibited behaviors; any depiction of a unified Evangelical moral code is misleading. Nevertheless, the strong ethical agenda in late eighteenth- and early nineteenth-century Evangelicalism exaggerated the image of the world as a place full of snares and entanglements that could corrode godliness.[38]

Time and Eternity: The Limits of Social Reform

A third aspect of the Evangelical tendency to downplay the temporal sphere was a suspicion of the type of optimistic social reform projects that were born in the eighteenth-century enlightenment and came of age in nineteenth-century liberalism, socialism, and a general spirit of revolutionary radicalism. The nineteenth century was marked by a growing spirit of hopefulness toward the possibility of reforming the structures of temporal life, as manifested in Utopian communities such as that organized by Robert Owen (1771–1858) at New Lanark, in radical political views nourished by the radical experiments of the French and American revolutions, and in the basic commitment to progress and improvement

---

37. Hylson-Smith, *Evangelicals*, 34–35.

38. For a discussion of Evangelical taboos (and examples of some variation within proscribed activities), see Rosman, *Evangelicals and Culture*, esp. 70–80.

epitomized by liberals of all hues.[39] Such attitudes showed an awareness of the possibility of change over time and emphasized the potential of development and transformation within the temporal sphere.

There were several reasons why Evangelicals might dissent from such "progressive" views. First, Evangelicals believed in the debilitating effects of sin and were skeptical that humans could completely overcome its toxic pollution of all human activity. Reviewing proposals for reform of the Poor Laws, for example, the influential Evangelical newspaper, the *Record*, concluded that "all meddling . . . is sure to issue in disappointment and misery if a just estimate is not made of human nature, as described in the word of God."[40] Therefore, when Evangelicals participated in the public sphere their motivation tended not to be hopeful plans for reconstructing human society but rather the perception of some particularly sinful action that needed to be halted. The Evangelical social vision has therefore been described as a negative social agenda that attempted to reform only in order to remove barriers to the gospel, a gospel that was alone the solution to societal ills.[41] "Let [the religious reformer] labour for eternity alone," cried the *Christian Observer* in 1821. "Let him honestly endeavour to evangelize his people—and the Gospel will prove itself to be the best preparative for the reception of just principles of economics."[42]

A second reason for the Evangelical resistance to the reforming tendencies of nineteenth-century Britain was the basic conservatism of the movement. Evangelicals, especially those in the national churches of Great Britain and Ireland, wanted to guard against the destabilizing effects of social, political, and religious radicalism. They pointed out that those individuals who shouted loudest for the reform of society—French revolutionaries, American republicans—often dispensed with orthodox Christianity along with traditional hierarchical political institutions.[43]

39. Holladay, "Nineteenth-Century Evangelical Activism," 51.

40. *Record*, August 26, 1844.

41. Bebbington, *Evangelicalism in Modern Britain*, 133–35.

42. "Review of Chalmers' Christian and Civic Economy." *Christian Observer* 20 (1821), 495.

43. David Owen contends that "Evangelicals shared with their contemporaries a conception of class relationships that accepted the existing order of society as divinely ordained and more or less immutable." Owen, *English Philanthropy*, 95. Such analyses owe much to the theories of Élie Halévy concerning the way in which Methodism helped promote the values of individual thrift, hard work, and morality, and thus counseled its predominantly lower class adherents not to challenge the social order. Itzkin, "Halévy Thesis."

Boyd Hilton has extended this analysis of the conservatism of the movement. In his seminal *Age of Atonement*, an examination of the connection between nineteenth-century social attitudes and Christian theology, Hilton argues that Evangelicals rejected the concept of reform and progress because they actually dissented philosophically from the notion, increasingly prevalent in nineteenth-century intellect and culture, that "time" and history were linear and progressive media. Hilton suggests that many Evangelicals saw the temporal sphere as static and non-developmental, or perhaps even cyclical. He argues that for the majority of nineteenth-century Evangelicals the world was a probationary arena in which the individual was tested by God in order to prove herself fit for heaven. The world could not itself be improved "over time" because God had designed it only as a temporary school of discipline through which each generation must pass, with the same set of tests, on their way to their eternal destiny. It therefore could not, and indeed should not, be altered, only endured. Since the purpose of the world was to train the individual, the individual had no business in taming the world. "Temporal setbacks," argues Hilton, were interpreted by Evangelicals as "divine encouragement to [individual] reformation and redemption.... The sequence of sin, suffering, contrition, despair, comfort and grace ... shows that pain was regarded as an essential part of God's order."[44] The temporal sphere was a place of excoriating trial. Thus, concludes Hilton, Evangelicals "did not suppose that either beauty or happiness ... was to be found in the temporal world."[45] The best card in Hilton's historiographical pack is the well-documented support of leading Evangelicals such as John Bird Sumner (1780–1862) and Thomas Chalmers for the Poor Law Amendment Act (1834), which scaled back welfare provision for the poor in favor of encouraging personal responsibility. The reform embodied the idea that poverty was generally the result of a moral failure and ought to prompt personal reformation, not social amelioration.

Time and Eternity: The Danger of the Material World

Typical Evangelical rejections of the temporal-spatial sphere in favor of the things of the eternal realm can be noted in a fourth area. The constant calls to flee the temptations of the world easily slipped into a spirituality

---

44. Hilton, *Age of Atonement*, 11.
45. Ibid., 21.

and theology in which the actual fabric of the material world came under suspicion. This reflected the tendency identified by W. R. Ward that, from its inception in the eighteenth century, Evangelicalism was "all about salvation and not creation."[46] The crucial slippage here was between deprecation of "worldliness" on the one hand and disregard for the physical earth on the other. Because the worldly pursuits shunned by Evangelicals were played out on the terrestrial plane, and since Christian history had bequeathed to late eighteenth- and early nineteenth-century Evangelicals a rich tradition of imagining the eternal as a realm of distant light, ethereality and non-earthiness, it was no surprise that the fabric of the creation itself should be, if not explicitly rejected, then at least rarely lauded.[47]

This element of Evangelical attitudes toward the things of time was more noticeable by the lack of positive affirmations of the natural world rather than by outright statements of hostility toward it.[48] Thus Doreen Rosman has argued that although Evangelicals could acknowledge order and beauty in the natural world, they tended to see the created order in functional rather than aesthetic terms. Creation was seen as the proof that should convince unbelievers of the existence of God rather than the canvas of God's creative activity. "Believing that natural theology was a poor sister to the revelation of God as redeemer in his Word, Evangelicalism deprecated the work of creation in comparison with that of redemption."[49] This functional view of the world was evident in the pages of the *Christian Observer*, for example, when it was proposed that "the blessings of this world are necessary to the life, support, and comfort of man . . . they are means, not ends."[50] John Venn made a similarly equivocal statement about the benefits of the natural world: "The world is yours to enjoy it with moderation, thankful for the convenience it affords you while a pilgrim and stranger in it, on your way to a better and heavenly country."[51] Such attitudes were based once again on the Evangelical view of the power of sin, which produced a theology of nature "where the

---

46. Ward, *Early Evangelicalism*, 133.

47. McDannell and Lang, *Heaven: A History*, 154.

48. Evangelical enjoyment of the natural world increased as the Victorian era progressed, in part because of the kind of romantic predilections that are the major theme of this present study. See Smith, "The Mountain and the Flower" and Atherstone, "Frances Ridley Havergal's Theology of Nature."

49. Rosman, *Evangelicals and Culture*, 47.

50. "Family Sermons—CCLVI." *Christian Observer*, 1st ser., 29 (1829), 346.

51. Rosman, *Evangelicals and Culture*, 50.

dysfunctional aspects of creation were given their due, illustrating the corrupting effects of Adam's fall."[52] As Rosman and Hilton have argued, echoing later nineteenth-century critics from within Evangelicalism such as R. W. Dale (1829–95), this outlook was also related to the failure of Evangelical theology to account properly for the incarnation as an integral part of how God related to the material world.[53]

The Evangelical suspicion of the created order found expression in the Evangelical approbation of Thomas Malthus' "dismal" ideas about the limited capacity of the world to support a growing population. Malthusian economics, which were supported by Evangelicals such as Thomas Chalmers, had a low view of the capacity of agriculture to sustain a growing population. Boyd Hilton argues that the Evangelical acceptance of Malthus gave rise only to a "paradox" concerning how a good God could allow suffering, famine, and poverty in his creation. Hilton contends that such apparent failures in the created order were resolved by the idea outlined in the previous section; namely, that the world was intended not as a place of Elysian delight, but as a testing ground, its limitations acting as the trials that prepared one's soul for the future life of heaven. Grace could overcome nature and heaven would be a reward for those who had passed through the world's trials and deficiencies. "Nature and grace being so obviously distinct, no one expected earth to partake of the blissfulness that is Heaven."[54] This leads to the fifth and final nuance of Evangelical attitudes toward time and eternity.

Time and Eternity: Heading for Heaven

This suspicion of the material world was most evident in Evangelical eschatology. Eschatology is the branch of theology that seeks to know how, when, and where God will inaugurate the final settlement of his ultimate purposes. Eschatology is never simply about the future, however. It also speaks about the overall conception of reality constructed by a religious community. As David Livingstone contends, "eschatologies, no less than creation stories, are comprehensive cosmologies. They situate their adherents in conceptual frameworks that make sense of their particular

---

52. Brooke, "Science and Dissent," 25.
53. Rosman, *Evangelicals and Culture*, 47, 89, 245–46.
54. Hilton, *Age of Atonement*, 300.

historical setting and in an entire system of beliefs and behaviour appropriate for the regulation of the social order."[55]

The eschatological priorities of nineteenth-century Evangelicalism have seemed unproblematic to many historians. Richard J. Helmstadter, for example, was confident that "salvation, for most Evangelicals, meant going to heaven after death."[56] Given the dualism within Evangelical thought between "time" and "eternity"—and thus between the "world" and "heaven"—many Evangelicals imagined the nature of the heavenly future life to be discontinuous with life on earth. For example, John Venn argued that "the real Christian . . . dwells, fondly dwells, upon the contemplation of heaven as his true home; and he values it, not on account of its likeness to this world, but its dissimilarity."[57] Such dualism could give rise to an ontological differentiation; a contrast between flesh and spirit, body and soul, matter and ether. An appeal was often made to the vivid imagery of 1 Peter in which it was said that the material earth would be burned up in the last day, a clear indication, according to some Evangelicals, that the heavenly realm was going to be completely unlike terrestrial existence. Thus Venn wrote: "Thou that buryest all thy hope in the earth upon which thy foot treadeth, see what a state of immortality and glory remains after this earth is burned up, and the elements have been dissolved with fervent heat!"[58] Similarly, an anonymous contributor to the *Christian Observer* wrote: "What is the whole world but a city of the plague? And shall not all that it contains be soon burned up and the elements melt with fervent heat?"[59]

Such language suggested that the physical substance of the globe would not survive into the heavenly future. In fact, to suggest otherwise was felt by many Evangelicals to be an affront to the very nature of God. "It is more than probable that the scene of the last judgement will be in the air or clouds," wrote a correspondent to the *Christian Observer*, because "it would detract from the dignity of the person, and the sublimity of the subject, to conceive that the Being who, though once 'despised and rejected of men,' should ever again stoop so low as to set his foot upon

---

55. Livingstone, "Evolution and Eschatology," 33.
56. Helmstadter, "Nonconformist Conscience," 67.
57. Venn, *Sermons*, 1:343.
58. Ibid., 1:332.
59. "Forms of Prayer Against Pestilence," *Christian Observer*, 1st ser., 32 (1832), 334.

this globe."[60] Another reviewer thought that "the most glorious bodies in the whole range of this materialism, which we do witness, will have no place in that mighty renovation."[61]

The idea that the future hope was immaterial was nowhere more evident than in the Evangelical fascination with portraying deathbed scenes.[62] If death was the entry point to eternity, then it was imperative for a Christian to die well, professing faith, and even signaling to their friends and family that they could glimpse something of the heavenly realm during their final minutes on earth. As one popular poet put it: "Blessed Jesus! while we live,\ All that's needful freely give; \ When we on a death-bed lie, \ Come, and teach us, \ Teach us, Saviour, how to die."[63] Countless tracts, novels, and biographies included detailed descriptions of deathbed scenes.[64] "Philosophy is afraid of death," wrote a contributor to the *Christian Observer*. "Christianity glories and triumphs in it. It is to its chamber . . . that the Christian teacher chooses to carry us, that he may shew us a 'father in Israel' expiring there, and call upon us, in the contemplation of his dying hours, to devote ourselves afresh to the service of the Redeemer."[65]

Underlying this fascination with the moment of death was an important theological point: if at the moment of departing this world one could expect to enter immediately into the heavenly realm, then salvation must be a purely spiritual matter, for clearly the human body was left cold on the deathbed and was itself not necessary in order to experience heavenly bliss. In other words, it was clear to many Evangelicals that the glories of heaven could be experienced in a non-physical way. The Scottish hymn writer James Drummond Burns (1823–64) thus penned such typical lines as "So when the Christian's eyelid droops and closes / In nature's parting strife, / A friendly Angel stands where he reposes, / To wake him up to life." In such a conceptual universe, it was a small step from the death-bed to heavenly glory.[66] Such sentiments made good sense within

---

60. "Thoughts on the Millennium," *Christian Observer*, 1st ser., 27 (1827), 717.

61. "Review of Chalmers' Sermons," *Christian Observer*, 1st ser., 24 (1824), 445.

62. Knight, *Nineteenth-Century Church*, 49; Hempton, *Methodism and Politics*, 66–68.

63. "See a Christian Die," *Christian Observer*, 1st ser., 33 (1833), 541.

64. For a discussion of this phenomenon, see Rack, "Evangelical Endings."

65. "Review of Wilson's two sermons on the Death of Scott," *Christian Observer*, 1st ser., 21 (1821), 361.

66. Castle, *Sing a New Song*, 35.

a framework that urged leaving behind the things of time for the glories of eternity. As a contributor to the *Christian Observer* put it:

> The body and soul ... must be separated: the former must become senseless, motionless, breathless; it must decay; it must mix with its native dust; it must lose all that distinguished it as a living body. ... The soul in the mean time, disentangled from the flesh, has winged its flight to the presence of God ... it survives, either a happy spirit before the throne of God, or a condemned spirit in the world of darkness and despair.[67]

Relatively few Evangelical leaders made an explicit rejection of either the created order or of the resurrection of the body. The historic creeds of the church upheld by Evangelicals maintained the goodness of the original creation and looked forward to the resurrection of the body. Orthodoxy thus constrained Evangelical sentiment. Nevertheless, the frequent contrasts made between time and eternity, earth and heaven, created an atmosphere in which heaven was widely depicted as non-physical and non-terrestrial. Even if educated Christian leaders might be able to reconcile a sense of heavenly otherness with a commitment to historic Christian claims about eschatological materialism, it was by no means clear that this would have been the impression left in the popular mind by Evangelical discourse about time and eternity. As one astute contributor to the *Christian Observer* put it (he was answering an opponent who challenged him to produce evidence that Evangelicals *actually* rejected the resurrection of the body in any creedal statement): "Popular impression is a subtle thing, eluding argument, surviving refutation, and often colouring unconsciously even the thoughts of those who are attempting its correction[;] ... it exists, not in the shape of defined tenets, but of a diffused atmosphere of thought."[68] As this short survey has suggested, it was the fact that the antithetical discourse resonated at several levels that made it a powerful and all-pervasive element of Evangelical discourse.

Revising Time and Eternity

The description of Evangelical attitudes toward "time" and "eternity" outlined above may be styled the classic position. The use of the term

---

67. "Family Sermons—CCXXI," *Christian Observer*, 1st ser., 27 (1827) 268.

68. "Christian Prospects of the World to Come," *Christian Observer*, 2nd ser., 18 (1855), 151.

"classic" implies two things. First, it alludes to the fact that the shifts in how Evangelicals imagined "time" and "eternity" that will be described in subsequent chapters were, in part, an aspect of the generational reappraisal of older Evangelical ideas that started to occur in the 1820s. This revisionism, which sometimes occurred quite explicitly and deliberately, will thus be contrasted with the "classic" emphases of the previous generation, although, of course, the "classic" and the "revisionist" often co-existed in somewhat ambiguous tension.

Second, the term "classic" refers to the synthetic description of Evangelical attitudes toward "time" and "eternity," or "earth" and "heaven," that has been constructed by historians. This of course includes the sketch that I have just drawn. If I have done injustice to the Hanoverian Evangelicals, I will be glad to hear a revision of my caricature. However, my interpretation proposes that the classic late eighteenth- and early nineteenth-century Evangelical dichotomization of time and eternity does indeed have descriptive power up until around the 1820s, but has wrongly been allowed by historians to continue to define Evangelicalism for all time, as if Evangelical thought never changed or mutated.

This is part of a wider problem, namely, that Victorian Evangelicalism is all too often defined by the attitudes and actions of the Hanoverian Evangelicals. Of course, no sharp lines of religious differentiation can be drawn on the basis of periodization determined by the reigning British monarch, but historians have worked for too long with a somewhat leaden conception of Evangelical belief systems. This is in part because of a prejudice that Evangelicalism is an action-based, not an idea-based, movement. Many historians have therefore assumed that one can quite quickly dispense with what Evangelicals *thought*, because it was simple, unsophisticated, and static, and spend most of their time delineating the nature of the very many Evangelical activities and public postures. The result is that the first generations of establishment Evangelicals, among whom happen to number the great heroes of the movement such as William Wilberforce and Hannah More, get the privilege of defining subsequent generations—they are, as Ford K. Brown put it, "fathers of the Victorians." Potential shifts in ideology and theology are downplayed because of an assumption that there were no great intellectuals in the Evangelical movement. It is, after all, a reasonable assumption that there is little point in exploring the intellectual development of a movement that is assumed to be inherently intellectually "simple . . . artless and largely uncontroversial."[69]

All of this is magnified in the period between 1820 and 1870 because so many scholars have, for reasons of intellectual stimulation (mixed, no doubt, with a dash of intellectual snobbery), preferred to spend time with Anglo-Catholic and Broad Church ecclesiastics—Newman, Pusey, Keble, Arnold, Maurice *et al.*—than with the Evangelicals. Early scholar-critics of the movement such as R. W. Church (1815–90) and Mark Pattison (1813–84) constructed a roadblock around the study of the Evangelical movement after about 1830, which diverted people away from a Christian community that they viewed as having lost its warmth and energy, and which had become "extreme, barren, sterile."[70] Twentieth-century historians followed suit. In an influential essay written in 1955, Noel Annan hallowed the Clapham Sect as part of the Victorian "intellectual aristocracy," but traced their legacy mainly among their decidedly non-Evangelical offspring.[71] The result of such assumptions meant that for much of the twentieth century "the Evangelical Movement is studied until the death of Wilberforce in 1833 or possibly that of Simeon in 1836, [but] after that no one knows what happened to the Evangelicals or much cares."[72]

This book is part of a historiographical re-engagement with mid-nineteenth-century Evangelicalism that has been occurring slowly since the 1980s.[73] I will argue that we need to re-examine this "classic" Evangelical discourse toward time and eternity. In so doing I am affirming the need to re-appraise the whole character of the mid-nineteenth-century Evangelical movement.

The essence of the shift that will be explored in this book can be described as a conceptual softening of the temporal and the eternal, of the material and the spiritual, of this life and the life to come. This was essentially a process of equalization. The temporal sphere came to be

---

69. Hylson-Smith, *Evangelicals in the Church of England*, 52.

70. R. W. Church concluded that by the early 1830s the Evangelical school "presented all the characteristics of an exhausted teaching and a spent enthusiasm." Church, *Oxford Movement*, 15. Mark Pattison remembered that "in 1833 Evangelism [sic] was already effete." Pattison, "Learning in the Church of England," 269.

71. Annan, "*Intellectual Aristocracy.*" A similar approach was taken by Tolley in his *Domestic Biography*.

72. Clarke, *Making of Victorian Britain*, 23.

73. D. M. Lewis, *Lighten Their Darkness*, 3; Stunt, *From Awakening to Secession*.

accorded a far greater dignity and honor than it had once been given, precisely because the realm of eternity came to be imagined as similar to and continuous with earthly, temporal life. Evangelicals in fact began to yearn, in the words of one Evangelical leader writing in the 1820s, for "an intermediate and defined condition between the two—*terrestrial and heavenly, temporal and spiritual.*"[74]

This change in temperament was, of course, by no means an unambiguous or complete revision. The rhetorical contrast between time and eternity was too deeply ingrained within Evangelical discourse and too much "part of the stamped and accredited currency of the language of Zion," to borrow a phrase from the Glaswegian Congregational minister, Ralph Wardlaw (1779–1853).[75] The essence of the Evangelical message was still well served by drawing attention to the need to prioritize eternal salvation over human ambition. In fact, the extent of change in Evangelical priorities was more or less the inverse of the order in which each layer of discourse was introduced above: the largest shift was in eschatological reasoning, the smallest in the broad evangelistic cry to take care of one's eternal interests. Evangelicals who took part in consciously revising eschatological views therefore continued happily using the contrast between time and eternity to urge repentance on their flock, while they might also attend conferences that explicitly rejected an immaterial view of heaven.

This book will therefore focus a large amount of attention on shifts in Evangelical eschatology in the middle decades of the nineteenth century. Although this focus means there is a certain limitation to the topics discussed in this book (it is not the definitive work on everything that could be said about Evangelical views of time and eternity), it is perhaps the most fruitful line of research to pursue when trying to grasp the nature of the mid-century Evangelical movement. This is because, as alluded to already, eschatology reveals much not only about "the end times" but also about how one imagines that God relates to all the dimensions of reality. Eschatology, as Bernard McGinn has stressed, is concerned with "the relation between time and eternity, between man's life in history and the heavenly realm."[76] The eschatological synthesis explored in this book is important to understand in its own right, but plotting its contours ac-

---

74. Way, *Thoughts on the Scriptural Expectations*, 62.
75. Wardlaw, *Discourses on the Sabbath*, 109.
76. Reeves, "Preface," xiv.

curately also has the potential to unlock the door to a new perspective on nineteenth-century Evangelicalism as a whole. Indeed, as one of the opponents of premillennialism noted, this eschatological doctrine

> is a school of Scripture interpretation [which] impinges upon and affects some of the most commanding points of the Christian faith; and when suffered to work its unimpeded way, it stops not till it has pervaded with its own genius the entire system of one's theology, and the whole tone of his spiritual character, constructing, I had almost said, a world of its own.[77]

Premillennialism was not a dilettantish pursuit, but a powerful catalyst of theological transformation. The biographer of William Hepburn Hewitson (1812–50), the Free Church of Scotland minister of Dirleton, for example, noted that premillennialism exercised in his subject "so mighty a motive-power . . . that he used to speak of it ever afterwards as bringing with it a kind of second conversion."[78]

Given the importance of this doctrine, it is troubling that there exist serious misconceptions about Evangelical eschatology in the mid-nineteenth century. In particular, the type of eschatological thought that will be examined in this book, cumbersomely labelled as "historicist premillennialism," has often been seen as a gloomy, pessimistic, reactionary, world-denying, and Manichean creed. Kenneth Newport is representative of the scholarly consensus when he argues that:

> Premillennialists held (and hold) to a very negative view of humankind. They generally consider that humanity and/or human society is rotten to the core, and that this state of things can be overcome only by the direct, cataclysmic intervention of God. Things are bad and will get worse. Individuals and society at large will slip further and further into the moral chaos until this world is so totally wicked that God will himself act (as he did in Noah's day) to put things right.[79]

Given the importance of eschatology as a key to understanding an entire theological worldview, by accepting this description unquestioned we are in danger of severely misunderstanding large parts of the Victorian Evangelical movement. Furthermore, given the dominance of this network of Christians in the nineteenth century, when we get this wrong,

---

77. Brown, *Christ's Return*, 6–7.
78. Baillee, *Memoir*, 49.
79. Newport, *Apocalypse and Millennium*, 12–13.

we also potentially forestall some important insights into the nature of all nineteenth-century theological traditions. This conviction that rightly understanding a seemingly obscure part of the mid-century Evangelical mind actually unlocks a significant element of the nineteenth-century theological mind is the central rationale for this book.

Although descriptions of premillennialism such as that given by Kenneth Newport might seem to us to make logical sense (if we know anything about premillennialism it is its assertion that Christ will have to come back to earth before anything gets better in the world—so it must logically be a pessimistic creed, must it not?) we need to ask whether they cohere with what specific premillennialists have *actually* thought and said. Susan Sizer has observed that too often "scholars treat religion as composed of belief systems—systems which the scholars have constructed—rather than as it appears in the forms which are its vehicles."[80] In fact, by spending time reading the sources of nineteenth-century premillennialism, it not only becomes hard to uphold this reductionist description of premillennialism but possible to argue that much of premillennialism expressed a sentiment almost diametrically opposed to the kind of views that are bestowed upon it by the abstract definitions of historians and theologians.

By contextualizing the study of this premillennialism eschatology within the framework of shifts in Evangelical attitudes to "time and eternity," I will argue that nineteenth-century Evangelicalism, even when apparently at its most gloomy and reactionary, was set more firmly in the mainstream of Victorian intellectual and theological life than has been previously imagined. All nineteenth-century theology was resolutely moving toward a higher appreciation of the temporal-spatial sphere. Premillennialists, as surprising as it may seem to anyone who has grown used to the pre-digested description of this element of nineteenth- and twentieth-century Evangelicalism, were in several important ways on the cutting edge of such developments. In the next chapter I will introduce the specific group of Evangelicals who broke with the "classic" discourse of time and eternity and proposed a different eschatological synthesis.

---

80. Susan Sizer, *Gospel Hymns*, 129.

2
Eschatology and the Evangelical Imagination

"The Triumphs of Mercy and Religion": Evangelical Postmillennialism

IN 1822 THE CHRISTIAN *Observer* reviewed the events of the previous year with great excitement.[1] It noted "the progress of morals, education, religion, and general improvement in various parts of the world"; it observed "the growth of that religious and moral zeal, of that spirit of disinterested philanthropy"; and it claimed that all over the world "Christians [are] mustering with united strength 'to the battle of the Lord against the mighty.'" Such activities, it concluded, represented "the triumphs of mercy and religion."[2] The evidence the journal adduced to support its optimism was drawn from the huge range of missionary and cultural initiatives to which the Evangelical revival had given rise: foreign missions, campaigns against slavery and deprivation, the extension of Christian principles throughout society, a spirit of co-operation between denominations, and the wide distribution of Bibles and other religious literature throughout Europe and beyond. This was indeed the triumph of mercy and religion. It was also the triumph of Evangelicalism.

The Millennial Tradition

Underpinning this ebullient confidence in the ability of mission agencies, churches, and philanthropic societies to spread the gospel was an

---

1. For the *Christian Observer,* see Altholz, "Religious Periodical Press," 16–17.
2. "Preface" to bound edition of *The Christian Observer . . . for 1821, Being the Twentieth Volume,* iv.

eschatological position called "millennialism." This term relates to the belief that the events described in the twentieth chapter of the book of Revelation will transpire on the earth. This text describes a future one-thousand year era—a "millennium"—during which Christ imprisons Satan and reigns in glory on the earth alongside re-animated Christian believers. The passage is highly poetic. It has therefore given rise to numerous interpretations throughout church history. Formative voices in the second- and third-century church, including Justin Martyr (AD 100–165), Irenaeus (d.c.AD 202) and Lactantius (c.AD 240–c.320), claimed that the text was a prediction of an imminent new era on the earth, an interpretation that came to be known as *chiliasm*, from the Greek for "thousand." This belief flowed from an early Christian tradition that pursued eschatological theology in the context of the Jewish apocalyptic hope for the dawning of a messianic kingdom. If Jesus was the promised Messiah then he would fulfill the Old Testament promise for the establishment of a visible, earthly kingdom. The Christian millennium answered such an expectation.[3]

As the Christian community pulled away from its Jewish roots in the late second and third century, so this chiliastic eschatological vision also dimmed. After the Emperor Constantine converted to Christianity in the fourth century, the increasing wealth and security of the church dulled aspirations for a radically new world order of the kind promised by the millennialist tradition. The historian Eusebius (AD 260/265–339/340) claimed that perhaps the millennium had already dawned within the splendors of the imperial church.

This eschatological vision was itself displaced in the early fifth century as the western Roman Empire cracked under the weight of its own internal political failures and the increasing political ambitions of Germanic allies such as the Goths, Ostrogoths, and Vandals. When Alaric the Goth (AD 370–410) sacked Rome in AD 410, many wondered why God had let such a calamity befall his church. It seemed as though God's eschatological plans had been thwarted. An explanation of this troubling situation was given by the North African Christian leader, Augustine of Hippo (AD 354–430). His views re-oriented millennialism for the rest of Christian history. In his *City of God* (AD 410–425), Augustine argued that the millennium should not be interpreted as a particular moment of earthly history but rather as an image of the spiritual reality enjoyed by all who

---

3. Daley, "Apocalypticism in Early Christian Theology," 3–10.

loved God, entry into which was granted by the sacraments of the church. Christians were members of the "city of God," an eternal heavenly city that transcended all political transmogrifications. Augustine did not reduce eschatology down to the present in the manner of late nineteenth-century proponents of the so-called "Social Gospel." He continued to believe in the second coming of Christ, a final judgment, and the inauguration of a final eternal state. However, he argued that all these things would occur in a supra-historical *dénouement*, not as part of any temporal system.[4] For Augustine, "the millennium was spiritual, not physical."[5]

In accounts of historiography Augustine is often credited with bequeathing a firm commitment to linearity to the Western mind.[6] Although he did indeed reject a Platonic idea of temporal cyclicity, he also eschewed a meta-narrative of Christian redemption that embedded divine salvific activity in the flow of historical time. He claimed that apocalyptic scripture was simply too complex and variegated to be matched to an historical timeline.[7] Those who taught an earthly millennium, thought Augustine, fell back into the carnal principles of the Jews and had not understood the spiritual treasures of Christ. Augustine's de-historicizing of eschatology, including the millennium, has been the default position of many Christian traditions throughout history.[8]

Despite the hegemony of the Augustinian position, the implicit hope of a period of earthly redemption has always bubbled under the surface of Christian communities. In the later Middle Ages it was evident in the idea of the "Last Emperor" who would bring peace and prosperity to Europe, as well as in the medieval "Peace of God" movement which hankered after a new era of social and religious harmony, expecting it to dawn around the year AD 1000.[9] Such prognostications did not have high hopes for this era of peace, however. Rather, most thought this brief interlude of holiness would be destroyed with the arrival of Antichrist, a figure associated with the beast described in Rev 13, but actually only called "Antichrist" in the Epistles of John. The most important statement

---

4. Frederickson, "Apocalypse and Redemption," 160–8.

5. Anderson, "Soteriological Impact," 29.

6. For an example of this view, see Bernstein, *Progress and the Quest*, 31.

7. Anderson, "Soteriological Impact," 30; Lerner, "Refreshment of the Saints," 97; Lerner, "Medieval Return," 52–3.

8. Lerner, "Millennialism," 326.

9. For an overview of the theme, see Landes "The Apocalyptic Year 1000." For a selection of essays on the theme, see Landes et al., *The Apocalyptic Year 1000*.

of such views was *De Antichristo* by the French Cluniac monk, Adso of Montier-en-Der (d. 922).

In the twelfth century the Italian monk Joachim of Fiore (ca. 1135–1202) looked forward to a dawning "age of the spirit," which he believed would come *after* the destruction of the Antichrist—thereby implying the greater permanence of such an era—although Joachim did not explicitly identify this age with the millennium. He proposed that the Age of the Spirit would begin in AD 1260. Other medieval Christians embraced a tradition called *refrigerium sanctorum*, or "refreshment of the saints." This was believed to be brief era that would follow the destruction of the Antichrist, but proceed the end of all things, during which true Christians could rejoice that they had survived the onslaught of the Antichrist (hence the idea of "refreshment").[10] These ideas blended with a tradition of eschatological Sabbatism, a belief in a seventh age of history (although not typically identified with the thousand years) before the return of Christ, a view that had first been proposed by the Northumbrian monk, Bede (AD 672/3–735).[11]

The first writer to identify the *refrigerium* of the saints and the sabbath of the church with a literal one-thousand year earthly millennium was probably John of Roquetaillade (d.1366). His writings were thus the first time an explicitly chiliastic millennialism had surfaced since it had been discredited in the early church. Like others in the *refrigerium* tradition, Roquetaillade linked this era with the conversion of the Gentiles and the Jews and looked forward to the re-establishment of the Jewish nation centered on a rebuilt Jerusalem.[12] In this late medieval apocalypticism one finds the seeds of what came to be known as *postmillennialism*, a belief that a revived church would preside over a universal millennial era preceding the final return of Christ, during which godliness and divine peace would spread throughout the earth.

This late medieval revival of the idea of a coming golden age cohered with the growing optimism of the so-called "renaissance." "Inherited

---

10. Lerner, "Refreshment of the Saints," 102, 109. Lerner demonstrates that this concept was embraced by theologians such as Jerome and Bede who *rejected* a millennial kingdom, yet, due to some complicated mathematics, found that they had some prophetic days left over when constructing their explanation of the chronology of apocalyptic scripture. They associated these days with the concept of "refreshment," thereby allowing "millennialism" proper to return to medieval eschatology by "a back door."

11. Lerner, "Medieval Return," 154–55.

12. Lerner, "Refreshment of the Saints," 132.

prophetic traditions that awaited a future time of deliverance could and did blend easily with the humanistic vision of a returning golden age[;] . . . the joys of classical learning, the growing sense of the power of language, the desire to find dignity in creative human pursuits were all able to build on medieval dreams of a *renovatio mundi*."[13] Indeed, by the time that Christopher Columbus made landfall in the Americas and Vasco de Gama reached India via the Cape of Good Hope, belief in an approaching golden age of earthly bounty was causing Augustine's de-historicization of eschatology to creak under the strain of the enticing prospect of exploration and discovery. "In other words, a wondrous earthly future was growing just when Western Europeans were poised to storm the globe and survey the heavens."[14] This new optimism prevailed for the next two hundred years and eventually blended into the cultural optimism of the Enlightenment.

The disruptive effects of religious reformation in the late medieval and early modern period also prompted a revival of more radical and disruptive forms of millennialism. Numerous groups, including fifteenth-century Czech Taborites, sixteenth-century German Anabaptists, and seventeenth-century English Puritans, actually acted out their millennial aspirations. During the British civil wars of the 1640s, for example, groups such as the Fifth Monarchists, Levellers, and Diggers drew on the millennial images of a new world order to justify radical political and economic revolutions. Even moderate Puritans nurtured a hope that the kingdom of God might be about to dawn within England's godly commonwealth.[15] More broadly, the seventeenth-century Anglo-American Puritan tradition was infused with a belief that extraordinary events—such as the end of Catholicism and the conversion of the Jews—were about to transpire on earth. Although some believed that Christ's return would have to occur before these events occurred, many believed they would be achieved through an extraordinary outpouring of the Holy Spirit—plus a dash of deftly-deployed English foreign policy.[16]

In the British Isles, after the restoration of the monarchy in 1660, the kind of radical millennialism which had encouraged individuals to preempt divine action by taking the political initiative lay in tatters, and even

---

13. Barnes, "Images of Hope and Despair," 145; Eschabo, "Millennial Border," 26.
14. Lerner, "Medieval Return," 71.
15. Gribben *Evangelical Millennialism*, 37–50.
16. Ibid., 32–35.

the aspirations of the more moderate Puritans had been muted by the bitter memories of how hopes for a new world order had created bloodshed and political turmoil during the era of the Civil War and Commonwealth. This distaste for religious visions of social and political change meshed with the general European weariness of religiously-inspired violence that had ravaged Europe during the Wars of Religion. After 1660, with apocalyptic thought at a discount, there was a tendency "to discard the traditional forms of Christian apocalypticism . . . and to reduce all eschatology to the doctrine of personal immortality."[17]

However, millennial belief continued to circulate in European and North American Protestantism. The German Lutheran Pietist movement, with its emphasis on transformative religious experience and active expressions of charity and mission, encouraged excitement that God was at work in the world. "The dawn of the gospel of the Kingdom is breaking through with its shining splendour," wrote Pietist leader Johann Wilhelm Peterson in 1692.[18] In the early eighteenth century, Pietist theologian Johann Albrecht Bengel made millennialism a key part of his theological system.[19] Pietist millennialism looked forward to an age in which converted and regenerated individuals would be active and happy in their service to God throughout the world. The beginning of this millennium would come not through dramatic political cataclysm, but rather through the sure and steady progress of true religion, one individual at a time. This was an eschatology that stressed continuity and progress rather than a radical inversion of the social order.

In the Anglo-American context, this optimistic millennialism found its earliest and fullest expression in the writings of the Anglican clergyman Daniel Whitby (1638–1726), whose Enlightenment sensibilities also led him to embrace Unitarianism. Whitby's vision of a coming golden age was a religiously-tinged version of the broader Enlightenment hope for a better world achieved through the progressive efforts of the individual. Whitby was not doctrinally of one mind with any of the leaders of the set of events that came to be known as the "Evangelical revival," but his vision of a millennium proved attractive to those who reflected on the growth of religious fervor in the 1730s and 1740s. In particular Daniel Whitby's writings influenced the New England Congregational

---

17. Barnes, "Images of Hope and Despair," 169.
18. Rast, "Pietism and Mission," 299–300.
19. Ward, *Early Evangelicalism*, 136–8.

pastor, Jonathan Edwards (1703-58). Edwards interpreted the revivals in Massachusetts and beyond as part of God's millennial plans. "'Tis not unlikely that this work of God's Spirit, that is so extraordinary and wonderful is the dawning, or at least a prelude, of that glorious work of God, so often foretold in Scripture, which in the progress and issue of it, shall renew the world of mankind," he wrote.[20] Edwards helped this vision of millennialism to become the default outlook of the Evangelical revival that was occurring across the English-speaking world in the mid-eighteenth century.[21] For example, Welsh Calvinistic Methodist Thomas Charles (1755-1814) observed that "the coming of the Lord amongst us has been with such majesty, glory, and irresistible power . . . I am not without hopes, but these are dawnings of the promised millennium, and showers that precede the storm which will entirely overturn the kingdom of darkness."[22]

This Evangelical version of millennialism, which is the vision known to posterity as "postmillennialism," became the default eschatological view of most British Evangelicals. Its re-emergence in the eighteenth century was surprising to some, since it reversed the suspicion of millennial anticipation that had prevailed since the 1660s. "For some considerable time past," explained Thomas Scott in the early nineteenth century, "the question concerning a Millennium . . . gains more general credence; is supported, or allowed, by writers of widely discordant theological opinions; and has lost by far the greater part of that odium and contempt which formerly attached to it."[23]

The Evangelical Postmillennialist Vision

Eighteenth- and early nineteenth-century Anglo-American Evangelicals believed that the millennium would be an era marked by the universal diffusion of Christianity, the end of war and conflict, and the overthrowing of false religion. The conversion of the Jewish nation to Christianity

---

20. Quoted in Marsden, *Jonathan Edwards*, 264.
21. Gribben, *Evangelical Millennialism*, 58-62.
22. Murray, *Puritan Hope*, 121-22.
23. Scott, *Holy Bible*, 5:778. Despite the dominance of postmillennialism, a dissenting premillennialist tradition was also evident. Charles Wesley—known, of course, for writing the eschatological hymn, "Lo! He Comes With Clouds Descending!"—is the most notable example. Gribben, *Evangelical Millennialism*, 67-70.

was also one of the central components of the postmillennial hope.[24] In short, "a time shall yet arrive," wrote John Newton (1725–1807) in a characteristic statement of the belief, "when the love of God and man, of truth and righteousness, shall obtain throughout the earth."[25]

The early church vision of Irenaeus and Justin Martyr had associated the inauguration of such a millennium with the coming of Christ, an assumption grounded in the obvious textual assertion of Rev 20 that Jesus would reign during the millennium alongside his resurrected saints. Eighteenth- and early nineteenth-century Evangelicals rejected this interpretation. Christ would indeed return, but *after* the millennium, not before it. "There will be, I think, no visible appearance of Christ, but a peculiar outpouring of the Spirit," concluded Thomas Scott.[26] For this reason these Evangelicals are called *post*-millennialists, the "post" of this designation referring to the timing of Christ's return in relation to the millennium. This attitude reflected their disinclination toward the millennium being construed as a socially disruptive event, for what could be more disruptive than the return of Christ? Instead, they saw the millennium as a time of increased spiritual activity among individual Christians, leading to a crescendo of godliness. Thomas Chalmers, for example, thought that God "plieth his many millions of instruments for bringing about this magnificent result. It is enough for each of us to be one of these instruments, to contribute his little item to the cause."[27] Thus, when the *Christian Observer* suggested that the signs of the very human-led Evangelical success were the "auspicious dawn, as we trust, of a brighter day, which is about to open upon us!" it was clearly exciting hopes among its readers that the millennium might not be far distant, not because Christ was about to return, but rather because Christian activism was so ebullient.[28]

How distant was the millennium for these Evangelicals? Timing was somewhat vague. As W. R. Ward has contended, this was not a vision of prophecy that had much interest in setting time and dates. This reflected the general aversion of Evangelicals to constructing so-called "systems"

---

24. Murray, *Puritan Hope*, 113, 152.

25. Newton, "Extent of Messiah's Spiritual Kingdom," 153.

26. Pratt, *Eclectic Notes*, 256.

27. Chalmers, *Political Economy*, 1:223.

28. "Preface" to bound edition of the *Christian Observer . . . for 1821, Being the Twentieth Volume*, iv.

of theological speculation.[29] Some individuals did dabble in date-setting, however. John Wesley, following Bengal, thought that the millennium would begin in 1836; but even this millennium, he argued, would be invisible and spiritual, not an event announced with a blaze of glory. In many ways, the image of an impending yet somewhat hazy millennium was more useful than an exactly-dated version.[30] After all, there was always more work to be done; there were always more souls to be converted. The millennium was thus invariably, and conveniently, a generation away. John Clayton (1754–1843), Congregational minister of the King's Weigh House chapel, London, noted that "it is a comfort to me and my wife, that we are training up children who will bring on the Millennium."[31]

This fuzziness about timing was acceptable to the Evangelical mind because the millennium was not conceptualized as a radical break with the present. There was thus little expectation that the millennium would start dramatically or disruptively. The present, in fact, may already have had tinges of the millennial dawn, and the millennium itself would retain streaks of the present era. Indeed, postmillennialists did not generally think that the millennium would be a perfect world, merely a much improved one. It will "not exclude evil men from the world, though it will be very extensive," concluded John Clayton.[32]

Most importantly, postmillennial Evangelicals did not want the millennium to be equated with heaven or the eternal state. At the end of the thousand years Christians would, to put it crudely, "go up to heaven." Indeed, Thomas Scott said that one of the joys of millennial life would be "the prospects of a happy meeting in heaven," noting that for all its delights, the millennium would be "inferior to heavenly felicity."[33] This millennium was a period of human history, not the divine eschatological *dénouement* in which Christians should place their ultimate hope.

I will argue shortly that this view of the millennium contrasted with a *higher* view of earthly felicity proposed by the Evangelicals under discussion in this study, Evangelicals who, ironically, have been styled as "pessimists" in their view of the earth. This new breed of Evangelicals, which

---

29. For example, Charles Simeon wrote: "God has not revealed his truth in a system: the Bible has no system as such . . . be Bible Christians not system Christians." Brown, *Recollections of . . . Charles Simeon*, 269.
30. Ward, *Evangelical Identity*, 138–39.
31. Pratt, *Eclectic Notes*, 260
32. Ibid., 257.
33. Scott, *Holy Bible*, 778.

emerged in the 1820s, was styled *pre*-millennialist because of a revision of opinion about when Christ would return relative to the millennium. However, their revisionism was far more profound than this seemingly minor shift of prophetic chronology. Before exploring this eschatological vision in more detail, however, it is necessary to contextualize its emergence in terms of the changing configuration of mid-nineteenth-century Evangelicalism.

The Younger Evangelicals

In 1823 the editorial voice of the *Christian Observer* sensed a generational shift within the Evangelical movement. "Men who have devoted the spring time of life to the furtherance of the cause of God, and have been permitted to outlive the summer, bearing the burden and heat of the day, have necessarily been overtaken by the decays of autumn," the writer noted in melancholy mood.

> In such visitations as these, it is natural . . . to cast around an anxious inquiry, Who shall advance to the vacated posts in these "noble armies" of zealous Christians? Whom have they left behind to whom their mantle may have fallen? . . . It is in this view particularly that our appeal to the "sons and daughters of sainted sires"—the members of a new generation, whose parents have ceased, or are soon to cease, from their earthly labours in the rest of heaven—is highly important.[34]

The journal was correct to be concerned about the Evangelical inheritance. The offspring of the Hanoverian Evangelicals were starting to rebel against their aging parents. Some of these "sons and daughters of sainted sires" rejected Evangelicalism altogether and moved into Catholicism, broad church liberalism, or even principled agnosticism. Their stories have been told in detail elsewhere.[35] Meanwhile, others rebelled not by rejecting the faith of their fathers but by suggesting that it had been too weak. During the 1820s a sharp spirit of criticism emerged that took to task many of the institutions and assumptions held by Evangelicals of the late eighteenth and early nineteenth centuries.

---

34. "Suggestions addressed to the Offspring of Religious Parents," *Christian Observer*, 1st ser., 23 (1823), 401–2.

35. Examples include: Brown, *Fathers of the Victorians*; Newsome, *Parting of Friends*; Stunt, "John Henry Newman."

This new acerbic strain within Evangelicalism worried some religious leaders, who looked back with nostalgia to the pragmatism, moderation, optimism, and warmth of the age of Wilberforce and Scott. Such nostalgia was exemplified in an often-quoted passage from Sir James Stephen (1789–1859), the son of Clapham Sect member, James Stephen (1758–1832). Writing to his wife in 1845 he declaimed: "Oh, where are the people who are at once really cultivated in heart and understanding—the people with whom we could associate as our fathers used to associate with each other? No 'Clapham Sect' nowadays."[36] In place of the broad-minded, pragmatic, tolerant, and optimistic Evangelicalism of the early nineteenth century, a new sectarian Evangelical subculture appeared to have emerged. These younger Evangelicals, so it seemed, were obsessed with doctrinal and ecclesiastical purity, elevated pet topics to dogmatic certainty, and preferred to look to the outward conventions of belief than to inner piety.[37]

In 1853 W. J. Conybeare (1815–57) fixed our image of this new Evangelicalism in a famous analysis of contemporary "church parties" in the *Edinburgh Review*.[38] Conybeare argued that these "ultra-Evangelicals" drew attention to what they thought was a stress on outward formulae of faith, which represented the "shibboleths of the sect" rather than inward marks of spiritual grace.[39] Similarly, the satirical invective used against Evangelicalism by Charles Dickens (1812–70), Anthony Trollope (1815–82), and George Eliot (1819–90) helped create the image of mid-century Evangelicals as a dilapidated, risible, hypocritical, and obscurantist sect. It was in this era that the headmaster of Rugby and broad churchman Thomas Arnold (1795–1842) gave his infamous definition of an Evangelical as "a good Christian, with a low understanding, a bad education and ignorance of the world."[40] Such characterizations have surely been in

---

36. Stephen, *Letters*, 87.

37. Elliott-Binns, *Evangelical Movement*, 43, 49.

38. Conybeare, *Church Parties*, 284.

39. Ibid., 285. The *QJP* thought that Conybeare attacked Evangelicals "with an excess of bitterness which is not easily accounted for, flinging against them all missiles that came to hand—jests, gossip, tattle &c." Review of *The Evangelicals and the Edinburgh. A Reply to the Article on Church Parties*, by the Revd. Samuel Minton, *QJP* 6 (1854), 193. Minton was a premillennialist who later became a supporter of Conditional Immortality.

40. Stanley, *Life . . . of Thomas Arnold*, 221.

part responsible for repelling historians from serious study of the movement in the early Victorian era.

At the heart of the younger Evangelicals' critique was a stinging indictment of the panoply of the religious organizations, agencies, meetings, publications, and so-called "machinery" that had characterized the early-nineteenth-century Evangelical world. In other words, they appeared to reject the very things that the *Christian Observer* had in 1821 interpreted as indications of the coming millennium.

An early version of this critique can be detected in a book by the minister of Percy Chapel, London, James Haldane Stewart (1776–1854), titled *Thoughts on the Importance of Special Prayer for the General Outpouring of the Holy Spirit* (1822). In this work Stewart contended that Evangelicals had placed too much trust in the ability of human agency to spread the gospel. "It has been observed of the works of man, that they are complex in their construction, and trivial in their effects," wrote Stewart, sardonically. "A machine of a thousand wheels is employed to produce a silken thread."[41] Stewart urged the Christian community to rediscover the role of the Holy Spirit in the life of the church, and thereby to acknowledge that the prerogative of missionary work rested with God alone, not with human ingenuity and effort.[42]

In a similar vein, in 1824 Edward Irving (1792–1834) launched a searing diatribe against the modern missionary movement in a sermon given before the London Missionary Society, one of the greatest mission institutions and a source of considerable Evangelical pride. Irving was a Church of Scotland minister who had served an apprenticeship under Thomas Chalmers in Glasgow. In 1822 he became minister of one of the Church of Scotland's London churches, the Caledonian Chapel in Hatton Garden. In his sermon, which was later republished under the title *For Missionaries After the Apostolical School* (1825), Irving accused the Evangelical world of supplanting reliance on God with a commitment to organization, careful financing, and rationalist strategizing. "This is the age of expediency, both in the Church and out of the Church; and all institutions are modeled upon the principles of expediency, and carried into effect by the rules of prudence," he fulminated.[43] Irving spoke with the radical romantic tone of the day. He was a friend of Samuel

---

41. J. H. Stewart, *Thoughts on . . . Special Prayer*, 3.

42. Stunt, *From Awakening to Secession*, 117–46.

43. Irving, *For Missionaries After the Apostolic School*, xiv. For discussions of Irving and the Catholic Apostolic Church, see Grass, *Edward Irving*.

Taylor Coleridge (1772–1834), who described him as "the freest, bravest, brotherliest human soul mine ever came in contact with."[44] Irving's critique of religious pragmatism and utilitarianism matched Coleridge's hatred of rationalism and utilitarianism. It also resonated more broadly with the early nineteenth-century romantic critique of the dehumanizing tendencies of industrialization and the amoral economic rationalism of burgeoning middle class capitalism.

Undergirding this new radical strand of Evangelicalism was a desire for passion, drama, enthusiasm, and effusions of the supernatural.[45] To this desire for authentic spiritual experience was tethered a desire for ecclesiastical purity, and particularly a call to "apostolicity," meaning the recovery of the presumed purity, simplicity, and trust in God demonstrated by the early church.[46] Essex Evangelical William Marsh (1775–1864) set out such an agenda in *The Spirit of Primitive Christianity* (1826), and the theme was also adopted by Alexander John Scott (1805–66), a Scottish Presbyterian minister and later a Christian socialist who had also served for two years as assistant to Edward Irving in the late 1820s.[47] The conviction that the established church was corrupt and stood under the judgment of God led several Evangelical groups to believe that it was necessary to separate themselves from the traditional denominations during this era.[48] One of the most notable secessions of this era was that of the group of Evangelicals who gathered around Edward Irving within the Catholic Apostolic Church after his deposition from the Presbyterian Church of Scotland over allegedly heretical statements concerning the human nature of Christ.[49] A second major example of secession was the fissure in the Church of Ireland created by John Nelson Darby (1800–1882) who became the organizing genius of the separatist Brethren movement.

This new spirit of criticism and sectarianism created considerable turbulence within the Evangelical community in the late 1820s. Timothy

44. "Edward Irving" in Geedes, *Viri Ilustres*, 66.

45. Carter, *Anglican Evangelicals*, 167.

46. The call for primitive apostolicity linked Anglican Evangelicals with the early emphases of the Oxford Movement. Hylson-Smith, *Evangelicals in the Church of England*, 114.

47. For an introduction, see Newell, "Scottish Intimations."

48. Carter, *Anglican Evangelicals*.

49. On this "heresy" and its relationship to historicist premillennialism, see below, 171.

Stunt has documented the emergence of a stricter attitude that pulled asunder the Bible Society over the issues of whether the Apocrypha should be included with Bibles distributed to Catholic areas of Europe. Further debates occurred in the early 1830s about whether Unitarians could belong to the membership of this Trinitarian institution.[50] The radical Evangelicals leading these campaigns—"a sort of Evangelical 'vigilante' group," as Stunt puts it—established new vehicles for the propagation of their views.[51] Among these was the Continental Society for the Diffusion of Religious Knowledge, founded in 1819 by Robert Haldane (1764–1842) who, fresh from his experience in helping lead a period of revival in Switzerland (the so-called Genevan *réveil*) desired to "reform both the Socinian tendencies of the Protestant denominations and those suffering under Popish Christianity" in mainland Europe.[52]

This new strident variety of Evangelicalism is also associated in particular with the *Record*, a newspaper founded in 1828. It was edited by Robert Haldane's nephew, Alexander Haldane (1800–1882).[53] The *Record* promoted a vigorous, uncompromising Evangelicalism that took issue with some of the decisions of the past generation of Evangelical leaders, particularly on pressure-point issues such as relaxing civil disabilities placed on Catholics. Ian Rennie and Ian Bradley have both drawn attention to the emergence of a distinct "Recordite" body of opinion in Parliament that championed stricter and more controversial views in the 1830s, including the need to uphold Sabbath laws, to defend the Protestant establishment, and to assume a theonomic approach to law-making which sought to enforce godliness by statute.[54] This attitude was noticeably different from those of the older moderate and conciliatory group of "Saints," led by William Wilberforce, who practiced a non-partisan and pragmatic approach to Christian politics.[55]

Although it is possible to detect a revival of vociferous Calvinism among these younger Evangelicals, criticisms of Evangelical missionary

---

50. Stunt, *From Awakening to Secession*, 239–46. See also Oliver, *Prophets and Millennialists*, 125; Rosman, *Evangelicals and Culture*, 28–32.

51. Stunt, *From Awakening to Secession*, 102.

52. Quoted in Carter, *Anglican Evangelicals*, 163. See also Stunt, *From Awakening to Secession*, 95ff.

53. Altholz, "Alexander Haldane," 24–29.

54. Wolffe, "Recordites."

55. Bradley, "Politics of Godliness," esp. 251–69; Rennie, "Evangelicalism and English Public Life."

activity were not a return to the anti-mission sentiments exhibited by some eighteenth-century Protestants who had been unfavorable to the new Pietist missionary zeal that dawned during the Evangelical revival.[56] In fact, as Stunt has demonstrated, many of these Evangelicals drew their energy from the ongoing *réveil* in Switzerland, a movement which combined Calvinist convictions with an intense desire for mission.[57] One of the radicals, Lewis Way (1772–1840), could even sound an apparently old-fashioned Evangelical theme when he told the Continental Society in 1826 that the "very existence" of mission societies, was one of the "signs of the *latter times*[,] . . . those days which immediately precede the establishment of that universal kingdom."[58] The argument of these Evangelicals was not that missionary activity was wrong *per se*, but rather that Evangelicals had come to view the plethora of religious agencies as an end in themselves and, in their commitment to making Evangelicalism a successful and even fashionable religious enterprise, had hedged-in the radical implications of the gospel by an attitude of pragmatism, compromise, and vacillating moderation.

The New Millennialism

In terms of eschatology, many of the younger Evangelicals continued their characteristic theme that the older generation had confused human effort with divine initiative. Mission was necessary and even a sign of God's impending kingdom, but its results were not in and of themselves constitutive of the coming millennium.[59] For example, Edward Thomas Vaughan (1777–1829), the vicar of All Saints and St. Martin's, Leicester, claimed that mission effort should not be focused upon conversion of the world, as much as it should be like John the Baptist, announcing the (second) advent of the Messiah. Success was to be measured more by fidelity to the message than by the results achieved by preaching and proselyting. Mission did not build the millennium.

The most obvious eschatological revision that many (but, as I shall show later, not all) younger Evangelicals made was to switch the timing of

---

56. Carter, *Anglican Evangelicals*, 163; Bebbington, *Evangelicalism in Modern Britain*, 77.

57. Stunt, *From Awakening to Secession*, esp. 91–116.

58. Froom, *Prophetic Faith*, 3:443.

59. Vaughan, *Letter*, 8–12.

the return of Christ. They argued that Christ would return not at the end of the millennium but at the beginning. For this reason they are called *pre*-millennialists. This chronological change clearly fitted with the broad theological thesis of the younger Evangelicals: only divine intervention could produce a transformed world. Postmillennialism had placed unwarrantable hope in human effort.[60] "Until Christ comes again," wrote Baptist premillennialist John Cox (1802–78) "the world will continue unblest, and nature unredeemed. Man will go on chasing shadows, and creation will groan under its heavy burden."[61]

Furthermore, for leaders such as Edward Irving and John Nelson Darby, who insisted that the whole church was currently under God's judgment for its compromise and doctrinal flabbiness, the premillennial scheme reignited the sense of discontinuity between this age and the next that had been subdued in the postmillennial vision. For Evangelical separatists, as for the early church, the return of Christ stood as a hiatus between one age and the next.

Pulling the return of Christ to the start of the millennium also had another effect: it quite simply heightened the role of the second advent as an object of prophetical concern. After all, in the postmillennial scheme one would never expect to be alive at the time of Christ's return since it was always at least one thousand years in the future. "It would be an abuse of the rational intellect to suppose a man could be daily in expectation of the Lord's advent and at the same time be looking for a thousand years blessedness to precede that event," explained the prophetical writer George Montagu (1799–1855), Viscount Mandeville from 1799 to 1843, and, from 1843, the Sixth Duke of Manchester.[62] Although postmillennialists acknowledged divine influence in creating the conditions necessary for the millennium, the millennium belonged to a church animated by the Holy Spirit, not to the person of Christ. Postmillennialists were therefore not greatly concerned with talking about Christ's return in any more than general terms. In fact, postmillennialist Charles Simeon (1759–1836) wrote that, although he did not object in principle to the concept of a visible return of Christ, spending too much time dwelling on this doctrine "intoxicates the imagination" with "vain conceits."[63]

60. Stunt, *From Awakening to Secession*, 19; Gribben and Stunt, *Prisoners of Hope?*, 10.
61. J. Cox, *Themes for Thought*, 81.
62. Montagu, *Things Hoped For*, 8.
63. Carus, *Memoirs of . . . Charles Simeon*, 460.

In the premillennial scheme, by contrast, the return of Christ could, at least in theory, be expected within one's own lifetime. Assertions of a bodily (sometimes termed "literal," although I will argue later that this is a word with many nuanced meanings) return of Christ to rule on the earth increased in number from around 1820. An early statement was made by James Hatley Frere.[64] Further affirmations of the physical return of Christ were offered by William Cuninghame,[65] John Fry (1775–1849),[66] John Bayford (n.d.)[67] and Lewis Way, who wrote a series of letters in 1816 under the pen-name "Basilicus" that were reprinted in the *Jewish Expositor* between 1820 and 1822.[68] Most of these writers linked the return of Christ with the assertion of his millennial rule. Premillennialists believed the millennium would only be created and sustained by the return of Christ.

Historicists and Futurists

Premillennialism grew in popularity during the 1820s and 1830s. Thomas Macaulay wrote in 1840 that "many Christians believe that the Messiah will shortly establish a kingdom on the earth, and reign visibly over all its inhabitants. . . . It is preached from pulpits, both of the Scottish and of the English."[69] The view did not, however, gain much ground among Nonconformists, who continued to posit the postmillennial view. "This millenarian theory is held by very few among the Dissenters," thought Francis Close (1797–1882), the well-known Cheltenham clergyman.[70]

As premillennialism grew, it diversified. Two particular flavors of the doctrine emerged, but only one form embodied the new emphasis on

64. Frere, *Combined View*, 210–16. Bebbington argues that Frere did *not* believe in a personal advent but rather a metaphorical or spiritual return. It is true that he was not as explicit about the bodily return of Christ as some other premillennialists, but I think that his work appears to suggest a somewhat more "personal" return than Bebbington credits. Bebbington, *Evangelicalism in Modern Britain*, 82.

65. Cuninghame, *Dissertation* .

66. Fry, *Lyra Davidis*; Fry, *Second Advent*.

67. Bayford, *Messiah's Kingdom*.

68. These were reprinted as: Way, *Letters*. See also Way, *Palingenesis*.

69. Macaulay, "Civil Disabilities," 467. Macaulay made this comment in the context of a somewhat disingenuous argument that, since many individuals of rank and authority held such "fifth-monarchy" views, which Macaulay thought were very similar to Jewish beliefs, there was thus no reason to prevent Jews from sitting in Parliament.

70. Close, *Catholic Doctrine*, 24. Close himself also rejected the idea of an earthly millennium and argued that the earth would be destroyed in the *eschaton*.

temporal-spatial renewal with which this book is concerned. This form was called *historicist premillennialism*. The alternate stream was called *futurist premillennialism*. There were similarities between the two versions of premillennialism, not least the belief that Christ would return in person very soon, but there were also significant distinctions.

The most obvious divergence between the two schools of premillennialism was on how to interpret the myriad symbols of apocalyptic literature, particularly those images contained in the books of Daniel and Revelation. Historicists argued that prophetic biblical texts was a coded version of real historical events. The interpretative method that made this reading of prophetic texts possible was the belief that a "day" spoken of in prophetic biblical texts should be understood as representing one year of ordinary time, the so-called "year-day" theory. When reading prophetic passages that referred to an activity that lasted for a certain number of days, the historicist interpreter stretched this "day" to comprehend many centuries of history. The historicist did not think that *everything* had yet been fulfilled, since there were always a few more symbols yet to be matched to historical events. Indeed, the art of historicism was to decide exactly where on the prophetic timetable one stood and then to plot out which contemporary leader or event might assume the mantle of the prophetic events that remained unfulfilled. There was thus some dabbling in fortune-telling among historicists, who were always eager to identify the latest political figure or world event that might warrant being draped with prophetic garb. Nevertheless, unlike the alternative futurist scheme, the burden of historicism was to assert that much of prophecy was *already* fulfilled.

The futurist interpretation rejected the "year-day" theory. It contended that when a "day" was mentioned in prophetic biblical texts it meant, quite simply, a twenty-four hour period of time. The prophetic timetable was thus drastically curtailed to just a few dramatic years of apocalyptic activity. Since it was obvious that there had not yet been any such period of intense eschatological turmoil in world history, the logical conclusion was that all prophecy was as yet unfulfilled and thus awaiting a future accomplishment. As Henry Grattan Guinness (1835–1910), one of the last prominent defenders of historicism, explained in 1878: "it stands to reason, that if these emblematic visions [of the book of Revelation] are read under the impression that these things are to come to pass literally, the conclusion that the book consists entirely of unfulfilled prophecies is inevitable, for most assuredly no such things ever have come to pass."[71]

Until the 1820s futurism was almost exclusively favored by Catholic interpreters of prophetic biblical texts. This was because historicism unswervingly identified the historical Roman Catholic Church with one or more of the dark figures of the apocalypse—be that a beast, a vial of judgment, or even Antichrist itself. Yet if prophecy did not refer to history, as futurists contended, then it became much more difficult to suggest that the Pope and his church labored under prophetic condemnation. This was because prophetic parts of Scripture were not about any person or institution that had existed in history up to the present day; and yet clearly the Roman Catholic church *had* existed for many centuries and so it was *de jure* acquitted of the many crimes and misdemeanors described in biblical prophecy.

Futurism took hold among Protestants through the work of a group of scholars at Trinity College, Dublin, including Samuel Roffey Maitland (1792–1866), James Todd (1805–69), and William Burgh (d.1866).[72] These scholars were more interested in discrediting prophetic speculation altogether—by soberly asserting that reason behooved scriptural commentators to affirm that a "day" must mean a "day" and not a year—than they were themselves animated by prophetic fervor. However, futurism was taken up among the more prophetically-minded among Irish Evangelicals, including the Archbishop of Cashel, Robert Daly (1783–1872), Lady Theodosia Powerscourt (d.1836), the patron of Irish prophetic conferences, and John Nelson Darby, the Irish Anglican clergyman and founder of the Brethren.[73] Darby made futurism into one of the foundational planks of his innovative premillennial scheme, which is known as *dispensationalist premillennialism*.[74]

A more detailed examination of Darby's "dispensationalist" version of premillennialism will be offered in chapter 4. However, it is important

---

71. Guinness, *Approaching End*, 111.

72. Maitland wrote a series of books and pamphlets between 1826 and 1834, the first of which was Maitland, *Enquiry*.

73. The most extensive study of the prophetic currents in Irish Evangelicalism is Liechty, "Irish Evangelicalism." See also Stunt, *From Awakening to Secession*, 147–82; Gribben, "Introduction," in Gribben and Holmes, *Protestant Millennialism*, 3–20.

74. While futurism is a particular mode of expounding prophetic symbolism, dispensationalism is a broader package of assumptions about God's involvement with history, the relationship between Israel and the Church, and the correct method of reading Scripture.

to note here that Darby is a major reason that historians have partially misrepresented the premillennialist movement in nineteenth-century Britain. The stream of premillennialism associated with him became the dominant form of millennial belief in American and British Evangelicalism from the late nineteenth century onward,[75] partly through the influence of the Brethren movement, and then through the adoption of this version of premillennialism by evangelist Dwight L. Moody (1837–99), and by its inclusion in the extensive footnotes attached to the hugely popular Scofield Reference Bible (1909, revised 1917). Dispensationalist premillenialism became an integral part of religious, cultural, and even political assumptions, particularly in the United States.[76] The phenomenal success of the *Left Behind* series of apocalyptic novels, rooted in Darby's type of futurist premillennialist eschatology, in the late 1990s and early 2000s testified to its significance.[77]

Predictably, then, more scholarly attention has been focused on this successful tradition than the one which it eclipsed, and there has been a tendency to imagine that all premillennialists in the nineteenth century were essentially similar in all but esoteric matters of prophetic debate. "The basic tenets of the millenarian creed . . . were held with a surprising degree of unanimity," concluded Ernest Sandeen after reviewing the divergences between historicists and futurists in the nineteenth century. "Diversity existed, of course, but in the elaboration of prophetic chronologies, not in the fundamentals," he concluded.[78]

This is wrong. Premillennialists were indeed united on several points, not least by their common rejection of postmillennialism, but, as the historicist premillennialist Gerard Noel pointed out, the question at stake in all eschatological discussion is not just about the timing of the return of Christ, but more especially about *"the nature of [God's] ultimate kingdom."* By examining beliefs about this "ultimate kingdom"—the millennium and beyond—it is evident that the version of premillennialism associated with John Nelson Darby was distinct from the version embraced by the individuals with whom this book is concerned. A full

---

75. Mangum and Sweetnam, *Scofield Reference Bible*, 53–92.

76. This influence is traced in Frykholm, *Rapture Culture*, esp. 13–38. A 2006 Pew Survey found that 83 percent of American Christians believed in the rapture, one of the central planks of the dispensationalist premillennialist package that descends from John Nelson Darby. Quoted in Smith, *More Desired*, 151.

77. The contours of this genre are sketched in Gribben, *Rapture Fiction*.

78. Sandeen, *Roots of Fundamentalism*, 39.

delineation of this argument will be made in chapter 4, but to anticipate briefly the content of that chapter here, it is notable that Darby's version of premillennialism denied a materialistic future for Christians. In fact this "millennialist" leader did not actually believe that the millennium would be experienced by Christians, which is perhaps one reason why some historians have sensed the millennium was not important to British premillennialists.[79] Darby's futurist reading of prophecy also tended to remove God from the historical process and thus created a sharper sense of dichotomy between this world and the next than that held by historicists. Furthermore, this view also promoted a far more negative view about the role of Christian institutions within society, particularly the established church. As was exemplified in the Brethren movement—within the boundaries of which Darbyite premillennialism prospered—this eschatology suited a sectarian group who believed they were a chosen remnant, rescued from the chaos of a decadent world and church.

By contrast, historicist premillennialism offered a quite different eschatological synthesis. Historicist premillennialists were optimists, progressives, and materialists. While Darbyite premillennialism became an important constituent element of the early twentieth-century Protestant movement called "Fundamentalism," historicist premillennialism was far more closely aligned with trends in nineteenth-century theology to which twentieth-century Fundamentalists would object.[80] Historicist premillennialism was a liberalizing creed and provided one of the most important discursive spaces within which mid-nineteenth-century Evangelicals could re-envision the relationship between time and eternity. It was both an expression of broader re-conceptualization and one of the most powerful catalysts for such theological and ideological change within the Evangelical world. Clearly, since dispensationalist premillennialism became dominant in the late nineteenth century, we already know that the vision described in this book did not "win" in terms of shaping Evangelical eschatology in the long term. I will discuss some reasons why

79. David Bebbington argued of British premillennialists that "their eyes were fixed less on the blessing of the millennium to come than on the Second Advent of Jesus Christ that would precede it." Bebbington, "Advent Hope," 103. cf. Rennie, "Evangelicalism and English Public Life," 85–87.

80. The argument of this book must therefore problematize any attempt at describing the theological package of mid-nineteenth-century Evangelicals—of which the turn to premillennialism is often accounted as one of the most acute symptoms—as symptoms of proto-fundamentalism. This is the main thesis of Sandeen. The argument is rehearsed in Rennie, "Fundamentalism."

this was the case in the conclusion. Nevertheless, historicist premillennialism did anticipate and advance much of the later nineteenth-century debate in the broader Victorian church about the kingdom of God, the importance of the incarnation, the widening scope of salvation, and the essential earthiness of Christianity. The surprise of the book will be to show how this apparently reactionary and conservative movement, which most historians have seen as just one more element of the obscurantist gloom of mid-century Evangelicalism, was actually one of the first to demonstrate the shift of nineteenth-century theology into an optimistic vision of the redemption of space and time.

The Growth of Historicist Premillennialism

Historicism had existed as the dominant exegetical mode of scriptural apocalypse amongst Protestants since the sixteenth-century Reformation. The "year-day theory" that was its lynchpin in fact had a lineage that could be traced, in broad outline, to the prophetically-minded twelfth-century monk, Joachim of Fiore.[81] The father of Protestant historicism was the seventeenth-century commentator, Cambridge scholar Joseph Mede (1586–1638). His seminal *Clavis Apocalypticae* was still being republished in this era (in 1833, for example, by Robert Bransby Cooper (1762–1845)). Mede's concern had been to demonstrate the overriding plot of God's providence by viewing the prophecies of Old and New Testament as a unified whole and outlining the course of history to the present. He conjectured that the prophetic story might conclude in 1718. His work was the foundation for the prophetic exegesis of Isaac Newton (1642–1727) and William Whiston (1667–1752), among others. The works of these authors were sober and weighty considerations of the way in which prophecy was fulfilled in historical time. The authors of such works were eager to use their mathematical and scientific skills to unlock the chronology of prophetic biblical texts.

Historicism was not tied to a particular millennialist scheme, nor did it necessarily imply a particular doctrine of the second advent. It was concerned with God and history rather than Christ and the millennium. In fact, historicism was used in the late eighteenth century to confirm the postmillennial conviction that history was moving toward a period of millennial righteousness and to encourage the missionary activity that

---

81. Oddy, "Eschatological Prophecy," 13–14.

would achieve this goal. The influential early nineteenth-century expositor of biblical prophecy, George Stanley Faber (1773–1854), was a postmillennialist in his convictions.[82]

Until the 1830s, there was little question that a Protestant with an interest in prophecy would have been historicist. What was new in this era was the assertion of the premillennial advent. Some of the early defenders of the premillennial advent, such as John Fry, John Bayford, and Lewis Way, did not, in fact, make much appeal to any particular mode of prophetic chronology, although neither is there evidence that they dissented from the historicist scheme. Their concern was more with proving that Scripture supported the personal advent than with precise questions of days and years. Meanwhile the prophetic chronologers of this era—the successors to Mede and Newton, including William Cunninghame[83] and James Hatley Frere[84]—*did* affirm a premillennial advent but made relatively little of the doctrine in preference for focusing on the more precise questions of decoding prophetic symbolism.

Therefore, the honor of producing the era's first full-blooded defense of the personal, bodily premillennial advent interwoven with an historicist chronology went to the Presbyterian minister Edward Irving who, in 1827, translated the work of the Chilean Jesuit, Manuel Lacunza Y Diaz (1731–1801) (writing under the pen name "Juan Josafat Ben Ezra"), *The Coming of the Messiah in Glory and Majesty* (1827). Although Lacunza was actually a futurist in his interpretation of biblical prophecy, he was also stridently premillennial in regards to his belief about Christ's return to preside over an earthly millennium. Irving, who had previously believed only in a spiritual second coming, thus combined Lacunza's commitment to a personal, physical return of Christ and an earthly millennium, with his own historicist chronology, which he had learned from James Hatley Frere.

Irving's book became very well-known and he is therefore sometimes regarded as the father of the new historicist premillennialist movement, a sobriquet which is problematic, both because it overlooks the growth of all the component aspects of the movement in the late 1810s and early 1820s, and also because Irving was not entirely representative

---

82. Orchard, "English Evangelical Eschatology," 66.

83. Cuninghame, for example, affirmed the personal advent and the millennium although he resisted an extensive discussion of either, recognizing that they were contentious issues. Cuninghame, *Dissertation*, vi, 346.

84. Frere, *Combined View*, 210–16.

of the ways in which historicist premillennialism developed in the decades that followed.[85] Nevertheless, his peculiarly strident character and argumentation won notoriety for the premillennialist movement.

The idea gained further momentum through a series of conferences organized by the wealthy banker and politician, Henry Drummond, at his estate at Albury Park, Surrey, between 1826 and 1830.[86] Among the twenty or so men present were Irving, William Cuninghame, James Hatley Frere, Edward Vaughan, William Marsh, Hugh McNeile (1796–1879), George Montagu, James Haldane Stewart, and Charles Hawtrey (1780–1831).[87] The Albury meetings were a mixture of prophetic interpreters like Cuninghame and Frere, who largely worked within a tradition of scholarly chronology that stretched back to Newton and Mede, and interested clergy and laity like McNeile, Marsh and Drummond, who were eager to convey the fruits of prophecy to a wider audience. Henry Drummond delineated the six points of the prophetic future upon which he believed the 1829 Albury conference had agreed. These included the belief that judgment, falling particularly on the Christian church, would close the current era of history; that the Jewish nation would be restored during this time of judgment; and that Christ would then return to inaugurate the millennium.[88]

Looking at the outcome of these meetings, which gave considerable space to discussing the failures of the church, W. H. Oliver concluded that premillennialism was "more interested in calamities than in happiness."[89] Some contemporaries agreed with this analysis. Premillennialists "speak in strong terms of the deteriorated and deteriorating state of the world; they view Christendom as verging to its downfall; they consider our Bible and missionary societies, not as instruments for ushering in the latter-day glory, not as harbingers of mercy to the wide world, but only as messengers to gather out a few elect vessels . . . till God in his wrath shall consume the world of the ungodly, and bring in a wholly new dispensation," complained the *Christian Observer* in 1828.[90]

85. Bebbington, *Evangelicalism in Modern Britain*, 82.

86. Drummond acted as a kind of prophetic *impresario*. His *Dialogues on Prophecy* were an edited account of the Albury meetings. On the Albury conference, see Patterson, "Designing the Last Days," 53–98.

87. Sandeen, *Roots of Fundamentalism*, 19; Oliver, *Prophets and Millennialists*, 107.

88. Sandeen, *Roots of Fundamentalism*, 21.

89. Oliver, *Prophets and Millennialists*, 63.

90. Review of *An Inquiry into the Grounds on which the Prophetic Period of Daniel*

There is no doubt that this early stage of the historicist premillennialist movement was somewhat bleak in tone. There were good reasons for this outlook, not least the fact that much of British society as a whole suffered from a similarly gloomy malaise in the late 1820s. One does not have to agree with E. P. Thompson's famous assertion that in this era Britain was "within an ace of revolution" to recognize that the agitation of Catholic Emancipation and radical pressure for political reform created a looming sense of crisis. This crisis was a coda to a generation constantly alarmed by the dangers of radicalism and the specter of revolution. "Those who can remember the era of the French Revolution," wrote the historicist premillennialist vicar of Hamstall, Staffordshire, Edward Cooper (1770–1833) in 1826, "must call to mind with appalling recollections the danger which appeared to threaten this country."[91]

However, premillennialism did not stay in its vale of despair, just as British society also moved on from the crises of the late 1820s and early 1830s. With the dawning of the Victorian age, Britain entered a more optimistic, progressive, liberalizing era during which technology and innovation were beginning to have a visible and exciting impact on the quality of life. Similarly, after the heat and light of Irvingism died down, historicist premillennialism broadened out to become the creed of men and women in the national churches of Britain and Ireland who were temperamentally as moderate and catholic as their postmillennial forbears.[92] Albury, Irving, Darby, and the late 1820s version of premillennialism, combined with our ongoing encounters with dispensationalist premillennialism, have wrongly been allowed to set the tone for how all nineteenth-century premillennialism has been interpreted.[93]

. . . by Rev S. R. Maitland. *CO*, 1st ser., 28 (1828), 398.

91. Cooper, *Crisis*, 218.

92. Burnham argues that the decision to embrace premillennialism was a matter of temperament. Burnham, *Story of Conflict*, 103. Although it is true that individuals like Darby and Irving had somewhat morbid personalities, not least because of their experiences of illness and personal tragedy, the decision to embrace premillennial belief was, on the whole, theological and cultural and did not appear to reflect either a sanguine or morbid personality type. I agree with the argument of Timothy Weber in regard to American premillennialism in the late nineteenth and early twentieth centuries: "In the long run . . . psychological explanations of premillennialism fail. For the vast majority of premillennialists, the religious or doctrinal appeal is more important than the personal one." Weber, *Living in the Shadow*, 230.

93. W. H. Oliver interprets the Albury Conferences as the "high point" of premillennial excitement, an analysis which gives a misleading view of the longevity of historicist premillennialism and thus allows this early period an unwarranted privileged

The transition to a more measured premillennialism was evident in several Anglicans who, in the early 1830s, deliberately distanced themselves from their past radical stances. Hugh McNeile (1795–1879), whose name would go on to be associated with Liverpool Protestantism, exemplified this retreat from the most gloomy implications of early premillennialism. McNeile was the rector of Albury in the late 1820s and moderated the early conferences at Henry Drummond's home. However, in the early 1830s McNeile quit his association with Drummond and Irving, preaching a public recantation in which he fully exposed their "heretical views."[94] McNeile did not, though, give up his premillennialist eschatology. Instead he adopted a more measured premillennialism articulated from within the Anglican Evangelical establishment.[95] Similarly William Marsh, the curate of Colchester, nicknamed "Millennial Marsh" for his well-known eschatological opinions, also pulled away from the Irvingites in the early 1830s and went on to have a highly successful career as an historicist premillennialist clergyman in the Church of England.[96]

Meanwhile Evangelicals who could legitimately be seen as heirs of the Clapham Sect were swelling the historicist premillennialist ranks. Most notable among these was Edward Bickersteth, a former Church Missionary Society missionary in Sierra Leone. In 1830 he became Vicar of Watton, Hertfordshire. Bickersteth adopted historicist premillennialist views in 1832.[97] Bickersteth narrated his conversion to premillennialism not so much as a switch in timing in regard to the second advent, nor as issuing from any particular sense of impending social catastrophe, but rather as primarily being grounded in a new conviction

---

position in defining the overall character of the movement. Oliver, *Prophets and Millennialists*, 107.

94. This was published as McNeile, *Letters to a Friend*. See also *Random Recollections*, 109–10.

95. Carter is wrong when he suggests that McNeile "abandoned the English prophetic movement altogether." Carter, *Anglican Evangelicals*, 187. McNeile objected to secessionist premillennialism, and to some of the proto-pentecostalist elements of the Catholic Apostolic Church, but *not* to premillennialism in general. He was, in fact, one of the foremost advocates of premillennialism over the next twenty years.

96. C. Marsh, *Life of William Marsh*, 185. Marsh was given this name by Birmingham political radicals who "took for granted" that the millennium Marsh spoke of would "be of a similar nature with 'the golden age' which they had been led to expect." Ibid., 146.

97. Birks, *Memoir of the Rev. Edward Bickersteth*, 2:38–42; E. Bickersteth, *Practical Guide*, 64.

that the kingdom of Christ would be earthly and physical, rather than spiritual and inward, as he had been taught by the previous generation of Evangelical teachers.[98]

The acquisition of such moderate supporters gave the movement a rather different hue. Bickersteth, for example, said he wished to view the subject "more in the practical application than in minute anticipated declaration of future events."[99] The strong pastoral and devotional element to Bickersteth's thought was indicative of a shift away from Irvingite drama and invective. Thomas Rawson Birks, Bickersteth's son-in-law and himself a leading premillennialist writer and speaker, noted of his father-in-law that there was "no one whose character and example had so wide an influence in rescuing the study of prophecy alike, from the censure of its opponents, and the perversion of mistaken friends."[100] Bickersteth was not afraid to restate the basic tenets of the historicist interpretation but, along with many of his colleagues in Anglican and Presbyterian pastoral ministry, he did not devote large amounts of time to discussing questions of chronology or making predictions. As Edwin Leroy Froom—whose dense survey of the historicist tradition, *The Prophetic Faith of our Fathers* (1950), remains both an essential and a frustrating *vade mecum* for all scholars of the movement—observed, after the mid-1830s, "specific expectation had given way to generalities."[101]

Historicist premillennialism was not, then, the opinion of a small sectarian fanatics. E. B. Elliott (1793–1875) noted in the preface to an 1851 reprint of his *Horæ Apocalypticæ* that since "the date of the first publication of my own work on the Apocalypse [in 1844], so rapid had been the progress of these views in England, that instead of its appearing as a thing strange and half-heretical to hold them, as when Irving published his translation of Ben-Ezra, the leaven had evidently now deeply penetrated the religious mind."[102] Mourant Brock (1802–56), the his-

98. E. Bickersteth, *Practical Guide*, 312.

99. Ibid., 52.

100. Birks, *Memoir of the Rev. Edward Bickersteth*, 2:44. Birks has recently attracted scholarly attention. See R. S. Brown, "Evangelicalism, Cultural Influences, and Theological Change."

101. Froom, *Prophetic Faith*, 3:704. Froom, whose own volumes are filled with details of prophetic minutiae, probably did not intend this to be a compliment.

102. Elliott, *Horæ Apocalypticæ*: 4:552. I have been unable to find any comparable estimates for Scotland, although there was clearly strong support from Presbyterians such as Horatius Bonar. There is little evidence of particular support for premillennialism from Welsh Evangelicals, probably reflecting the prevalence of Nonconformist

toricist premillennialist curate of Christ Church, Clifton, estimated that there were seven hundred historicist premillennialists in the Church of England in 1845.[103] Thomas Rawson Birks thought in 1857 that the "view is now entertained by a majority of the Evangelical clergy of England and Ireland."[104] Scottish journalist James Grant (1802–79) opposed millennial theology in his important work, *The End of All Things* (1866), but he nevertheless admitted that many of his friends were premillennialists.

> A large number of my most revered private friends are . . . firm believers in the doctrine of a personal reign of Christ on earth. . . . They are alike *eminent* for the greatness of their talents, for their deep and sustained spirituality of mind, for their habitually close walk with God, for their exemplary conduct in the society and sight of their fellow men, and for their devotedness to the cause of Christ and of souls.[105]

Grant left no doubt that these premillennialists were thoroughly mainstream, catholic and, in all respects other than their eschatology, paradigms of Christian zeal and charity.

This new theological worldview was disseminated through a host of conferences, lectures, journals, and sermons. One of the earliest of these organizations was the Society for the Investigation of Prophecy. This group had begun to meet in London in the mid-1820s under the direction of James Hatley Frere, Edward Irving, and Lewis Way.[106] A second significant group was the Powerscourt conferences. This group, which first met in 1831, was initially a mix of historicists and futurists, and was chaired by the Bishop of Cashel, Robert Daly.[107] The conference became increasingly acrimonious due to the influence of John Nelson Darby. Disagreement

---

postmillennialism among the Presbyterian Church of Wales, although the usage of Welsh as the medium for theological debate during the nineteenth century has made it difficult for the current author to confirm or deny the presence of a premillennial tradition. However, research currently being undertaken at the School of Welsh at Cardiff University on millennialism in nineteenth-century Wales may shed greater light on this under-studied issue. I am grateful to Dr. David Ceri Jones and Prof. E. Wyn Jones for conversation on this issue.

103. "Advent Tracts," 2:135, quoted in Spicer, *Our Day*, 274.

104. Steane, *Religious Condition of Christendom*, 64.

105. Grant, *End of All Things*, Preface. Italics in original.

106. Froom, *Prophetic Faith* 3: 449–54, 498; Burnham, *Story of Conflict*, 110. Their ruminations were published as *Papers Read Before the Society for the Investigation of Prophecy* (1828).

107. An account can be found in the *Christian Herald*, Dec. 1831, 287.

with Darby's sharp criticism of the established church, his doctrine of the pre-tribulation rapture of Christians, and divisions between historicism and futurism led to many historicists and establishmentarians withdrawing by 1833.[108] Many other groups were more successful and less acrimonious. These included personal meetings organized by William Marsh in both Colchester and Birmingham,[109] the Prophetical Alliance, under the leadership of William Pennefather (1816–73) at Barnet (c.1859–64),[110] and the Edinburgh Association for Promoting the Study of Prophecy (founded 1841), chaired by William Bonar.[111]

Some of the most important meetings were those of the Anglican clergy who established the Prophecy Investigation Society (not to be confused with the Society for the Investigation of Prophecy) in 1842. The Society comprised of forty-two clergymen and eight laymen.[112] The main activity of the Society was to organize an annual prophetic lecture series. Many of the clergy involved had given lectures on prophetic subjects at the Episcopal Chapel, West Street, Soho in 1841. After the official foundation of the society, an annual Lent lecture series was held from 1842 to 1858 at St. George's, Bloomsbury, where [Henry] Montagu Villiers (1813–61)

---

108. Burnham, *Story of Conflict*, 114–21.

109. C. Marsh, *Life of William Marsh*, 139.

110. Sandeen thought that the Prophetical Alliance may have been an abbreviation for the Society for the Investigation of Prophecy. However, William Pennefather's biographer made a distinction between Pennefather's attendance at meetings of the Society for the Investigation of Prophecy (or "Prophetical Society" as he styled it) on the one hand, and his later leadership of a group called the Prophetical Alliance on the other. Pennefather himself was dispensationalist and argued for a rapture of the saints before the millennium. However, in keeping with his irenic spirit "he was convinced that those who differed as to the details of prophetic interpretation might meet together in loving harmony." Sandeen, *Roots*, 86; Braithwaite, *Life . . . of William Pennefather*, 253–54, 321.

111. The rules of the Association were published as part of the Edinburgh Association for Promoting the Study of Prophecy's *Lectures on Subjects Connected with Prophecy* (1842).

112. Grant, *End of All Things*, 114–15. This means that I do not think that this is institutionally the same organization as the Society for the Investigation of Prophecy, founded in 1826 by James Hatley Frere as argued, for example, in: Froom, *Prophetic Faith*, 3:498–99; Brown, "Evangelicalism, Cultural Influences," 44; Bebbington, *Evangelicalism in Modern Britain*, 85. Indeed, James Haldane Stewart noted that he had in May 1842 "aided in forming a Society for the Investigation of Prophecy," which would meet in November for the first time in St. George's, Bloomsbury. D. D. Stewart, *Memoir . . . of James Haldane Stewart*, 307.

and Emilius Bayley ministered successively.[113] Edward Bickersteth was a driving force behind the foundation of these lectures.[114] These addresses were exhortatory, speculative, and intended to inspire hope and devotion. They were not primarily concerned with prophetic chronology, nor with apocalyptic catastrophe.[115] The gatherings of the Prophecy Investigation Society inspired many regional historicist premillennialist gatherings. Montagu Villiers claimed in 1849 that he was aware of thousands who had gathered to hear similar prophetic lectures in Scotland, India, and the United States.[116]

A slew of journals also promoted historicist premillennialist views, including Irving's mouthpiece, *Morning Watch* (1829–33), *The Christian Herald* (1830–35), edited by Edward N. Hoare (1800–1877) and *The Investigator, or Monthly Expositor and Register, on Prophecy* (1831–36), edited by Joshua W. Brooks (1790–1882), the rector of Clarborough, Retford. Brooks assumed the role of *de facto* head of premillennial publicity in the 1830s. The Scottish Evangelical Presbyterian Horatius Bonar edited the *Quarterly Journal of Prophecy* (1848–73).[117] Other journals integrated historicist premillennialist thought into their broader concerns. Particularly significant in this regard was the *Churchman's Monthly Review* (1841–47) and the *Christian Lady's Magazine* (1834–49), edited by Charlotte Elizabeth Tonna. This book draws on all of these periodicals, following the example of Simon Skinner in taking mid-nineteenth-century religious journals seriously as a rich source of primary material.[118] Interestingly, one journal that did *not* share premillennialist views was the *Record*, the publication usually seen as symptomatic of the modern

---

113. Villiers was described as "perhaps at present the most influential clergyman in London" by the anonymous author of a primer on London clergy commissioned by the editor of the *Times*, Mr. Delane. "The Principle Clergy of London," 19.

114. Birks, *Memoir of the Rev. Edward Bickersteth*, 2:164

115. Ernest Sandeen could only find one collection of these lectures in the British Library; Donald Lewis found nine in the Bodleian Library, Oxford. Sandeen, *Roots*, 25; Lewis, *Lighten Their Darkness*, 306. In fact, the entire series is deposited in both the British and Bodleian Libraries. The British Library electronic catalogue also has entries for each contributor and lecture title, as well as the title and editor of the volume.

116. Villiers, "Advent of the Lord," 368.

117. "The originators of the *QJP* were opposed to Futurism and . . . combat it through the medium of their pages." "Reviews." *Free Church Magazine* 8 (1851), 29; Sandeen, *Roots*, 84–85. This is not to be confused with the subtitle of Irving's *Morning Watch*, which was "a Quarterly Journal on Prophecy and Theological Review."

118. Skinner, *Tractarians and "the condition of England,"* 61.

Evangelical pessimism and obscurantism of which premillennialism is assumed to be a constituent part. Clearly the younger Evangelical generation were more complex a group than we sometimes imagine. I will have more to say about this in chapter 6.

There were also many books and pamphlets on prophecy produced during this era. Froom estimated that at least one hundred historicist premillennialist works were produced in this period, although with the aid of electronic library catalogues to search keywords this number now appears conservative.[119] Many of these works were derivative, but there were also significant new contributions. The ranks of scholarly prophetic interpreters in the vein of Mede were swollen in the 1840s by Edward Bishop Elliott, who produced the summation of historicism, a massive commentary on the book of Revelation, *Horæ Apocalypticæ* (1844). This book was the high point of the historicist tradition in British Evangelicalism.[120]

The Pre-Millennial Optimists

Boyd Hilton accused premillennialists of "philistinism and morose, intolerant barrenness,"[121] and Clyde Binfield claims that premillennialists were "world-denying."[122] While this may be true for the futurist dispensationalist premillennialism of Darby and the Brethren, and while it is to some extent true of the opening *salvos* of historicist premillennialism from Irving and the Albury conferences, it is highly misleading to characterize the bulk of mid-nineteenth-century historicist premillennialists in this way. Of course, these individuals remained committed to a supernatural conclusion to history, and to a view of a transcendent God who alone could achieve the salvation of humankind. To those who doubt such premises, all religious views are to an extent "pessimistic" as they place a limitation on human ability to perfect the world. However, my description of the premillennialist optimism is meant to make sense when viewed *within* the world of Protestant religious discourse, and particularly, within the assumptions shared by those Evangelicals who have given considerable thought to the end times.

119. Froom, *Prophetic Faith*, 3:266.
120. Orchard, "Evangelical Eschatology," 178.
121. Hilton, *Age of Atonement*, 212.
122. Binfield, "Jews in Evangelical Dissent," 234.

Far from abandoning the positive view of the world held by the Hanoverian postmillennialists, these mid-nineteenth-century Evangelicals were robustly positive about the created order. In fact, they were *far more* positive about time and space than their postmillennial forbears. The basic reason for this is relatively simple to explain. In premillennial thought Christ would return before the dawn of the millennium; thus the millennial era represented not so much the culmination of church history but rather the beginning of eternity and the opening chapter of the final state to which scripture pointed. After all, if Christ was present in person, how could one have anything but high hopes for what might be achieved! The divine energy would blaze from day one of the millennium, transforming the world into its divinely-ordained eternal state. Indeed, it will become clear that these Evangelicals were not concerned simply with a narrow doctrine of a millennium so much as they were interested in proposing a broad thesis concerning the materiality of Christian salvation. They were temporal-spatial optimists, believing that God intended to bring about heaven on earth. By contrast, their postmillennial forbears had little place for the material universe in their eschatological vision.

It is important to understand that many postmillennialists (and, indeed, Evangelicals without a subscription to any particular eschatological doctrine) found such a vision repellent, not only because of divergent exegetical methods about prophecy, but because of an *a priori* rejection of the idea that space and time could be the final destiny of Christians, least of all Christians who had already been excused from the earth by virtue of their death. "We cannot conceive," Thomas Scott had written, "that it could add to the felicity of those, who, being 'absent from the body, are present with the Lord,' to come again to dwell on the earth; which must be in some degree a scene of pain, suffering, imperfection, and death, till the present state of things is fully ended."[123]

Conversely, an *a priori* commitment to eschatological physicality also undergirded the premillennialist commitment to the return of Christ. Most historians have simply interpreted the focus on Christ's return as a token of contemporary Evangelical despair, and as part of a nagging doubt that the efforts of the church could achieve the universal reign of peace and godliness of which the millennium was assumed to consist. It is certainly true that, because premillennialists had such high hopes for the millennial age as part of God's final purpose toward the earth, they

---

123. Scott, *Holy Bible*, 777.

did not believe that human effort alone could inaugurate this state. But to imagine that they simply saw the return of Christ as a kind of "last resort" of the desperate and despairing is severely misleading. This is because it was not just the *timing* of the advent about which premillennialists were concerned, it was also its *nature*.

Premillennialists stressed that Christ's return would be the coming of the human—the flesh and blood former carpenter of Nazareth—Jesus Christ to earth. This was a position that distinguished nineteenth-century premillennialists from eighteenth-century postmillennialists, who believed that during the millennium "Christ will not come down from heaven *personally* to reign on earth; but that he will reign *spiritually* in the prevalence of his gospel, and by his Holy Spirit in the hearts of men in general."[124] Premillennialists mounted an objection not only to the timing of Christ's return. They claimed that the postmillennial vision had lost sight of Christ's humanity. "The Christian world is blinded by a 'mystical application' concerning the advent," wrote William Cuningham in an early statement of this belief, going on to contend that it was time to return "to a primitive doctrine of the personal advent of Messiah."[125]

In reply, postmillennialists objected not simply to the revised timing of the second advent but more particularly to the way in which the premillennialist conception of the return of Christ offered a robust endorsement of the physical world as a site of divine concern. As David Bogue put it, "How wise and pious men could ever suppose that the saints, whose souls are now in heaven, should ... descend to live on earth again; and that Jesus Christ should quit the throne of his glory above, and descend and reign personally over them here below ... may justly excite our astonishment."[126]

Ironically, then, although there was indeed some criticism of the early premillennial indictment of Evangelical mission societies, and of the tendency of men like Irving and Darby toward sectarianism, the real problem that contemporary critics saw with premillennialism was *not* that it was world-denying but that it was *world-affirming*! Anti-premillennialist writer Susannah Henderson thus warned against the "millenarian heresy" of talking of the future glory of the earth "in such prospective charms as tend to heighten its present attractions," not because she had

124. Ibid.

125. Froom, *Prophetic Faith*, 3:373.

126. Quoted in review of *Discourses on the Millennium* by David Bogue. *CO*, 17 (1818), 746.

a particularly detailed scriptural refutation of the concept, but rather because she thought that people did not "need any incentive to cleave unto the dust."[127] It is significant that contemporaries perceived clearly how the premillennialist vision undermined the multi-layered Evangelical anti-worldliness discussed in the previous chapter. By contrast, many modern historians have failed to register quite how subversive premillennialism was of traditional Evangelical language about time and eternity, and they have therefore been unable to perceive how closely such re-evaluation of the temporal-spatial sphere was aligned with similar revisionist trends across the spectrum of Victorian theology.

Structure of the Remainder of this Book

I propose to show that the signature historicist premillennialist hope in the imminent return of Christ was rooted not simply in a view of the *parousia* as the last resort of a world that had exhausted all other possibilities for reform. Rather, it was a conviction that Christ would come to fulfill a comprehensive redemptive plan which had been in operation since the beginning of the world. Central to the architecture of their thought was the belief that the temporal-spatial world was the site of all significant divine interest and activity. The divine purpose stretched from initial creation, pervaded the historical process, energized the present moment, and would stretch onward toward the millennium and eternity. They believed the sole concern of the divine plan was not with saving individual souls for translation to heaven, but with the universal establishment of the kingdom of God upon earth. The remainder of this book explores this new Evangelical temporal-spatial optimism from four perspectives.

In chapter 3, I will argue that this central conviction that the earth was the sole concern of God led to a robust confidence in the historical process. God worked in and through time. In chapter 4, I will discuss the premillennial belief that heaven would come about on earth, and the conviction that believers would experience a resurrection of the physical body. In chapter 5, I will explore some of the broader theological consequences of this belief in renovation of the material world. I will demonstrate that some premillennialists argued that the progressive and dynamic nature of the age to come might allow time for moral and spiritual growth and education, so that even those who appeared to have

---

127. Henderson, *Modern Fanaticism Unveiled*, 210.

rejected God would have time enough to repent. In this chapter I will also show that, because premillennialists believed that heaven would dawn on earth, they were encouraged to hope that eternity could be experienced in the present life of the believer. Such views had significant resonances to non-Evangelical thinkers such as F. D. Maurice as well as to the growing nineteenth-century emphasis on the incarnation and immanence of Christ. Finally, in chapter 6, I will argue that this optimistic assessment of the sphere of temporal-spatial relationships helps explain why many historicist premillennialists became involved in programs of ameliorative social reform during this era, despite their ostensible rejection of human efforts to improve their world.

Although a large part of this book will focus on the position called historicist premillennialism, it will be clear that sometimes dividing lines between viewpoints were fluid, particularly on the complex matter of prophecy. Indeed, it will be suggested that the premillennialist stance is in fact best seen as the most prominent and sophisticated expression of a broader tendency within the Evangelical culture, which non-millennialists also increasingly exhibited, toward finding a greater role for the things of time and space.

Two Explanatory Keys

Explanations are sometimes best placed at the end of an investigation. However, two explanatory ideas will recur throughout the book and it is necessary for the reader to be conversant with them at the beginning to save laborious diversions within subsequent chapters. In expressing these new ideas about time and eternity, Evangelicalism was reflecting two inter-related aspects of the broader nineteenth-century *zeitgeist*. The first was the broad cultural phenomenon termed romanticism; the second was the all-pervasive awareness of "time" within mid-nineteenth-century British society.

Romanticism

The leading historian of British Evangelicalism, David Bebbington, has contended that, just as Enlightenment ideals governed the tone and temperament of the eighteenth-century Evangelical revival, so the Evangelical world of the period from 1820 until around the end of the century was dominated by the influences of cultural romanticism. This romantic temper, he argues, was a reaction against the rational assumptions of the eighteenth century, which had been rooted in the virtues of balance, science, optimism, and progress. In place of these attitudes came a taste for the supernatural, the dramatic or bizarre, a greater sense of the numinous, a spiritualizing of nature, and an increased emphasis on the inner life, on emotions and psychology.[128] Historians including Stephen Prickett and Bernard Reardon have provided ample evidence to confirm that romantic thought formed many of the characteristics of religious life in mid-nineteenth-century Britain.[129]

The romantic elements of historicist premillennialism can be detected in at least four related ways, which will be briefly outlined here, with more detailed discussion deferred to appropriate points in this book. First, the longing for a unification between the temporal and the eternal was a central romantic theme. "There is something in the human mind which makes it known that in all finite Quantity there is an Infinite, in all measures of Time an Eternal; that the latter are the basis, the substance, the true and abiding *reality* of the former," wrote Samuel Taylor Coleridge.[130] Historicist premillennialists understood the symbols of biblical prophecy as revealing eternal principles within temporal images; they conceived of history as a sacramental disclosure of the eternal mind of God; and they longed for the reunification of spirit and matter which would occur in the *eschaton*, and which might be prefigured among the faithful even in the present. The belief that Christ would come back in flesh as he had appeared at his first advent affirmed the historicist premillennialist belief in the solidarity of God with humanity and the capacity of the eternal to dwell within the temporal.

The second resonance between historicist premillennialism and romanticism flowed from the first. It was a conviction that religion was not something over and above the physical or natural world, but was contained within it.[131] Such romantic thought, learned in part from Coleridge, was the basis of the conviction articulated by the influential Christian theologian F. D. Maurice (1805–72), that the kingdom of Christ was a pre-existing reality that Christians should strive to actualize

---

128. Bebbington, *Evangelicalism in Modern Britain*, 80–81.

129. Prickett, *Romanticism and Religion*; Reardon, *Religion in the Age of Romanticism*.

130. Coleridge, *Aids to Reflection* (Coleridge, *Collected Works*, vol. 9), 54.

131. Prickett, *Romanticism and Religion*, 127.

within the existing structures of the world, rather than a hope for a future state of affairs. While many historicist premillennialists of course maintained a future aspect to their hope, the fact of physical continuity between this age and the age to come led them to stress that redemption consisted of the maturation of what was already in existence rather than a radically different mode of existence. Several talked explicitly about the present dimension of the kingdom of Christ and the need to see heaven as a state of mind or act of obedience to God in the present, as much as a geographical location of the future. This belief led to a conviction, common to some historicist premillennialists as well as to seminal romantic theologians such as Friedrich Schleiermacher (1768–1834), that salvation consisted not just of confessing the truth, but also in an experiential engagement with it.

This high view of physicality led to the historicist premillennialist hope for a restitution of the created world, which is the third connection with the romantic movement. The historicist premillennialist hope in the restitution of all things echoed the romantic longing after wholeness and unity, and romantic yearnings for a world free from the fleeting and transitory experience of much of life. The romantic artist saw this recombination of disparate elements of nature and human experience as one of the key purposes of his or her artistic endeavor. Indeed, the idea of "restitution" was to be found in poets such as William Blake (1757–1827).[132] The detailed descriptions of millennial and eternal felicity offered by historicist premillennialists may be considered as in some sense a parallel act of creative imagination, in which the dislocated experiences of life were healed by a poetic image of the future realm.

Fourthly, historicist premillennialism had a strong sense of the progressive development of historical time, which resonated with what Bernard Reardon has called the deep awareness within romantic thought of the "eternal flow of things."[133] Romanticism was a movement deeply aware of the restless pulse of human existence, and of the flow of history that was continually pointing forward to a future realization.[134] This point is expanded in the following section.

---

132. See Ferber, *Social Vision*, 187–89.
133. Reardon, *Religion in the Age of Romanticism*, 7.
134. Prickett, *Romanticism and Religion*, 142.

The Apprehension of Time

This discussion of the sense of restless motion within romanticism connects to the second main argument concerning the relationship between historicist premillennialism and the broader cultural and social milieu. This argument, which is a central thread woven through the specific discussions of this book, relates to the deep awareness of time displayed by premillennialist discourse. This awareness of time was, in part, a romantic concern. As George Poulett argued:

> Romanticism is first of all a rediscovery of the mysteries of the world, a more vivid sentiment of the wonders of nature, a more acute consciousness of the enigmas of the self. Now there is nothing so mysterious, so enigmatic, so wonderful as Time. It is ... [the problem] which is perpetually experienced not only as a *thought*, but as the very essence of our being. We are not only living *in* time; we are living time, we *are* time.[135]

The sharp awareness of time was also derived from sources broader than intellectual curiosity. In 1967 Jerome H. Buckley contended that the trope of time was all-pervasive in nineteenth-century literary discourse. He argued that, although a consciousness of time was not unique to the nineteenth century, individuals in this era became more deeply aware of time as an external and inescapable force which rendered life both open to opportunity and vulnerable to insecurity. There was, he argued, a new conception of public time, an unprecedented notion that society was embedded within a matrix of temporality and that time was decisively important to all aspects of communal life.[136]

This new sense of time was shared by many Evangelicals. Evangelicals had, of course, always exhibited a concern with the issue of time. The phrase, "to redeem the time," was a synonym for conscientious and strenuous action and a wise husbandry of the units of one's life. Time, understood in this sense, was a gift from God that ought to be correctly married with holy and moral action. This sense of time-thriftiness was certainly evident amongst Evangelicals of the mid-nineteenth century. However, Evangelicals in this period, in common with the wider society of which they were a part, developed a deep awareness of time as a transcendent phenomenon or an external force. Time became not simply

---

135. Poulett, "Timelessness and Romanticism," 3.
136. Buckley, *Triumph of Time*, viii, 5–13.

that which was measured and organized by the individual, but an almost concrete energy that shaped and controlled social and personal life. The historicist premillennialist social reformer Lord Ashley, for example, spoke of the "stream of time, like waters of a loamy river, unceasingly depositing, acquiring, and confusing its alluvial soils."[137] There arose, then, a profound sense of the *temporality* of things, an awareness that individuals and communities lived within a flow of time, and within a dynamic, moving, and fluctuating sphere. "TIME! What is Time?" mused Robert Maguire (1826–90), Rector of St. Olave's, Southwark in 1860. "It is a monosyllable, easily pronounced, oft uttered, frequently trifled with, but containing within it millions of ideas[;] . . . that mysterious principle which operates on everything, and yet touches nothing."[138] The acute sense of the pressures of time and the speed of society led several Evangelicals into supporting movements to arrest working hours and prevent overwork in this period.

The reasons for this new temporal awareness in nineteenth-century society were myriad. The arrival of mechanized work practices, the associated rise of factory discipline and clocks, and the coming of the railways and telegraph communications were all important factors in altering perceptions of time.[139] If technological developments portended a sense of motion, speed, and dynamism, other temporal discourses moved people to encounter the vast and expansive nature of the course of time throughout history. Developments in geological science, especially associated with James Hutton (1726–97) and the theory of "deep time," proposed that geological formations had taken eons to reach their current state.[140] This led Hutton to state, famously, that the world bore "no vestige of a beginning, no prospect of an end."[141] Meanwhile, the "uniformitarian" theory of Charles Lyell (1797–1875) argued that geological changes had been caused gradually by natural processes operating over a long period of time, not by sudden bursts of catastrophic activity as many geologists

---

137. Hodder, *Life . . . of Shaftesbury*, 3:54.

138. Maguire, *Time: Its Lessons*, 2.

139. Thompson, "Time, Work-Discipline"; Mumford, *Technics and Civilization*; Landes, *Revolution in Time*; Bergmann, "The Problem of Time"; Schivelbusch, *Railway Journey*, 20–21, 33–44.

140. Henri de Saussure (1740–99), Georges Cuvier (1769–1832), and Gottlieb Werner (1749–1817), among others, came to conclusions similar to those reached by Hutton concerning "deep time" in around the same period.

141. Hutton, *Theory of the Earth*, 96.

held. This affirmed the notion of "deep time" and added to it a sense of imperceptible but steady motion and mutability in the universe. Tennyson drew on Lyell's geology in his poetic conception of a world in constant motion. "The hills are shadows, and they flow / from form to form, and nothing stands / They melt like mist, the solid lands, / Like clouds they shape themselves and go."[142] Geology thus produced a giddying insight into the vastness of time.[143]

Geological science attempted to plot the history of the earth. It was thus one part of the heightened attention to history and to the movement of time over many centuries. Of course, history—understood as the succession of all events—is in one sense only another word for time, and so this historical sensibility did not simply add another dimension to heightened temporal perception; rather it was perhaps the broadest and most all-pervasive manifestation of an awareness that communities exist within a flow of development and change, and of the conviction that historical time is a realm of contingency and possibility.[144] This perception, that human relationships and societies exist as temporal objects, is a state of awareness commonly labeled "historicism."

To talk of nineteenth-century "historicism" is to note not simply an interest among contemporaries in the events of the past—although this was markedly evident amongst nineteenth-century protagonists—but is also to discern a basic mode of thinking that was pervaded by an awareness of living within a successive, eventful sequence of time. John Stuart Mill (1806–73) identified the phenomenon in a series of articles in the *Political Examiner* in 1831. He explained that "the idea of comparing one's own age with former ages . . . is an idea essentially belonging to an age of change."[145] In other words, the turn to historical investigation arose from the general atmosphere of temporal fluidity and development. The historicist predisposition, which was bound into the wider romantic movement and found its earliest expression among German intellectuals such as Barthold Niebuhr (1776–1831), Georg Hegel (1770–1831), Johann Gottlieb Fichte (1762–1814), and Leopold von Ranke (1795–1886), was governed by the idea that to understand a society, one must look to the particular historical processes that had given it shape and form. It

---

142. Tennyson, "In Memoriam" (1850).
143. Rudwick, *Meaning of Fossils*, 201.
144. Buckley, *Triumph of Time*, 5.
145. Mill, "Spirit of the Age," 228.

proposed that each society or culture was a unique organism, marked by the peculiar set of antecedents from which it had grown and developed.[146]

Here was the point, then, at which romanticism and the broader social-cultural temporal awareness met, as the romantic interest in national history and organic growth was nourished by the broader alertness to temporal motion. Liberal thinkers as diverse as Thomas Macaulay (1800–1859) and Augustus Comte (1798–1857) found in this sense of temporal dynamism a basis for their belief in ongoing material and intellectual improvement. Conservative thinkers found such an idea of progress somewhat harder to reconcile with the providence of God, or the sinfulness of humanity. However, they also had a basic commitment to the "progressiveness" of historical time and thus married a "romantic" interest in finding eternal laws to an "enlightenment" desire to map a meta-narrative of historical development.[147] The school of thought associated with Samuel Taylor Coleridge, which drew on the German Idealist philosophy of Fichte, Schelling, and Hegel, proposed that the historical and natural worlds were in a process of gradual disclosure and self-realization. Historical time could be viewed as a process by which "the transcendent reveals itself in history by becoming selectively immanent in it," a grand pattern of progressive revelation in which God or a higher being worked through time, and particularly within communities and nations, to fulfill his purposes.[148]

Nineteenth-century thinkers believed their world to be changing, developing, and mutable. This gave rise to a sense of temporal decisiveness, a belief that the current era was unparalleled and in some sense a climax of all that had gone before, and that the world was rushing on toward its ultimate destiny. Indeed, the essence of the secular historicist outlook was awareness that the current epoch was fundamentally different from any other era, possessed by a different "spirit" or *zeitgeist*. The new attitude led to the belief that historical writing should not look to the past as a mine of examples that could be applied to the present day, but rather as a profoundly different place. This in turn led to a sense

146. Mandelbaum, *History, Men and Reason*, 42.

147. Bowler, *Invention of Progress*, 49. Walter Houghton suggests that the scientific progressivism of liberal optimism and the idealist, transcendental developmentalism of conservative or romantic understandings of historical development existed as a "loose blending" in the popular mind. Houghton, *Victorian Frame of Mind*, 30.

148. Baldacchino, "Value-Centered Historicism." See also Ryn, "Defining Historicism."

of temporal novelty that was widely felt among nineteenth-century protagonists. "I cannot, I am sure, be mistaken as to this, that the state of society in England at this moment was never yet paralleled in history," wrote Thomas Arnold to Thomas Carlyle in 1840.[149]

This emphasis on the uniqueness of the present moment, combined with the perception that all things were alive with movement and significance, led to the conviction that something dramatic and decisive was looming and gave rise to the kind of feeling of "temporal momentousness." A whole swathe of British society was convulsed with a prophetic sensibility in the early nineteenth century. Judeo-Christian imagery was deployed by a range of thinkers to describe the unmatched sense of the importance of the moment in the early nineteenth century.[150] While the prophetic turn in nineteenth-century society was a signal of uncertainty, it also reflected the more general sense of ascribing importance to the current age, a tendency that could produce optimism and hope as much as pessimism and depression. As David Newsome summarized, "as the pace of life was increased . . . so the motion of mankind towards the fulfillment of its destiny was immeasurably accelerated. This might mean progress—or it could mean ruin. On this men were divided."[151]

Prophetic discourse, rather than being simply an expression of hopelessness, was in fact able to reconcile the competing trends of optimism and uncertainty by overlaying the course of material, social, and political history with another posited dimension of reality—the divine, supernatural, or eternal realm. What appeared to be decadence and catastrophe in the first sphere could thus be interpreted as progress and triumph in the other. Those with a deep awareness of time therefore also tended to have a strong sense of eternity, or at least, a desire to discover the overarching laws or principles with which historical time moved and pulsed. The heightened awareness of time cannot be divorced from a desire to look through the events and circumstances of the temporal world and discover the foundation of historical time in the depths of eternity, and thereby to reconcile motion and stability, uncertainty and confidence, despair and triumph.

---

149. Stanley, *Life of . . . Arnold*, 500–501.

150. The many guises of apocalyptic thought in this era have been documented in Garrett, *Respectable Folly*; Oliver, *Prophets and Millennialists*; Harrison, *Second Coming*; Lockley, *Visionary Religion and Radicalism*.

151. Newsome, *Parting of Friends*, 6; Buckley, *Triumph of Time*, 53–89.

Historicist premillennialism should be understood as an important aspect of the Evangelical apprehension of time and temporality in this era, and therefore as a significant element of the broader nineteenth-century temporal awareness. While on the one hand the movement sprang from a clear uncertainty and feeling of dislocation brought about by contemporary social and political events, its rhetoric infused history and contemporary society with a sense of progressive and optimistic certainty by interpolating the idea of the rule of God in and through the temporal process. Furthermore, the heightened interest in the temporal realm (meaning the sphere of material, temporal-spatial relations), was connected with the experiential apprehension of time (that is, the registering of time as an external, potent force) that pervaded the era. In experiencing and talking about the deep currents of time that washed over society, historicist premillennialists were led to find meaning and purpose in the temporal realm. Historicist premillennialism was, therefore, a deeply temporal discourse not only in the sense of being a *response* to societal unrest, but also in the sense of being an eschatological vision that ascribed to time and temporality a central role in its understanding of how God worked.

Therefore, although one might at first suspect, as many treatments of the movement would seem to imply, that the rise of historicist premillennialism signaled horror at the nauseous sea of motion and change and an expression of desire for the beatific stasis and rest that Christian eschatology had long promised the faithful, the Evangelicals of this study in fact proposed a vision of the final purposes of God that re-created their time-saturated world. They embraced the historical process as part of the divine order and hoped for a renovation of the temporal-spatial realm, a world in which time would still flow and progress was still possible. Above all, it may be said that historicist premillennialists sought God and Eternity *in time* rather than positing a salvation that removed believers from the pulse of temporal-spatial life. This is the essential thesis of this book.

3

The Romance of History

To the student of prophecy, the annals of the day and the hour rushing past are full of interest. He hears in the events of the present the echoes of ancient prophecies. He sees the inspired word translating itself into facts. To his mind, great statesmen and soldiers are not the sculptors, but the chisels only in the hands of the Divine Sculptor; and the policy of cabinet, and congress, and divan is merely the filling up of the grand programme laid down nearly two thousand years ago. God is in prophecy its inspiration; God is in history its actor.

—JOHN CUMMING, *REDEMPTION DRAWETH NIGH*

The Prophetic Past

TODAY PREMILLENNIALISM IS ASSOCIATED with sandwich-board predictions of the end of the world, or with science-fiction-style novels and movies that depict a post-parousial dystopia. Premillennialism appears to be a movement restlessly concerned with the future, ever alert to the sounds of "distant thunder."[1] There is even a premillennialist website that publishes a "rapture index" that forecasts the likelihood of Christ's return to take his faithful to heaven, based on the presumed biblical significance of current world affairs.[2] So pervasive has our modern understanding of end-times speculation become that it is difficult to imagine that the notion of prophecy ever related to the *past* rather than the future. But nineteenth-century historicist premillennialists insisted that they were

---

1. The title of a well-known "rapture" movie (1978).
2. It can be consulted at http://www.raptureready.com/rap2.html.

plain-speaking, common sensical, and reasonable women and men, precisely because their interpretation of prophecy was not wide-eyed speculation about the future, but sober and verifiable assertions about the past. "It is no dream that four monarchies have in succession displayed their strength," wrote Gerard Noel (1782–1851), alluding to the fulfillment of the prophecies recorded in Daniel: "the subject belongs to recorded facts—to prophecies fulfilled, not conjectured."[3] The QJP affirmed that the past took priority: "Those who engage in prophetic study . . . have help and guidance as to the future if they will seek where they ought to seek it from the experience of the past. In every single instance where Scripture has been its own witness as to fulfillment the predicted event will be seen to have proved alphabetically true."[4]

Historicist premillennialists certainly did not entirely avoid future-gazing. They were convinced that they were living toward the end of a long prophetic drama, but with a few more scenes left to play out. They were therefore naturally excited about the future. "We are looking in breathless anxiety for the next movement among the powers of Europe," wrote Charlotte Elizabeth Tonna.[5] Indeed, if futurists and historicists looked in two different directions concerning whether prophetic biblical texts interpreted the past or predicted the future, they nevertheless tended to converge on the idea that the present was pregnant with prophetic significance. These ruminations about the final events of the apocalyptic drama are the most famous aspect of the nineteenth-century prophetic speculation because they appeared to contemporaries to be the most outlandish. George Eliot, for example, satirized those "Evangelical ladies" who "regard as a sort of 'light reading' the demonstration . . . that the French are the very frogs predicted in the Revelations."[6]

The purpose of this chapter, however, is not to weary the reader with detailed analysis of the precise signs and symbols that constituted the historicist world.[7] While historicist premillennialists could tend towards the bizarre or abstruse in their discussions of the particular details of prophetic interpretation, their philosophy of history was thoroughly modern and mainstream. They were products of the Victorian fascination with

3. G. T. Noel, *Brief Enquiry*, 252.
4. "Inspired Literality of Scripture," *QJP* 2 (1850), 299.
5. Elizabeth (Tonna), *Personal Recollections*, 353.
6. Eliot, "Evangelical Teaching," 121.
7. Orchard, "English Eschatology" and Oddy, "Eschatological Prophecy" both have both extensive discussions of the historicist tradition.

time, development, progress, and history. In their attempt at describing God's involvement in the rise and fall of world empires—Babylonian, Persian, Abbasid, Ottoman, French—they were also products of Victorian imperialism. It was no coincidence that the great lines of world history were expected to converge during Britannia's stint as the pre-eminent global superpower.

The Historicist Premillennialists

Historicist premillennialists had a panoramic vision of history. They believed that secular and sacred history were parts of the same divine sphere of concern. "Civilization is the handmaid to divine truth, and the redemption of nature to the service of man advances by parallel steps with the redemption of man himself to the service of his Maker," it was argued in the *CMR* in the journal's first edition in January 1841. "The history of society is the stately porch—the history of the church of God the magnificent temple to which it leads."[8] Historicist premillennialists had little time for pursuing a spiritualized history that was separated from the rest of the story of human existence. Instead, they talked of God's plans being "blended in with the whole range of history; and all the events recorded in profane historians."[9] This vision was expanded upon by William Robert Fremantle (1807–95), a founding member of the Prophecy Investigation Society who also served as its president from 1862 until his death in 1895. The history of civilization, marked by art, learning, and knowledge, was concomitant with the progressive establishment of the kingdom of God on earth, argued Fremantle. "Let us realize the fact," he instructed his audience at the Prophecy Investigation Society lecture series of 1849, "that all things and all events, material and moral, are working together to increase the unsearchable riches of the heir. . . . The Almighty Architect made nothing in vain."[10] Such a view of the past hallowed all human events: "What a sanctified and calming light this throws upon all the works of God, all the dispensations of Providence, all the events of nations," mused Fremantle. "Every moment of time, every act of man, every production of art, every discovery of science . . . contributes

---

8. Review of *The Natural Order of Society* by Dr W. C. Taylor, *CMR* 1 (1841), 18.
9. Birks, *First Elements*, 430.
10. W. R. Fremantle, "Christ the Heir," 20.

its quota of praise."[11] This totalizing view of the past was echoed in 1850 by the *QJP*, which proposed that even the minutest element of the world was invested with a genetic code that strained towards a future fulfilment:

> [In] every Being, and Planet, and Atom, of which the World consists, there was incorporated, when their spheres were first assigned, a tendency, which ... would lead on to the development of God's idea in Creation ... the Collective Mind of Nature is impregnated with hope ... it is ready, like as was Lazarus, to burst its bandages and cerements, and walk again amid the sunshine of its early splendour.[12]

This concept of an all-pervasive "mind of Nature" (note the rather unorthodox upper-case "N") that drove history forward was highly romantic.

To be a student of prophecy, then, one needed to be a scholar of history. "Prophecy cannot therefore be complete without history, for its fulfillment must be sought in history; history is not only the light of the times, but the light of prophecy," argued Edward Bickersteth.[13] Since historical knowledge was demanded, the historian was held in high regard. "There are few offices more important or more difficult than that of the historian," wrote the reviewer of Robert Wilberforce's *The Five Empires, an Outline of Ancient History* in the *CMR* in 1841,

> especially when he records the events of other times than his own ... he who goes back to remote ages, and travels afar to foreign climes, for the material of his work, requires many and great qualifications to enable him to make it such as shall reflect true honour upon himself, and confer real benefit on others.[14]

Premillennialists showed particular gratitude to historians who had outlined the history of the periods and events to which they believed prophecy alluded. Edward Gibbon was the historicist premillennialists' favorite infidel. A writer in the *CMR* in 1845 concluded that "the student who is now prepared to enter upon the examination of the vith chapter [of Revelation] should take Mr. Elliott's commentary in one hand and Gibbon's history in the other: Indeed, it would be difficult to say which of the twain—the infidel or the believer—has contributed most largely

---

11. Ibid.
12. "The Earth: Its Curse and Regeneration," *QJP* 2 (1850), 450.
13. E. Bickersteth, *Practical Guide*, 25.
14. Review of *The Five Empires* by Robert Isaac Wilberforce. *CMR* 1 (1841), 288.

to the elucidation of the Apocalypse."[15] Gibbon was, of course, no friend to the kind of providential schema that premillennialists were trying to construct, but Edward Elliott praised the God who had "overruled the intellectual tendencies of a mind like *Gibbon's*" and had thus allowed him to fashion a reliable and accessible work which could be used by the student of prophecy to illuminate the word of God.[16] Elliott even thought that "his pictorial graphic mode of giving his historical sketches assimilated them to the pictorial form of ... the Apocalypse."[17]

There was praise for other historians who turned their attention to elucidating the dark corners of the historical record. The *CMR* in 1841 deployed a geological metaphor in their praise for the work of German scholars such as Leopold von Ranke and Barthold Niebuhr who, they believed, "have toiled in the mine of ages; they have pierced through the superincumbent mass; they have descended to and examined the primary strata; they have brought the treasures of antiquity to light; and have exhumed facts that lay buried under the ruins of a primeval world."[18] These geological metaphors were not casually chosen. They arose from knowledge of the way in which geological studies were revealing the vast and awe-inspiring hegemony of time. These premillennialists shared the contemporary wonder at temporal boundlessness. "The present is an era of fossil geology," wrote one reviewer in 1844.

> In all directions the buried remains of past ages are dug up and brought to light with persevering zeal. ... A thoughtful mind will perhaps discern, in this rage for the discovery of antiquities, this rehearsal of all past history, a sign of some great change that is approaching, the consummation of the whole course of Providence for six thousand years.[19]

Historicist premillennialists enjoyed living in an era where historical study was coming of age because it confirmed the climactic significance of the current era.

These premillennialists shared with other Victorians not only an interest in historical study but also a fascination with discovering an

---

15. "Recent Works on Prophecy," *CMR*, 5 (1845), 941.

16. Elliott, *Horæ Apocalypticæ* 1:117.

17. Elliott, "Counter-Retrospective," in *CO*, 2nd ser., 30 (1867), 575.

18. Review of *The Ecclesiastical and Political History of the Popes of Rome* by Leopold Ranke. *CMR* 1 (1841), 69.

19. Review of *Vigilantius and His Times* by W.S. Gilly. *CMR* 4 (1844), 473.

underlying meaning to the historical process. There was, in fact, some recognition that historicist premillennialists and romantic historians were working toward the same goal of uncovering the hidden "laws" of history. Edward Elliott, for example, lavished much praise on the German romantic thinker Frederick von Schlegel (1772–1829) for articulating a philosophy of history that attended to the role of providence in shaping the course of temporal development, and for proposing that "the highest object of *philosophy* is the restoration of God's image in man, so the great object of the *philosophy of history* must be to trace historically the progress of this restoration."[20] He believed that Schlegel had argued that "without the idea of a Godhead regulating the course of human destiny, of an all-ruling Providence . . . the history of the world would be a labyrinth without an outlet, a confused pile of ages buried upon ages, a mighty tragedy without a right beginning, or a proper ending."[21] Elliott agreed that Christians must similarly search out the "moral philosophy of the history of Christendom."[22]

This desire for meaning in history meant that pure, hard data was not enough; a deeper narrative pulse was also necessary. "The facts of history are but half the battle, without its rationale: they are only the body without the spirit," claimed a writer in the *CMR* in 1841.[23] "Without the grid to map out this central thread we lose our way in a wilderness of curious anecdotes, instead of tracing the main stream of providence, till it opens into a wide ocean of everlasting peace."[24] Thomas Rawson Birks argued that understanding history in light of the divine spirit that pulsed through all events provided a unifying and edifying interpretative structure for grasping the significance of all the events of time. "When we read and understand the fulfillment of prophecy, History, otherwise a dark and cheerless ocean, becomes bright with the sunshine of the divine presence," he concluded.[25] The prophetic biblical texts of course functioned

20. Elliott, *Horæ Apocalypticæ*, 4:244.

21. Ibid., 245.

22. Elliott, *Horæ Apocalypticæ* 4:243. It is worth noting here that premillennialists were generally eager to adopt elements of German thought that upheld their vision. The *QJP*, while admitting that they dissented from some elements of modern German theology, thought that "much progress has been made towards soundness in the faith by German theologians." "German Prophetical Interpretation," *QJP* 1 (1848–49), 339.

23. Review of *The Five Empires*. *CMR* 1 (1841), 288.

24. Ibid., 285.

25. Birks, *First Principles*, 426.

as the key to discerning the ontology of the historical process. "In the Scripture we have the true philosophy of history, and the historians of our day would do well to learn more of such philosophy than they have done," noted the *QJP* in 1849, with a wry glance at the rage for idealist historical expatiations.[26]

For historicist premillennialists, prophecy was a poetic, symbolic, allusive, temporalized description of an eternal reality. Far from the apocalypse being about odd things, it was about normal things transfigured by the light of the eternal. "The essential character, then, of the book [of Revelation] is simply—the unveiling of Jesus Christ. It is a removal, for the instruction of the Church, of that veil which conceals her Lord now that He is ascended into heaven," claimed Birks.[27] "The symbols are fantastic," he admitted, but one must not read them "with a gross and wonder-making spirit." Rather, "they remind us . . . that the ordinary course of the world, when portrayed by the colours of inspiration, and seen in the light of heaven, may constitute a series of moral prodigies, no less wonderful, and more deeply instructive, than those natural signs and wonders on which a sportive fancy ever delights to dwell."[28] In centering their thoughts on the prophetic, historicist premillennialists believed they were affirming, not denying, the significance of the temporal-spatial sphere as the central locus of divine concern.

Decoding History: Reason or Romanticism?

This understanding of the historicist premillennialist approach to history complicates the prevailing view of premillennialism established by Ernest Sandeen in *The Roots of Fundamentalism*. Sandeen argued that Victorian premillennialists were the pioneers of a "scientific" or "inductive" biblical hermeneutic in which the reader approached the Bible believing that it contained transparent data about historical and prophetic events.[29] San-

26. "The Double Fulfilment of Prophecy," *QJP* 1 (1848–49), 570.
27. Birks, *First Elements*, 266.
28. Ibid., 274.
29. Harriet Harris defines an inductive approach as "the conviction that the biblical records inform us not of ideas or interpretations of events but of events themselves." This gives rise to the belief "that the biblical text gives us objective, factual accounts of real states of affairs; and that the 'plain sense' of scripture is available wherever the reader does not obscure the text with subjective interpretation." Harris, *Fundamentalism and Evangelicals*, 116–7; cf. Barr, *Fundamentalism*, 48, 64. See also Marsden,

deen believed that such an inductive approach to interpreting Scripture, which he called a "literal" methodology, was central to the emergence of early twentieth-century American Fundamentalism, which was marked, argued Sandeen, by a belief that the Bible could be scanned for exact, scientifically precise data, particularly about creation and the last things. Fundamentalists derived their commitment to a "literal" reading of Scripture (and their opposition to reading the biblical text as metaphor or poetry) from their prophetic heritage. Because this way of reading of Scripture was first articulated in nineteenth-century premillennialism, Sandeen concluded that the "roots" of American Fundamentalism lay in the mid-nineteenth-century British premillennialist movement.[30]

Sandeen's claim that premillennialism "gave life and shape to the Fundamentalist movement" has been subjected to rigorous criticism. It is now clear that Fundamentalism was the product of many converging streams in late nineteenth- and early twentieth-century history, not just premillennialism.[31] But what of his argument, that Victorian premillennialists were the pioneers of a new inductive, or literal, method of scriptural exegesis?

In one sense, Sandeen was indeed correct. The historicist version of premillennialism involved an assumption that the symbols and narratives of biblical prophecy could be matched precisely with historical events from the time of Christ up to the present. The premillennialist vicar of Prittlewell, Frederick Nolan (1784–1864), explained in 1831 that "by the scale which it supplies, the descriptions of the Prophet, when divested of their figurative garb, and presented in the nakedness of the letter, may be measured in the minutest proportions."[32] James Hatley Frere meanwhile aimed to make the subject of prophetic enquiry into "the object . . . of scientific research." The attempt at devising a set of rules by which one might interpret prophetic symbols would produce a

---

Understanding Fundamentalism, 122–52; Marsden, *Fundamentalism and American Culture*, 55–62.

30. Sandeen, "Toward A Historical Interpretation"; Sandeen, *Roots of Fundamentalism*, 13, 103–13.

31. Sandeen, *Roots of Fundamentalism*, xv. Sandeen's ideas in relation to fundamentalism were critiqued in Moore, "Another Look at Fundamentalism" and Marsden, "Defining Fundamentalism." Sandeen replied to the latter in "Defining Fundamentalism."

32. Nolan, *Time of the Millennium*, 46.

situation in which "prophecy will be admitted to be, what it undoubtedly is in reality, a perfect system," according to Frere.[33]

Both futurists and historicists believed that prophecy was a description of actual events that either had taken place, or would take place. It is true, then, that nineteenth-century premillennialism exemplified an interpretive strategy that was continued and extended by twentieth-century premillennialists in the Fundamentalist movement and that has continued to have great purchase over the modern conservative Evangelical mindset, particularly in the United States. This is a strategy that searches the Bible for precise descriptions of what one might today call "real-time" events. George Marsden's description of Fundamentalist premillennialists in the early twentieth century would seem to hold good for historicist premillennialists in the mid-nineteenth century when he wrote that "they were absolutely convinced that all they were doing was taking the hard facts of Scripture, carefully arranging and classifying them, and thus discovering the clear patterns which Scripture revealed."[34]

However, there are two objections to Sandeen's thesis, and to the characterization of historicist premillennialists as rationalistic "literalists." One objection will be delayed until chapter 4 when I will return to the concept of "literalism" in relation to historicist premillennialist eschatology and will argue that the term was actually deployed in a far more specific way than that assumed by Sandeen and other modern commentators.

The other objection, with which I will deal here, relates to a distinction between historicists and futurists on the issue of "literalism." Scholars who have examined twentieth-century Fundamentalism have associated its "literalist" approach to prophetic biblical texts with the on-going influence of Enlightenment values over the American intellect. George Marsden said Fundamentalist scriptural interpretation, particularly its prophetic dimension, represented a "Baconian inductivism" governed by the conviction that "with the Scriptures at hand as a compendium of facts, there was no need to go further."[35] He attributed the success of this approach in part to the failure of romanticism, with its greater sensitivity to image and metaphor, to percolate into American intellectual life.[36]

33. Frere, *Combined View*, iv.
34. Marsden, *Fundamentalism and American Culture*, 56.
35. Ibid., 56.
36. Ibid., 226.

I make no judgment as to the validity of Marsden's analysis in regard to twentieth-century American Fundamentalism, but it is an essential thesis of this book that historicism premillennialism was a thoroughly romantic movement. While it is true that the historicist premillennialist methodology of matching prophetic symbols to an historical timeline (whether past or future) was coolly rationalistic, the attempt at decoding history also reflected the prevailing tendency among the most romantic thinkers to posit grand schemes of historical development and to adapt, rather than abandon, the "Enlightenment" ideas of reason and progress. Indeed, much contemporary scholarship on romanticism no longer recognizes the sharp division between "Enlightenment" and "romantic" thought, ascribing the division in part to misleading contemporary self-categorization, and in part to subsequent literary critics' desire for over-schematization.[37] John Wolffe is helpful when he describes the return to system within prophetic Evangelicalism as exemplifying "a transmuted legacy of Enlightenment rationality in the construction of grand theological and exegetical schemes in an attempt to make sense of the action of God in history in the face of the disorder of contemporary events."[38]

The historicist premillennialist desire for a "science" of prophecy was not just abstract scholasticism, but rather an expression of the growing nineteenth-century romantic intoxication with the accumulation of knowledge and the appreciation of the unity of the natural and physical world.[39] It expressed a characteristically romantic desire to stand on the mountain-top and enjoy the splendor of a transcendent, comprehensive experience of the whole. Henry Drummond exemplified this attitude in 1828:

> Men study the prophecies, as too many do other parts of Christian doctrine, as if they were unconnected and isolated facts. They are like persons who look through the windows of a building which contains a very large and complicated piece of machinery; by dint of some pains they arrive at the knowledge of the uses of all that they see, but, for want of being able to get inside the building, they cannot perceive how all the various

---

37. Rieder, "Institutional Overdetermination"; Bone, "The Question of a European Romanticism."

38. Wolffe, *Protestant Crusade*, 30.

39. Knight, "Romanticism and the Sciences."

movements are connected, so as to produce one grand, and consistent, and uniform operation.[40]

Similarly, the Irish missionary and historicist premillennialist Alexander Dallas (1791–1869) complained in 1831 that "one of the greatest hindrances to the student of prophecy is the want of a defined conception of the grand scheme, of which all the subjects of divine prophecy form a part."[41] These were characteristically romantic criticisms of the perceived Enlightenment atomization of knowledge and a desire for comprehensive and totalizing visions of reality. Because historicism had a wider field of vision than futurist premillennialism—the entire past, not just the immediate present and apocalyptic future—it tended to be more amenable to such romantic longings for holistic knowledge than its futurist counterpart. "What a field for historic research lies here before us!" exclaimed Edward Elliott with excitement. "A field extending over seventeen centuries, and over countries many more than those of European Christendom."[42]

Recognizing this holistic vision is important because, while Sandeen used the term "literalist" to refer to the shared premillennialist commitment to using the Bible as a textbook of prophetic concern, historicists in fact used the term "literalist" to refer contemptuously to the *futurist* concern with the minutiae of times, dates, and symbols, and to allude to what was seen as the risible decision by futurists to abandon the idea that prophecy was a metaphor for history and instead to imagine that the apocalypse would occur in some odd set of beasts roaming, and plagues convulsing, the earth for a couple of years in the imminent future. The *QJP* thought that "the extreme minuteness of detail into which some literalists have gone as to future events . . . by the puzzles and perplexities it thus introduced, has repelled not a few [and] has made many who wished to study the subject shrink back in despair."[43] The *CMR* similarly rejected William Burgh's futurist scheme because of its "distinguishing characteristic of . . . insisting upon the most literal and obvious interpretation which can possibly be adopted."[44]

---

40. Drummond, *Dialogues*, 1:3.
41. Dallas, *Introduction to Prophetical Researches*, i.
42. Elliott, *Horæ Apocalypticæ*, 1:115–16.
43. "Our Last," *QJP* 25 (1873), 319.
44. "The Year-Day Interpretation," *CMR* 2 (1842), 781.

Historicists thus rejected the arcane and wooden nature of futurist literalist interpretation. In typically romantic vein, they felt that the imagination was necessary for a proper interpretation of prophetic literature. Thomas Rawson Birks pointed to this when he admitted that: "The utmost which the literal exposition, properly so called, can do, is to place us in the position of the Seer at the time when the visions were seen. But to interpret the signs is a deeper question of spiritual wisdom and scriptural research, not of grammatical skill."[45]

The romantic sensibility of these historicist premillennialists led them to eschew strict literality in prophetic interpretation on the matter of times and dates. Not least among the reasons for this was their foundational denial that a "day" of prophetic biblical texts literally meant a "day," and the corresponding idea that prophetic biblical texts had encoded historical events in metaphor and symbol. In their reading of prophetic texts they were by necessity far from being literalists because they *a priori* believed that it was impossible so to be. Thomas Rawson argued sardonically that even the self-professed "literalist" (i.e., the futurist) "forsakes the letter at every turn, when it strikes him at the moment as inconvenient."[46]

Furthermore, while it is true that historicists constructed a grand scheme of prophetic interpretation with some similarities to later Fundamentalist-premillennialist cosmologies, for historicists this methodology reflected as much their belief that Evangelicals had become too individualistic in their conceptions of salvation and had lost sight of the comprehensive nature of biblical theology as it did an *a priori* rationalistic commitment to an "inductive" approach to scriptural hermeneutics. Although historicists could analyze times and dates forensically, they were more interested in articulating an entire philosophy of history that comprehended the entire human condition and that invested the temporal sphere with divine significance.

The historicist vision was a far more totalizing and universal one than that of the futurist. Their divergence on prophetic chronology was thus only one element of a more profound divergence about the interaction between time and eternity. Futurism turned its face from the long course of historical time and towards a future burst of catastrophic activity. By rejecting the year-day theory, futurists imagined that the events

---

45. Birks, *First Elements*, 253.
46. Ibid., 254.

of prophetic biblical texts would occur in a dramatic, contracted time period sometime in the near future, thereby providing little incentive to explore God's activity in history.

Historicists were very aware of the difference between their own position and that of futurism. "Futurists," complained the *QJP* in 1851, "love extremes. They reckon both past and present by far too commonplace to be matter of prophecy, and have conjured up a future crowded with strange scenes and visions, which have little in common either with this earth or the race which inhabit it."[47] In other words, futurism was seen as distant and unearthly, whereas historicism was imagined to be a down-to-earth, realistic interpretation. The writers of the *CMR* described the futurist view of prophecy as "a sectarian and contracted exposition which shuts it up within one corner of time."[48] Their own understanding, by contrast, was described as "wide and comprehensive."[49] This accusation of sectarianism and extremism was significant. It suggested that the futurist interpretation constructed an idea of redemption in which God acted dramatically to bring an end to time and space and to rescue believers from this destruction.

It can be argued, then, that historicist premillennialists were, in fact, "historicists" in the more familiar (and romantic) sense of that term when applied to nineteenth-century culture: they were fascinated with historical mutability, development, change, growth, and progress—the very ideological underpinnings of nineteenth-century historicism that George Marsden argues later American Fundamentalist premillennialists mobilized their "scientific" and literalist approach to Scripture to resist.[50]

The God of Progress

What, then, was the shape of history for historicist premillennialists? John Burrow drew attention to what he believed to be the transition in the nineteenth century "from a characteristic (though far from universal) disposition to the representation of history in terms of eventfulness, even of a catastrophic, apocalyptic kind, to the subtler representation of it as

47. "Elliott's 'Horæ Apocalypticæ,'" *QJP* 3 (1851), 371.
48. Review of *The Revelation of St. John, Literal and Future* by Rev. R. Govett. *CMR* 3 (1843), 268.
49. "Govett on the Apocalypse," *CMR* 3 (1843), 268.
50. Marsden, *Fundamentalism and American Culture*, 226–27.

a kind of sedimentary process, whose longer-term significance lay far beyond the knowledge of the actors engaged in it."[51] The former kind of understanding of time, argued Burrow, drew inspiration from the theory of geological catastrophism—the belief that changes in the rock formations occur by short, sharp, dramatic events in a relatively short time period. By contrast, the latter conception of gradual, sedimentary temporal change derived from geological uniformitarianism, which argued that change occurred by the effect of almost indiscernible natural forces over an elongated time period. Burrow linked the interest in apocalypse in the early nineteenth century with a temporal understanding that "deals in shocks and endings, or types of the end, of the moments when the order of time and nature is suspended."[52]

Premillennialism, with its obvious interest in divine intervention and an unfolding divine drama, could be interpreted as falling within the former "catastrophic" approach to time. The dispensationalist version of premillennialism certainly appears to fit this model. But, despite its ostensible concern with "apocalyptic" history, historicist premillennialism in fact fits better with the new "sedimentary" approach to historical change. The belief that prophecy was fulfilled in history, and that the whole course of historical development was part of an unfolding of God's plans, implied that God need time to enact his purposes. "It is obvious that all the blessing of Christ's redemption will not, we may truly say, *cannot* be communicated at once, but must await a gradual development," contended the *QJP* in 1850.[53] Historicist premillennialists believed in the slow but progressive enactment of divine truth and action. "When time was young, revealed truth was small in stature, though of perfect proportion and most attractive beauty. These proportions have gradually expanded," explained the *QJP* in 1858. "Prophecies have been turned into facts, and promises into blessings ... all time becomes vocal with truth; God's eternal thoughts are written on the face of time."[54]

---

51. Burrow, "Images of Time," 199.

52. Ibid., 204.

53. "The Scripture Testimony to the State of the Departed," *QJP* 2 (1850), 310. The article was concerned, in part, with the gradual restoration of humans to the *imago Dei*. It was at pains to point out that "it is impossible that the redemption ... can be at death," but must await the further return of Christ and resurrection of the dead. This connected with the premillennial rejection of Evangelical idealization of death, of which I will have more to say in chapter 4.

54. "The Dial and the Bible," *QJP* 10 (1858), 60.

A writer in the *CMR* captured this sense of gradual progressivism which underlay historicist premillennialist thought in an article about Peel's Irish policy in 1845. "We are no advocates for sudden reform," (s)he opined, "God's changes in nature are all gradual; infancy, childhood, and manhood are slowly progressive steps, and the ceremonial law gradually opened the way for the light of the gospel."[55] Such a sentiment of course sprang from the political conservatism of the authors and readership of the journal, but it was not merely a reaction against radicalism. It was underpinned by a theological conviction that God enacted his plan on a grand, vast scale, which needed time to expand and develop. In a review of Henry Drummond's pamphlets on prophecy, the same journal had stated in 1842 that:

> The plan discernible, in the prophecies of the coming Saviour, was that of gradual development . . . step by step, point by point, "here a little and there a little," by successive revelations, often separated from each other by whole centuries, was the grand outline sketched and filled up. . . . The Divine plan is usually that of gradual development.[56]

Gerard Noel similarly believed that "it is impossible to survey the events of the past, and prospects of the future, without being struck by the *gradual manner* in which the work of redemption will have realized its hopes to man . . . how *slowly* has God effected the purposes of his grace to mankind."[57] "God's . . . greatest works rise slowly," confirmed a writer in the *QJP*. "His trees grow slowly . . . His flowers grow slowly . . . His creatures grow slowly . . . God can afford to take His time."[58]

The commitment to temporal gradualism also led to a strong sense of the *directionality* of historical time. Contrary to Boyd Hilton's suggestion that for Evangelicals "the world appeared to be locked in stasis, subject merely to cyclical fluctuation" before 1850, the historicist premillennialist view of historical time was both dynamic and linear.[59] The *CMR* in 1847 explained:

---

55. Review of *Report . . . in respect of the Occupation of Land in Ireland. CMR* 5 (1845), 199.

56. Review of *On Government by the Queen* and *Reasons Wherefore a Clergyman . . .* by Henry Drummond. *CMR* 2 (1842), 250.

57. G. T. Noel, *Brief Enquiry*, 224.

58. "The Life of a Justified Man," *QJP* 25 (1873), 42.

59. Hilton, *Age of Atonement*, 300.

Doubtless there are many persons, even in "the religious world," who please themselves with the idea, that "to-morrow shall be as this day, and much more abundant," and who expect that 1856 shall be like 1846,—not perceiving, that 1846 was *not* like 1836, nor 1836 like 1826, nor 1826 like 1816. But the truth is, that, whether we are pleased with it or not, and whether we perceive it or not, a change is perpetually going on, and our yesterdays, instead of re-appearing to-morrow, will never return again.[60]

Such a sense of historical development allowed historicist premillennialists to claim that, in a society where the cry of "progress" was frequently uttered, they had some claim to be the true progressives. "Progress, we know well, is a favourite watchword in the mouths of revolutionists and infidels of every grade; but few of them ever caught a glimpse of that vast and majestic bourn, towards which the course of time is fast hurrying us along," claimed the *CMR* in 1841.[61] Birks affirmed such a view in his 1853 St. George's lecture, arguing that "the history of our world, when seen in its true light, is all moving swiftly onward, and converging on great result, the coming of the Son of God, and his reign for ever over a ransomed universe. . . . There is no real rest in this rapid progress."[62] In its opening issue, the *QJP* claimed that the church must stake its claim as the only ones who had a firm ground for a belief in progress. Living in the latter days, it claimed, Christians now had a far greater sense of truth than ever before. In a statement that echoed the optimistic language of a Thomas Macaulay, the journal concluded that "our ground is now surer; our way less intricate; our steps are firmer. We must now be considerably nearer truth, if we have not wholly reached it. We see, at least, more clearly the direction in which it lies."[63]

What kind of God acted in this way? Boyd Hilton depicted the premillennialist God as prone to cataclysmic unpredictability. The approaching judgment of God was the final blast of unexpected and invasive activity of a deity who regularly suspended the laws of the nature to enact judgment upon the world. Hilton was correct to suggest that historicist premillennialists rejected any view of divine activity that supposed that God was in some way absent from the processes of history,

60. Review of *A Pastoral Letter to His Parishioners* by Rev. William J. Bennett. *CMR* 7 (1847), 321.

61. Review of *The Natural History of Society. CMR* 1 (1841), 21.

62. Birks, "Signs of the Lord's Coming," 229.

63. "Our Connexion with the Future," *QJP* 1 (1848-49), 3.

content to let the "natural laws" he had originally established take their course. Indeed, they claimed that God was profoundly involved in the historical process; but the manner of this involvement was not wildly interventionist or chaotic. "It is possible to conceive how the Almighty works," argued the *QJP* in 1855 in an article affirming the premillennial advent of Christ, "not by sudden miraculous effect, but by natural law, long order and progress, seeing the end from the beginning, and advancing, it is probable, men and angels, and the world they inhabit, to higher charges, each grander and more perfect than the preceding."[64] Thomas Rawson Birks uttered similar views the previous year at the St. George's Lectures. Birks had no doubt that God could, if he wanted, intervene in the wild and dramatic way that Hilton ascribed to the premillennialist imagination. "All creation, then, down to each dew-drop and blade of grass, is stored with hidden fire," noted Birks, "and it needs but one touch from the finger of the Almighty ... to produce a tempest of fire that would consume the whole human race, and completely change all the physical features of the planet on which we live."[65] But God did *not* work in this way, concluded Birks, for it was not in his interests to transform and convert in an instant, but rather to display his love in an ever-progressing manifestation of his benevolence. "If almighty power were capable, from its nature, of condensing all its vast results into a moment of time," he concluded, "the Divine eternity would become a barren and sterile waste, instead of a fitting theatre for the ever-enlarging display of wisdom, holiness, and love."[66] God pervaded all time in order, slowly but certainly, to win his creation back to him; he did not act chaotically or arbitrarily, argued historicist premillennialists. "Our God is not a God of expedients like man: surprised as it were by this event, and suddenly called upon to provide for that emergency," affirmed William Pym, but rather "from the unfathomable recesses of his own eternity, he has looked forth over all the future concerns of time, fore-ordaining everything according to his pre-determinate counsel; and, consistently with that sure rule, shall each be unfolded in its season."[67]

A commitment to temporal gradualism, and to the vastness of time necessary for adequate divine disclosure, was evident in the use made

64. "Is the Advent of Christ Premillennial?" *QJP* 6 (1855), 362.
65. Birks, "Unbelief of Pretended Science," 87.
66. Birks, *Ways of God*, 23.
67. Pym, "Doctrine of the New Testament," 56.

by some historicist premillennialists of the "gap" theory of creation. This was the belief that a distinction was to be drawn between the age of humanity—which many, following the calculations of Archbishop James Ussher (1581–1656) in the seventeenth century, thought was around six thousand years—and the age of the physical earth on the other. The "gap" in question was between the first and second verse of Genesis. It was supposed that between the first verse, which narrated the formation of matter, and the second, which narrated the creation of humanity, there might exist eons of time. "All that geology really demands for its phenomena is time," noted a reviewer of Robert Chambers' controversial *Vestiges of the Natural History of Creation* (1844) in the *CMR* in 1845, and went on to stress the Bible's willingness to grant the demand.[68] "The Bible, so far from denying, absolutely declares the existence of the earth and of the waters, before the six-days' work of creation began: and if it did exist in darkness, without form and void, it may as well have been for ages as for hours," it concluded.[69] Similarly, the *QJP* refused to dogmatize on the age of the earth. "God gives us no date for his creation. . . . It may be six thousand or it might be sixty thousand years ago."[70] "Six thousand years . . . [is] a strange period to limit the productive powers of an eternally existing and eternally operating God!" remarked Northamptonshire premillennialist James Brown.[71] The *QJP* even proposed that planet earth was replete with life prior to the "beginning" of the story narrated in Genesis. "It is not the

68. Review of *Vestiges of the Natural History of Creation*, CMR 5 (1845), 254.
69. Ibid.
70. "Genesis," *QJP* 4 (1852), 18.
71. J. Brown, *Restitution of All Things*, 35. James Brown, a missionary to the colony of Georgia before becoming minister of Barnwell, Northamptonshire (1796–1812), articulated a doctrine of the "restitution of all things" some time before it became fashionable. The first edition of his book was published in 1785. The second enlarged edition, published in 1824, showed little awareness of other writers on prophecy. He took a broadly historicist view of prophecy, believing that prophetic biblical texts related "to the whole duration of the present administration of Providence." He was equivocal about whether "the thousand years" of Rev 20 was meant to be read as implying exactly a millennium or whether it might actually represent "myriads of ages," but "there cannot be a doubt but that a period of innocence and happiness under the more immediate auspices of the Redeemer is there pointed out and that this period is described as prior to the New Heavens and New Earth and the universal revolution of Nature afterward mentioned." Brown associated this millennial era with the "second coming of Christ," "and though the scene here set forth does not amount to the full Restitution of all Things it is certainly an important crisis of the Times of that Restitution." J. Brown, *Restitution of All Things*, 37, 84–86, 90.

infancy of a new creation that we behold [in Genesis 1] but the mangled and corrupting corpse of the old which must be buried out of sight ere the new can be begun."[72]

This willingness to hypothecate that human history, and the biblical witness to divine involvement with that story, was, in fact, only a small element of the overall length of time that God and matter (and possibly even sentient life?) had existed, fitted with the belief argued by several premillennialists that eternity itself was an endless cycle of time, "a new and wondrous calendar, whose days are millennial and whose years immeasurable ages."[73] In other words, premillennialists were aware of being a speck in the midst of vast eons of unchartered temporality. Their vision resonated with Hutton's sense of deep time: it was without vestige of beginning or prospect of an end.

Signs of the Times

While there was clearly a commitment to the idea that time was a broad and gradually unfolding media, it would be inaccurate to portray historicist premillennialism as unambiguously committed to sedimentary, gradualist views of change and progress. Combined with the emphasis upon the length and breadth of the historical process was a clear emphasis upon the decisive and tumultuous nature of time and space in the present moment. Historiographical representations of premillennialism have typically stressed the attention paid by these women and men to the way in which contemporary world events were read as matching the series of judgments that the book of Revelation promised would be poured out in the final days of history. These multiple representations of time, both gradualist and cataclysmic, reflected the basic ambiguity of the broader nineteenth-century engagement with questions of temporal awareness.

The heightened awareness of time was created by several layers of social and cultural change, from the temporal breadth and majesty of history and geology to the temporal frenzy and speed of industry and modern communications. This sense of motion and convulsion could sometimes create a sense of a world out of control. Some historicist premillennialists, at various times, expressed a strong conviction that the world was in a state of nervous dissolution. "The kingdoms of the

---

72. "Genesis," *QJP* 4 (1852), 18.
73. Birks, "First Resurrection," 245–46.

world are shaking under commotions more impressive and emphatic than any that have preceded our day; portentous events are becoming so frequent as to become familiar; and the veil is being raised from the approaching dreadful scene—a scene more frightful than the sons of Adam ever beheld," summarized the pseudonymous "Colvinus," in 1854.[74] "The world is in motion everywhere: yet it is the motion of fever, not the healthy action of the frame," observed the *QJP* in 1848.[75] Thomas Rawson Birks also noted the "uneasy, feverish expectation of some great, indescribable revolution."[76]

It is true, then, that premillennialists were giddied by the speed and motion that pervaded the society in which they lived. They could sometimes fear that all things were in a state of nervous dissolution. They were not, of course, the only ones to experience such psychological dislocation. John Stuart Mill noted that "the conviction is already not far from being universal, that the times are pregnant with change."[77] Literary historian Wendell V. Harris suggests that the phrase "'sign of the times' . . . appears with such frequency in early nineteenth-century essays that it seems to sum up an almost obsessive preoccupation with the state and prospects of the nation."[78] Most Victorians had a melancholic streak, but they were also irrepressible optimists. Historicist premillennialists shared these dual personality traits,[79] but their eschatological confidence actually meant that it was often the latter characteristic that dominated. While on the one hand they could feel giddied by the speed of technology, communications, science, and politics, they could also be intoxicated by the excitement of the day.

Commonly, then, the "signs of the times" were described by premillennialists with fascination rather than fear. "Ought we not to be deeply grateful for the privilege of living in times when the great map of the world's progress is being unfolded with unheard-of rapidity?" asked the *QJP* in 1854 in an article that saw both imperial expansion in China and the Californian gold rush as signs of the approaching kingdom of God.[80]

---

74. Colvinus, *Impending Doom*, 32.
75. "Our Connexion With the Future" *QJP* 1 (1848–49), 6.
76. Birks, "Signs of the Lord's Coming," 41.
77. Mill, "Spirit of the Age," 228–29.
78. Harris, "Interpretive Historicism," 444.
79. Brown, R. "Victorian Anglican Evangelicalism," 692.
80. "God's Doings," *QJP* 5 (1854), 23.

The *CMR* similarly described "activity, bustle, excitement, contest" as marks of "the external kingdom of God."[81] Similarly, although Evangelicals have gained a reputation for deploring the effects of urbanization,[82] historicist premillennialists saw the growing cosmopolitan excitement of the city as a glimpse of an eternity that would be firmly metropolitan—busy, restless, commercial. "Thou are no child of the city / Hadst thou known it as I have done," versified Horatius Bonar—perhaps rebuking those who followed the late eighteenth-century Evangelical poet William Cowper's idea that "God made the country, and man made the town."[83] Bonar continued:

> You call it life's weary common,
> At least but an idle fair,
> The market of man and woman,—
> But the choice of the race are there.
> In your lone lake's still face yonder,
> By your rivulet's bursting glee,
> Deep truth I may read and ponder,
> Of the earth and its mystery.
> There seems, in yon city's motion,
> Yet a mightier truth for me;
> 'Tis the sound of life's great ocean,
> 'Tis the tides of the human sea.[84]

Much that impressed Victorians in general about their society also impressed the historicist premillennialists as indications of the coming of the kingdom of God, including its speed and motion. For example, the technology of communication in particular fascinated them. Discussing the new electric telegraph, George Croly (1780–1860) noted that "three months, and six thousand miles of ocean, were virtually *annihilated* by a matchless mechanical invention, put into the hands of mankind."[85] Croly argued that such innovations portended the coming of a universal society in which time and space were no longer barriers to free

---

81. Review of *Offices of Prayer for Private Devotion. CMR* 2 (1842), 53.
82. Brown, C., *Death of Christian Britain*, 18–30.
83. Cowper, "The Task" (1785), l. 749
84. "The City," QJP 7 (1855), 201. The poem was published here anonymously, but its author is identified as Bonar in C. Marsh, *Life of William Marsh*, 143.
85. Croly, *Universal Kingdom*, 15.

communication.⁸⁶ Edward Bickersteth was also optimistic that the signs of peace, prosperity, and technological innovation were harbingers of the return of Christ.⁸⁷

Revolutions in transportation—the invention of stream ships and railways—were another sign of the times for some premillennialists. "At the present day even, we are able, by the improvements in steam navigation, to reach the antipodes in two months . . . and a year or two may see us sending a message to the East Indies *in ten minutes*," speculated the *QJP*.⁸⁸ Edward Hoare (1812–94),⁸⁹ curate of Richmond, Surrey, noted "that, just before the advent, there shall be an increase of science and travelling. . . . Thousands and tens of thousands have now become travelers, who, a few years since, had scarcely quitted the immediate neighbourhood of their native town."⁹⁰ A prophetic text commonly deployed to interpret this surge in global human movement was Dan 10 which stated that in the last days "many shall run to and fro, and knowledge shall increase." "Steam and colonization, united, have multiplied our travelers certainly more than a hundredfold," noted the *CMR*.

> You now meet a man at Charing-Cross, and exclaim, "Why, I thought you were in New Zealand!" "So I was," is the reply,— "the other day; but some business required me here; so I just came over for a few weeks, but shall return again on the first of next month." . . . These are the days of which the prophet Daniel spoke . . . the nineteenth century may safely be described as the age of rapid, earnest, and perpetual locomotion, and of amazing extension of human knowledge.⁹¹

As such talk of "steam and colonization" suggests, the phenomenon that most impressed these premillennialists was the British Empire. "There is, perhaps, no spectacle in all of history so marvelous as the present greatness of the British Empire," wrote Thomas Rawson Birks. "It is one on which the sun is always rising, and always setting."⁹² Indeed, the sin-

---

86. Ibid., 16.
87. E. Bickersteth, *Signs of the Times*, 34.
88. "God's Doings in the Earth," *QJP* 5 (1854), 23.
89. This Edward Hoare is not to be confused with Edward Newenham Hoare, the Irish evangelical who edited the historicist premillennialist journal, *The Christian Herald*.
90. Ibid, 13–14.
91. Review of *The Kings of the East*. *CMR* 2 (1842), 53.
92. Birks, *Truth and Life*, 2.

ews of nineteenth-century British global hegemony were precisely the technological marvels that annihilated both time and space. Thus the imperialist Birks delighted in "steamboats and railroads, electric telegraphs, submarine telegraphs, new lines of steamers, surpassing all the triumphs of science and art in former ages in size and swiftness."[93] Transport and communication innovations allowed an unprecedented trans-national transfer of people, data, commerce, and ideas. No wonder the historicist premillennialists desired an account of history that encompassed global history (or, at least, about as global as they could imagine given some inherent western European biases).

This imperial context reminds us that there was a spatial as well as temporal dimension to the historicist premillennialist vision. The very idea of the formation of a universal society rising up from within the current order was the consequence of thinking about the kingdom of God while living within the core of the world's largest maritime empire. "In Isaiah 24 we find Tarshish ships are used in God's service to bring sons of Israel," reflected Mourant Brock. "And is it to this that we are to look as the happy future of our country? . . . Are we to be of the isles of the sea that shall thus wait for the Lord?"[94] The confidence that all things were converging within the present era of history was a reflection of imperial cultural and economic confidence. "ENGLAND WILL NOT GO DOWN IN THE CATASTROPHE OF NATIONS. IT WILL LAST TO THE END, STRONG, PROSPEROUS AND GREAT," opined John Cumming, the minister of Crown Court Church of Scotland congregation in London.[95]

The art of parsing prophetic texts to match them with great world empires of the past, and the implicit conclusion that it was within the age of *Pax Britannica* that God would bring about his final purposes, was an *apologia* for the present global order. Victorian imperialism thus re-energized the pre-existing historicist pride in the Protestant credentials of Great Britain with a new sense of momentousness. "The chief Protestant nation, Britain," ruminated Bickersteth, "touches America with one hand and China with the other, plants one foot on the Cape of Good Hope and another on North West America and the children of mercy send forth the messengers of mercy east and west, north and south." He believed that the British Empire "betokens a preparation of the whole earth for some

---

93. Birks, "Spread of Knowledge," 72.
94. Brock, "Position of England," 105–6.
95. Cumming, *Destiny of Nations*, 282. Upper-case typography in original.

great event affecting the whole human race."⁹⁶ On occasion, a historicist premillennialist discourse on the spatial glories of the Empire actually exhibited a discursive slippage between the Empire of Victoria and the kingdom of God. John Cumming reflected:

> The children of today are the future inhabitants of our different colonies and if we send them out converted and Christianized, instead of being repealers of the connection between the parent country and the colonies, they will be indissoluble links between them[;] . . . these children will be champions of a throne under the shadow of which they have been blessed, and sticklers for the national institutions which have been to them springs of refreshment[,] . . . for in such cases we have been instrumental in adding subjects to the kingdom of God, and building up living temples that will last for ever and ever.⁹⁷

These premillennialists were simultaneously mesmerized, excited, and overawed by the age in which they lived. Yet historicist premillennialists, unlike their futurist dispensationalist counterparts (or, indeed, unlike Tennyson in his gloomiest moments), did not believe that all earthly things were creeping to destruction. Rather, "it is . . . the assured conviction that all things are tending under the influence of divine control towards its advent, that enables the children of God to look upon the changes and controversies of the day, not indeed with apathy, but with an interest that has not one element of despondency."⁹⁸ Moreover, as I shall show in the next chapter, their prophetic vision of the future was too robustly positive toward the material sphere for such gloominess. They had little sense that the approaching second advent was the "end of the world," but rather a fulcrum within God's perpetual involvement with the earth. Charles Goodhart argued that the parousia was that "event towards which all converges from *one* eternity that it may diverge for *another*; or, to restrict our view a little, that event to which all the events and circumstances of our life here converge, that they may diverge again for the life to come."⁹⁹ Although premillennialists might talk of history moving toward its conclusion at the second advent, this referred to the current "age," not the basic fabric of time and space, Goodhart explained:

---

96. E. Bickersteth, *Signs of the Times*, 33–34.
97. Cumming, *Church Before Flood*, 132
98. Review of *Horæ Apocalypticæ* by Rev. E. B. Elliott. *CMR* 4 (1844), 443.
99. Goodhart, "Established Holiness," 80.

> If the illustration is not too remote, we may liken all the thought and feeling and conduct of our present condition to so many pencils of rays, which, instead of being abruptly terminated at the close of our present existence, are to be refracted through the prism of coming judgment, then to be contracted or expanded from their apparent to their true dimensions, and thenceforth to assume their true colour of greater or less brilliancy throughout the eternal existence that is to follow.[100]

So whether one rejoiced or despaired about the signs of the times, the current era was *critical* and not *terminal*, a preparation for a restitution, and not a destruction, of the world.[101] "No doubt prophecy deals with *crises*," noted the *QJP* in 1851, "but *crisis* and *end* are not the same."[102] Congregational minister William Leask (1812–84) agreed, pointing out that when the Bible spoke of the end of the world it meant "not *kosmos*, the material world, but *aionos*, the age or dispensation; that is to say, the course or flow of time during which the Gospel of the kingdom will be preached."[103] The "coming of the Lord" should not be "regarded as the final dealing of God with mankind and the earth, as the end of all history and of time itself," suggested the *QJP* in 1854 for "when the Lord comes he has much to do upon the earth."[104] Time and space had a vast history, but as I shall argue in the next chapter, for these premillennialists the past was only the beginning of the history of the world.

Conclusion

Premillennialists had no doubt that a great momentous event was about to occur. The signs of the times were everywhere. According to the *QJP*, the world was like a "falling mass," which increased with speed as it neared the end of its gravitational descent.[105] The historicist premillennialist concern for tracing the ways in which God had acted in the course of history in fulfillment of prophetic biblical texts was perhaps the most obvious way in which historicist premillennialism exhibited the deep

---

100. Ibid., 112.
101. Houghton, *Victorian Frame of Mind*, 31.
102. "Elliott's 'Horæ Apocalypticæ,'" *QJP* 3 (1851), 371.
103. Leask, *Earth's Curse and Restitution*, 18.
104. "God's Purpose Concerning Man and the Earth," *QJP* 5 (1854), 264.
105. "God's Doings," *QJP* 5 (1854), 23.

temporal awareness of the society of which it was a part. This stress on the importance of the historical process and the concern to trace the working of the eternal God in the realm of space and time undergirded the historicist premillennialist theological commitment to upholding the temporal realm as a significant, enduring, and divinely-ordered realm. The world was not a static realm of probation or excoriating moral trial for the individual, but a complex organic mechanism that was in the process of eternally-driven transformation. They believed that all of history—sacred and secular—was alive with the purposes and plans of God.

Underpinning this conviction about history was the set of themes that will be explored in the following chapter, namely the belief that God was less concerned with saving an elect that he would remove to an immaterial heaven, than he was with a process of cosmic redemption to recover the entire temporal-spatial sphere. God (occasionally pictured as being just a little a bit like Queen Victoria) had only one imperial dominion. He did not just work in history to achieve some other, suprahistorical end; rather his work was profoundly and inherently historical, concerned with the processes and relationships of which temporal life was constituted. "He reigns from everlasting to everlasting," contended Thomas Rawson Birks. "He sitteth in the heavens over all from the beginning. This essential dominion began with the first act of creation, and must endure through eternity."[106] This belief in the unitary dominion of God led historicist premillennialists to view historical time as a process of dynamic redemptive activity in which the whole material universe was not moving towards a catastrophic destruction, but rather was growing into a magnificent consummation.

---

106. Birks, *Outlines of Unfulfilled Prophecy*, 186.

4

The Renewal of Time and Space

In a radical departure from traditional belief, [N. T.] Wright says that Christians are not ultimately destined for a spiritual place called heaven. He says that at the end of time as we know it, God will literally remake our physical bodies and return us to a newly restored planet.

—MARTIN BASHIR, ABC NIGHTLINE, 2008

IN 1828, GERARD NOEL, the curate of Richmond, Surrey, declared that a revolution had occurred in his understanding of the afterlife. Noel admitted that, in common with Christians throughout "successive ages," he had for a long time believed that the "future glory" of a Christian believer would consist in translation to a heavenly realm where he would enjoy "*spiritual* and *divine* fellowship" with God. This "heaven," explained Noel, was often portrayed as "a world at once ethereal, distant, and unseen, separate in all its usages and enjoyments from that which we now inhabit."[1] Noel admitted that this view of the future was all-pervasive in the Christian world and that it had been "fastened to my own mind . . . by all the associations of the past, and by all the habits of education and converse with other Christians."[2] However, he confessed that, after further study, he was now "at length compelled to separate from it."[3] The "continued popularity" of the view, Noel declared, was due neither to

---

1. G. T. Noel, *Brief Enquiry*, 12.
2. Ibid., 17
3. Ibid.

Scripture nor to reason but rather "to the prescriptive force of habit, and to the despotism of accredited interpretation."[4]

Noel had become a premillennialist. However, by choosing to open his *apologia* for premillennial belief neither with a detailed exposition of prophetic chronology, nor with a simple focus upon the personal second advent of Christ, but rather with an explanation of his revised views about the nature of the future life, Noel signaled that his eschatological shift had profound implications far beyond an esoteric interest in predicting dates for the end of the world.

Noel explained that God would fulfill his plan of redemption not by removing an elected group from the world and translating them to an immaterial heaven, but rather through the personal return of Christ to earth, who would transform and repair the entire terrestrial sphere, "converting a moral wilderness into a scene of culture, fertility, and concord."[5] Christ, he reminded his readers, "directs us to pray for the establishment of his kingdom, and this kingdom appears to belong exclusively to this *material Earth*."[6] When Christ returned, explained Noel, he would "render visible the power of his *Kingly* office, and stretch forth his redeeming scepter from shore to shore" and the "redeemed church, thus united to her Lord, [shall] reign with him on the earth."[7] In place of the hope for a spiritual heaven, Noel proposed that the future hope of believers was the reinvigoration of the temporal-spatial sphere. "The conviction has fastened strongly upon my mind, that the honour of our blessed Lord and Master is connected, in a peculiar manner, with this renovation of the earth," he concluded.[8] Noel had come to believe that heaven would be a place on earth.

Noel's eschatological breakthrough was far from unique. Many other Evangelicals also came to talk in glowing terms about the future destiny of the world. Like Noel, these new premillennialists were ambivalent toward the traditional notion of "going to heaven when you die."[9] Premillennialists "find nothing in Scripture of what we old-fashioned

---

4. Ibid., 17.
5. Ibid., 15.
6. Ibid., 26.
7. Ibid., 20, 32.
8. Ibid., 29, 96
9. "On Going to Heaven When I Die," *CO*, 2nd ser., 17 (1855), 228.

Christians call 'heaven,'" noted the *Christian Observer* acerbically.[10] These premillennialists instead devoted much time to describing the world that would dawn when Christ returned, a world that they believed would be full of physical people living within communities alive with science, art, and technological progress. They claimed biblical warrant for their vision, but their vision for the future was also shaped profoundly by the society and culture in which they lived.[11]

The Restitution of All Things

Premillennialists called their doctrine of the material future life "the restitution of all things." William Pym (1792–1852), the rector of Willian, Hertfordshire, explained the import of the phrase:

> By the restitution of all things, therefore, in this earth, we understand to mean, that almighty act whereby every thing, which has been cursed for the sin of man, shall be restored to at least its primitive state of perfection and blessing, though, we conceive, to a higher degree; and shall thus harmonize with that moral renovation, which shall then be introduced among the children of men.[12]

The phrase was derived from Acts 3.20, when the apostle Peter is recorded as preaching the following words:

> Repent ye therefore, and be converted, that your sins may be blotted out, when the times of refreshing shall come from the presence of the Lord. And he shall send Jesus Christ, which before was preached unto you: Whom the heaven must receive

---

10. Review of "An Inquiry into the Grounds . . ." *CO*, 1st ser., 28 (1828), 400.

11. In this chapter, and in all subsequent chapters, I am going to drop the adjective "historicist" (apart from where I want deliberately to make a contrast between historicists and futurists, in which cases I will resurrect it) and simply refer to "premillennialism." This is intended to serve two purposes. First, it promotes economy of style. Second, although historicism was clearly the bedrock of the views discussed, and thus the reader should assume that the individuals under question were historicist, interpretations of Scripture were not the main theme of the works cited in this chapter. In some cases there is no actual evidence one way or another about a particular individual's views of prophetic chronology. I thus do not want to constrain artificially by the use of narrow labels what was, as I will argue below, a broad-ranging revision of eschatology among Evangelicals. I would rather let the words of these protagonists define the essence of their views.

12. Pym, *Restitution of All Things*, xi.

until the times of restitution of all things, which God hath spoken by the mouth of all his holy prophets since the world began.[13]

The word rendered "restitution" in this passage was the Greek term *apokatastasis*, a concept used in ancient medical practice to mean "healing" or "return to health."[14] Premillennialists argued that this term was found at several junctures in the New Testament to refer to an eschatological restoration and renewal (e.g., Matt 11.13; 17:2; Acts 1:6). Edward. B. Elliott explained: "*Katastasis* means the actual state, condition, or constitution; and, consequently, *apokatastasis* must most naturally mean a *new and different constitution* of things, generally by *restoration* to what it was originally."[15]

The focus on this concept of *apokatastasis* by Evangelicals is in some ways surprising because the concept is most commonly associated with universalist soteriology—the belief that everyone will receive salvation from God. Origen (ca. AD 185–ca. 254) and Gregory of Nyssa (ca. 335–ca. 394) both used the term to indicate that the world operated in a cyclical motion with all things proceeding from, and eventually returning to, God. It will become evident in the next chapter that some premillennialists did in fact move toward a doctrine of universalism because of their commitment to the idea of restitution, but it is also important to note that the logic of their argument tended to flow from assertion of *material* restitution (i.e., restoration of the physical world) to *moral* restitution (i.e., some kind of salvation for all humanity), not from an *a priori* commitment to the notion of universal salvation.

For these premillennialists, the idea of restitution was rooted in the belief that God had promised to establish a kingdom on earth in the last days. Joshua W. Brooks argued that the essence of the premillennial vision was centered on "a king and a kingdom."[16] As already explained in chapter 2, one of the sources to which premillennialists looked to prove this contention was the proof text of Christian millennialism, Rev 20. An appeal to this text, which spoke of Satan being bound and righteousness

---

13. Acts 3:20.

14. González, *Essential Theological Terms*, 12. Lewis Way was among the first historicist premillennialists to explore the meaning of the term, and suggested that it meant "convalescence". Way, *Thought on Scriptural Expectations*, 38. The word can also be spelt "apocatastasis."

15. Elliott, *Horæ Apocalypticæ*, 5th edn, 209. See also Brooks, *Essays*, xxii.

16. Brooks, *Essays*, 10.

being established on earth for a thousand years, gained this group the sobriquet "pre-millennialist." This, as chapter 2 explained, was a compound term describing both their belief in a millennium, and their assertion that Christ would return before the start of such an era.

However, in many ways the label of "millennialist" or "premillennialist" is, if not inaccurate, then at least somewhat misleading. This is because the essence of premillennial belief was not exclusively in the millennium, but rather in an earthly jurisdiction that would be established by the physical presence of the Messiah, Jesus Christ.[17] Revelation 20 was one biblical text which suggested that such a kingdom would be inaugurated, but premillennialists founded their argument on a much wider biblical basis than has often been appreciated. "It indicates great ignorance, to suppose that all our system is built on a chapter or two of the Revelation of the Apostle John," noted Brooks.[18] It was, in fact, possible to deny a precise millennium but still believe in the return of Christ to establish an earthly kingdom. James Haldane Stewart is a good example of someone who took such a view.[19]

Indeed, if premillennialists wanted to say anything meaningful about the future, they *had* to be more than millennialists. After all, the text of Rev 20 is very stark. It says very little about what would happen during the millennium. Acts 3 and the notion of "restitution" provided a creative way forward for these "millennialists" in search of further details of what an earthly kingdom of righteousness might actually look like. As one anonymous advocate admitted candidly, "unless we identify the Millennium with the restitution of all things, there is not the least hint regarding the Millennium to be found in the Prophets."[20]

---

17. Ibid., 26.

18. Ibid., 10.

19. Stewart wrote in the 1820s that he wished to talk about the second coming "entirely distinct... from all sentiments concerning the millennium." Oliver, *Prophets and Millennialists*, 71. His son and biographer affirmed that "he seldom, if ever, preached upon the millennium." D. D. Stewart, *Memoir of... Haldane Stewart,* 137. However, reticence about the millennium did not stop Stewart from talking extensively about the physical nature of the world to come, as quotations from his lectures later in this chapter demonstrate. Even those who technically dissented from a millennium often shared in the "millennialist' reconceptualization of the world to come. Oliver's implication that Haldane Stewart was one of the gloomy premillennialists who "took pains to clear away all millennialist associations, as if it were possible to write of the second coming without an implicit millennialism," is therefore misleading.

20. A Preacher of the Church of Scotland, *Restitution of All Things*, 5.

Of course, the passage from Acts contained no more clues about the exact nature of "restitution" than the text of Rev 20 did about the nature of a "millennium." Nevertheless, the context of Peter's sermon to a group of Jews, and his reference to the Old Testament prophets predicting a divine "restitution," allowed nineteenth-century premillennialists to extrapolate that this passage linked the return of Christ to the promise in the Old Testament of the restoration of the Jewish people from captivity. Because the Old Testament tended to describe the establishment of the final kingdom of God with images of material fecundity (a classic example is Isa 35), premillennialists contended that the "restitution of all things" was to be construed as a cosmic event in which the whole created order was renewed. "The restoration of Israel is spoken of in connection with, or under the figure of, the new creation," explained Gerard Noel. "The restitution of all things" was thus used as a description of the whole gamut of biblical prophetic promises for God's cosmic redemption. William Pym could therefore claim that the doctrine "has formed the burden of inspired song: it has awoke the harp of Judah: it has embodied the visions of seers, and filled with gladness the hearts of holy men of God, who spake as they were moved by the Spirit of Christ that was in them, and testified to these things."[21]

Although some premillennialists were cautious about speculating whether this earthly restitution would continue after the millennium had ended (thus allowing for some the possibility that an ethereal "heaven" might be the venue for life *after* the millennium), most believed that renewal of time and space was not restricted to a period of one thousand years. Thomas Nolan (1809–82) was typical when he affirmed that the promises sometimes associated with the "millennium" could, in fact, be read as pertaining to the whole span of eternal life:

> This blessed period begins with the coming in glory of Christ at the commencement of the millennium. . . . It is not, however, necessary to suppose that it is terminate at the close of that period, especially when so many passages speak of [Christ] reigning for ever and ever.[22]

The *CMR* similarly affirmed that "the twenty first and twenty second chapters of the Apocalypse" should be interpreted as referring to the "post-millennial glory of the church through all the generations of the

---

21. Pym, *Restitution of All Things*, x.
22. T. Nolan, "Saviour's Throne," 323–24.

age of ages,"[23] and the *QJP* asserted that "after the glorious appearance of our great God and Saviour Jesus Christ this earth will become the abode of liberty and joy and that this glorious state of things will last eternally."[24]

This belief that the personal reign of Christ would extend indefinitely meant that an emphasis on material restitution became not only an explanation of the nature of the millennium but also emerged as a new vision of the entire eschatological *dénouement*. This attitude was exemplified in a fictional dialogue between "John" and his "Minister," published in the Irish Evangelicalism journal *The Christian Herald*, edited by Edward N. Hoare (1800–1877):

> **Minister**—Well, John, whenever you see the thorns springing up in your garden, in spite of all your labour and toil, which costs you the sweat of your face—think of Jesus; think *of his first coming* to bear the curse for us; and think of *his second coming* to put an end to the curse altogether; and this is the way to turn the curse into a blessing.
>
> **John**—But, Sir, about *this earth* being the place where Jesus and his people are to be in glory;—I thought we were to go to *heaven* to Him, and not for Him to come down to us.
>
> **Minister**—Wherever Jesus is, that is heaven; and when this earth is changed, and made new, and as glorious as it was when first God created it; and when Jesus will "reign in Mount Zion and at Jerusalem and before his ancients gloriously," *then* this earth will be all that we are used to fancy heaven would be.[25]

The final line in the dialogue nicely captures the iconoclasm of Evangelical eschatological revisionism: heaven was an old-fashioned, fanciful idea that had now been superseded by a new doctrine concerning the earthliness of salvation. Critics of millennialism were well aware of its tendency to dismiss classical ideas of the heavenly future: "The doctrine of these modern Millenarians extends, as we understand it, to this, that there is not a syllable in Scripture about what *we* call heaven; that all that is said of heaven applies *only* to the Millennium," scoffed the *Christian*

---

23. "Some Recent Works on Prophecy," *CMR* 5 (1845), 933. Note here that the term "post-millennial" refers not to the timing of Christ's return, but to anything that happens after the millennium.

24. "The Year of Jubilee," *QJP* 3 (1851), 26.

25. *Christian Herald*, September 1830, 159.

Observer.²⁶ The postmillennialist *Eclectic Review* similarly dismissed the premillennial notion that "deprives us of Paradise, and offers us the Millennium in its stead."²⁷

Evangelical premillennialists did not, of course, pluck this new attitude out of thin air. Its origins lay in the fusing of a theological argument with a cultural predisposition. The theological argument concerned the correct way to interpret biblical passages relating to the Jewish people. The cultural predisposition was romanticism. Before examining in more detail the colorful content of their vision for the world remade, it is necessary to spend some time exploring this background to the emergence of an Evangelical commitment to temporal-spatial renewal.

The Roots of Restitution

Biblical Literalism and the Common Sense Reading of Scripture

As discussed briefly in chapter 3, it has been claimed that Evangelicals in the mid-nineteenth century adopted a new approach to the Bible called "literalism." This was an attitude that eventually became tethered to the doctrine of biblical inerrancy and served as the foundation for the fundamentalist defense of biblical authority and veracity against liberal biblical criticism in the early twentieth century, particularly among conservative Protestants in the United States.

I highlighted in chapter 3 that in reference to the interpretation of prophetic chronology and symbols, historicists sometimes associated the word "literalist" with the futurist scheme from which they dissented. Nevertheless, they also made frequent positive appeals to the idea of literalism, an ostensible paradox that demonstrates that "literalism" was a more complex and multifaceted idea than is often appreciated.²⁸

---

26. "Review of Works on Prophecy and the Millennium," *CO*, 1st ser, no. 284 (August 1825), 497.

27. Review of *A Brief Enquiry* . . . by Hon. Gerard T. Noel. *Eclectic Review*, new ser. 30 (1828), 216.

28. The complexity of the term and an implicit warning against the very casual way in which scholars deploy it to describe Evangelical and Fundamentalist hermeneutics—as if the term has a univocal objective meaning in the realm of critical analysis, rather than being an historically-conditioned and modulating concept within Evangelical discourse itself—can be found in Boone, *Bible Tells Them So*, 39–60.

When historicists appealed positively to literalism they were at one level expressing a broad premillennial commitment to "common sense" realism. This was the eighteenth-century school of thought associated with a number of influential Scottish philosophers, which asserted all humans have an inherent capacity to grasp ideas about natural and moral reality because the universe is intelligible: the way things appear to be to individuals is, in fact, the way they really are. In regard to the interpretation of the Bible, common-sense realism gave purchase to the doctrine of the perspicuity of Scripture, the idea that the words of the Bible are intelligible to every individual because God desired his Word to be understood by all.[29] By extension, it suggested that Scripture was a transparent medium for the communication of reality, not an occluded set of literary reflections that needed to be decoded by complex interpretative strategies. As Harriet Harris has explained: "a 'common sense' or inductive approach to scripture" sustains "the conviction that the biblical records inform us not of ideas or interpretations of events but of events themselves." This gives rise to the belief "that the biblical text gives us objective, factual accounts of real states of affairs; and that the 'plain sense' of scripture is available wherever the reader does not obscure the text with subjective interpretation."[30]

All premillennialists sounded this "common sense" note in regard to prophetic interpretation. "We cannot but agree in supposing that that Spirit who influenced the minds of His instruments [i.e. the biblical authors] acted at least as honestly as any human author of probity and credit. He used words in their simple and usual sense," argued the premillennialist prebendary of Blackrath (County Kilkenny), Samuel Madden.[31] This commitment to an accessible text led to the idea that words in Scripture should not be implied to have a hidden or higher meaning other than the one that would commend itself by the plain, surface meaning of words to the common reader. Premillennialists thus spoke constantly of their commitment to a "plain and literal" reading of Scripture.[32] "What do we mean by a literal interpretation?" asked Thomas Rawson Birks. "One in

---

29. H. A. Harris, *Fundamentalism and Evangelicalism*, 96–100; Noll, *America's God*, 93–113; Gribben, *Evangelical Millennialism*, 71–72.
30. H. A. Harris, *Fundamentalism and Evangelicalism*, 116–17.
31. S. Madden, *Nature and Time*, 21.
32. Brooks, *Essays*, 26, 63.

which words have the same sense ascribed to them which they usually bear in daily life."[33]

Pervading premillennialist literature, then, was the hum of Ockham's razor, shaving away what premillennialists thought were fanciful, allegorical, or mystical interpretations of texts, in an attempt to reach what they believed to be the most straightforward, simplest meaning of biblical words. Gerard Noel, for example, stated that his exposition of prophecy would take as its theme those scriptural passages "scattered over the surface of scripture, in language plain, literal, and popular."[34] Premillennialists were committed to the general usefulness of Scripture, which they believed was occluded when esoteric interpretations and glosses were placed on biblical texts, and particularly on prophetic passages. They wanted to use prophecy to strengthen faith by showing that God actually fulfilled, in real life events, the promises he made. Edward Bickersteth thus condemned the "figurative interpretation of plain expressions" because he believed them to have "thrown away much of the prophetical *use and instruction* of lengthened and important predictions."[35]

However, precisely because literalism was defined as a "common sense" reading of Scripture, it did not actually mean denying emblems and symbols in prophecy. In other words, somewhat confusingly, a commitment to literalism did not mean taking everything literally. "It is possible to be unwisely literal," warned the *QJP*.[36] Rather, commonsense literalism meant asserting that Scripture was itself clear about where it was speaking emblematically and clear about when its words were not symbols or metaphors. "In most cases, what is symbolical is manifestly so; and there is need only of the ordinary judgment of a sober mind so to interpret it," argued Bickersteth.[37] In other words, at times the best way to take Scripture "literally" was to acknowledge that it was speaking symbolically, as long as it seemed plain or "manifest" that the text justified such a reading.

This would all be well if, of course, everyone really did share a "common sense" that consistently alerted them to whether it was better to interpret a passage as symbolic or non-figurative. In reality, as Crawford

33. Birks, *First Elements*, 250.
34. G. T. Noel, *Brief Enquiry*, 2.
35. E. Bickersteth, *Practical Guide*, 71. (Italics added.)
36. "The New Heavens and Earth," *QJP* 12 (1860), 212.
37. E. Bickersteth, *Practical Guide*, 22

Gribben observes, "Evangelical interpreters could not agree on what the results of the application of that hermeneutic actually signified."[38] The very divergence between futurists and historicists on whether prophecy was about the past or the future was proof that such a shared faculty did not actually exist.

In fact, as one probes historicist premillennialist literalism more deeply, it becomes clear that the appeal to literalism was not a general principle for interpreting all Scripture. It was an appeal made to support a more precise theological point about the correct way to interpret *specific parts* of prophetic biblical texts. It is probable that the interpretative outcome preceded a commitment to a literal methodology.

In appealing to a literal reading of Scripture historicist premillennialists were specifically objecting to what they called "the viscous system" of "spiritualising" prophetic biblical texts that, they believed, had led the church astray in its vision of the future destiny of humans.[39] "Millenarianism takes for granted a simplicity and literality of interpretation which utterly repelled the heretical advances of Origenism," explained the *QJP*.[40] The reference to "Origenism" was an allusion to the interpretative principle pioneered by this church father, and kept alive in the medieval *quadriga*, or "fourfold" method of interpreting Scripture, which claimed that, in addition to the "literal" sense of a passage (relating to the event that actually occurred) one should also seek after three higher (or deeper) meanings: namely, the moral (relating to practice), allegorical (relating to belief and doctrine), and anagogical (relating to the future) senses.[41] These applications of a passage, proposed the theory, must be reached by contemplation and spiritual insight and may not even have been known to the original author. In this approach, Scripture was not as plain or obvious as it might at first seem and it was not intelligible to the average reader.

Premillennialists objected vehemently to such mystical or metaphorical interpretation. "We reject the metaphorical or mystical hypothesis with all the energy of our souls. It is a well without water, a mirage of the desert, a delusion, and a snare," argued William Leask (1812–84).[42]

38. Gribben, *Evangelical Millennialism* 72.
39. Brooks, *Essays*, 10.
40. "The History of Chiliasm," *QJP* 2 (1850), 270.
41. de Lubac, *Medieval Exegesis*, 1:15–74. Premillennialists often lumped the three non-literal meanings together as "allegorical" interpretations.
42. Leask, *Earth's Curse and Restitution*, 12.

The *QJP* agreed, arguing that the "figurative interpretation has been, in all ages, the downward pathway to error; literal interpretation has been as invariably the upward road to truth."[43]

However, it was not really patristic Origenism in the abstract that worried premillennialists. Rather the allusion to this church father was a code to describe the classic Evangelical habit of taking what appeared to be some very physical, earthy, eschatological promises and arguing that they were only images or figures of an inward, individual, and spiritual reality. William Anderson, minister of the United Presbyterian Church, John Street, Glasgow, wondered why these "scholastic theologians" think that the phrase "the Coming of the Son of Man . . . does not mean the Coming of the Son of Man by any means, but the Coming of the Romans, or the Coming of Death, or the Coming of any thing which the fancy most conceits, save and except, of the Son of Man himself."[44] And Lewis Way caustically noted that those who took the "allegorical" view directly inverted plain biblical language on every point:

> The plainest expressions submitted to [the allegorical] ordeal change their import. "Kingdom Of Israel," thus transmuted, signifies *Gentile dynasty*—"Coming Down," is interpreted "*a strong metaphor for an ascension upwards.*" "Time," becomes the synchronism of *eternity;* and "Earth," the synonyme [sic] of *heaven!*"[45]

An appeal to literalism was not, then, an *a priori* method for interpreting Scripture, but was itself a theological doctrine, a belief in the materiality—that is, the literality—of God's prophetic promises; a belief that God had promised redemption on earth, not heaven; that Christ would come down, rather than the soul go up, and that God would enact redemption within time, not eternity. In other words, the historicist appeal to literalism really had nothing to do with a general method of treatment of prophetic texts (for as I showed in chapter 3, on this issue historicists actually dismissed futurist "literalism"), but was actually another way of underscoring the type of eschatological materialism that was the pervasive theme of all premillennial theology. The enemy of "literalism" was an

---

43. This article expressed pleasure that German biblical scholarship also appeared to be embracing a non-allegorical "literal" approach to Scripture. "History of Chiliasm," *QJP* 2 (1850), 340–41.

44. W. Anderson, *Apology for Millenarianism*, 11.

45. Way, *Thoughts on Scriptural Expectations*, 92. Upper case emphasis in original.

Evangelical anti-materialism that not only claimed that much of Scripture was figurative, but also restricted its prophetic *outcome* to a non-physical, heavenly, soul-ish fulfillment. This de-materializing of eschatology was the enemy that the premillennialist campaign for "literal" interpretation was mobilized to vanquish.

In fact, we can make this analysis still more specific. In the parody of typical "spiritualization" of eschatology offered by Way, one point soared above the rest and is the nub of the link between literalism and material restitution, namely his assertion of the literal restoration of a territorial nation of Israel. What premillennialists specifically meant by a desire to interpret the Bible "literally" was that it must be interpreted in a way that affirmed the physical reconstitution of God's chosen people as promised in the Old Testament. It was this *particular* theological point (which also included the physical return of the Messiah as the ruling King of this kingdom) that premillennialists believed an appeal to a more *general* common sense reading of Scripture would support.

Biblical Literalism and the Destiny of Israel

The emergence of this more specific doctrine of "literalism" concerning the restoration of Israel was a resurrection of one side of a Reformation debate about God's purposes toward Israel.[46] The position that premillennialism sought to oppose was that upheld by both Martin Luther (1483–1564) and John Calvin (1509–64). This argument proposed that God had finished his dealings with his wayward chosen people, the Jews.[47] In this interpretation, the Gentile church had replaced the Jewish nation as the sole recipient of the grace of God toward humanity. Any promises made to Israel in the Old Testament must therefore be interpreted as having been fulfilled in the new covenant established by Christ. There was now no specific divine purpose toward the Jews as a distinct, chosen people. Jews could be saved, but like the rest of humanity they would have to become Christians and their Jewishness would count for no more than any other national or ethnic identity.

The Puritan Bible commentator Matthew Henry (1662–1714), a favorite of many nineteenth-century Evangelicals, provided a good

---

46. There are, in fact, hints that this belief had older roots. See Lerner. "Refreshment of the Saints," 110.

47. Sizer, Stephen, *Christian Zionism*, 27; Murray, *Puritan Hope*, 62.

example of this view in his commentary, which was republished in the early nineteenth century by Nonconformist ministers George Burder (1752–1832) and Joseph Hughes (1769–1833): "Christ came to set up his own kingdom, and that a kingdom of heaven, not to *restore the kingdom to Israel,* an earthly kingdom . . . we are bid to expect *the cross* in this world, and to wait for *the kingdom* in the other world . . . how apt we are to misunderstand scripture, and to understand *that* literally, which is spoken figuratively."[48] Henry was, of course, writing in the aftermath of a disastrous "literalist" experiment at introducing a theocratic republic in the British Isles during the seventeenth-century civil wars.

Premillennialists denounced the kind of interpretation pioneered by Henry, and often repeated by non-premillennialists in the nineteenth century. As Way put it, in the context of that same statement given above, in such a standard reading "The Gentile, enjoying the figure, [wrongly] overlooks a literal fulfillment to the Jew. Canaan is transferred to his own bosom, or placed in the heavens above: *any where,* but in the Land Of Promise."[49]

At the heart of the premillennialist re-inversion of the Evangelical "mystical" concept of eschatology was an attempt to recover an alternative Reformation idea about the Jews that had been first proposed by Theodore Beza (1519–1605) and Martin Bucer (1491–1551), and which was popularized by a marginal note in the Geneva Bible, the favored translation of English Puritans.[50] This interpretation of the Old Testament contended that Israel was not simply replaced by the church. Rather, it argued that God would fulfill his purposes for the restoration and salvation of Israel. "Where Israel, Judah, Zion and Jerusalem are named . . . these and such like are not allegories . . . but meant really and literally the Jews," explained the Puritan leader Sir Henry Finch (1558–1625) in 1621.[51] This position was the original Protestant "biblical literalism." Again, it was not a method for general scriptural exegesis, but a proposition about the role of Israel in the redemptive purposes of God. Israel would be "really and literally" restored, thus prophecy must account for this earthly dimension of the establishment of God's final kingdom. It was this argument, that Old Testament prophecies have a "primary and literal reference to

48. Henry, *Exposition,* 9.
49. Way, *Thoughts on Scriptural Expectations,* 92.
50. Stephen Sizer, *Christian Zionism,* 27; Murray, *Puritan Hope,* 41.
51. Quoted in Stephen Sizer, *Christian Zionism,* 29.

the Jews," that was reinvigorated by nineteenth-century premillennialists and which explains, and is explained by, their broader commitment to a "literal" reading of Scripture.[52]

This approach to Israel entailed a modification of inherited ideas that Old Testament prophecy found its typological fulfillment in the church (so-called "replacement theology"). Edward Bickersteth confessed that he had for a long time made the common mistake "of confining their [i.e., the Old Testament prophets] meaning simply to the Christian church, and not taking their literal application to the Jewish nation."[53] It also led to the conviction that Israel would be saved as Israel, rather than as a conglomeration of individual Jews converted to Christianity. "All Israel shall yet be saved.... They shall be grafted in again. They shall glory in Jesus their Lord, they shall be a full blessing to the whole earth," wrote Bickersteth.[54]

Implicit in the idea that God still had plans for Israel was an idea that must be held as at least partly responsible for reinvigorating the literalist argument in the early nineteenth century, namely belief in "Jewish restorationism." Restorationism, which was the root of late-nineteenth century Zionism, was the belief that God intended Israel not only to be converted *en masse,* but also to be reconstituted as a distinct nation, existing within its ancient territorial boundaries in the Levant. The idea was not inherent to literalism, but it was certainly its logical conclusion. In the first decades of the nineteenth century an eschatological hope for the conversion of the Jews, which had been present among Evangelicals and Puritans since the Reformation, became inextricably linked with hopes for the physical reconstitution of dispersed European Jews into a geopolitical entity in the Eastern Mediterranean.[55] The reasons for this rise of Jewish restorationism had much to do with the growing spirit of philo-Semitism across early-nineteenth century Europe.[56] In 1791, during the French Revolution, France became the first European country to grant

---

52. Way, *Thoughts on Scriptural Expectations,* 51.

53. E. Bickersteth, *Practical Guide,* 71–72.

54. E. Bickersteth, *Restoration,* 197.

55. The history of nineteenth-century evangelical attitudes to Israel, and the emergence of Evangelical Zionism, is interwoven with (although broader than) premillennial eschatology and is treated most fully in D. M. Lewis, *Origins of Christian Zionism.* For broader discussions of Jewish restorationism in nineteenth-century society, see Kobler, *Vision Was There;* Tuchman, *Bible and Sword;* Polowetzky, *Jerusalem Recovered.*

56. Binfield, "Jews in Evangelical Dissent," 226.

full citizenship to its Jewish population, a policy continued by Napoleon throughout his conquered territories in the early 1800s and given added prescience because Napoleon seized land in Palestine, thus opening the Holy Land to a western power for the first time since the fall of Acre, the last Crusader state, in 1291.[57]

Restorationism developed in the nineteenth century in various ways, many of which in fact drained the movement of its eschatological significance and interpreted Jewish emancipation as a priority of a liberal agenda that also pushed for the rights of people groups living in multi-ethnic empires, or under alien rule, to form their own nation-state.[58] However, given the prophetic significance with which many Evangelicals invested the French Revolution, it was natural that the gains made by Jewish groups in the early nineteenth-century French Empire were interpreted by many Christians as a harbinger of the millennial day, and that interest in the fortunes of the Jewish people should merge with those who were interested to track the prophetic timetable.

In short, it is vital to recognize that early nineteenth-century European history fed the Evangelical prophetic mindset not only by alarming it with stories of terror, radicalism, and revolution (the common interpretation of the origins of premillennial pessimism) but, much more positively, by generating a belief that God was acting to fulfill scriptural prophecy within the temporal sphere, particularly in relation to the restoration of the Jewish people to their ancient homeland. This feeling grew exponentially throughout the first half of the nineteenth century as philo-Semitism became widespread among British intellectuals and political leaders, and events throughout Europe appeared to portend the growing possibility of Jewish re-settlement.[59] In particular, the crumbling Ottoman Empire was seen by premillennialists as having been prefigured in prophecy by the image of the drying up of the river Euphrates (Rev 11:12), an event they believed would precede the return of the Jews to their homeland.[60]

---

57. Perry, *British Mission*, 1. On Napoleon's relationship with the Jews, see Kobler, *Napoleon and the Jews*.

58. For the broader history of attitudes toward Jews in the nineteenth century, see Rubenstein and Rubenstein, *Philosemitism*.

59. Edward Bickersteth summarized the events that he believed were augurs of Jewish restorationism, and thus of the end times, in *Restoration of the Jews*, lxxvi–xcviii.

60. See, for example, Grimshaw, "Introductory Lecture," 29.

The key institution for promoting the dual agenda of Jewish conversion and Jewish restoration among Evangelicals was the London Society for Promoting Christianity Among the Jews (LSPCJ), sometimes known as "The Jews Society." Founded in 1809 by the converted Jew Christian Friedrich Frey (1771–1850), the LSPCJ stood as a symbol of early nineteenth-century Evangelical co-operation. The society was initially constituted to undertake missionary and apologetic work among the local London Jewish populace. The LSPCJ subtly changed in tone during the late 1810s, moving away from evangelization of London Jews, toward a more aspirational conviction that their work was concerned with the conversion of the entire global Jewish people.[61]

This change of priority was particularly associated with Lewis Way, whose ideas have already been quoted. Way was a barrister turned Anglican priest who had inherited a small fortune and spent it on re-endowing the LSPCJ. Way was concerned not only with the conversion of the Jews, but also with their physical restoration to Palestine. He lobbied for the Congress of Vienna (1815) to uphold this principle and then turned to the Russian Tsar, Alexander I. Eager to collect data to present to Alexander, Way and several colleagues went on tour in Europe in 1817 and met Jews in Russia, Germany, and the Netherlands. As well as evangelizing Jews, he continued pushing his agenda "to obtain for the descendants of Abraham greater civil and political privileges than they are now permitted to enjoy."[62]

The endeavors of Way were reported in the mouthpiece of the society, *The Jewish Expositor*, edited by Charles Hawtrey, the secretary of the LSPCJ. It was while on his European tour that Way became convinced of the premillennial advent of Christ, a view he put forward in a series of letters in the *Jewish Expositor* in 1820 under the pen-name "Basilicus." These letters were also one of the earliest statements of the doctrine of the premillennial advent among Evangelicals.[63]

Across the Evangelical world in the 1810s and 1820s, this literalist, restorationist theology took hold. Gerard Noel, for example, delivering the Anniversary Sermon of the Jews Society in 1820, eight years before his *apologia* for fully-fledged premillennialism, waxed lyrically for the restorationist cause: "Oh where is now the nation once beloved of God.

---

61. For the history of the LSPCJ, see Gidney, *History of the LSPCJ*. Gidney was eager to play down the premillennial dimension of the Society.

62. "Return of the Rev. Lewis Way," *Jewish Expositor* 4 (1819), 38.

63. Perry, *British Mission*, 33.

Oh where the land once the fruitful paradise of the earth?"[64] Similarly, William Marsh (1775–1864), the rector of Colchester who would become a leading advocate of premillennialism, was alerted to the Jewish cause by Cambridge Evangelical leader Charles Simeon (1759–1836), who had asked him to deputize for him at a Jews Society event in 1818. Preparing for a sermon on a subject in which he had not previously felt any interest, Marsh undertook a crash course in biblical prophecy relating to Israel and emerged a strong proponent of the idea that Israel would be saved as a nation.[65] During the 1830s, lectures on the restoration of the Jews were held in Glasgow, Liverpool, and Leamington Spa and the first meeting of the annual Bloomsbury prophecy conference took Jewish restorationism as its theme.[66] The definitive statement on Jewish national restoration was made by the statesman of mid-century Evangelicalism, Edward Bickersteth, in his *The Restoration of the Jews to Their Own Land* (1841).

The point to underline is that the theological logic seems often to have run from a literal Jewish conversion to a literal second advent of Christ, not the other way round. As Hugh McNeile, who gave a series of lectures in 1827 on the future prospects of the Jews, concluded: "Of the portions of passages which apply to the *nation* and the *land,* be thus admitted to the favour of a literal interpretation . . . upon what principle of consistency, or canon of analogy, is it, that a similar interpretation is denied to the interwoven portions of the same passages, which apply to The King?"[67] The premillennial advent of Christ was not really the cry of despair of common caricature, but rather a theological proposition concerning the fulfillment of Old Testament prophecy relating to the kingdom of God on earth: a real kingdom, needing a real king—the Jewish carpenter–Messiah, Jesus Christ. This was the basis for asserting the "literal" second coming of Christ before the millennium. As Charlotte Elizabeth Tonna put it: "Israel is the key-note, by which every chord must be tuned."[68]

---

64. Quoted in "London Society for the Conversion of the Jews," in "Religious Intelligence," *Appendix to the bound edition of the Christian Observer for 1820, Being the nineteenth volume* (1821), 882.
65. C. Marsh, *Life of William Marsh,* 65–68.
66. E. Bickersteth, *Restoration of the Jews,* lxxx.
67. McNeile, Sermons on *Second Advent,* xviii. Upper case emphasis in original.
68. "The Protestant," *CLM* 13 (Jan–June 1840), 576.

One People or Two? The Division of Premillennialism on the Issue of Israel and the Church

The new interest in the literal restoration of Israel was the theological underpinning for the seismic shift in Evangelical eschatology. Suddenly, things that had once been thought to apply to a heavenly, spiritual future were rendered as belonging to a temporal, earthly sphere. The "earthiness" of Old Testament prophecy was not just a metaphor for a spiritual salvation, but a real, temporal-spatial event that was perhaps beginning right in front of people's eyes! But why should belief in Jewish restoration entail that Christians—the New Covenant people of God—would share in this material restoration or earthly hope? After all, the logic of literalist theology might imply quite the opposite. Perhaps the Old Testament might promise an *earthly* kingdom to Jews, and a *heavenly* inheritance for Christians? Indeed, this should have been an attractive option because it would keep intact the in-built Evangelical sensibility that the things of the spiritual and heavenly world trump the things of the material and earthly sphere.

In fact, this *was* exactly the idea embraced by the most famous and, in the long term most influential, premillennialist, John Nelson Darby. As we saw in the previous chapter, Darby argued that God had dealt with Israel in six dispensations, or eras, each of which represented a kind of test that God's people had failed. Throughout the Old Testament, Israel had hoped for the coming of a Messiah to bring about a promised earthly inheritance, but had, in the end, rejected Christ. This rejection was, in fact, the termination of the sixth Jewish dispensation. Because of this rejection, God had put his dealings with Israel on hold, paused Jewish history, and thrown open the offer of salvation to the Gentiles. This offer to the church, as recorded in the pages of the New Testament, was not the earthly hope of Israel, said Darby, but rather the promise of a spiritual or heavenly inheritance.[69] Darby therefore argued that the Bible contained two sets of promises, one to Israel and one to the church. Darby said this distinction was "the hinge upon which the understanding of scripture turns."[70] This interpretation of the Bible became known as "dispensationalism," because its organizing theme was the distinction between the way in which God dealt with his people in different eras and, in particular, the

---

69. Burnham, *Story of Conflict*, 35–38.
70. Darby, "Reflections," *Collected Works*, 2:18.

two differing eschatological outcomes promised to people of the Jewish and Christian dispensations.[71]

This dispensationalist interpretation led to certain hermeneutical conclusions about biblical prophecy according to Darby, namely:

> In prophecy, when the Jewish church or nation ... is concerned, i.e., when the address is directly to the Jews, there we may look for a plain and direct testimony, because earthly things were the Jews' proper portion. And on the contrary, where the address is to the Gentiles ... there we may look for symbol, because earthly things were not their portion and the system of revelation to them must be symbolical.... When therefore facts are addressed to the Jewish church as a subsisting body... I look for a plain, common-sense, literal statement.... On the other hand, as the church was a system of grace and heavenly hopes ... it is ... symbolized by analogous agencies.[72]

Darby meant by this statement that Old Testament prophecies should be read "literally," that is, as pertaining to things of the earth. But the New Testament, addressed to a "spiritual" people, should be interpreted according to symbol and analogy. Like other premillennialists, when Darby talked about a "literal" interpretation of scripture, he meant not simply a plain or common sense reading of all Scripture, nor merely a belief that things like the return of Christ or the millennium would really occur, rather than being symbols of inward spiritual change. Rather he used the word "literal" to refer to an interpretation of the Old Testament which avoided the common tendency to see the promise to Israel as fulfilled in the church.[73] But for Darby, the corollary of this view was that the destiny of the church was *not* "literal," that is not "earthly," but was rather "spiritual" and "heavenly." Indeed, he argued that the hope of the church was to be taken away secretly, before these events described by prophecy,

---

71. The idea of distinct "dispensations" of salvation history was not, in itself, unique to Darby and was shared by historicists. However, the notion of a two-track salvation process, and a related hermeneutic of scripture, which came to be the most distinctive parts of Darby's "dispensationalism," was not common.

72. Darby, "On Days Signifying Years," *Collected Writings*, 2:35.

73. Burnham, *Story of Conflict*, 37–38; Sweetnam, "Two Peoples". I am indebted to Mark Sweetnam for the idea that "literalism" for Darby was a theological presupposition, which must be explained by looking to Darby's own education and experience, not simply a hermeneutical method. For a further elucidation of literalism as a prior theological commitment, not a neutral interpretive strategy, see Donaldson, *The Last Days of Dispensationalism*, 1–30.

to enjoy an exclusively heavenly, spiritual inheritance. This was the event that came to be known as the "rapture."[74]

Darby's literalism was not, therefore, a simple catchall for understanding Scripture. It was an *a priori* hermeneutical assumption about a two-state salvation solution. Darby thought Scripture was only literal (i.e., earthly) when talking about the Jews, but was symbolic and allegorical (i.e., heavenly) when talking to the Gentiles. He wanted Irenaeus for Israel and Origen for the church. It was a highly idiosyncratic, and amazingly successful thesis, although not without a number of significant critics, not least from within the Brethren movement itself.[75]

Darby had, in fact, found a way to keep intact the classic Evangelical hope for a heaven, non-earthly future as part of a broader "spiritual" (one might even say "mystical" because, as both Timothy Stunt and Gary L. Nebeker have suggested, Darby may have been influenced by emphases in continental European mysticism) approach to Christian identity.[76] Darby's Christian hope was entirely non-earthly, or "non-literal." "The one proper hope of the church has no more to do with the world than Christ has, who is in heaven," he concluded.[77] The reason for Darby's conclusion owed much to his theological journey and his deep sense of pessimism concerning the state of his own Church of Ireland. His despair at the state of the world and the church led him to create a vision of Christian hope that posited an entirely spiritual other-worldly *dénouement* to God's plans for those who followed Christ, one which rejected all earthly structures, whether ecclesiastical or physical.[78] Darby held what Jonathan Burnham has called "a position of radical dualism between material and spiritual matters."[79] Indeed, the most startling fact about the version of

---

74. Sandeen, *Roots of Fundamentalism*, 62–64; Weber, *Living in the Shadow*, 20–23.

75. Burnham, *Story of Conflict*, 114–21.

76. See Stunt, "Influences in the . . . Development of J. N. Darby," 61–65; Nebeker, "Ecstasy of Perfected Love."

77. Darby, "The Hopes of the Church of God," *Complete Writings*, 2: 382–83.

78. This mystical sense was related to Darby's early career as a high churchman and perhaps also to what Timothy Stunt has called a tradition of "exact churchmanship" within the Irish church in the early nineteenth century. It is, of course, notable that Darby's critique of the worldliness of the church was paralleled by the language of the contemporaneous Oxford Movement. In fact, Darby claimed that he had once admired the rigorous spirituality of Catholicism and thought of himself as having pioneered Tractarian themes before the Oxford Movement came to birth. Stunt, *From Awakening to Secession*, 154–55; Carter, *Anglican Evangelicals*, 228–29.

79. Burnham, *Story of Conflict*, 135.

premillennialism flowing from Darby's vision was that the millennium was in fact abandoned as an object of Christian hope because Christians would be removed from the earth before it began.[80] "The Christian's hope is not a prophetic subject at all," concluded Darby.[81] He thus tethered dispensationalism to futurist prophetic chronology because, he argued, the events of prophecy would only happen *after* Christians had been raptured out of their way—which clearly could only mean in the future, not in the past.

Much of historicist premillennialism differed from Darby concerning the destiny of the Gentiles (i.e., the Christian church) in relation to the Jews. While historicist premillennialists agreed with Darby and his followers that the material promises made to the nation of Israel should not be spiritualized, they resisted the notion that there were therefore two peoples of God and two sets of promises.[82] Embracing an Old Testament literalism, but rejecting the "two people" hypothesis of Darby, meant only one option was open to historicist premillennialists, namely to argue that Christian hope was, like that of Israel, an earthly (or a "literal") one. Thus, as William Pym put it, "by a wondrous ordinance, the destinies of Zion are linked with the whole family of man."[83] Therefore, for historicists, the Old Testament, with its promise of earthly restoration, was a set of predictions not only for the Jews, but for the Gentiles as well. Charlotte Elizabeth Tonna told the readers of her *CLM* in 1845: "we shall find that this restitution of all things, is dwelt on by all the *New* Testament writers, as well as the Old; indeed, it is the one bright spot on which, in the eternity before us, the eye is taught to rest."[84]

Why did historicist premillennialists choose this "unified" option rather than follow Darby to propose a dualistic eschatology? There are three considerations that help account for this fact. First, traditional

80. Nebeker, "John Nelson Darby," 107.

81. Darby, "The Rapture," *Collected Writings*, 11:156.

82. In modern terminology, this attitude marks these premillennialists as "historic premillennialists." This term has the meaning of "classical" and is used by those who reject the prevailing dispensationalist interpretation to suggest this form of premillennialism was the "original" (and thus authentic) version. The use of this term is not to be confused with "historicist," which denotes the view of *when* prophetic biblical texts is fulfilled. For an introduction to historic premillennialism, see Blomberg and Sung, *Case for Historic Premillennialism*

83. Pym, "The Redeemer's Return," 316.

84. "Our Years are Numbered," *CLM* 25 (Jan.–June 1845), 50 [emphasis in original]; Pym, *Restitution*, 73.

doctrinal convictions about Scripture undergirded the historicist premillennialist attitude. Darby's interpretation of Scripture was eccentric. It is therefore quasi-Marcionism that needs to be explained more than the historicist premillennialist commitment to the unity of the Bible. Historicist premillennialists believed both Old and New Testaments were applicable to Christian life. "Many who *formally* assent to the truth, 'ALL Scripture is given by inspiration of God, and is profitable . . .' do *in effect* deny it. Some are not ashamed to assert, that the rule of *Christian* conduct is contained in the New Testament alone, and acting on the principle they avow, altogether neglect the Old," complained James A. Begg (d.1869).[85] "We maintain, that [the Old Testament] continues the great Standard Revelation of God's Will to the world," affirmed Joshua Brooks.[86] Thus historicist premillennialists thought that to limit application of Old Testament prophecy to the Jewish nation alone was, as Edward Bickersteth saw it, to "carry the literal interpretation too far."[87] Thus, once literalism was established as the proper way to interpret the Old Testament, it was in many ways natural for individuals who believed the Old Testament remained relevant to Christians to assume that the church must somehow be incorporated in its promises of earthly felicity.

Second, ecclesiastical loyalty was a contributing factor. The historicist interpretation of prophecy was a Protestant, establishment conviction that held that God had not only acted in history, but also in the magisterial churches of Great Britain and Ireland. As Ralph Brown has argued, shared social networks, educational backgrounds, and sense of national responsibility meant that, after the furor of the late 1820s and early 1830s, most historicist premillennialists tended to resist sectarianism and embrace comprehension.[88] It was no coincidence, then, that a comprehensive, unifying view of eschatology was held by those who remained committed to a national, "catholic" church, while the view of the removal of individuals from the earth became associated with a sectarian and separatist stream of nineteenth-century Evangelical Protestantism (and also went on to be profoundly connected with a separatist strand

---

85. Begg, *Connected View*, 13. James A. Begg should not be confused with James Begg (1808–83), the Free Church of Scotland minister and social reformer. He later became a leading advocate of Seventh-Day Adventism. Froom, *Prophetic Faith*, 3:560; *Seventh Day Baptists*, 67–68.

86. Brooks, *Essays on the Advent*, 10.

87. E. Bickersteth, *Practical Guide*, 77.

88. R. Brown, "Victorian Anglican Evangelicalism," 683–85.

of twentieth-century American Protestantism). Nor was it a coincidence that a willingness to endorse the materialism of Christian hope was found among those who valued Christian faith expressed through a visible national church that held out grace through the ministry of Word and Sacrament. "Spiritual men," wrote Edward Bickersteth, alluding sardonically to Dissenters as well as to the "spiritualizers" of scriptural prophecy,

> deny the value of sacraments, or of national establishments, or the grateful use of earthly things, or the restoration of the Jews; and the merely infidel men of the world, delighted with such aid, join them in the hope of overthrowing the whole of God's word. But the outward ordinances, and the union of Church and State, and the right enjoyment of God's creation, and the restoration of Israel, are as real a part of God's design of love to men, as the invisible and spiritual glories of his church.[89]

Ideologically, ecclesiastically, and temperamentally, historicist premillennialists were committed to inclusivity and to the manifestation of divine purposes through concrete, visible, and comprehensive entities.

Third, the historicist view of God's involvement in all history (not, *pace* Ralph Brown, only magisterial Protestant history) meant these premillennialists saw God as a far more comprehensive, universal force than Darby's image of the deity. As we saw in the previous chapter, Darby's "futurism" restricted divine activity to a short burst of apocalyptic activity in the imminent future. God was absent from history. Moreover, Darby's belief that each "dispensation" ended with failure implied that history was a sad tale of human failure rather than of divine progress. There were, of course, futurists who rejected Darby's dispensationalist/rapture hypothesis and it was not inherently impossible for a non-dispensationalist futurist to be a believer in an earthly restitution as the object of Christian hope. However, a comprehensive restitution to which all history was moving made more sense for historicists than futurists because restitution for historicists was envisaged as the climax of a process of recovery that had been the pattern of God's interaction with the temporal-spatial sphere since creation. As Thomas Rawson Birks put it, in the era of restitution "the separate elements, prepared for thousands of

---

89. E. Bickersteth, *Restoration of the Jews*, cxviii. Donald Lewis has identified a new "Calvinist apologetic" for church establishments in the 1830s that drew particularly on the notion of the "covenant" and looked to the Old Testament as a model for British society. Some of these themes will be revisited in chapter 6. D. M. Lewis, *Lighten Their Darkness*, 17–25.

years, are all to be combined in one vast and glorious exhibition of the moral dominion of God."[90] There was thus an obvious synergy between historicism and restitution.

Romanticism and Restitution

I have summarized the logic by which the idea of restitution became prominent among a section of Evangelical premillennialists, but logical argument is not always enough to explain the purchase that an idea gains over a group of people. Evangelicals devoted much time to studying and arguing about the meaning of prophetic biblical texts, but the biblical and theological framework was like a valley carved out into the eschatological landscape. Into that valley rushed a flood of socio-cultural predilections and ideas, in particular the values described by the term "romanticism."

The theme of "restitution" was an important element of European romantic thought. In the eighteenth century, the idea of restitution had found favor among several romantic theologians, including Freiderich Schleiermacher (1768–1834), for whom it cohered with an understanding of the solidarity and brotherhood of the human race, and the mystically-inclined Friedrich Christoph Oetinger (1702–82) who articulated a scriptural justification for the doctrine.[91] The idea of *apokatastasis* also appealed to romantic thinkers such as Johann Gottlieb Fichte (1762–1814) and Friedrich Schelling (1775–1854) because of their belief that the universe was in a process of self-realization, the final goal being a form of completeness or "oneness." The same resonance between premillennialist commitment to restitution and the broader romantic culture was also evident in the other, less commonly-used, term which some premillennialists used as shorthand for their eschatological expectations—*palingenesia*. This was a word used by Jesus in the Gospel of Matthew to describe the "re-generation" of all things at the Last Judgment. Lewis Way popularized the term in an eschatological epic poem, summarizing the doctrine of the restitution of all things, entitled *Palingenesia. The world to come* (1824).[92] The term had currency in German romantic philosophy

---

90. Birks, "Resurrection to Glory," 253.

91. Schwarz, *Eschatology*, 339–41.

92. The *Literary Gazette* wrote of this work that the author "is parabolical beyond all parabolists. . . . He treats of a Millennium . . . . This is the *third* world. The first was before the flood; the second is our present world; and as the *Literary Gazette* does not expect (however deserving) to be read in the next, we shall save ourselves the trouble

(Thomas Carlyle parodied it in *Sartor Resartus*) and also in scientific, and quasi-scientific, speculation about, and experimentation with, the notion of generation and re-generation in organic entities.[93] The Swiss naturalist Charles Bonnet (1720-93), for example, articulated a theory that all animal life would reach inherent perfection in a future state in his popular *Palingénésie philosophique* (1769-70).

Nowhere is the symbiosis between premillennialism and romanticism clearer than in the thought of the intellectual leader of English romanticism, Samuel Taylor Coleridge (1772-1834). Coleridge, though rejecting the idea of a strict earthly millennium as proposed by his friend Edward Irving, nevertheless expressed his entire agreement with the idea of a reconstituted natural world, affirming

> that the objects of the Christian Redemption will be perfected on this earth;—that the kingdom of God and his Word, the latter as the Son of Man, in which the divine will shall *be done on earth as it is in heaven,* will *come;*—and that the whole march of nature and history, from the first impregnation of Chaos by the Spirit, converges toward this kingdom as the final cause of the world. Life begins in detachment from Nature, and ends in union with God.[94]

Coleridge was perfectly in harmony with the majority of premillennialists in this eschatological statement. His statement suggests that belief in a material restitution was a doctrine that transcended the specific nuances of prophetic interpretation, and could exist even among people who did not subscribe to a conventional "historicist premillennialist" outlook.

All romantic thinkers longed for the reunion of what was disparate and fragmented. As Hoxie Fairchild concluded, "beneath the entire [romantic] movement one perceives the desire to bring God, man, and nature, finite and infinite, real and ideal, familiar and strange, into a thrilling unity of diverse elements."[95] Edward Bickersteth recognized

---

of reviewing *Palingenesia.*" Review of *Palingensia, Literary Gazette* 8 (1824), 808.

93. *The New Monthly Magazine* reported, with some mockery, that: "At the meeting of naturalists, held at Stuttgard in 1834, a Swiss savant revived the subject of the Palingenesia of the alchemists, with a receipt for an experiment of that kind, extracted from a work by Oetinger.... This so called Palingenesia... was the art of reproducing from the ashes of an object the form which it originally possessed". "The Palingensia of the Alchemists," *The New Monthly Magazine and Humorist* 83 (1848), 136.

94. Coleridge, "Notes on Irving's Ben-Ezra," 513.

95. Fairchild, "Romantic Movement in England," 22.

that theological arguments about Israel were actually part of a broader ideal, which one can see in retrospect was the romantic hope for restitution. "The difference respecting the literal and spiritual restoration of Israel," he noted, "is a part of that question which relates to the redemption of all earthly things. It is the design of Christ to bring what is visible, and sensible, and material into full subjection to ... and entire sanctified combination with the spiritual and invisible."[96]

The image of the restitution and recovery of the world and the regeneration of nature thus proved irresistible to a certain section of women and men living in a cultural universe pervaded by ideas of discovering the eternal within the temporal and thus uniting the spiritual and physical in one grand *dénouement*. The anti-premillennialist writer David Bogue believed that premillennialists indulged a "licentious imagination, which ... [has] wandered into the fairy scenes of its own creation."[97] This was a cynical view, although not entirely inaccurate. Many lectures and books written about the nature of the world to come must be seen as a corpus of imaginative romantic literature. As Thomas Rawson Birks told his auditors at St. George's, Bloomsbury, in 1843, "the hope of the Millennium has thus a fullness, and breadth, and grandeur which no words can describe. ... What larger wish can even our imagination conceive?"[98] Premillennialists were not content with bald statements of fact about the nature of the world to come. Their romantic sensibility led them to colorful and lyrical meditations on the nature of the future. Their vision of the destiny of the earth was a curious mix of scriptural exactitude and poetic license.

"In saecula saeculorum": The Premillennialist Vision of the Age to Come

Rejecting the Evangelical tendency to present heaven and earth as different kinds of place, premillennialists were eager to stress continuity and similarity between this age and the next. "The happiness of the world to come," opined the *CLM*, "far from being of another species and complexion to that which we are here capable of tasting, is described to us in the word of God by every image most naturally attractive to the

---

96. E. Bickersteth, *Restoration of the Jews*, cxviii.

97. "On the Personal and Spiritual Reign of Messiah," *The Evangelical Magazine and Missionary Chronicle* 5 (1827), 464.

98. Birks, "First Resurrection," 260.

human mind."[99] "All the revelations, indeed, which are given to us of a future state, connect it with this life," agreed James Haldane Stewart (1776–1854).[100] The *CMR* similarly urged the believer to look positively on the current sphere of existence because the age to come would be "a perpetuity and perfection of *his present chief delights*."[101] This idea of organic connection between this age and the next was evident in the two controlling ideas of the premillennialist discourse: the renewal of the earth, and the resurrection of the body.

The Renewal of the Earth

As already argued, the reinvigoration of the entire terrestrial globe was at the heart of the premillennialist vision for the future. In addition to the images of material felicity found in the Old Testament, the key text in proving the renewal of the natural world was Rev 22:3. This promised the removal of the "curse" placed on creation because of human sin. Non-premillennialist Evangelicals had interpreted this verse as referring to the relief from toil and pain in heaven. For example, George Townsend (1778–1857), Canon of Durham Cathedral, argued: "When man ascends with Christ to heaven, we are expressly told there shall be no more curse; and this enables us to understand that happiness of heaven to which Christ our Lord shall raise us."[102] But, as might now appear entirely predictable, premillennialists thought such sentiments were logically inconsistent. The earth, not heaven, had been cursed, so earth must be liberated from its curse: "for this plain reason,—the words, '*No more curse*' necessarily imply the *previous existence* of a curse, and its *ceasing to exist* in the same place or state in which it had before existed," argued the *QJP*.[103]

It was therefore contended that the world to come would see a complete reinvigoration of the natural order. "Even now," wrote the Independent minister John Pyer (1790–1859) in romantic vein, "the creatures in nature . . . the rocks, and trees, and flowers—the seas, and clouds, and rivers—. . . participate in this great unitary and universal posture of expectation—this necessary condition of a vast, secret, silent waiting for the

---

99. "Anticipations," *CLM.* 8 (July–December 1837), 59.
100. J. H. Stewart, "Recognition of the Saints," 279.
101. Review of *Life in the Sick Room* by Miss Martineau. *CMR* 4 (1844), 262.
102. G. Townsend, "Christ's Glorious Ascension," 318.
103. "The Kingdom of Christ," *QJP*. 22 (1860), 249.

grand Apocalypse of these coming times."[104] James A. Begg, meanwhile, anticipated the renewal of non-human life forms in the future, reminding his readers that "from the accounts of Millennial holiness and felicity, given by the Prophets . . . we learn that even the inferior Animals are, at the Restitution of all things, to have their natures restored, that they may live in the state of harmony in which they existed at creation's dawn."[105] Premillennialists presented a vision of harmony, healing, and peace in which all that now existed in a broken state would be repaired and unified. Hugh McNeile concluded: "The whole of what we call the animal, vegetable, and mineral creations, which, because of their harmony and mutual dependence, and because they all together compose one world, are spoken of in the singular number as the creature or the creation. This creation is personified [in Scripture] . . . it fell under a curse . . . [but] Yes there shall be deliverance[;] . . . the Lord Shall make all things new; a new earth, new animals, new fruits!"[106]

Although the logic of the argument was that what was currently diseased would be restored to health, these statements about the future destiny of the world clearly reflected a love of the natural world, even in its "cursed" state. "Even in the disjointed ruins we may discern something of the magnificence and splendour of the original building," remarked McNeile.[107] Gerard Noel suggested that the doctrine of the restitution of all things "consecrates all the variety and loveliness of the material objects around us, by their connexion with a Paradise yet to be restored to our full, and perhaps eternal enjoyment."[108] Similarly, John Cumming drew his images of the future life explicitly from his travels in the British Isles: "I could not wish a brighter or more beautiful nook in heaven than some of the sweet glens in the Highlands, or some of the sequestered, beautiful spots in various parts of England."[109]

As Cumming's appeal to the bucolic delights of Britain suggests, this premillennialist hope for the renewal of creation reflected a well-known theme of nineteenth-century literary romanticism, a delight in

104. Pyer, *Coming Hour*, 7.
105. Begg, *First Resurrection*, 7.
106. McNeile, *Sermons on Second Advent*, 169–73.
107. Ibid., 106.
108. G. T. Noel, *Brief Enquiry*, 65.
109. Cumming, *Redemption Draweth Nigh*, 100. This statement is an example of how the use "heaven" continued to be used by some Evangelicals, even while they redefined its location and character.

the natural world and a conviction that ultimate reality could be found in and through the created order, not in an ethereal, distant place.[110] As Pamela Edwards has argued, in the British romantic tradition true felicity was to be found neither in spirit nor matter alone, but in the synthesis of the two dimensions.[111] This view was captured well in famous lines of the lake poet, William Wordsworth (1770–1850):

> Not in Utopia, subterranean fields,
> Or some secreted island, Heaven knows where!
> But in the very world, which is the world
> Of all of us,—the place where in the end
> We find our happiness, or not at all![112]

Premillennialists were highly Wordsworthian in their descriptions of the age to come. Indeed, the editor of the *Jewish Expositor*, Thomas Boys (1792–1880), echoed Wordsworth's sentiments in verse, summoning up the reinvigoration of nature thus:

> . . .creation, trembling
> And groaning, also was redeemed.
> In that new heaven and new earth, not alone
> Our souls in holy bliss shall live, but when
> Creation shall be perfect and renewed,
> As from the hand of God; no mind can grasp
> The joy and bliss our senses may receive
> From sight, from sound, from scent, from Nature's touch.[113]

Boys' capitalization of "Nature" even reflected the tendency of romantic poets to slip into pantheism.

For premillennialists, the age that would dawn when Christ returned would be the moment when earth joined with heaven, and when eternity met time. All that was good would be combined into a blended whole. "It will thus be one main excellence of this promised kingdom to restore the orderly connexion between heaven and earth, between the

---

110. Prickett, *Romanticism and Religion*, 127ff.

111. Edwards, *Statesman's Science*, 141.

112. William Wordsworth. "French Revolution As It Appeared To Enthusiasts At Its Commencement," *The Complete Poetical Works*. London: Macmillan and Co., 1888, Bartleby.com, 1999. www.bartleby.com/145/.

113. Boys, *God and Man*, 19–20.

unseen world of spiritual being, and the visible constitution of this lower universe," argued Thomas Rawson Birks.[114] When Christ returns, argued William Cadman: "The broken link of union and communion between the heavenly and the earthly, which was broken by man's sin, will be repaired... there will be the closest possible connexion and communication between the new heavens and the new earth."[115] This hope of reunification allowed premillennialists to maintain a strong supernaturalism. The world to come would not be a different world, but neither would it be simply the old world. It would be the temporal-spatial sphere renewed and refreshed through combination with the eternal and spiritual realm. "Every blessing, indeed, originates with God, and is dependent upon a *spiritual* energy, but the scene on which it operates is this material world," contended Gerard Noel.[116]

It is worth noting that some premillennialists articulated a kind of graduated system of degrees of glory in the *eschaton*. Some of these interpretations did appear to acknowledge the more traditional Evangelical languages concerning the "heavenly" destiny of believers. They thus proposed that Christian believers might "hover" somewhere above the earth, while Jews and non-Christian Gentiles would have their feet on the ground. William Lincoln, the rector of St. John's Episcopal Chapel, London Road, for example, said that Christian saints would live just above the earthly Jerusalem in a cloud of glory "so close to Jerusalem that it may be said 'the land is married' to heaven and its king."[117] However, whether these Christians were really in "heaven" or just in "the air"—that is, still part of a reconstituted material cosmos—was often ambiguous. Charles Goodhart, for example, proposed that Christian saints may live in a "heavenly Jerusalem," but by this term he meant a Jerusalem of the ether—"the heaven of our earth," as he put it with marvelous ambiguity—to be found high in the atmosphere of the world, and therefore still clearly part of the material universe. Thus even those millennialists whose Evangelical terminology bound them to place Christians in "heaven" still found it necessary to bring the location of that heaven as close as possible to the physical earth.[118]

---

114. Birks, "On the Order," 75.
115. Cadman, "Spread of the Knowledge," 219.
116. Noel, *Brief Enquiry*, 234.
117. Lincoln, *Sermons*, 74.
118. G. T. Noel, *Brief Enquiry*, 234.

Excursus: *Thomas Chalmers and the New Creation*

Although the vast majority of Evangelicals came to eschatologically materialistic and premillennialist doctrines in tandem, there are some notable cases in which the vision of a renewed creation was not explicitly linked to premillennialism. I spent some time earlier in this chapter explaining the theological logic of the prophetic hope for a material future. However, it is also an essential part of my argument that, while premillennialism certainly accelerated people's journey into a new vision for the future and was the most coherent and well-worked expression of such an eschatology, it should be seen as just one of the venues for the expression of a growing spirit of Christian materialism in British Christianity that can also be detected elsewhere, often also because of the growing purchase of romantic ideas across nineteenth-century religion.

One important individual who adopted a materialistic eschatology from a non-premillennialist position was Thomas Chalmers. In 1823 he published a version of a sermon that he had preached at St. John's Church, Glasgow, endorsing the "materialism" of a new earth.[119] Somewhat problematically for Hilton's depiction of Chalmers' gloominess and his contention that Chalmers had no hope that the earth would experience redemption (and perhaps problematic even for my own use of him to characterize the old Evangelical sentiment in chapter 1), the sermon is a robust endorsement of the goodness of creation and its place within the eternal purposes of God. "The object of the administration we are under, is to expiate sin, but it is not to sweep away materialism," Chalmers claimed.[120] Many of the themes that would later circulate within premillennialism were sounded in this little text: the goodness of creation, the embodied nature of the future life, the greater attraction of a "heaven" that connected with the present scene, a gentle attack on popular sentiment concerning the ethereality of the world to come, and a stress on the importance of the incarnation in signaling God's endorsement of the physical world.

On the one hand, Chalmers said that he did not believe that he was stating anything other than historical, biblical teaching. To some extent he simply exemplified the dissonance between the ability of educated clergy to state creedal truth and the more popular view of earth and heaven that circulated within Evangelical sub-culture. However, Chalmers' sermon

119. Chalmers, "New Heavens and the New Earth."
120. Ibid., 197.

did show some awareness that he was challenging demotic orthodoxy. He was, he said, aware of "the strangeness of impression which is felt by you . . . that in place of eternal blessedness there will be ground to walk upon; or scenes of luxuriance to delight the corporeal senses . . . having bodies such as we now wear, and faculties of perception . . . such as we now exercise."[121]

Chalmers' early endorsement of the goodness of creation and the eschatological "new materialism"[122] occurred at a time when he was still an avowed postmillennialist. Although this was certainly unusual, it actually underlines my broader contention that while the premillennialist movement that arose in the late 1820s clearly galvanized and accelerated the shift of Evangelical sentiment toward eschatological materialism, it was also but the most dominant expression of this move, not its sole cause. Premillennialism became a venue for discursive realignments about the relationship of God to history, society, and the material world, but these realignments were already occurring within religious thought in the decade before the full burst of premillennialist energy, not least because of the wide-ranging purchase of romanticism on the religious mind. In chapter 4 I will introduce another early adopter of eschatological restitution, Joseph Adam Stephenson, who made his affirmation of a new creation at around the same time as Chalmers, thus pre-figuring the larger move toward earthly salvation that occurred in the 1830s. This trickle toward eschatological materialism, which became a flood from the 1830s, underlines again that the premillennial turn was far from a cry of gloomy despair at the state of the world but was actually itself an expression of the growing optimism toward the temporal-spatial sphere.

It is also worth noting that despite the rather static picture of Chalmers in Hilton's *Age of Atonement*, Chalmers was, in fact, a man on a theological, and perhaps also a socio-economic, journey. I will return to his ideas of social reform in chapter 6. In terms of his eschatology, it is important to note that Chalmers did become a premillennialist. In the early 1830s, Chalmers began to study prophecy more deeply and embraced the premillennial advent. He wrote to Suffolk Evangelical Charles Bridges (1794–1896) in 1836 urging him to update Edward Bickersteth, with whom Chalmers had previously talked about eschatological matters, that "I am now far more confident than I wont to be that there is

---

121. Ibid., 195.
122. Ibid., 197.

to be a coming of Christ which precedes the millennium."[123] The *QJP* admitted that many would be surprised by the revelation of Chalmers' prophetic views.[124] It noted that, although Chalmers was not the most ardent champion of the doctrine, he had moved over the threshold enough to be counted among the premillennialists. "There can be no doubt that though his views were not matured, that his leanings were all in favour of Premillennialism. He had been struck with the strength of the scriptural evidence and he was not afraid nor ashamed to let that evidence weigh with him."[125]

We should probably view Chalmers as a somewhat unusual, although not unique, case of an individual who got to his earthly restitutionism before he got to his premillennial eschatology. Did his prior commitment to the former make the latter easier to swallow? There is not enough evidence to decide on this, but there can be no doubt he would have found much to commend in the ideas of Edward Bickersteth or Gerard Noel (and, indeed, his fellow Scottish Presbyterian premillennialists), who shared not only his commitment to the renewal of the earth, but also embedded this idea within a vision for a sacramental, national church presiding over a Christian society—the idea dearest to Chalmers' heart. Indeed, Chalmers explicitly looked forward to the millennial age when "the kingdoms of the world shall become the kingdoms of our Lord and Saviour Jesus Christ; or, in other words, the Governments of the world shall all be Christianized."[126] What we can claim is that both elements of his eschatology were probably products of the increasing romantic materialism that was washing over the mid-century Evangelical movement.

---

123. Hanna, *Selection from the Correspondence*, 326.

124. The revelation of Chalmers' endorsement of premillennialism, noted the reviewer in the *QJP*, was "one for which many, we apprehend, may scarcely be prepared." Review of *Memoir of the Revd Edward Bickersteth*. By T. R. Birks. *QJP* 3 (1851), 413. In a nice coincidence, the memoirs of Bickersteth and the third volume of the memoirs of Chalmers were published in the same year, allowing the *QJP* to point to the interaction on issues of prophecy between the two men in both reviews in the same edition.

125. Review of *Memoirs of the Life and Writings of Dr. Chalmers* Vol III. *QJP* 3 (1851), 416.

126. Hanna, *Memoirs of . . . Thomas Chalmers*, 4:489.

The Resurrection of the Body

The second way in which premillennialists stressed the continuity between this age and the age to come was the argument that individual identity would be transferred into the future. William Fremantle (1807–95) believed there would be "a complete regeneration of body and soul, accompanied by a real identity of person with all its earthly associations."[127] The central plank of this belief concerned the resurrection of the body, the corollary to the doctrine of the recovery of the earth. "The resurrection is ever presented as the end of our hope," argued Charles Goodhart.[128] In technical terms, premillennialists believed that the resurrection of Christians would occur at the start of the millennial period, a doctrine they justified with several passages from the letters of Paul and the book of Revelation. They called this the "first resurrection" to distinguish it from the general resurrection of the wicked at the end of the millennial era.[129] However, this specific doctrine expanded into a more general statement of hope concerning the place of the physical body within the age to come.

Many premillennialists believed that too often this historical Christian doctrine of resurrection was ignored or mutilated. "The salvation of the soul is all in all with them: the redemption of the body is comparatively of little concern," complained Lewis Way of his imagined "allegorizing" opponents.[130] James A. Begg agreed: "the resurrection of the body has a much more prominent place in Scripture than is now generally assigned to it."[131] Joseph Wolff (1795–1862), the star of the LSPCJ's missionary efforts, suggested that "the greater part of the Christian church have swerved from the plain sense of scripture; and have turned to the phantomizing system of the Buddhists, who believe that the future happiness of mankind will consist in moving about in the air."[132]

These premillennialists, by contrast, wished to assert that that there could be no separation of the body from the soul in the *eschaton*. "My body is not something that does not belong to me," contended John Cumming. "Man is soul and body. If I am not redeemed as a man I am

127. W. R. Fremantle, "Unveiling of Hidden Wonders," 293.

128. Goodhart, "Powers of the World to Come," 201.

129. For a typical statement of the doctrine see Brooks, *Essays on the Advent*, 59–69.

130. Way, Thoughts on *Scriptural Expectations*, 91.

131. Begg, *First Resurrection*, 3.

132. Wolff, *Journal*, 96.

not redeemed at all." He then added, somewhat vaingloriously: "I do not want another body; I shall be content with the one I have."[133] Benjamin Philpot told the St. George's audience in 1841 that he had searched the scriptures to find the version of purely spiritual salvation that was commonly talked of in religious circles, but was unable to locate any such idea. "I can find in the Bible," he concluded "no other happiness provided for redeemed man than one which involves the corporeal condition in which he came from the hand of the Creator. We can have no sympathies with any other condition."[134] A contributor to the *CLM* in 1841 went even further, suggesting that those who denied the resurrection of the body were nearly heretics:

> I do not say that anything of absolute Gnostic heresy is to be found in the teaching of those who try to improve on God's plan by never dwelling on the glorious theme of resurrection; but I do say that the Gnostic heresy first led men to look with this feeling of abhorrence on anything material as connected with our everlasting state.[135]

The *QJP* also hinted that heresy might be abroad, reminding its readers that the "primitive Church had to expel from her communion those . . . who denied the resurrection of the body."[136] The allegorizing, or spiritualizing, of future promises about the body was treated as harshly as interpreting biblical statements about the earth as metaphors for an immaterial heaven. Premillennialists saw resurrection as a moment of romantic recombination. Birks thus stressed that "the resurrection is . . . an act of Divine power, wherein the exalted Saviour will . . . restore that union between the body and the immortal soul."[137]

Because of bodily resurrection, premillennialists expected that people would recognize each other and live in vibrant communities in the new age. William Cadman was convinced that "there will be recognition—how else to explain multitudes coming to sit down with Abraham and Isaac and Jacob in the kingdom of heaven?"[138] James Haldane Stewart thought that "this recognition might seem highly probable,

133. Cumming, *Millennial Rest*, 71.
134. Philpot, "Last Invitations," 121.
135. "Erchomena," *CLM* 15 (Jan–June 1841), 259.
136. "Scripture Testimony to the State of the Departed," *QJP* 2 (1850), 312.
137. Birks, "Resurrection to Glory," 233.
138. Cadman, "Gathering of the Saints," 147.

from the character of our great Creator. One of His peculiar attributes is His goodness, or communicative benevolence; His delight in making His creatures happy: and assuredly this recognition will tend much to increase the felicity of the redeemed."[139] John Cumming similarly argued: "I look on the future as the restoration of scattered families, of suspended friendships, of broken circles; the reanimation of departed images."[140] Thomas Boys put such hopes into verse:

> Then, oh how great the joyous blessedness
> Of recognition in the holy host,
> of those whom we on earth so loved, whose hearts
> And ours were intertwined as one.[141]

To help this process of recognition, argued Fremantle, "memory will be infinitely strengthened, so that not a scrap of the past, not a link in the long series of earthly association will be missing."[142] The interest in memory was again a romantic theme. Wordsworth famously called the moments of personal connection with one's vanished past "spots of time" that broke down the dislocated nature of life and captured the unity of existence within one transcendent vision.[143] The strengthening of memory in the future world would allow individuals to enjoy a personal, experiential unity between time and eternity. Their resurrection as full human beings affirmed that God intended to bring the spiritual and eternal to bear upon the physical and material world. The old Evangelical idea where individual souls found their eternal rest in an ethereal heaven entirely remote from the world was entirely discredited by a vision of a physical, social, terrestrial future.

Killing the King of Terrors

One significant consequence of this strong belief in the resurrection of the body and the renewal of the world among premillennialists was a sharp critique of the Evangelical fetish of death. As was suggested in chapter 1, the "deathbed scene" was a staple of Victorian religious discourse, and

---

139. J. H. Stewart, "Recognition of the Saints," 279.
140. Cumming, *Apocalyptic Sketches*, 243.
141. Boys, *God and Man*, 20-21.
142. W. R. Fremantle, "Unveiling of Hidden Wonders," 289-90.
143. On the romantic interest in memory, see Springer, "History and Memory."

proceeded on the assumption that the soul proceeded directly to heaven upon quitting the world.[144] "It may be generally remarked, of ministers and other members of the church, that the attention and expectation of both are *exclusively* directed, by the received mode of interpretation, to what is generally understood by the expression of *going to heaven,* by an *immediate* translation to the celestial glory," noted Lewis Way.[145] Joshua W. Brooks similarly argued: "I [do not] mean to assert, that Christians generally deny the Advent [and] Resurrection. . . . What I mean to insist on is, that Christians, in their ordinary expositions and discourse, make these truths *subordinate,* and the intermediate prospect of death *pre-eminent.*"[146]

Premillennialists were chary of the doctrine of the intermediate state because of its tendency to usurp the return of Christ and resurrection of the body, and thus to imply that salvation was ethereal and immaterial. George Montagu noted that "not a few of the advocates for our Lord's personal reign upon earth have maintained views with regard to the intermediate state of the soul, which are adverse to the doctrine upon that subject most generally held amongst Protestant divines." Montagu himself did not reject the intermediate state, but he admitted that it needed a firmer biblical grounding than that commonly given to it in Evangelical discourse.[147]

Even those premillennialists who did not explicitly reject the idea that the soul went to be with God at the point of death nevertheless dethroned the doctrine as the object of Christian hope. "Paul does not console those who have lost friends in the modern way, by telling that soon they would die, and that thus they would join the spirits of their departed friends in heaven," complained the *Christian Herald* in 1830.[148] William Pym, alluding to the idea that one could claim the soul of the departed was in a perfect state of rest, asked those who held this position, "whether the condition of the spirits of the just is a perfect condition? I know that their *spirits* are perfect, but where are their *bodies*?"[149] Joshua Brooks, while admitting that "the believer at death enjoys a conscious fellowship,"

144. F. Knight, *Nineteenth-Century Church,* 49–54.
145. Way, *Thoughts on Scriptural Expectations,* 86.
146. Brooks, *Essays on the Advent,* 18.
147. Montagu, *Intermediate State,* 5.
148. *Christian Herald,* Mar. 1830, 6; W. Hamilton, *Defence of the Scriptural Doctrine,* 94.
149. Pym, "Jerusalem's Glory," 153.

did not believe this was heaven, and claimed "that in the primitive church they held those not to be Christians who maintained that souls are received up into heaven immediately after death."[150]

The true hope of the believer, premillennialists contended, should not be death, but the second coming of Christ. Edward Bickersteth claimed that Evangelicalism had made a mistake in its insistence on limiting eschatological thought to the realm of death. "REGARD THE LORD'S COMING RATHER THAN DEATH AS THE GREAT EVENT FOR WHICH YOU ARE TO PREPARE," he thundered.[151] Charles Sabine, a lawyer from Oswestry, Shropshire (writing under the name "Laicus"), also had sharp words to offer to the contemporary religious world: "I know well that the individual believer is taught to concentrate all his hopes in the article of death, when the spirit ascends to God who gave it, and when he is told that he shall receive his crown of glory," he admitted, but such thought "was not the teaching of the apostles who preached Jesus and *the resurrection*—not Jesus and *death*—as the hope of the Church." Sabine concluded acerbically that "the Church has fallen in love with the king of terrors."[152]

Instructively, John Nelson Darby *objected* to the critique of death present among many historicist premillennialists. Reviewing a work by Edward Irving, who was a strong critic of the Evangelical fascination with death as the hope of the believer (Irving critiqued "the strange and unnatural use they [i.e., leaders of Christian opinion] make of death"),[153] Darby endorsed death as an object of Christian hope: "In evincing . . . that the resurrection at Christ's coming is the substantive hope of the Church, he [i.e., Irving] attempts this by throwing every cloud upon the hope of the dying Christian. . . . Death to the believer is not a parting but a meeting, if our central and supreme affections are with Christ."[154] Such a sentiment fitted Darby's worldview and demonstrates again that his version of dispensationalist premillennialism kept alive a more typical Evangelical dualism, while historicist premillennialism pushed people toward a more robust view of the material world.

---

150. Brooks, *Elements of Prophetical Interpretation*, 52.

151. E. Bickersteth, "Waiting for Christ," 31. Upper-case emphasis in original.

152. Laicus, *Second Advent*, 16–17. Laicus was identified as Charles Sabine in a later anthology of premillennial texts, *Time of the End*, 378.

153. Irving, *Preliminary Discourse*, lvi.

154. Darby, "Reflections upon the Prophetic Inquiry," *Collected Writings*, 2: 12.

The most thoroughgoing refutation of popular Evangelical sentiment on death was that contained in Thomas Birks' *Victory of Divine Goodness*. This book, published in 1867 but which Birks claimed represented the summation of his developing views on eschatological topics over the last thirty years,[155] dealt explicitly with the tendency "to represent this world as wretched and illusive, and one from which our hearts ought to be longing hourly to be released." This was, Birks admitted, "a view which you sometimes hear from Evangelical preachers with just views of the Divine benevolence."[156] However, Birks thought that "[this] tone of thought . . . is no characteristic of Evangelical teaching, but belongs rather to a monastic and mediaeval theology."[157] Unfortunately, conceded Birks, such views still prevailed in contemporary thought, and their consequence was that death had become a longed-for release from the temporal world.

> It is a serious defect in our popular theology that death has been made to occupy the place which the Bible every where assigns to the great contrast of death, the resurrection. Our hymns and popular treatises abound in this substitution, which distorts and obscures, even when it does not subvert and destroy, the whole outline of Christian revelation.[158]

Death for Birks, as for other premillennialists, was no happy release, but "the triumph of the enemy, the dissolution of the godly workmanship of God, the breaking down of a once holy sanctuary."[159] This fetish of death, he concluded, resulted in "a large amount of sickly, unreal, sentimental feeling." Too many Christians, he argued, "content themselves with Protestant traditions, received at second hand from hymns and religious manuals," rather than turning to the scriptural hope of resurrection.[160] Not death, then, he argued, but life, should be the great hope of the Christian—a resurrected life, which, he added with romantic accent, "is the re-uniting what death has severed, the undoing of what death has done."[161] The doctrine of restitution and resurrection was offered as a

---

155. Birks, *Victory of Divine Goodness*, vi.
156. Ibid., 10.
157. Ibid., 11.
158. Ibid.
159. Ibid., 245.
160. Ibid., 13.
161. Birks, "Resurrection to Glory," 233.

clear and self-conscious critique of popular Evangelical sentiments about death and the afterlife. Premillennialist Evangelicals did *not* believe that salvation meant "going to heaven after death."[162]

Time, Motion, and Progress in the Age to Come

Just as premillennialists believed that time was important in the present age (the theme explored in chapter 3), so they also imagined the future as essentially *temporal*—a domain of progress, work, business, growth, education, and movement.

First, premillennialists believed there would be natural fertility and growth in population in the age to come. In terms of human reproduction, whereas some limited this to the millennial reign, others thought reproduction would continue indefinitely.[163] Birks quoted the ordinance of Genesis to "go forth and multiply," which he said was given

> so that the absolute infinity of the Godhead might be imaged in the relative infinity of holy, intelligent creatures, of whose increase there might be no end. . . . [W]e can have no reason, *a priori*, to . . . restrict within the narrow limit of two or three hundred generations, the opening which the wisdom of the All-wise Creator has made for a perpetual manifestation of His own goodness and love.[164]

Edward Bickersteth agreed that the earth would continue to be fertile and bountiful in the age to come, providing adequate resources for an expanded population. "Even now," he noted, "two-third of our world is ocean, incapable of increase, half of the rest, and perhaps more, is almost desert, and of the remainder, the largest part is very imperfectly tilled. There is room even in the latter, for a vast increase, when the whole earth might become like the garden of the Lord."[165] An anonymous writer agreed with these sentiments: "these subjects will be exceedingly numerous, in the regenerated world, which will be enriched in an extraordinary degree, and its habitable parts enlarged: there will be neither sea nor deserts. With this increase of surface and fertility, its population

---

162. Helmstadter, "Nonconformist Conscience," 67.
163. Philpot, "Deliverance of the Meek," 180.
164. Birks, *Outlines of Unfulfilled Prophecy*, 333–34.
165. E. Bickersteth, "Earth Yielding Her Increase," 337–38.

may be multiplied a thousand fold."¹⁶⁶ The *QJP* believed that getting rid of the water would allow more space for an expanded population and pointed to the Netherlands as supporting evidence. "Large tracts now covered with water, caves, and arms of the sea, may be drained . . . as in Holland, and this will enlarge the Earth," it suggested.¹⁶⁷ There was also good news for gardeners: "noxious weeds" would be eliminated, affirmed Hugh McNeile.¹⁶⁸ These sentiments provide a significant background to the association of Evangelical premillennialism with opposition to Malthusian demographic theories: unlike proponents of the "dismal science," premillennialists believed that the created order was capable of perpetual increase and could sustain an exponential increase in population.¹⁶⁹ "The *material* world will become again what it was at first, beautiful in all its parts, fertile to the utmost extent of man's necessities, and salubrious throughout every place and every clime," concluded William Cadman.¹⁷⁰

Second, premillennialists insisted that eternity was a busy place, full of social interaction and exertion. "Ours shall be an eternity of *holy activity* as well as heartfelt praise," argued the Vicar of St. Paul's, Wolverhampton, William Dalton (1805–80).¹⁷¹ Mourant Brock asserted that "*a place of society*, as well as a place of meeting, is this City of God. The future state is not figured by solitude, and by eremites, but by a *city* and its *inhabitants*; every thing replete with life, and with society."¹⁷² John Cumming assured his listeners that "the future is a social place. This city is not to consist of tiers of cells, cold, insulated, disconnected with each other, like the cells of prisoners undergoing solitary confinement. What a miserable idea of heaven that would be!"¹⁷³ John Cox contended that "the life of glory which the Church will realize, will be one of great activity, of dignified service as regards God, and of honourable rule as respects other beings and things."¹⁷⁴ Charles Goodhart agreed with this description. "We cannot conceive of anything short of a mighty stirring activity

---

166. A Church of Scotland Preacher, *Restitution of All Things*, 26.
167. "The Earth: Its Curse and Regeneration," in *QJP* 2 (1850), 257.
168. McNeile, *Sermons on the Second Advent*, 100.
169. See chapter 6 for a further discussion of this theme.
170. Cadman, "Liberty of Christ's Kingdom," 52.
171. Dalton, W., "Delay of the Second Advent," 133.
172. Brock, "City Which Hath Foundations," 317.
173. Cumming, *Millennial Rest*, 205.
174. J. Cox, *Future*, 118.

of busy holiness," he contended."[175] William Cadman even proposed that the reason that the future was a place of society was because God himself did not want to be alone: "His desire for their society and communion is far more intense than their desire to be with Him."[176] Horatius Bonar concluded his paean to the urban environment, from which I quoted in the last chapter, by explaining that he would prefer to dwell in the "smoke and din" of the city, precisely because

> the home to which I'm hasting,
> Is not in some silent glen,—
> The place where my hopes are resting,
> Is a city of living men.[177]

Third, premillennialists believed that the future realm would be one of great exploration and discovery. The growth of science and learning in the millennial era was an obvious illustration for the theme of millennial progress. Knowledge and innovation were, after all, arenas in which the nineteenth century had witnessed great strides. John Cumming wrote that in the *eschaton*:

> We shall grow in all kinds and in all degrees of knowledge. The telescope gives us now but a glimpse of the magnificence of that universe which we shall then see no more through a glass darkly. The mere outposts and sentinels of that brilliant army are all that even the telescope can overtake.[178]

If these premillennialists were pessimistic about the power of human ability to transform the world before the return of Christ, this belief was inverted for the world they imagined would dawn when Christ returned. Charles Goodhart believed that in the future human capacity would be increased to include "the *unlimited use of, and power over, all the material universe.*"[179] George Croly looked forward to the Messiah creating a reign of peace where nations would stop investing in warfare and devote money and time to technological innovation. "Thus, the whole opulence of matter and mind, would be applicable to the arts of peace, to civilization, to science, to brilliant invention, and to the general productiveness

---

175. Goodhart "Powers of the World to Come," 216.
176. Cadman, "Gathering of the Saints," 155.
177. "The City," *QJP* 7 (1855), 201–2.
178. Cumming, *Millennial Rest*, 363.
179. Goodhart, "Powers of the World to Come," 212–13.

of the globe."[180] In what must be one of the most ambitious predictions of the future, Joshua Brooks thought that humans would be able to fly in the age to come. He called this the "locomotive power" of the risen saints.[181] Birks agreed: "To be tied down to one little spot alone is rather a humiliation than a natural condition," he argued.[182] In fact, in this premillennial vision, anything was possible. The energies and inventions of the present era would flourish. Bickersteth thought that "all is to be used in God's service. All the skill and invention and genius of art consecrated, and each artifice busy in yielding up every store to his glory."[183]

Boyd Hilton argues that premillennialists were against science.[184] Clearly this is wrong. Indeed, several premillennialists, including John Cumming, Thomas Rawson Birks, and the widely respected Rector of St-Dunstan's-in-the-West, Edward Auriol (1805–80), were involved in attempting to place scientific discoveries within a Christian framework. They each contributed to lecture series to young men on the merits of scientific study.[185] Their embrace of science was not antithetical to their premillennialism. Rather, it was profoundly connected to their belief in an infinite, eternal God who, they believed, had created a vast and rich landscape upon which scientists and inventors could discover and innovate and thereby bring eternal praise to the creator. John Cumming could thus encourage those involved in scientific research that their work was not in vain:

> Let that chemist work in his laboratory; encourage that astronomer, who spends the night in cataloguing groups of stars; let that mathematician pore over books, and waste the midnight oil[;] . . . it is the rush of the waves of science, and literature, and knowledge, that roll onward and upward to the presence of the everlasting throne, there to reflect the glory of Him that made them, and the riches of Him who is throned upon the very riches of the universe itself.[186]

Fourth, premillennialists also suggested that the world to come would be a place of education. Human beings would not just work with

180. Croly, *Universal Kingdom*, 22.
181. Brooks, *Essays on the Advent*, 99.
182. Birks, *Ways of God*, 114.
183. E. Bickersteth, "Earth Yielding Her Increase," 337.
184. Hilton, *Age of Atonement*, 22.
185. For example, Cumming, "'God in Science.'"
186. Cumming, *Apocalyptic Sketches*, 496–97.

all their might, but would *grow* in knowledge and ability. Edward Bickersteth contended that there would be an increase in the capacities of the human mind: "The knowledge we may attain of the depths of the earth, and of the heights of the heavens, or of the laws of animal or of vegetable life; the insight we may gain of the human body, or of the world's history, will all be made to yield in increase of love and gratitude to the great Author of all."[187] Thomas Boys wrote about this developmental tendency in the *eschaton*, prefiguring A. C. Benson's similarly optimistic vision—"wider still and wider"—of the scope of the British Empire:[188]

> And as eternity rolls ages on,
> Wider and wider, higher and higher still
> Shall be developed man's progressive powers.[189]

William Harrison (1811–82), the rector of Birch, Essex, proposed in his 1852 St. George's, Bloomsbury, lecture that growth in human knowledge would actually somehow involve the expansion of the bounds of the millennial kingdom itself:

> We can conceive some little of what is unknown in the secrets of science and nature; but how much remains to be understood of Him who is the ineffable Infinite! Yet as the knowledge and power of each member of the heavenly kingdom enlarges, in that degree the kingdom itself will increase.[190]

Far from decrying the idea of progress in favor of a pessimistic catastrophism, then, premillennialists were full believers in the concept. Unlike contemporary utopians, however, they threw their vision of progress forward into the *eschaton* rather than believing it was the unqualified characteristic of human effort in the present realm. "That is the age of PROGRESS! What progress, when God shall set his hand to it! In the light of that ever-widening knowledge, in the blaze of that ever-brightening glory, how poor, how vile shall seem the progress of the dishonoured past!" ruminated the *QJP*.[191] The premillennialist concept of progress was not, of course, the vision of progress and development in which many nineteenth-century liberals or utopians believed, nor was it necessarily

---

187. E. Bickersteth, "Earth Yielding Her Increase," 339–40.
188. I.e., "Land of Hope and Glory" (1902).
189. Boys, *God and Man*, 23.
190. W. Harrison, "Vastness of Christ's Kingdom," 330.
191. "The Apostolicity of Chiliasm" *QJP* 2 (850), 15.

the progress hoped for by postmillennial forbears; but it was, nevertheless, a loud echo of the idea of development and growth that was all-pervasive in nineteenth-century society. Indeed, that a group of people who believed in an infinite degree of *future* progress should be denied a claim to share in Victorian optimism because they had some doubts about the *current* capacity of humans to enact this change is somewhat paradoxical! Premillennialists were incurable progressives and relentless optimists. Their vision of the future was fully temporal: a world marked by progress, education, and growth; a world remade.

Conclusion

The underlying theme of premillennialist thought was that the Bible spoke not of a heaven to which believers went after death, but rather of a theocratic kingdom on a renewed earth that would last for at least a millennium and quite probably for all eternity. They found justification for such a belief in a theological proposition about the role of Israel in the prophetic purposes of God, and they buttressed the argument by an appeal to a particular way of reading Scripture. Having established the proposition, they were unafraid to provide color and definition to the idea of temporal-spatial hope drawing not only on prophetical passages of Scripture, but also on the poetic imagination taught to them by the broad cultural disposition to which the short-hand term "romanticism" is often given.

In painting images of the world to come, premillennialists argued that the future life would be the fullness and culmination of all that currently existed, and stressed that the elements of the current world would mature and flourish in the millennial and eternal sphere. Any eschatological vision that implied that the soul alone could find eternal rest was dismissed, an opinion that had implications for the Evangelical view of death as an entry point into heaven. Humans would participate in a new age that was earthly, physical, and social, a world where "time" continued to operate on creatures living a spatial existence and where there might even be a possibility for the reprobate to find redemption. Beneath the crust of the seemingly obscurantist ideas about prophetical times and dates was an iconoclastic set of ideas about eschatology and salvation. Such ideas could lead premillennialists to speak in even more radical terms, as the next chapter will show.

5

Premillennialism and "The Age of Incarnation"

> Then shall be shown, that but in name
> Time and eternity were both the same.
>
> —JAMES MONTGOMERY (1771–1854), "TIME—A RHAPSODY"

THE RE-IMAGINING OF HEAVEN was an iconoclastic act. It carried with it several further radical theological implications, each of which were in keeping with the liberalizing drift of nineteenth-century theology. From the 1840s an increasing number of theologians and Christian leaders proposed that the goal of the Christian life was less to ensure safe posthumous entrance to heaven and more to make visible the hidden kingdom of God within the current temporal order. This revision of eschatology was part of a broader updating of Christian doctrine and practice to account for developments in understanding of the historical accuracy of Scripture, widespread acceptance of geological and biological evolution, and the perceived alienation of large parts of the population from the church.

This "liberal" Christianity—so-called because it was prepared to act with liberty toward some traditional Christian doctrines in order to save the heart of Christian spirituality and ethics from some of the challenges of modern science and scholarship, and because it shared with other forms of liberalism a belief in the continual improvement of individuals and society—emphasized that God had not simply saved humans from a future divine judgment but had also empowered them to live renewed and reconciled lives in union with their creator and with their fellow human beings. This vision increasingly downplayed the judicial and retributive nature of God in favor of emphasizing his love and mercy. Hell began to slip from view. The new theological synthesis thus increasingly downplayed judgment in favor of emphasizing the possibility that God would give all human beings time enough to amend their lives.

Boyd Hilton dubbed the entire theological synthesis that he believed dawned around 1860 an "age of incarnation." He contended that the early nineteenth-century Evangelical-influenced "age of atonement," with its focus on the world as a place of excoriating preparation for heaven, was displaced by a kinder, more socially alert, and more immanent vision of God. In this model, Christ was imagined not as the penal sacrifice appeasing a wrathful God, but as a compassionate brother and ethical role model, full of love and transformative forgiveness. On the cross, Christ did not so much pay a debt to God but instead demonstrated the eternal forgiving and transformative love of God within history.[1] Hilton argued that such theology fit with the more progressive and reforming sentiments of later Victorian British society.[2]

Hilton associated these new theological impulses with the waning of Evangelicalism and the emergence of a new "broad church" hegemony within British Christianity.[3] In this chapter, I offer a revision of this view by arguing that the eschatological revisionism of the premillennialist movement pushed at least some of its adherents into territory commonly thought to have been inhabited mainly by non-Evangelical Christians. The themes which this chapter will explore are first, the possibility of universal salvation and downgrading of hell and punishment; second, a stress on the incarnation of Christ; and, third, a subtle (and, of course, ironic) downplaying of the future nature of salvation in favor of an emphasis on enjoying the eternal in the present.

Premillennial Universalism

In the previous chapter, I argued that premillennialists hoped for a comprehensive restoration of the material world, and for physical continuity between "time" and "eternity." The idea of complete material restoration, and a vision of the age to come as a time of progress and development, raised a question for some premillennialists: might it be possible that

---

1. Hilton, *Age of Atonement*, 292, 296, 299.
2. Ibid., 332.
3. Ibid., 315.

God intended to educate and transform all human beings, not just those who claimed the name "Christian"? Was salvation, in fact, possible for everyone? Moreover, if even animals and plants were to be restored to a pristine state in the new creation, might not God intend the healing of the whole human race? Indeed, would not such a universal forgiveness actually be, in fact, the only way that God could enact the type of universal, all-encompassing victory over sin, death, and the devil for which premillennialists hoped? Universalism bubbled under the surface of premillennialist discourse.[4]

The Millennial Schoolhouse

A growing unease with notions of hell and eternal punishment has been well documented in nineteenth-century religious history.[5] In 1849 Fenton Hort (1828–92) wrote to F. D. Maurice claiming that "disbelief in the existence of retributive justice . . . is now so widely spread through nearly all classes of people."[6] Although there was a variety of reasons for the growing soft-pedaling of the doctrine of physical punishment, Geoffrey Rowell and David Powys have contended that the nineteenth-century commitment to progress, development, and education undermined the belief that death fixed an irrevocable judgment upon individuals.[7] Repentance, conversion, and moral progress, it came to be held, were still possible after death.[8] Meanwhile new assessments of penal theory led to a decline in the nature of retributive justice in favor of the idea of reformative punishment, a theme which also grew from the broad cultural

---

4. Ralph Brown has noted that a broadening of soteriology was "particularly prominent among adventist Evangelical Churchman" in the nineteenth century. R. Brown, "Victorian," 700. However, Brown offers little explanation for why this should have occurred. The materialistic element of premillennialist thought outlined in the previous chapter is the essential context for understanding this drift toward universalistic thought. For my direct reply to Brown, and his interlocutor, Boyd Hilton, see Spence, "Renewal."

5. David Walker has contended that discomfort concerning the physical nature of hell had existed since at least the seventeenth century, although theologians were anxious about expressing their uncertainty about the doctrine because of the function of the notion of hell as a deterrent against immorality. Walker, *Decline of Hell*, 4ff.

6. Hilton, *Age of Atonement*, 274.

7. Rowell, *Hell and the Victorians*, 56, 213–16; Powys "Nineteenth and Twentieth-Century Debates," 100.

8. Bauckham, "Universalism," 51.

commitment to improvement and growth. There was, then, a significant "temporal" aspect to these revisions of hell. They were rooted in the idea of development and progress over and against finality and immutability.[9]

One alternative to arguing that death irrevocably fixed an individual's everlasting punishment was the doctrine of a conscious, active, intermediate state in which individuals might still have the chance to reform even after death. This belief had been proscribed in Protestantism since the sixteenth-century reformers dispensed with purgatory. However, the idea made a comeback in the nineteenth century. This doctrine was central to the contribution made by H. B. Wilson (1804–88) to the controversial and influential volume of *Essays and Reviews* published in 1860. Wilson hoped that after the final judgment there would be found "nurseries as it were and seed-grounds, where the undeveloped may grow up under new conditions—the stunted may become strong, and the perverted restored."[10] In a study of Victorian revisions of hell, Michael Wheeler suggested in passing that the popularity of the doctrine of the millennium was one example of a revival of interest in the intermediate state in Victorian Britain. Wheeler suggests that the belief that Christ would return to reign over a renovated earth for a period of one thousand years was one aspect of the desire for intermediary stages of post-mortem or post-*parousial* existence, which itself was part of an understanding of a world in motion and development.[11]

Wheeler did not explore this argument in depth, but it is clearly astute given all the themes of premillennial discourse discussed so far. Indeed, Lewis Way explicitly called the millennium an "intermediate state" between time and eternity.[12] Thomas Rawson Birks also saw the millennium as a "middle term" that functioned to bring "eternity near to us, in the very regions of time."[13] Inherent in this idea was the concept that the millennium functioned as a period of tutelage by which individuals and nations were drawn into the ambit of God. Many premillennialists suggested that the millennial era would thus be one of gradual progress and transformation, which is not surprising given their commitment to

---

9. This problematizes Boyd Hilton's claim that premillennialists favored retributive punishment, in contrast to moderate Evangelicals, who preferred reformative theories of punishment. Hilton, *Age of Atonement*, 215–16.

10. Rowell, *Hell and the Victorians*, 116–17.

11. Wheeler, *Death and the Future Life*, 78–83.

12. Way, *Thoughts on Scriptural Expectations*, 36.

13. Birks, "First Resurrection," 243–44.

temporal gradualism outlined in chapter 3. "Perhaps the *entire* curse shall not be *at once* repealed," speculated the *QJP*. "Yet it may be, that not until a later epoch shall the whole cosmogony of the world be revised, and the commencement, but the close, of the millennial parenthesis may witness the final expulsion of all that is evil."[14] Thus the millennium was pictured as an educative and developmental era. It would witness, as William Marsh put it, "a race of men preparing for a higher state."[15] Alexander Dallas similarly called it "the educational period of the sons of Adam." Birks described it as "the time when the nations shall repent of their vanities, and earth bear once more some resemblance of heaven[;] ... heaven itself shall stoop down to earth; and that the Lord Jesus, in visible glory, shall welcome back the rebellious prodigal within the happy bounds of the unfallen universe."[16] Bickersteth proposed a similar idea: "The common conception among Christians has often been as if the redeeming love of God was exhausted in the company of the elect who meet the Lord at his appearing, and are thenceforth ever with the Lord." However, he continued, "a deeper and closer search of Scripture reveals this further mystery of Divine goodness."[17] Mourant Brock repeated Bickersteth's claim *verbatim*, and then added: "The present is a dispensation of election, that of universality. In this way will ascend to the Lamb from successive and endless generations successive and endless praise."[18]

This view of the millennium as a period of education was very close to that held by the early church theologian Irenaeus, the father of millennialism.[19] He believed that "humans must advance toward fulfillment in God by a slow, at times frustrating process of learning and becoming."[20] Irenaeus saw Christ as a "recapitulation" of Adam who, unlike Adam, fulfilled completely the purpose of humanity toward God. In turn, he argued, the new creation that would dawn at the return of Christ was a recapitulation of Eden. It would be a sphere in which individuals who followed Christ, the Second Adam, could learn again to walk in the path of righteousness, as God had originally intended. For Irenaeus, the

---

14. "The Earth," *QJP* 2 (1850), 466.
15. C. Marsh, *Life of William Marsh*, 330.
16. Birks, "First Resurrection," 259.
17. E. Bickersteth, "Kingdom of Christ," 414.
18. Brock, "City Which Hath Foundations," 305.
19. Horrocks, *Laws of the Spiritual Order*, 175.
20. Daley, "Apocalypticism," 9.

millennium was a period of acculturation and education, allowing individuals to experience proximity to God within the renewed creation.[21] In seeking reasons for the revival of millennialism in the mid-nineteenth century, it should be of no surprise that this deeply "temporal" doctrine, which received its earliest support from a church father acknowledged to have been strongly committed to the notion of the temporal, progressive nature of redemption, found fertile soil among a society that was preoccupied with notions of development, improvement, and growth.

This notion of an educational apocalypse was also central to the thought of Gerard Noel, with whose story of "conversion" to premillennialism the previous chapter began. Towards the end of his *Brief Enquiry* Noel posed the question: what might a king do with his rebellious subjects? Noel suggested, in what must be read as a caricature of popular Evangelical eschatology, that "he might send a special commission into the land—he might accompany this commission with an overwhelming force, before which all the resources of the rebellious must at once be annihilated."[22] Noel argued there was another option open to the returning king, an option that Noel obviously endorsed:

> He might send a commission, not to annihilate but to repair—not to crush by violence, but to restore by wisdom—not to erase the title from his brows, but to restore allegiance to his laws . . . he might educate, enlighten, protect, and reward—he might bring into exercise the latent sympathies of the misguided and the ignorant . . . and he might succeed in the high and generous effort, of converting a moral wilderness into a scene of culture, fertility and concord.[23]

Noel's vision was rooted in his conviction that the returning king would not "transfer" the elect "as far as might be, to the peaceful regions of his empire" and "lay waste" the earth, but that he would restore the earth to its original state.[24] The significant addition was, of course, that this restoration involved the education and restoration of the rebellious creatures, so that all the earth—and Noel at least appears to imply its human

---

21. Daley, *Hope of the Early Church*, 31.
22. G. T. Noel, *Brief Enquiry*, 14.
23. Ibid. 14–15.
24. Ibid. 14.

inhabitants—would be converted and transformed. Implicit in such teaching is a move toward restorative, and against retributive, theories of divine justice.[25]

It would be misleading to describe Noel as a universalist. His writing could also display a belief in the judgment of the "wicked."[26] Yet his rhetoric was clearly poised ambiguously between a traditional Evangelical Calvinist emphasis upon election and a notion of ultimate reconciliation and the triumph of divine love. The significance of Noel's language in this regard is magnified because of his friendship with the more well-known "universalist," Thomas Erskine of Linlathen (1778–1870). While in the case of many of the people discussed in this book prophetic views have obscured more "liberal" theological inclinations, Erskine has suffered the opposite fate. He has often been portrayed as one of a number of notable mid-nineteenth century "progressives," who moved from a harsh Evangelicalism (and in this case from Presbyterian Calvinism) to a more generous soteriology.[27] As always, the distinctions are not as clear as historians have sometimes imagined. Erskine certainly was on a theological journey, but as well as more usual "broad church" themes, his theology also included a resolute commitment to the kind of prophetic outlook shared with many premillennialists. For example, in 1827 he wrote to his sister, urging her to read Edward Irving's work on the *Prophecies*, and telling her that he was impressed with Irving's interpretation of the fulfillment of prophecy in recent times.[28] Erskine's *Brazen Serpent* (1831) contained a strong prophetic element in which he claimed that the waning of the Turkish Empire was a sign that the great convulsion that would end the age was near at hand.

> I speak of a fixed and longing expectation, of the sure and fast approaching accomplishment of those promises which announce the final triumph of the Messiah, the establishment of his reign upon earth, the manifestation of the sons of God, and the full development of all those high privileges which arise out

---

25. Rowell, *Hell*, 44.

26. Noel could, for example, affirm an orthodox view of judgment in his *Sermons* (although these were written before his public conversion to premillennialism) suggesting that there was no pardon on the further side of death. G. T. Noel, *Sermons . . . for the Use of Families*, 306.

27. Horrocks, *Laws of the Spiritual Order*, 8, 29, 31, 76, 131–59.

28. Hanna, *Letters of Thomas Erskine* 1:109.

of their union with their divine Head. This doctrine appears to me now in a very different light from what it once did.[29]

Recognizing Erskine's prophetic view sheds new light on our understanding of Erskine's better-known theological speculations concerning the scope of God's redemptive activity. Erskine argued that, in Christ, God had issued a universal pardon. Forgiveness for sin was secured, and humanity had been healed of its rebellion. The demand of the gospel was for a response to this universal offer of forgiveness. Only by understanding that Christ had died for all could an individual reach an assurance that this salvation was indeed efficacious for her or him. "A very common idea of the object of the gospel is, that it is to show how men *may obtain pardon*; whereas, in truth, its object is to show how *pardon for men has been obtained*," he contended.[30] Erskine stressed that all humans must come to a personal realization of the reality of this pardon; but he believed that God would not cease working in the heart and mind of the unregenerate until such a realization had been obtained. Erskine held that God's purpose was educative and transformative. "He who waited so long for the formation of a piece of old red sandstone will surely wait with much long-suffering for the perfecting of a human spirit," he claimed, echoing the premillennial interest in the vastness of geological time.[31] Erskine's commitment to a God who longed for righteousness and "will not cease from using the best means for accomplishing it in us all" led him into a belief in the doctrine of the restitution of all things. He lamented that "the expectation of the restitution of all things occupies much less space in the common announcements of the gospel, or in the thoughts of Christians, than it ought to do."[32]

Evidence of the influence Erskine might have had upon Noel (or, indeed, vice-versa) is frustratingly absent. Erskine spent time with Gerard Noel while touring the Continent in 1823 and described Noel as "so

---

29. Ibid., 380.

30. Ibid. 379.

31. Hanna, *Letters of Thomas Erskine* 2:242. Erskine's analogy was not casually chosen. He was referring to the recent publication of Scottish amateur geologist Hugh Miller's study of the old red sandstone of the British Isles—another appropriately geological/temporal metaphor for God's gradual redemptive process. Miller himself spoke of looking forward "to the recreation yet future" at the return of Christ. Quoted in *Time of the End*, 374–75.

32. Erskine, *Unconditional Freeness*, 111. Cf. Hanna, *Letters of Thomas Erskine*, 2:242.

likeable" and a "very great comfort to me."[33] Noel, meanwhile, included Erskine under the pseudonym "St Clair" in his account of his time in continental Europe, *Avendel* (1826). Gerard Noel's daughter, the hymn writer Caroline Noel (1817–77), wrote an elegy on Erskine's death, suggesting a life-long family friendship.[34] While it is not possible to prove that Erskine influenced Noel, Erskine's conviction "that He who came to bruise the serpent's head will not cease his work of compassion until he has expelled the fatal poison from every individual of our race"[35] and his avowed commitment to *apokatastasis* was the same broad thesis pervading Noel's *A Brief Enquiry*. For Noel, as for Erskine, divine allegiance would be restored amongst humanity in the eschaton; the wilderness would be converted to a fertile realm and Christ would act to win back humanity through educative transformation. Both men were part of the same theological ambit in which hope for a progressive restoration of all things was becoming increasingly prominent in nineteenth-century Britain.

The Wideness of God's Mercy

Of course, talk of the millennium being a period of education and acculturation left more questions than it answered. Did premillennialists mean that *everyone* who had ever lived would participate in this era, or just those who were alive when Christ returned? There was no clear answer given to this question. There were, however, other intimations of universalism among premillennialists that tended to stress not so much the educative dimensions of the millennial era but rather the comprehensive scope of the settlement that God would enact in the final reckoning of all things. Here it was indeed evident that premillennialists wanted a broad, if not universal, salvation involving many people who did not claim the name Christian during their lifetime. John Cumming, for example,

33. Ibid., 89, 59.

34. Hanna, *Letters of Thomas Erskine*, 2:379. Caroline Noel's most famous hymn, "At the Name of Jesus" (1870), begins with a sentiment shared with both Erskine and her father: "At the name of Jesus every knee shall bow / every tongue confess him, king of glory now." This was, of course, rigorously biblical, and yet also, when read in the context of the type of thought being expounded in this chapter, gently allusive to the comprehensive eschatological event of the type of which Gerard Noel and Erskine spoke.

35. Hanna, *Letters of Thomas Erskine*, 1:92.

admitted that he still believed in eternal punishment but was prepared to suggest that contemporary views of the scope of salvation were too conservative.[36] "I dare not infer from the Bible that the vast multitudes of Hindoos and Mahommetans will be lost for ever . . . if saved, it must be by the name of Christ; but God may have secret modes of applying the efficacy of that name to the souls of them that never heard it."[37] Those who will be saved, he concluded, "are not a few, as certain ultra-Calvinists believe; and they are not all, as certain Universalists believe; but they are a vastly larger body than the most sanguine of us are sometimes disposed to admit."[38] Thomas Boys versified similar beliefs:

> Numbers within, numbers without the door
> Of Christ's Church visible on earth to men,
> A great multitude no man can number,
> Love bids us hope salvation still may find;
> . . .
> Almighty is the love of God in power,
> And by that boundless love there may be found
> Among the heathen a goodly number,
> Saved, as they only can be saved,
> By the all-sufficient grace of JESUS.[39]

A further factor in pushing some premillennialists toward a more comprehensive soteriology was the concept of national restoration. Many premillennialists were committed to the idea that nations were real and important entities. This view arose from their reading of prophetic biblical texts in which, they believed, it was suggested that God worked through nations and empires in historical time to enact his plans. Moreover, the communal nature of the Jewish restoration, and the obvious fact that if Israel was to be restored, then this was an example of the salvation of non-Christians, provided a basis for speculating about the incorporation of other nations into the final settlement that God would enact.[40] The re-

---

36. Cumming, *Millennial Rest*, 91.
37. Ibid., 146.
38. Ibid., 483.
39. Boys, *God and Man*, 34–35; 36.
40. "As the Lord Jesus, at his second coming, will restore the Jews to their own land; it follows, that whatever change may have taken place on the earth, the geographical distinctions of countries will remain discernible, so far, at least, as will be necessary to distinguish Palestine from all the other countries of the earth." McNeile, *Popular*

curring premillennialist idea that nations, including Israel, might exist in the millennium was significant enough to make a tendency toward universalism evident to contemporary critics of the movement. For example, Samuel Waldegrave (1817–69) gave a damning assessment of premillennialist thought in his 1854 Bampton Lecture. He argued that universalism was the logical consequence of premillennialist thought concerning the restoration of nations in the eschaton, and warned that Christians should be alarmed at this implicit liberalizing drift of premillennialism.[41]

Evidence of this hope for a "universal" turning of nations was manifold. The *QJP* in 1849 expressed its hope that in the age to come there would be a "conversion of nations," and also a universal turning to Christ. "In many cases, in the majority of cases—perhaps in all, there shall be the real conversion of the heart," it claimed—an idea that suggested that all would indeed be saved through faith in Christ, although such repentance would, it seemed, be almost inevitable in the millennial era.[42] Similarly, the *CMR* asked:

> Is it a wild Utopian and unwarrantable expectation, that God's written rule should ultimately be known to, and govern, all nations. . . . Is it more than God has promised, that the moral, political, and religious wilderness of this world shall rejoice and blossom as the rose? that as all the heathen—i.e. the nations, are the inheritance of the incarnate Christ, so also shall they be his possession, and all flesh see the Salvation of God?[43]

This writer went on to imagine that "one harmonious result appears in the conformity of nations, governments, churches, and individuals, to the high standard of his will."[44] Such statements seemed to override traditional Evangelical emphases on individual responsibility in the hope that God might act to redeem and recreate communities and nations as corporate entities.

Despite these seemingly radical statements premillennialists continued to preach the need for repentance and faith and the sole sufficiency of the saving grace of Christ Jesus. Yet they also believed in a total

Lectures, 159.

41. Waldegrave, *New Testament Millenarianism*, 183, 565.

42. "The Dominion of the Second Adam," *QJP* 1 (1848–49), 399.

43. Review of *La Christianisme et la Revolution*, by Par E. Quinet, *CMR* 5 (1845), 787.

44. Ibid.

restitution, a position that had led many Christians before them into a belief that all would be saved. This was a paradox. Put starkly, the problem centered upon asking what place there was for the darkness of hell in a world restored to goodness. "To assume the perpetual continuance of active malice and permitted blasphemies," observed Thomas Rawson Birks, "is to ascribe to God a dominion shared for ever with the powers of evil. It makes hell the scene of Satan's triumphant malice, just as heaven is that of the Creator's triumphant love."[45] This ambiguity led several premillennialists to attempt a logical reconciliation between their commitment to the justice and judgment of God on the one hand, and their belief in a complete renovation of the universe on the other. Two solutions emerged. Neither received universal endorsement, but they were indicative of the general drift of premillennialist soteriology.

Live and Let Die: Conditional Immortality

One attempt at reconciling justice with restitution was the idea of conditional immortality, the belief that humans are not inherently immortal but have immortality bestowed upon them conditionally by God. Immortality is the reward of salvation. Those who are not saved do not live forever in a state of punishment (since being raised to life again would itself make them participants in the reward of the faithful) but rather simply lose the right to life—their punishment is their annihilation at death. Conditional immortality gained popularity among some Evangelicals during the late nineteenth century. A conference in London in 1876 drew together proponents of the doctrine, and the Conditional Immortality League was founded in 1878.[46]

Some of the pioneering proponents of conditional immortality were premillennialists. In 1868, Samuel Minton [Samuel Minton-Steinhouse] (1820–94)—who had just the previous year put into print a trio of sermons given at Eaton Chapel outlining his belief that the historicist interpretation of prophecy pointed to the momentous significance of the year 1867[47]—published *The Glory of Christ In the Creation and Reconciliation*

---

45. Birks, *Victory of Divine Goodness*, 47.

46. This is chronicled in *Report of a Conference*.

47. Minton, *Our Present Position*. Minton was minister of St. Silas Church, Liverpool (1843–57), Percy Chapel, London (1857–64) (where he succeeded James

of All Things. This was a conditionalist manifesto premised on the conviction, rooted firmly in the millennialist tradition of which he was a part, that the restitution of all things was the ultimate eschatological purpose of God. His endorsement of this belief meant that he could find no place for eternal punishment of the reprobate in a restored universe. "Are sin and suffering to last for ever, or is the whole Universe to be reconciled to God?" demanded Minton. "My war is against the belief in Eternal Evil."[48]

The most prominent premillennialist exponent of conditional immortality in this era was William Leask, the Congregational minister of Maberly Chapel, London. In 1864 Leask became founder editor of *The Rainbow*, a journal devoted to providing a forum for premillennialist prophetic debate.[49] The journal was catholic in spirit and entertained some debate in its letters pages on the topic of conditional immortality during its early years.[50] In 1869, there appeared a full-length article by William Maude (d.1883), a premillennialist who had originally formed his prophetic views under the influence of Hugh McNeile. Maude argued explicitly for conditional immortality. Through the subsequent debate that followed the publication of this article, Leask was converted to the cause. Despite five hundred people cancelling their subscriptions in protest at the new views being propounded in the journal, Maude and Leask turned *The Rainbow* into the primary vehicle for the promotion of the doctrine of conditional immortality.[51] A brief survey of Leask's thought shows that, although not many premillennialists made this move, it was in fact only a short step from premillennial belief in the restitution of all things to conditional immortality.

First, when writing in favor of conditional immortality, Leask continued to work within the premillennialist paradigm of constructing an eschatology based on a "plain and literal" rendering of Scripture, with particular ire reserved for the way in which Greek philosophy was

---

Haldane Stewart), and Eaton Chapel, London (1864–74). Froom, *Conditionalist Faith*, 2:389–90.

48. Minton, *Glory of Christ*, xi–xii.

49. *The Rainbow* enjoyed renown as a premillennialist journal. It was described as "the accredited monthly organ of millenarianism." Review of *The End of All Things*, *The Gospel Magazine*, 5th ser, 3 (1866), 277.

50. An anonymous letter sparked the debate in June 1865. "An Inquirer, Letter to the editor," *The Rainbow* 2 (1865), 284.

51. This account is based on Froom, *Conditionalist Faith*, 2:338–50, 382. Leask edited *The Rainbow* until his death in 1884.

supposed to have mangled the teaching of the early church. "We [do not] mean to introduce counter interpretations, but to let the Holy Book speak for itself, taking its words in their primary and proper meaning, and accepting what is written as our sole authority in matters of religious belief. Our sole object is the restoration of apostolic doctrine."[52] Leask argued that the doctrine of the immortality of the soul was a Platonic concept and simply could not be found in the Bible. Moreover, he contended that taking words in their plain and obvious sense, "death," not "everlasting conscious punishment," seemed to be the natural meaning of Scripture. "The everlasting punishment of Scripture is by Scripture itself declared to mean everlasting destruction. Conscious torment for ever in the fires of hell is not a doctrine of revelation. We send it back with reprobation to its pagan source as an impossibility in the case of mortals, and an outrageous libel upon the character of the ever blessed God."[53]

Second, although not all conditionalists were premillennialists, conditionalism provided a solution to the problem posed by the premillennial doctrine of cosmic restitution: what place could there be for hell and punishment within the final purposes of God if he would, in the end, make all things new? Restitution, after all, was rescue, not retribution. Leask's solution prior to his conversion to conditional immortality had exhibited the same drift toward universalism as was shown by some fellow premillennialists. Thus in his *Royal Rights of Jesus* (1867), written before he embraced conditional immortality, Leask exulted in the comprehensive, restored universe, and hinted that restitution might mean a far broader salvation than Evangelical popular sentiment commonly imagined:

> The universe is safe, the redemption is completed. . . . Stupendous achievement! Most marvelous issue of that profoundest of divine thoughts, embodied in the single word Redemption! There is a tendency manifested in our pulpit ministrations and our religious books to limit the significance of this splendid word. . . . The salvation of a handful of the human race, that handful which receives *our* doctrine, holds our creed, and thinks with us, is the too prevalent idea, whilst it is quietly assumed that the overwhelming majority are doomed to remediless destruction, and the earth with all its wondrous wealth of beauty, notwithstanding the curse, to annihilating fires.[54]

52. Leask, "Scripture Doctrine," *The Rainbow* 7 (1870), 540.
53. Ibid., 543.
54. Leask, *Earth's Curse*, 28–30. This book was a reprint of an article that originally

Ironically, given that conditional immortality was resisted by a large number of Evangelicals as heretical (including, presumably, many of those premillennialists who cancelled their subscription to *The Rainbow*), Leask's conversion to conditional immortality actually allowed him to rein back some of these hints at universalism because it was now no longer necessary to find a place for the reprobate in a restored universe—they simply vanished. Thus in his *apologia* for conditional immortality, Leask was forthright in his support of a classical Evangelical notion of judgment. "The punishment of gospel rejecters is certain. Justice requires it, and it will undoubtedly be inflicted."[55] Leask could now enjoy the contemplation of the restored universe that his premillennialist convictions had taught him without worrying that the existence of the damned suffering torment was a blot on the landscape and perhaps even a kind of victory for the devil. Thus Leask, in seeking to prove conditional immortality, wrote:

> The gracious Creator could not have such a monster in his universe as a deathless sinner. . . . The life of the future is *all holy*, and consequently, all happy; for the life of the future is exclusively in the Holy One of God. . . . It is found that there are many mansions in the Father's house, but after the decision of the great white throne not a solitary dungeon in all His dominions. Evil is no more. . . . Life floods the universe. God in Christ, and Christ in men, for ever and for ever.[56]

Third, and finally, in his justification for conditional immortality, Leask sounded the classic premillennialist theme of the centrality of the resurrection of the body, and the consequent rejection of the idea that the soul proceeded directly to heaven at the moment of death. "The future life revealed in Scripture is connected with resurrection," he argued, although he admitted that "such a conclusion will be sufficiently startling to those who send all Christians to glory as soon as their eyes are closed in death."[57] Leask's point was that resurrection was in and of itself the essence of Christian hope. There could therefore be no resurrection to torment, for resurrection was a gift bestowed only on Christian believers.

---

appeared in *The Rainbow* 2 (1865), 247–62. Upper case emphasis in original.

55. Leask, "Scripture Doctrine," 543
56. Ibid., 542–43, 549.
57. Ibid., 544.

Death was the enemy and the annihilation of the individual at death the true "everlasting punishment."

> The real truth is that we have *no* revelation of a future life apart from resurrection. The resurrection, and the impartation of a life which is for ever to animate the incorruptible body, will take place at the same time. . . . Immortality and incorruption form the double boon of the children of God, the double glory of that portion of the human race, who through God's rich grace are to attain to the resurrection of life.[58]

Conditional immortality was one way of reconciling the notion of a restored universe with the question of the punishment of sin. Few premillennialists adopted this view, although a speculation on the matter is found in the Northampton premillennialist James Brown, who wrote: "*Everlasting Destruction from the presence of the Lord*, may with perfect propriety mean extinction, entire annihilation: that punishment may surely be said to be *everlasting*, which shall never end in restoration, or relief."[59] Perhaps, despite its general unpopularity and association with rational dissent, in some ways annihilationist was not radical enough. After all, premillennialists hated the idea of annihilation of the earth, so too they perhaps intuitively resisted the annihilation of the body? However, conditional immortality married to the restitution of all things was actually a more conservative doctrine than the universalistic tendencies of some other premillennialists.

---

58. Ibid., 545. This idea had actually been implicit in the thought of Edward Irving. "In scripture it is the resurrection, not the acquittal, which is continually presented to the righteous, so as to leave no doubt that the resurrection is itself the very act of acquittal, is in some way or other the distinction, the glorious distinction of the saints." Irving, "Preliminary Discourse," liv. There was also a resonance between the premillennialist rejection of the intermediate state of the soul or at least the suggestion that it is a state of privation, and the arguments of Unitarians such as Joseph Priestley and David Hartley. Many of the themes announced in this chapter also resonate with the Unitarian writer Richard Wright (1764–1836), particularly the stress upon the resurrection of the body, the criticism of the way in which death had become the hope of Christians, and a tendency toward conditional immortality. See Rowell, *Hell and the Victorians*, 33–37, 41–42.

59. J. Brown, *Restitution of All Things*, 23.

Love Wins

The other solution to the problem posed by restitution—the problem being, how could one reconcile the notion of punishment existing within an entirely righteous and good universe?—was a more radical one; namely that for sinners, participation in such a restored universe would itself equal a kind of punishment. This view was taken by William Harrison, for example, who believed that "there is not a soul upon this earth which will not eventually come within the comprehension of this vast and magnificent kingdom."[60] Harrison's view was that all would be held and related to Christ, but not all would feel the effects of that relationship in the same way. Those who had rejected him would be incapable of participating in the community of love: this would be very hell.

> Remember that nothing can escape his rule, not even the hearts of his enemies; for though they will not be governed by love, the law of terror will subdue them. Oh, the wretchedness of not being able to love,—to feel the power and admire the loveliness of unsullied goodness without the grace to live it. What will this be but to realize that awful description of the outer state?—"there shall be weeping and gnashing of teeth."[61]

In other words, the experience of absolute goodness would, for the rebel, be itself a kind of damnation; or, to put it the other way round, damnation would be a kind of salvation.

The most comprehensive statement of the idea that the reprobate might somehow be both punished and restored at the same time was offered by Thomas Rawson Birks. Birks had ruminated on the problem of the future destiny of the wicked for some time. In his *Outlines of Unfulfilled Prophecy* (1854) he had suggested that the future reign of God would be an era of "redeeming love, coextensive with the whole living race of mankind," and not just those who had been elected in the present dispensation. In other words, God would automatically include newly born people within his kingdom. "The thought of these ever-widening streams and blessing, in perpetual generations of holy and redeemed creatures, must be, in the highest degree, attractive and delightful," he concluded.[62]

---

60. W. Harrison, "Vastness of Christ's Kingdom" 336.
61. Ibid.
62. Birks, *Outlines of Unfulfilled Prophecy*, 353, 356.

This left the problem of those who had died without Christ before the millennium. In 1867, Birks published a solution to this dilemma in his *The Victory of Divine Goodness*. Birks argued that the unbeliever would participate in "the victory of divine goodness," but would not be able to find joy in this new state. Instead each individual would be fixed "into a trance of holy adoration in the presence of infinite and unsearchable Goodness."[63] The reprobate would lament their foolishness and be outside the bounds of fullness of joy, but they would admit the truth of their own position and in doing so would acknowledge the justice and goodness of God. Gazing onward from their position of humbled servitude they would be abased, "yet out of its depth there may arise such a passive but real view of the joys of a ransomed universe, and of the unveiled perfections of the Godhead, as to fulfill, even here, in a strange, mysterious way, the predicted office of the Redeemer of souls, and to swallow up death in victory."[64]

Birks nicely revealed the ambiguity of the position to which several premillennialists appeared to be moving. He did not want to be a doctrinaire universalist. He had, in fact, argued against the doctrine in *Outlines of Unfulfilled Prophecy*. Throughout *The Victory of Divine Goodness* his argument constantly swerved to avoid the conclusion that he was advocating universalism. Yet, in the end, he admitted that the reprobate, constrained by the triumph of love in a redeemed universe, would experience a type of salvation. "Will they not be saved, in a strange, mysterious sense, when the depth of their unchangeable shame and sorrow finds beneath it a still lower depth of Divine compassion, and the creature, and its most forlorn estate, is shut in by the vision of surpassing and infinite love?"[65] Birks' vision of a complete restoration was a hope in the "triumph of Divine love" that could cast hell and death into the lake of fire.[66]

In 1866 Edward Bickersteth's son (and thus Thomas Rawson Birks' brother-in-law) Edward Henry Bickersteth (1825–1906), at this time Vicar of Christ Church, Hampstead, but later Bishop of Gloucester (1885–1906), published a premillennial epic poem called *Yesterday, Today and Forever*. The poem—which sold 77,000 copies in Britain and America, and which some contemporaries somewhat hyperbolically

63. Birks, *Victory of Divine Goodness*, 47.
64. Ibid., 48.
65. Ibid., 190–92.
66. Ibid., 171.

claimed rivaled the oeuvre of Dante and Milton—reflected Birks' vision of the paradoxical salvation experienced by the reprobate in hell.[67] "Only thus fetter'd can we safely gaze / on that the final victory of love," intoned Bickersteth's Devil, leading the praise of those "whose hopeless ruin is their only hope."[68] Even this vision of the damned rejoicing in their ruin did not quite satisfy Bickersteth, who, in the final book, while himself sitting in the highest bliss, catches whiffs of smoke "rising from the Deep," and describes the sight of the mountain of hell as "a grief which chastn'd but not jarr'd our bliss." His grief is only rendered acceptable because it echoed Christ's sufferings. There were signs that Bickersteth was somewhat perplexed by his own vision of a future where the reprobate rejoiced and the redeemed felt grief.[69] "After twenty years of prayer I must solemnly believe in eternal punishment, but in what it consists is the question," mused Bickersteth.[70]

While Bickersteth's "sweet" verse[71] probably shielded his equivocations on divine punishment from public view, Birks' views on future punishment did not go without criticism. He was forced to resign from the Secretaryship of the Evangelical Alliance in 1869.[72] The Dean of Wells, Edward H. Plumptre (1821–91), thought that the similarity between Birks' *Victory* and the views of F. D. Maurice was uncanny. "In not a few passages it presents so close a verbal identity with the language of Mr. Maurice's *Theological Essays*, that in a writer of inferior calibre it would suggest the thought of a literary plagiarism," he observed.[73] Geoffrey Rowell suggests that this similarity was due to a shared "reaction against the harsh eschatology of popular Protestantism."[74] But it perhaps owed

---

67. Recovering from a serious illness in 1872, Princess Alexandra (the Princess of Wales, and from 1901 Queen Consort) read extracts from Bickersteth's poem to her sick husband, Albert Edward, Prince of Wales (from 1901, King Edward VII). Aglionby, *Life of Edward Henry Bickersteth*, 101, 112, 553.

68. E. Bickersteth, *Yesterday, Today, and Forever* bk. xi, lines 998–99, 1008.

69. Ibid., bk. xii, lines 569–99.

70. Aglionby, *Life of Edward Henry Bickersteth*, 36.

71. Ibid., 99.

72. Bromham, "More Charitable Eschatology," 98.

73. Plumptre, *Spirits in Prison*, 229.

74. Rowell, *Hell and the Victorians*, 127. In the same year, Andrew Jukes (1815–1901) published *The Second Death and The Restitution of All Things*. This was a far more unambiguous statement endorsing universal salvation than the positions outlined in this chapter. Jukes used the term "restitution of all things" to appeal to the Universalist tradition flowing from Origen and Gregory of Nysa. Nevertheless, Jukes'

rather more to a commitment that Birks shared with Maurice, as well as with a vast number of other premillennialists, concerning the renewal of space and time. I will turn to explore the explicit links between F. D. Maurice and premillennialists later in this chapter.

Quite what the elder Bickersteth—the paradigm of orthodox Evangelical premillennialism—would have made of these familial re-assessments of eternal punishment can only be conjectured, although both Birks and the younger Bickersteth claimed their ideas had been in gestation for at least twenty years, so it is possible he was well aware of at least the genesis of their ruminations. Indeed, Edward Bickersteth had himself spoken of "the mystery of divine goodness" in 1843.[75] In fact, there was really nothing remarkable about these speculations once we realize that they were grounded in the premillennial vision. These romantic reconsiderations of classic Christian orthodoxy concerning the nature, scope, and essence of salvation were rooted in a high view of God's involvement in the temporal-spatial sphere, a commitment to the possibility of cosmic renewal, and a belief in the triumph of progress and education. Premillennialism, a movement commonly seen as reactionary, conservative, and even proto-fundamentalist, was actually a manifestation of nineteenth-century romantic re-envisioning of the purposes of God toward the entire material and moral universe. This reappraisal did not just affect eschatological ruminations about the future, but also triggered the emergence of new themes in other parts of premillennialist theology. One of the most significant of such themes was the premillennialist stress on the doctrine of the incarnation.

The Return of God Incarnate

The story of nineteenth-century Christian belief and practice is often narrated as a shift away from belief in a retributive, distant, and partial deity, and toward a celebration of the love, mercy, and generosity of God. At the center of this new vision of God was the doctrine of the incarnation. The incarnation spoke to later Victorian Christians of God's imminence and solidarity with the world, displacing an emphasis on his judicial

---

work of course also exemplified the general embrace of eschatological restitution in the mid-nineteenth century of which premillennial revisionism was a significant component.

75. See f/n 17 in this chapter.

transcendence. R. W. Dale (1829–95), the Congregational minister of Carrs' Lane, Birmingham, noted that in the later nineteenth century the incarnation was no longer viewed as "a kind of after-thought in the mind of God" but rather as the central activity by which God had provided "that the race should be one with Christ, and should live in the power of Christ's life."[76] Emphasizing the humanness of Christ reflected a greater appreciation for the material world, the human body, and demonstrated a heightened Christian awareness of the struggles and privations of human life. The incarnation also showed Christ's solidarity with the whole human race, not just with an elect.

Premillennialism was a liminal belief system. Evangelicals who adopted the premillennial outlook did not abandon their belief in the atoning death of Christ on the cross, nor did they simply collapse salvation into the present, as some proponents of the so-called "social Gospel" tended to do in the late nineteenth century. Nevertheless, they were in the vanguard of the reorientation of Victorian theology toward an age of incarnation.

Premillennialists turned to the doctrine of the incarnation first as an apologetic tool to support their belief in the visible, personal return of Christ. They realized that those who opposed their belief in the bodily return of Christ to rule over the earth often contended that the premillennialist belief was vulgar and involved an act of *lèse majesté* against God. "The doctrine of Messiah coming in person to establish his kingdom and administer it in association with his glorified saints," observed John Cox, "has been stigmatised as low, gross, carnal, judaizing, and I know not what beside."[77] One answer to such criticism was to stress that Christ had already stooped to live on the terrestrial plane. Those who doubted the second advent, contended premillennialists, must surely call into doubt the reality of the first advent too. An anonymous Scottish author put the point forcibly in 1829, arguing that "They seem to imagine that it is too much condescension in the Saviour to dwell with men! Can any thing be too condescending for Him, who has already come in the likeness of sinful flesh, and subjected himself to temptations from the devil and insults from men? . . . Why talk of condescension, when the greatest condescension has already been shewn?"[78]

---

76. R. W. Dale, *Old Evangelicalism and the New*, 44–45.

77. J. Cox, *Future*, 27.

78. A Church of Scotland Preacher, *Restitution of All Things*, 16.

The doctrine of the incarnation thus set a precedent: God had already shown that he would assume a body and dwell on earth, so "may not the grace which accomplished the first be expected to accomplish the second?" asked Gerard Noel.[79] The incarnation showed that there were no grounds for supposing that the second coming was a spiritual, rather than physical, reality, for, in the words of James A. Begg, "what valid reason can be offered for putting a spiritual interpretation on the one class of predictions, in the above series, which was not extended to the other?"[80] An appeal to the incarnation was also another way of proving that the earth would be the site of the final state of God's kingdom. As Horatius Bonar put it:

> What region of the universe so likely to be the place of [Christ's eternal] throne as the earth whose soil has drunk in his blood; this earth which furnished both his cradle and his tomb; this earth where he hungered, and thirsted, and was weary, and slept, and awoke, and moved to and fro as one of its own inhabitants; this earth whose fruits he ate, whose waters he drank, whose air he breathed, whose fragrance he inhaled, whose hills he climbed, whose olives shaded him, whose sun lighted him by day, and whose moon and stars by night; what planet in all the firmament so likely to be the seat of his throne, the centre of his dominion, the metropolis of his empire as this?[81]

Premillennialists believed that the first advent was, in fact, constitutionally bound to the second coming of Christ. "The similarity of the two advents, therefore, really proceeds from the fact of the unity of the object accomplished by the Son of God," wrote Edward Auriol in 1849.[82] "Our Lord does not merely dwarf the interval between the two events, as the starry spheres are lost to our eyes, whenever we gaze on the midnight sky," ruminated Thomas Rawson Birks. "He affirms a close and intimate connexion between them."[83] "The two advents are eternally and gloriously connected. We may not separate the 'child born' to the house of David, from the Almighty Prince on David's throne," contended Benjamin Philpot.[84]

79. G. T. Noel, *Brief Enquiry*, 158–59.
80. Begg, *Connected View*, 53.
81. Quoted in J. Cox, *Premillennial Manual*, 209–10.
82. Auriol, "Similarities and Contrast," 38.
83. Birks, "Signs of the Lord's Coming," 228.
84. Philpot, "Christ's Past Offering," 272.

The expectation of the *parousia* was in this way a hope for a second incarnation, the fulfillment of God's promise to dwell on earth. Gerard Noel explained:

> If this humiliation of the Son of God to manhood and to death be a matter, not of speculation but of history . . . is it an expectation unwarranted . . . that he who is *already* become man in his *mortal* condition . . . should again appear as man in his *higher* and *immortal* condition, in order to realize that very end, and to restore that portion of his creation, which had received so terrific an injury, to rectitude, allegiance, and felicity?[85]

So crucial was this doctrine that "incarnation must be considered as the centre of the fulfillment of the great scheme of Redemption," argued Alexander Dallas in 1850.[86] Premillennialists endorsed the cry of Noel for the return of God incarnate: "Incarnate Saviour! exalted Jesus! come, then, according to thy promise!"[87]

Premillennialists also contended that God becoming man was not only an element of the divine initiative toward the earth but was an act that had in fact transformed the human nature before God. In the person of Christ the human and divine had touched, not just for a few years, but forever. Humanity was now connected to God and could therefore enjoy a new experience of the divine. "It is, perhaps, by virtue of this personal assumption of Humanity in the Mediator, that all sensible intercourse and communication between God and man is carried on," thought James Brown.[88] Christ had lifted humanity to new heights. Christ, at his incarnation, "took man's nature into union with His own," argued William Leask.[89] There was now an intimate connection between human and divine, and thus between time and eternity. The East Anglian minister Benjamin Philpot suggested that in Jesus "the two natures are again brought into union, under circumstances which, in the case of every regenerate soul, render it more spiritual and more happy than before."[90] By triumphing over sin, the flesh, and the devil as a man, Christ had become the second Adam, the head of a restored humanity. "Christ took hold of

---

85. G. T. Noel, *Brief Enquiry*, 159. Italics in original.
86. Dallas, *Introduction to Prophetical Researches*, 13.
87. G. T. Noel, *Brief Enquiry*, 66.
88. J. Brown, *Restitution of All Things*, 30.
89. Leask, *Earth's Curse and Restitution*, 8.
90. Philpot, "Glorious Bridal," 325.

the seed of Adam, and became perfect man, on order that, as man, He might do for man, that which Adam had failed to do," contended Gerard Noel.[91] Thus, standing at the head of the whole human race, "as man's new head and forerunner" all would ascend to glory just as he had.[92] "Why has He joined himself to the creature, but that the creature may eventually be blessed in Him?" asked Edward Vaughan.[93]

The incarnation was not, then, simply a theoretical construct. Premillennialists urged spiritual contemplation of, and devotion to, the ascended Jesus Christ, the "God-Man."[94] William Pym thus invited his audience to

> rise with me still higher in the scale, yea, in heart and mind let us ascend whither our Saviour Christ is gone before, and under the guidance of the Eternal Spirit and with his blessed book in our hand, we may scale the everlasting doors, and cast ourselves in holy contemplation before the throne of the Eternal. And what is there? First and foremost we behold God Incarnate: God in our flesh.[95]

Edward Hoare thought that the incarnated nature of Christ in heaven was the greatest comfort to all believers. "There is no greater joy to the children of God, than the perfect humanity of their blessed Saviour. It is his real and perfect manhood which enables us to go boldly to the throne of grace, in the full assurance than we have not an High Priest who cannot be touched with the feeling of our infirmities."[96] The incarnation was perceived as that which connected the temporal and eternal realms; it was, concluded Thomas Rawson Birks, that "wonderful bridge which unites the Creator with the creature, and eternity with time."[97]

This focus on the incarnation, occurring several decades before the idea is assumed to have become central within Victorian religious discourse, was, of course, linked with the premillennialist endorsement of the importance of materiality. There was nothing blasphemous in

91. G. T. Noel, *Sermons Preached at Romsey*, 10.
92. Ibid., 71.
93. Vaughan, *Church's Expectation*, 141.
94. For examples of this phrase, see H. Drummond, *Dialogues on Prophecy*, 1:163; *Christian Herald* 2 (1831), 104; Fry, *Second Advent*, 489; Montagu, *Things Hoped For*, 94; G. T. Noel, "Sufferings of Christ," 29.
95. Pym, "State of the World," 24–25.
96. Hoare, "Perfect Equity," 245–46.
97. Birks, *Village Discourses*, 40.

saying that Christ had assumed flesh precisely because there was nothing sinful about human flesh, or any type of matter, in and of itself. As Gerard Noel claimed in his *apologia* for material restitution, "Jesus Christ is linked to our world by ties less fragile than those which human theology has framed."[98] If ever one wanted a slogan for the dawning of the paradigm-shifting "age of incarnation," Noel surely provided it in this summary sentence!

Premillennialists therefore took their convictions about the *future* restitution of the world to imply that there was no inherent fault in material existence. If heaven would come to earth in the age to come, then it could not be physical existence *in and of itself* that was flawed. Charles Goodhart addressed those detractors of premillennialism who believed that their doctrines of the resurrection of the body and the restoration of the earth were overly "carnal" with a ringing endorsement that, even in the present imperfect state,

> our connexion with materiality is not to be considered a trifling or subordinate matter, or looked upon as a necessarily imperfect condition. It is natural, indeed, to think so, *first,* from the great limitation of our present circumstances; and, *secondly,* from the sin and corruption which are so intimately mingled up with them. But, as far as the Word of God gives us any light, an exclusively spiritual condition would be the imperfect one, and a material condition that which superadds the capacity for an infinitely increased amount of enjoyment and glory.[99]

This was a theme repeated in the *CLM* in 1834: "Every property of matter, in all its multiplied combinations and developments, must be of God, and therefore good: the evil only is in the use and application which is man's," it reminded its readers.[100] James A. Begg agreed that "there is no more necessary connection between materiality and sin, than between materiality and righteousness."[101] And the *QJP* in 1850 noted that "It is an error old as the date of Manichaeism, that matter is the seat of remediless infirmity and contamination," a view it categorically rejected.[102]

---

98. G. T. Noel, *Brief Enquiry,* 27.
99. Goodhart, "Powers of the World to Come," 221.
100. "Music," *CLM* 2 (July–Dec 1834), 145–46.
101. Begg, *First Resurrection,* 3.
102. "The Earth: Its Curse and Regeneration," *QJP* 2 (1850), 286.

By asserting the ongoing full humanity of Christ, and endorsing the potential of matter to be energized by the divine, premillennialists suggested that all human beings, especially those now living as part of the redeemed humanity of which the incarnated Christ was the head, could possess a direct and vivid experience of the eternal. Although this mode of communication was a consequence of the new status of humanity "taken up" into the Godhead by Christ, there was also a stress upon the role of the Holy Spirit as the mediator and transmitter of the divine to the human. Indeed, it was the presence of the Spirit that guaranteed that the material world, and even the human body, could be kept from sin. Sanctified flesh was powerful stuff: it combined God's physical creation with his eternal spiritual energy.

Sanctifying the Flesh

The belief that human flesh was no barrier to divine communication, and its connection with an "incarnational" theology was manifested particularly in the thought of Edward Irving, John McLeod Campbell (1800–72), and Edward Vaughan. These three men all proposed that it was the Holy Spirit who had kept the fully human incarnated Christ free from sin and thus the Spirit empowered his body to live a perfect life. This naturally led to the conclusion that all humans—who were no different from Christ because they shared the same flesh as his—could also experience the power of the Spirit in their fleshly existence.

John McLeod Campbell began his theological journey by reflecting upon the type of faith expressed by those under his pastoral care. McLeod believed that his congregation tended to seek salvation as a way to avert God's wrath, not as a joyful response to his love. This, he thought, produced a defensive faith that produced sorrowful contrition only in so far as people lamented that their sin would bring judgment upon themselves. Instead of a commitment to live a holy life there was "merely regret for the personal evil consequences of having exposed one's self to the wrath of God."[103] Campbell decided that it was a lack of any assurance of election that produced such a negative version of faith: "I was gradually taught to see that so long as the individual is uncertain of being the object of love to his God, and is still without any sure hold of his personal safety, in the prospect of eternity, it is in vain to attempt to induce him to serve

---

103. Stevenson, *God in Our Nature*, 282.

God under the power of any purer motive than the desire to win God's love for himself, and so to secure his own happiness."[104] The confidence of personal redemption was not to be found in an inner search for signs of election as the Scottish Presbyterian Calvinist tradition had maintained, argued Campbell; rather, every individual could be confident of salvation because Christ had made reconciliation between the whole human race and God. Campbell's notion of atonement thus switched from a forensic understanding of substitution or propitiation in which Christ satisfied the wrath of God, and toward a "filial" understanding where God was acting in Christ to restore a broken relationship between himself and humankind. This conviction led Campbell to claim that forgiveness—although *not* salvation—was universal and unconditional. All humanity had been forgiven and could trust in the reality of this forgiveness, although Campbell insisted that this offer was temporary and would one day be revoked.

Central to this statement of the atonement was the notion that Christ was incarnated in a fleshly body of the same nature as that possessed by the rest of humankind. This was essential to Campbell's idea that God was in Christ reconciling humanity to himself. If Christ was not truly human as well as truly God, there could be no meeting of the alienated parties. Assurance flowed from the fact that all human beings were included in the type of humanity that Christ had assumed. All humanity had died, and all humanity were raised to new life with Christ. "Now my dear friends," Campbell told his parishioners at Rhu, "you must at once feel that if we realise to ourselves that Jesus is our very brother, that he came in our very condition—that he partook of our very nature."[105] Campbell insisted that Christ was not a different sort of person from any other human. This meant stating that he assumed sinful flesh, although he was kept from sinning by the Holy Spirit. "The flesh of Christ differed not in one particle from mine; but Christ did present his flesh, which was even my flesh, without spot to God through the eternal spirit." Christ achieved victory over the flesh, in the flesh.[106]

Campbell contended that the ascension of Christ to the "right hand of God" was based upon his triumph over sin and temptation *as a man* and not upon his divine status as the Second Person of the Trinity. His

104. Ibid., 281.

105. Campbell, "Sermon on 1 Peter 2, 11–14," in Stevenson, *God In Our Nature*, 318.

106. Stevenson, *God in Our Nature*, 84.

right to be called king was by virtue of his perfect humanity. "The man Christ Jesus, our brother, bone of our bone, and flesh of our flesh, is, at this moment upon the throne of Almighty God," he argued, "and observe he is there, not because he is God, for that was his eternal glory; but he is there in his human nature—he is, in his humanity, exalted to that high place."[107]

For Campbell, all who were united with Christ could obtain the same victory over the sinful flesh by the indwelling of the Holy Spirit. Thus, the victory over sin was not achieved by simply following Christ as an ethical exemplar, but involved the regeneration of the believer by the inward work of Christ. "It is not calling upon you to imitate Christ as you would imitate a man such as I am," he explained. "It is not saying, 'Here is the example of perfection: walk ye after this example and be ye perfect.' There is this great difference, that it is Christ in you that is to make you what Christ was."[108]

Campbell's thought was echoed, somewhat less irenically, by Edward Irving. Irving was a great admirer of Campbell. He called him "the greatest gift ever bestowed on the people of Scotland since the days of Knox—yea, greater than he."[109] Irving met Campbell during a visit to Scotland in 1828, but Irving had already articulated controversial views about the incarnation, so it is unlikely that one man directly influenced the other.[110] In 1827, Edward Irving preached a sermon in which he claimed that Christ had assumed a fully human nature at the time of his incarnation.[111] Irving did not, apparently, think such a contention was controversial. He was unprepared to be taken to task on the matter by the Anglican cleric Henry Cole, who published a stinging indictment of Irving's alleged heresy.[112]

Like Campbell, Irving argued that to speak of Christ assuming complete human nature meant one could talk of him coming in *sinful* flesh, because all humans were born under the curse of Adam. This was an unfortunate phrase because, although Irving in fact agreed with contemporary orthodoxy that Christ did not sin, many believed that Irving believed that Jesus was, in his actions, a sinner. Irving argued that his

107. Campbell, "Sermon on Luke 8," in Stevenson, *God In Our Nature*, 215.
108. Campbell, "Sermon on 1 Peter 2,11–14," in Stevenson, *God In Our Nature*, 319.
109. Jones, *Biographical Sketch*, 303–4.
110. Oliphant, *Life of Edward Irving*, 2:232.
111. Ibid., 5.
112. Cole, H., *Letter to . . . Edward Irving*.

claim was not about whether Christ sinned or not (he believed that he had not), but was rather about the reason *why* he did not sin. He claimed that many people explained Christ's sinlessnes by pointing to the special flesh with which Christ was endowed. In contrast, Irving argued it was due to the act of the Holy Spirit who had kept Christ's normal flesh—the same type of body as possessed by any other human being—from suffering the consequences common to the descendants of Adam and Eve:

> The point at issue is simply this; Whether Christ's flesh had the grace of sinlessness and incorruption from its proper nature, or from the indwelling of the Holy Ghost. I say the latter. I assert, that in its proper nature it was as the flesh of his mother, but, by virtue of the Holy Ghost's quickening and inhabiting of it, it was preserved sinless and incorruptible.[113]

Irving firmly denied that Christ was a sinner. He insisted that his argument meant quite the opposite because the indwelling Spirit had kept Christ entirely free from sin. "What a calumny it is then, what a hideous lie, to represent us as making Christ unholy and sinful, because we maintain that he took his humanity completely and wholly from the substance, from the sinful substance, of the fallen creatures which he came to redeem," he protested.[114] The consequence of maintaining the alternative proposition, that Christ remained sinless because of his divinity, not because of the Holy Spirit, was two-fold, argued Irving. First, it suggested that Christ was not really human. If he had not taken on the flesh of all humanity, he could not have acted as a mediator between God and humanity. Second, it supposed that every other type of human flesh was inherently sinful. If one felt so repelled at the idea of Christ taking on normal human flesh, it implied a low view of human flesh in general. Irving argued that material flesh itself is not sinful—humans chose to use their body for sin. "Sinful flesh" thus referred not to the composition of flesh, but to the consistent and universal way in which every human from Adam onward had directed their bodies to the pursuit of sin. Christ also had this same flesh—sinful flesh, meaning flesh of the same kind possessed by every human—but was kept from turning this flesh toward sinful pursuits by the sanctifying power of the Holy Spirit. This belief that the divine could break into the world was vividly manifested in the localized incidents of *glossolalia* during the early 1830s, first in Rosneath,

---

113. Jones, *Biographical Sketch*, 233–34.
114. Ibid , 235.

Scotland and then in Edward Irving's church in London. The events in Scotland centered upon the ministry of the Reverend Alexander (Sandy) John Scott (1805-66), who had served as Edward Irving's assistant in London between 1828 and 1830. They were also influenced by the teaching of John McLeod Campbell.[115]

Such occurrences of speaking in tongues were localized. Moreover, many premillennialists attempted to distance themselves from Irving both because of his Christological heresy and his association with the "pentecostal" outbursts in Scotland and London. However, Irving's stress upon the essential goodness of flesh was actually a standard premillennialist theme, linked to the wider affirmation of the created order outlined throughout this book. A contributor to the *CLM*, for example, suggested sympathy with the Irvingite position concerning the deep humanness displayed by Christ in his temptations:

> When we remember that plain declaration of St. Paul that "in *all things* it behoved him to be made like unto his brethren" (Heb. ii.17.) and again (iv.5) that he "was in *all points* tempted like as we are, yet without sin," we cannot help feeling that the innocent infirmities of our nature must have adhered to his; that sinless weakness of the flesh, which would have inclined him to repose, and that natural feeling which would have suggested peace and rest, rather than the awful struggle of his suffering life and the tremendous sacrifice of the cross.[116]

As with so much of premillennial theology, a slight ambiguity lingered on these points of theological speculation. What exactly did it mean to suggest that the infirmities of human nature "adhered" to the nature of Christ?

Other examples of this emphasis on what the humanity of Christ might imply about Christ can be found. Gerard Noel echoed Irving's doctrine, explaining that "the Eternal Word became flesh, but in that flesh the divinity seemed, often, to repose quiescent, and left the manhood to the full influence of the Holy Ghost; left the man Christ Jesus, beneath that influence, to struggle, even as we do, with all the sorrows, pangs, and privations of life."[117] The *Christian Herald* was similarly explicit in its agreement with Irving's proposition about the role of the Spirit in keeping Christ from sin, reminding its readers in 1832 that the incarnation relied

115. For an account, see Newell, "Scottish Intimations."

116. "Notes of a Trinitarian. The Son of God—The Messiah," *CLM* 8 (July-Dec 1841), 132.

117. G. T. Noel, *Sermons Preached at Romsey,* 19-20.

upon the coalescence of the divine and the eternal with the empowering presence of the Holy Ghost. "Neither the manhood separately considered, nor the Godhead separately considered—nor even the Godhead and manhood united, and without the Spirit, constitute THE CHRIST; but THE CHRIST is the Godman anointed with the Holy Ghost," the paper explained.[118] This was a great comfort, argued the journal:

> To the tempted Christian, the oneness of the flesh of Christ with the flesh of David, and therefore, with *his* flesh, is of the greatest importance; and to every Christian, hope of victory and of glory can only be held out by pointing him to "God manifest in *flesh*," bearing our sins in his own body—in our flesh tempted—in our flesh slain—in our flesh (glorified indeed as ours too shall be when the Lord's people arise) victorious over death—and in our flesh sitting on the throne for ever.[119]

The man who shared most with Irving on this point concerning the human nature of Christ was the historicist premillennialist Edward Thomas Vaughan, who may actually have influenced Irving in developing this Christology.[120] The *Morning Watch*, the mouthpiece of Edward Irving, in 1829 described Vaughan as "a theologian of the first order, in any age, and in any church; and in our day, in the Church of England, absolutely without a rival." "He teaches the connection between God and man in Christ," the review affirmed.[121] Vaughan was similarly concerned to affirm that the proposition "Christ appeared in the likeness of sinful flesh" implied that he had possessed the very nature of all humankind:

> What is meant then by the expression of "likeness?" Why, that He not only was verily a man, but appeared verily as a man, and appeared as though He was only a man. It does not deny the reality of his manhood; but declare that with the reality He had the resemblance; that He had all the figure and form of a man, with the real properties, powers, and capacities of a man.[122]

Vaughan stressed that the incarnation was not a new mode of being for Christ but the making visible of the second person of the Trinity

---

118. *Christian Herald* 2 (1832), 262.

119. Ibid., 261.

120. Jones, *Biographical Sketch*, 231–32.

121. Review of *Self-manifestation* . . . by E. T. Vaughan. *Morning Watch* 1 , (1829), 691.

122. Vaughan, *Expository Sermons*, 282.

who had, in fact, always been conjoined with human nature. He argued that "the Second of the three Co-equals in the indivisible substance of Jehovah hath consented and covenanted to act, and that from the beginning, yea, from everlasting, has been acting ... as though He were only a creature, as though He were only a man."[123] The Son was "uniformly and universally, from everlasting" emptying himself of his Divinity. His triumph was achieved not because he was divine, but through the connection of his humanity with the Holy Spirit:

> the very glory of the Second Person to have put his Godhead into abeyance; and, whilst He can never cease to be God, to act, within the precincts of that substance, and within the precincts of its powers, as that substance shall be brought into action, having its powered sharpened and enabled by the Holy Ghost.[124]

For Vaughan, as for Irving, the consequence of this doctrine was that Christ had been kept from sinning by the "sharpening" power of the Holy Spirit. Vaughan linked his incarnationalist theology of Christ to the pentecostal experience of the early church, proclaiming that all believers might know the same experience of the Holy Spirit as that which had kept Christ pure from sin. When Jesus promised that "ye shall receive power," Vaughan argued that he meant "an operation upon the body by the Holy Ghost. I cannot see the fitness with which such an expression shall be applied, if the operation primarily be upon the spirit; much less, if the operation upon the body be excluded."[125] Vaughan therefore contended that there was free communication between humans and God, between time and eternity.

> What is between me and God? Are there any stoppages, any walls, any bulwarks, any battlements? Has the devil power to keep me out? No; here am I,—a poor worm of the earth, it is true—but I have reality of intercourse, even as I have reality of connection, even as the very thread of my life extends to—I think that is a very lovely way of representing it—the very thread of my being is let down, if I may so speak, into my soul from the right hand of God.[126]

123. Ibid., 35.
124. Ibid., 4.
125. Ibid., 5
126. Vaughan, *Expository Sermons*, 29–30.

Vaughan then took his line of thinking to its logical conclusion. If one could experience the divine and eternal here and now in the human body, was talk of heaven and eternity really anything to do with the future at all? "I am not going to heaven," he proclaimed, "I shall not be taken up where He is. My habitation of heaven is now. I am now in heaven, if I ever am to be there. I am to know that I am as good as sitting there; I am, as to reality, just as though I were sitting there."[127] This suggestion that the Christian should focus more on grasping the eternal from within time, than he or she should anticipate a future translation to the abode of God was, of course, ironic coming from the mouth of an individual subscribing to what is commonly assumed to be a robustly future-oriented and world-denying apocalyptic system. Yet it was in many ways the logical conclusion of the premillennialist journey concerning the goodness of creation and the expectation of a coalescence of earth and heaven, time and eternity.

Indeed, premillennialism and the re-orientation of the idea of salvation away from the future to the present (a characteristic theme of later nineteenth-century theology) grew up oddly intertwined with each other. This claim is demonstrated in the final section of this chapter, which examines the links between premillennialism and the theologian who is often regarded as paradigmatic of the drift of nineteenth-century British Christianity toward a this-worldly "age of incarnation," Frederick Denison Maurice.

Finding Eternity in Time:
F. D. Maurice and the Premillennialists

F. D. Maurice was an Anglican priest and Professor of Divinity at King's College, London. The clearest statement of Maurice's theology, and one of the best early examples of the new direction in which Victorian theology was moving, was *The Kingdom of Christ* (1838). In this work Maurice outlined a vision of a universal society in which individuals were bound together by their identity as the body of Christ. He argued that the "kingdom" was not a future state but was rather an entity that existed objectively in the present, even if sinful humans often failed to recognize its reality.[128] For Maurice "the Kingdom was the community of

---

127. Ibid., 26.
128. Christensen, *Origin and History*, 24.

righteousness about to be established upon earth. It was not an idealized target never fully to be attained in this life but rather a real, living and fully functioning community that would be realized through the social application of Christ's teachings."[129] Such a theology may be termed a "partially-realized" or perhaps even "fully-realized" eschatology in which eschatological hope was transferred to the expectation that the rule of God would break into the present world order to effect the temporal transformation of individuals and communities. For Maurice, salvation was therefore about waking up to a current reality. He proposed "that society . . . is to be regenerated by finding the law and ground of its order and harmony, the only secret of its existence, in God."[130]

Maurice is sometimes dubbed the "father" of "Christian Socialism" because of his belief that if God is already present in human society then all individuals have equal dignity and inherent fraternity. Maurice was indeed willing to support the efforts of Charles Kingsley (1819–75) and John Malcolm Ludlow (1821–1911) to establish a Christian Socialist movement in the early 1850s. Yet while his emphasis on the solidarity of the incarnated Christ with each individual laid the theological bedrock from which Christian socialists could quarry, Maurice was more of theological idealist than a social reformer. He was a progenitor and pattern of all the Victorian revisionist theology that echoed his emphasis on the imminence of the divine within the temporal.

In terms of this theological re-conceptualization, Maurice was influenced not so much by radicalism as by romanticism. He derived his idea of the kingdom of Christ from the Neoplatonic idealism that he learned from Coleridge, his friends in the *Conversazione* Society debating club, and his tutor at Trinity College, Cambridge, Julius Hare (1795–1855). All of these protagonists shared the characteristically romantic fascination with the means by which the supernatural, infinite, and eternal realm could be perceived by the temporally-bound creature. These, and other, romantics embraced the concept, inherited from Platonic thought, that there existed an eternal realm of ideals of which the temporal and material was an image, or a "symbol"—a kind of translucent window into the eternal realm.[131] William Blake famously summed up such a quest for eternity

---

129. Phillips, *Kingdom on Earth*, 1.
130. J. F. Maurice, *Life of F. D. Maurice*, 2:137.
131. Reardon, *Religious Thought*, 39–51.

in time as the desire "to see a world in a grain of sand and heaven in a wild flower, / Hold infinity in the palm of your hand and eternity in an hour."[132]

Within this romantic outlook, the search for the eternal was not a quest for an unrecognizable ethereal or mystical world but was rather an attempt to uncover the ground of reality. Coleridge, for example, thus told his students that "you are going not indeed in search of the New World, like Columbus and his adventurers, nor yet an *other* world, that is to come, but in search of the other world that *now* is, and ever has been though undreamt of by the many, and by the greater part even of the Few."[133] This emphasis upon finding the true depths of the world *that is*, rather than longing either for the world that *is to come*, or seeking translation to an occluded mystical world, was the heart of the romantic endeavor. It was a quest, as Maurice himself put it, to "recognize the Eternal State under our temporal conditions," a phrase that acted as the conceptual presupposition of all later incarnational Christianity.[134]

It is clear that premillennialists reflected this same kind of romantic hankering of finding eternity in time. While they clearly did not deny the future dimension to salvation (and neither, I shall argue, did F. D. Maurice), they expected to grasp the eternal now, as well as then. "Strange to no Christian, no believing ear, can be the mention of a heaven begun on earth," explained the *CMR*, "a difference only of degree between the bliss of this life and of the life to come."[135] Charles Goodhart believed that "the power of the resurrection life is felt and known even here. Even *now* the renewed soul possesses the felicity of heaven, in all its essential qualities."[136] "How near may be our contact with a higher world! How ready our intercourse with superior orders of intelligent creatures!" exclaimed Gerard Noel.[137]

The most controversial statement made by F. D. Maurice—and one commonly seen as indicative of the drift of Victorian theology—was about the meaning of the term "eternity." Maurice was removed from his position as Professor of Theology at King's College, London, in 1853

---

132. William Blake, "Auguries of Innocence," *English Poetry II: From Collins to Fitzgerald*. Vol. 41. The Harvard Classics. New York: P. F. Collier & Son, 1909-14, Bartleby.com, 2001, www.bartleby.com/41/.

133. Cutsinger, *Form of Transformed Vision*, 2.

134. J. F. Maurice, *Life of F. D. Maurice*, 2:219.

135. Review of *Life in the Sick Room* by Miss Martineau. CMR 4 (1844), CMR, 262.

136. Goodhart, "Powers of the World to Come," 209.

137. G. T. Noel, *Brief Enquiry*, 189.

following the publication of his *Theological Essays,* which seemed to call into doubt the reality of eternal punishment. In fact, his argument about "eternal punishment" was more subtle than is often realized. Maurice believed that the true state of humanity in Christ was an already established reality, although it was also occluded by the imperfect spiritual sensibility of individuals. He believed that the essential aim of the Christian pastor was to help "realize the union of the spiritual and eternal with the manifestations of it in time."[138] Maurice therefore contended that eternity was not a word that signified "life after death," but it was rather "something real, substantial, before all time." It was thus a quality of life that could be recognized and actualized from within historical time as much as it was a state confined to the future. "When I ask, 'Do I then know what eternity is? Do I mean by eternity a certain very, very long time?' I am shocked and startled at once by my want of faith and want of reason," he claimed. "Our Lord has been training us by His beautiful, blessed teaching to see eternity as something altogether out of time, to connect it with Him who is, and was, and is to come."[139] The biblical promise of eternal life was, for Maurice, not life going on forever, but rather the offer of a new quality of existence. "The eternal life is the righteousness, and truth, and love of God which are manifested in Christ Jesus; manifested to men that they may be partakers of them, that they may have fellowship with the Father and with the Son."[140]

Maurice believed that this understanding of eternity as the fullness of God was orthodox and catholic. He wrote to the *Clerical Journal* to explain his position: "I desire also to use the word eternal or everlasting in that sense in which I find it used in Scripture, in the creeds, and in the prayers of the Church, and in the devotions of good men, viz., as appertaining primarily and expressly to God, and therefore as distinct from and opposed to *temporal*."[141] Like other romantics, he blamed the rationalism of John Locke and the eighteenth-century philosophy known as "sensationalism" for teaching a notion of eternity that made it about duration and succession, rather than using it as qualitative description pertaining to the absolute impassibility of the divine realm. "When anyone ventures to say to an English audience, that Eternity . . . denotes something real,

---

138. J. F. Maurice *Life of F. D. Maurice,* 2:264.
139. Ibid.,17
140. F. D. Maurice, *Theological Essays,* 449.
141. J. F. Maurice, *Life of F. D. Maurice,* 2:370.

substantial, before all time, he is told at once that he is departing from the simple, intelligible meaning of words, that he is introducing novelties: that he is talking abstractions," he complained. "This language is perfectly honest in the mouths of those who use it. But they do not know where they learnt it. They did not get it from peasants, or women, or children; they did not get it from the Bible. They got it from Locke."[142]

This anti-Lockean concept of eternity led Maurice into his most controversial argument, in which he questioned the notion of "eternal punishment." He argued that "if it is right, if it is a duty, to say that Eternity in relation to God has nothing to do with time or duration, are we not bound to say that also in reference to life or to punishment, it has nothing to do with time or duration?"[143] In other words, if eternity is the absolute realm in which God dwells, to speak of "eternal punishment" is oxymoronic. Only God is eternal, and because eternity is righteousness, truth, goodness and all absolutes that pertain to God, then hell or punishment cannot also be eternal in the same sense as God is eternal. Contemporaries seized upon this aspect of Maurice's argument. They claimed that Maurice had denied the doctrine of divine punishment. He thus became the archetypal Victorian theological revisionist, one of many nineteenth-century theologians who damned the doctrine of hell to oblivion.

Subsequent commentators have also often assumed that this was the subject with which Maurice was primarily concerned. It was not. One should note in the paragraph quoted above, for example, that Maurice suggested that eternity was an inadmissible prefix to either "life" or "punishment." The basis of Maurice's argument was about the meaning of the word "eternal," not about the reality or otherwise of punishment. Indeed, Maurice claimed to agree with the Evangelical Alliance that there should be *more* talk of God's judgment. Maurice did not thus deny the reality of punishment. Rather he thought that "eternal punishment" should be understood as being in a state of existence disconnected from God, whether that state occurred in the past, present, or future.[144]

---

142. F. D. Maurice, *Theological Essays*, 465. Locke had argued that it was simply impossible to imagine a state of existence without time: "If our weak apprehensions cannot separate succession from any duration whatsoever, our idea of eternity can be nothing but of infinite succession, of moments of duration wherein any thing does exist." Locke, *Essay*, 137.

143. F. D. Maurice, *Theological Essays*, 450.

144. Ibid., 322-3.

Because eternity was not for Maurice a stage of temporal existence but rather a set of moral qualities—righteousness, truth, love—which flowed from God, time and eternity could mutually exist and intermingle. He thus criticized the "language of the preachers about the worthlessness of the things of time (the things of this earth)."[145] Instead he claimed "that time and eternity co-exist here. The difficulty is to recognise the eternal state under our temporal conditions; not to lose eternity in time."[146] In other words, by separating the meaning of eternity from the notion of temporality Maurice was also able to re-import the eternal back into the space-time universe and understand temporality and eternity as interwoven threads of the same reality. "Whilst you distinguish the Eternal and the Temporal, you can see their relation to each other; you can feel what a blessing appertains to each," he concluded.[147] Thus, while he despised Locke for associating "eternity" with the notion of extended temporality, he had no objection to the idea that time would extend indefinitely. "I have no business as far as I see at present, to speak of death as ending time."[148] Both temporality and eternity formed the basic interwoven fibers of human life, now and always. "If eternal things are not future things more than they are present, more than they are past, if they are distinct in kind from temporal things—each may have its own honour, they may be inseparably linked together in the nature of man."[149]

The Premillennialist Revision of Eternity

While many thought that Maurice proposed novel and disturbing statements, two Irish historicist premillennialists, Henry Woodward (1775–1863) and John Michael Hiffernan (1792/3–1879), had already made a very similar argument in the pages of the normally cautious *Christian Observer* and in the Irish Evangelical newspaper, the *Christian Examiner* (founded 1824) during the 1830s.

Henry Woodward was the son of Dr. Richard Woodward, the Bishop of Cloyne. Fellow premillennialist William Pennefather said that Woodward was "a holy man, gifted with the most brilliant mind I ever

145. J. F. Maurice, *Life of F. D. Maurice*, 2:473.
146. Ibid., 219.
147. Ibid., 473.
148. Ibid., 219.
149. Ibid., 473.

met with, full of imagination and originality."¹⁵⁰ Educated at Corpus Christi College, Oxford, Woodward began his clerical career in 1799 in fellowship with a tradition that Timothy Stunt has called "exact churchmanship," a term encompassing Irish Anglicans who were scrupulous in their observance of ecclesiastical sacramental discipline and offered some resistance to the "low church" pragmatism of Evangelicalism.¹⁵¹ This was a tradition to which also belonged Alexander Dallas, fellow historicist premillennialist and *de facto* leader of Protestant missionary campaigns in Ireland.¹⁵² Here again, of course, is an anomaly in strict demarcations of ecclesiastical traditions.

In 1804 Woodward read Paul's Letter to the Romans and experienced a conversion experience. He recorded that "a change, such as I neither looked for nor could have conceived, came over my whole soul, and passed upon my whole nature."¹⁵³ In 1812 he became rector of Fethard, in the Diocese of Cashel, an office that he held until his death. During the late 1820s, Woodward aligned himself more closely with the Evangelical party in the Church of Ireland.¹⁵⁴

As rector of Fethard between 1812 and 1863, Woodward worked under the Bishop of Cashel, Robert Daly (1783–1872), who himself had a strong interest in prophecy and had presided over several Irish prophetic conferences.¹⁵⁵ This may have been one factor in moving Woodward toward premillennialism, a doctrine to which he stated his adherence in 1836.¹⁵⁶ Robert Daly himself turned toward futurist premillennialism in the late 1830s, thus aligning himself with powerful currents in the Irish prophecy movement, such as those associated with the Powerscourt Conferences and the looming presence of John Nelson Darby. Woodward admitted that Daly's revised prophetic exegesis momentarily shook his own eschatological outlook but he subsequently resolved that an historicist,rather than futurist, interpretation of prophecy made the most sense of Scripture.¹⁵⁷

150. Braithwaite, *Life . . . of William Pennefather*, 24.
151. Stunt, *From Awakening to Secession*, 153–55.
152. Bowen, *Protestant Crusade*, 210.
153. Ibid. xvi.
154. Ibid., 456–62.
155. Burnham, *Story of Conflict*, 114–16.
156. Woodward, *Essays*, 65.
157. Ibid, 206.

John Hiffernan, meanwhile, was "for more than forty years Mr Woodward's most intimate and much-loved friend, for twenty years his fellow-labourer in the parish of Fethard."[158] He later became Rector of St. John's Newport. Like Woodward, Hiffernan was an historicist premillennialist.[159] Hiffernan was the more prolific writer of the two men. He published *Life Sketches from Scripture* (1854) and its sequel, *Scenes from Our Lord's History* (1855), as well as a three-volume series of "Thoughts" (1877–78). Unlike Woodward, however, he left neither memoirs nor correspondence.

Woodward and Hiffernan contributed scores of articles to the *Christian Observer* in the 1830s and 1840s, probably in part because of Woodward's friendship with the editor, Samuel C. Wilks (1789–1872).[160] Their essays were largely devotional but often speculative, pondering questions concerning the future life, memory, and the nature of authority. It is clear that not all readers found their views entirely palatable. A reviewer of Woodward's *Essays*, writing in the *Christian Observer*, noted that some of his ideas "are of a nature which scarcely allows us to hope for general concurrence; because they are based rather upon probabilities than on evidence."[161] Their reappraisal of eternity was certainly one of their more speculative ideas. It is striking how closely it resembles the argument that gained notoriety for Maurice.

Like Maurice, Woodward and Hiffernan believed that faith in God was not simply a hope for a better life in the future but that it involved a re-aligned perspective on the present. "To the eye of faith eternity opens upon time," contended Hiffernan: "God is seen reigning over and regulating both worlds: not as essentially different kingdoms, but as separated provinces of the same empire."[162] The basis of such an assertion was that belief, again shared with Maurice, that eternity was a layer of reality that could co-exist with time, not a description of everlasting life that would dawn only after time had ended, or after the believer had died. Eternity was what made time enjoyable. "Eternity and God are so vitally interwoven with their many rich and spiritual enjoyments, that

158. Hiffernan commissioned the memoir of Woodward's life from which I have been quoting. Woodward, *Essays*, xiv.

159. Hiffernan, *Sketches*, 47.

160. Ibid., Preface, n.p.

161. Review of *Short Readings for Family Prayers* by the Rev. Henry Woodward, *CO*, 2nd. ser., 11 (1848), 195.

162. J.M.H., "On Natural Affections," *CO*, 1st ser., 35 (1835), 713.

without eternity, and without God, the sorrows and joys of life would be alike insupportable."[163]

For these two writers, Christian faith was the faculty that allowed an individual to perceive that the eternal infuses the temporal, and in turn to recognize the realm of space and time as an authentic part of the Divine order. Conversion was thus the opening up of an eternal perspective upon the temporal world: "The first ray of spiritual light, by letting in eternity upon time, and re-admitting God into this his own world, from which sin and sinners have conspired to exclude him, shews that all the real interests of time and eternity are identical," suggested Hiffernan.[164] It was therefore possible to suggest that eternity was an experience of the present as much of the future since "the soul which changes from being earthly, sensual, and devilish, to being heavenly, pure, and Godlike, passes by that change, even here, into the state of blessedness—into the confines of another world—into the dawn of eternity, and into the kingdom of heaven."[165] In fact, Woodward described his own conversion experience by saying that "it was as if heaven was opened to my soul, as if eternity had begun."[166] Woodward thus concluded that "the passage from time to eternity were not that violent and startling thing, which the misgivings of the carnal mind and natural heart would make it," and endorsed the present as a locus for encountering the eternal.[167] People who imagined heaven to be a radical disjunction with the present "had no foretaste or anticipation of that which is the very soul of future blessedness; and therefore their own experience can bear no testimony to the fact, that the substance of heaven commences here."[168]

Like Maurice, the two men acknowledged that recognizing the eternal in time was not easy. The human experience was the fragmentation of life into days, hours, and minutes. The endemic problem of humans was an inability to grasp the whole. This was not a fault in the substance of material life, they argued, but was a flaw in the perceptive faculty of humans. "There is a something wanting, not in outward objects, but in ourselves,"

---

163. J. M. H., "Atheism of the Carnal Heart," *CO*, 2nd ser., 4 (1841), 133.

164. J. M. H., "On Worldly Affections," *CO*, 1st ser., 35 (1835), 650.

165. H. W. [i.e., Henry Woodward], "Family Readings—John XVII.17," *CO*, 2nd ser., 6 (1844), 421.

166. Woodward, *Essays*, xvi.

167. H. W., "On Anointing the Feet of Jesus," *CO*, 2nd ser., 9 (1846), 705.

168. Ibid., 514.

argued Hiffernan.[169] Despite such partial vision, humans clearly longed for wholeness and yearned for the ability to comprehend the fullness of space and time in one draft. For this reason humans traveled to mountaintops, Hiffernan continued, because aloft a mountain top "we strain our eyes and feel such anxiety to discover the most distant points we can; and if we catch the faintest glimpse of some remote and well-known spot, rejoice as if we yet gained some costly prize."[170] This was a desire for spatial completeness, "and as it is with space, so it is with time."[171]

It was this observation of the human yearning for the eternal that led Woodward to make the statement that most clearly prefigured F. D. Maurice. This hunger for eternity in the midst of temporality, Woodward argued, meant that the Christian belief in "eternal life" could not mean "everlasting life," for if the promise of God were simply for an extended period of never-ending time in the future then such a state of existence would suffer from the way in which time fragmented and split experiences into small, unsatisfying portions. Woodward therefore argued that:

> It is my belief, then, that the essential difference between time and eternity does not consist in this, that the one is terminable, and the other infinitely extended. They are not the same in kind, and different only in degree. But eternity is, altogether, another mode of existence from that of time. The latter is life dealt out to us in parts, and successive portions. The former is, on the contrary, a fullness of being, without succession; a state in which there is neither past nor future, but in which the whole exists together and at once.[172]

Despite the lack of vision endemic to humans, Woodward was convinced that the eternal could burst in on this earthly scene whenever a concentration of disparate things were suddenly grouped together, when humans were granted the ability to pierce the fragmentary nature of time and thus perceive its underlying eternal fundament. Woodward likened such visions of eternity to those "rare and felicitous moments, in which the face of nature and the features of the landscape seem as if touched with some mysterious enchantment."[173] Thus, although this full perception of

---

169. H. W., "On Antepasts of the Future State," *CO*, 2nd ser, 9 (1846), 515.
170. J. M. H., "On Memory," *CO*, 1st Ser., 34 (1834), 518.
171. Ibid., 518.
172. Woodward, *Essays* (1836), 103.
173. H. W., "On Antepasts of the Future State," *CO*, 2nd ser., 9 (1846), 514.

eternal life would have to await a future realization, the two men were hopeful that one could experience such glimpses in the present, precisely because eternity was not everlasting future time, but a mode of existence:

> If eternity differ from time simply in degree, the one being terminable and the other not, then indeed all such notions fall to the ground. But if the great distinction be that in time existence is doled out to us by little and little, but that in eternity we shall have a fullness of being and all united, then it would follow that whatever now seems to bring distant things, whether of time or space, unexpectedly together, must so far anticipate our future life.[174]

Eternal life did not, therefore, mean going off to another place after death, but rather it involved a re-aligned perspective upon the temporal-spatial world. Time and eternity existed together now, the authors insisted; it was human perception of the eternal dimension that still awaited redemption. "I do not call those two worlds a present and a future ... for both are present, both are co-existent—but I call them a natural and a spiritual, a temporal and an eternal," claimed Hiffernan.[175] Hiffernan in fact came close to rejecting a future heaven at all: "Dream not of future or fantastic happiness—of a vague or visionary heaven. Holiness *is* happiness—is heaven," he wrote.[176] Correspondingly, he also called into question the reality of a future material hell. Prefiguring Maurice by at least a decade, he suggested hell was really the state of separation from God, which could be as much a present reality as a future threat.

> Abandon those vague fancies, and inoperative contemplations of a mere material fire, and material hell, and look well to the state of your souls. Look to the manner, and to the spirit, with which you discharge the duties of the several relations of life. Look to the character, and to the tendency, of your pursuits and enjoyments: to the habits of your life: to the tastes and tempers of your mind.[177]

Hiffernan and Woodward were not alone in their proposals. In particular, there was a similarity between their conception of "heaven"

---

174. Ibid., 517.

175. J. M. H., "Count the Cost," *Christian Observer*, 1st ser., 34 (1834); cf. J. F. Maurice, *Life of F. D. Maurice*, 2:219

176. J. H. [i.e., John Hiffernan], "On the Advent and Offices of the Holy Spirit," *Christian Examiner and Church of Ireland Magazine*, new ser., 2 (1833), 541.

177. J. M. H., "The Vagueness ... of Popular Religion," *CO*, 2nd ser., 3 (1840), 323.

or "eternity" as an affective state of mind and the concept of heaven expressed by several other historicist premillennialists. Gerald Noel, for example, wondered,

> ought not our notion of heaven to be connected rather with the honour of God—with the manifestation of truth—with the service of Christ—with conformity to his will—with union to his person and cause? . . . Should we not do well to consider heaven rather as a *state of character*, than as a mere region of enjoyment? as *a condition of mind*, than as a *local separation* from the *material* structure of the present world?[178]

Christ, argued Noel, had come to "win back" the "affections" to God, and "Eternity" was "the world to which the warm affections of the heart are linked."[179] Noel had perhaps developed this idea in conversation with his friend Thomas Erskine, who also believed that "opposition to the Spirit of God is the only real evil and conformity to Him is the only real good."[180]

Woodward, Hiffernan, Noel, and Erskine also shared with Maurice a vision of redemption that asserted that salvation was more than a future deliverance from God's judgment on the basis of Christ's death. "If pardon of sin alone had been sufficient to man's salvation," argued Hiffernan, "the atoning sacrifice of Christ might have been offered upon the altar of heaven, while 'angels' alone 'bowed down to look into' the infinite and mysterious abysses of redeeming love."[181] These theologians wished to stress the entire re-orientation of human life into conformity to the pattern of God's will. "A very common idea of the object of the gospel is, that it is to show how men *may obtain pardon*; whereas, in truth, its object is to show how *pardon for men has been obtained*," contended Erskine, stressing that enjoyment of the new status of humanity was available now, and did not await a future acquittal at the bar of judgment.[182] Noel propounded a similar idea, complaining that the depths and riches of salvation available to the Christian were not appreciated by most individuals. "Men often account 'salvation' to be a mere deliverance from the penalties of the law," Noel complained, "whereas salvation is a complex term[:] . . . the conversion *of the heart*, the return of the affections to God, is in

---

178. G. T. Noel, *Brief Enquiry*, 233. Italics in original.
179. G. T. Noel, *Sermons Intended Chiefly for . . . Families*, 3, 55, 304.
180. Hanna, *Letters of Thomas Erskine*, 1: 357.
181. J. M. H., "The Redemption of Man," CO, 1st ser, 35 (1835), 203.
182. Ibid., 379. Italics in original.

very truth, *salvation*."[183] Erskine also explicitly questioned the notion of eternity as referring to a future period of life.[184] He argued that "eternity has nothing to do with duration." He linked this proposition with an internalized, present-focused experience of the heavenly life, contending that "a man who receives the will of God into his inner being is taking hold of eternal life, for God's life is in His will."[185]

In all of these thinkers, the conviction that the material world would be restored by God led them to believe that the physical world as it was now constituted was an authentic arena for encountering the divine. This belief led to a subtle shift of emphasis among some premillennialists toward arguing that the believer ought to be more concerned with pursuing a holy, happy, and eternally-oriented life in the present, than with longing for a future deliverance from the earth.

The Premillennialist F. D. Maurice

So far the argument of this book has been that premillennialists have been overlooked as theological revisionists. But the inverse is also true. Theological revisionists like F. D. Maurice have been equally overlooked as products of the prevalent apocalypticism of the early-nineteenth century. Indeed, once we dissolve the schematic ecclesiastical boundaries beloved of the Victorians and their interpreters, and once we realize that what is commonly called "premillennialism" was a very board and wide-ranging set of convictions about the relationship between God and creation, Maurice himself could actually himself be categorized as a "premillennialist" thinker. An avowed premillennialist thinker like Thomas Rawson Birks did not just plagiarize Maurice, as Edward H. Plumptre suspected; rather, he and Maurice came to similar conclusions because they shared similar cultural and theological premises.[186]

There is an initial clue to Maurice's eschatological framework in the title of his paradigmatic statement of partially-realized eschatology: *The*

183. G. T. Noel, *Sermons Intended Chiefly for . . . Families*, 9.

184. Maurice was also influenced by Erskine. See J. F. Maurice, *Life of F. D. Maurice* 1:28, 43, 108.

185. Hanna, *Letters of Thomas Erskine*, 2:235.

186. Birks and Maurice also experienced the same romantically-drenched educational milieu of Trinity College, Cambridge. Education created a common foundation of intellectual and cultural assumptions that cut across ecclesiastical partisanship in the Victorian church. Preyer, "The Romantic Tide."

Kingdom of Christ. The theme of an earthly kingdom was clearly a dominant premillennialist trope. "I believe, and have stated it in the plainest terms, as also have many others, that Christ is King now, and that there is a kingdom now," stated the Baptist premillennialist John Cox.[187] Edward Bickersteth agreed. "The just view of the Church of Christ now is that of a kingdom; and the person and character of the King gives unspeakable, universal and everlasting importance and glory to this kingdom," contended Bickersteth. Indeed, an appendix to his *Practical Guide*, Bickersteth included Maurice's *Kingdom of Christ* in a list of recommended works dealing with eschatology. "Although not directly prophetical," noted Bickersteth, "the book nonetheless contains many original, striking and useful thoughts."[188] Like Maurice, Bickersteth believed the reality of this kingdom was established by the incarnational solidarity of Christ with humanity. "It is through the incarnation of our Lord Jesus Christ, and in the person of the God-man, that this essential dominion becomes visibly manifested to the whole universe," noted Bickersteth. "In the language of the address of our beautiful Coronation Service to our Queen, Remember that the whole world is subject to the power and empire of Christ our Redeemer."[189] And on this point he recommended that people read F. D. Maurice's book, *The Religions of the World and Their Relations to Christianity*, which he described as "an original and striking work" proving that Christ was even king over "false religions."[190] Clearly Bickersteth recognized the similarities between his own theological views and those of Maurice.

Such resonances were not coincidental. F. D. Maurice formulated his views about the kingdom of Christ under the tutelage of Joseph Adam Stephenson (1783–1838), a Somerset Evangelical who articulated a variant of premillennialist eschatology. A brief introduction to Stephenson is therefore necessary to explain why Maurice adopted the accent of millennialism.

The core of Joseph Adam Stephenson's thought was a conviction that Christ ruled the world *now*. To support this view Stephenson turned to a mode of prophetical exegesis called præterism. Præterism was an interpretation of Scripture that contended that the prophecies of the Old and

---

187. J. Cox, J. *Divine Origin*, 25.
188. E. Bickersteth, *Practical Guide*, 306, 275.
189. E. Bickersteth, "Kingly Power," 118.
190. Ibid., 122.

New Testament were fulfilled in events that occurred relatively quickly after the prophecy was made. Like futurism, præterism was an exegetical position that was originally popular with Roman Catholic scholars because it avoided identifying the Roman Catholic Church or the Pope with any of the negative symbols of the Apocalypse. It was first popularized by a Jesuit Monk, the Sevillian Luis de Alcazar (1554–1613) in *Vestigatio Arcani Sensus in Apocalypsi [Investigation of the Hidden Sense of the Apocalypse]* (1614). The scheme was adopted by Protestant Hugo Grotius (1583–1645), who saw it as a way of bringing peace to the wars of religion racking Europe in the seventeenth century, and by English biblical critic Henry Hammond (1605–60), who believed it to be an Anglican antidote to Puritan fanaticism. The præterist interpretation was taken up in the eighteenth century by Johan Samuel Herrenschneider who published a work in 1786 interpreting Revelation as describing the overturning of Judaism, the overthrow of heathenism, and the final universal triumph of the Christian church.[191] This encouraged further German præterist scholarship, most notably the works of German romantic thinkers Johann Gottfried Eichhorn (1752–1827) and Johann Gottfried Herder (1744–1803). It was perhaps to these two German scholars to whom Stephenson alluded in acknowledging his debt to continental thought.[192]

Stephenson's adoption of præterism had some affinity with amillennialism in that it downplayed the coming millennium in favor of interpreting the *present* era as the time of Christ's earthly reign. However, it would be misleading to describe Stephenson as an amillennialist in so far as this term might be construed to imply an eschatological disposition distinct from the themes of historicist premillennialism discussed in this book. In fact, in making his claims about the kingdom of Christ the author of the preface to Stephenson's *The Christology of the Old and New Testaments* in 1838 claimed that he was "sympathising in those very feelings which had given birth to the popular notions respecting the Second Advent of our Lord."[193] Stephenson's outlook shared with historicist premillennialism

191. This was *Tentamen Apocalypseos illustrandae*.

192. In England the view was also propounded by the Cambridge Evangelical Anglican orientalist and Professor of Hebrew, Samuel Lee (1783–1852). His daughter recalled that "ever since his translation of Eusebius's 'Theophania,' my father's mind had been more or less occupied on the subject of Prophecy, and he became convinced that the views which he entertained, known as the Præterist, were those held by the early Church." A. M. Lee, *Scholar of Past Generation*, 190.

193. The anonymous author of this introductory tribute to Stephenson was, in fact, F. D. Maurice. Stephenson, *Christology* 1:v; J. F. Maurice, *Life of F. D. Maurice*, 1:148

the belief that the primary purpose of God was to restore his rule over the material universe and that he acted in historical time to achieve this end. Stephenson believed the second advent would be the time when this rule would became fully manifest. He also, of course, interpreted prophecy historically, even though he diverged from "historicist" premillennialism concerning which parts of history were signified by scripture.

Stephenson was the vicar of Lympsham in Somerset from 1809 to 1844, "a clergyman of the school of Cecil and Venn," as F. D. Maurice described him—in other words, an Evangelical.[194] His father was the Vicar of Olney and a good friend of the slave trader turned hymn writer, John Newton. Educated at Queen's College, Oxford, Stephenson served curacies in Beckenham, Kent, Hatfield Broad Oak, Essex, and finally, Lympsham where he remained until his death.[195] In his early career as a clergyman, Stephenson was concerned mainly with pastoral duties. Like many other Evangelicals in the 1820s he developed an increasing interest in studying the prophetic parts of Scripture. Rejecting the historicist interpretation, he formulated a new exegesis of prophetic biblical texts with "the greatest assistance from the theologians of modern Germany."[196] This allusion was to the præterist exegesis of Scripture, which held that "the inspired writers do not speak of events which were to happen long after they had left the world, but rather show what significance lay in events which were almost immediately to follow the announcement of them."[197]

The burden of Stephenson's only published work, *The Christology of the Old and New Testaments* (1838) was to provide a detailed account of how the first decades of the early church exactly fulfilled scriptural prophecy. He pursued this task with an exacting thoroughness that rivaled his historicist counterparts. Stephenson argued that in the book of Revelation "every form of language adapted to fix the assurance of its going to be almost immediately fulfilled would be found employed."[198] Stephenson claimed that "only a single paragraph [of prophecy] remains to be accomplished," that is, the second advent of Christ.[199] Stephenson argued that, if prophecy had already been fulfilled, then the promised

---

194. F. D. Maurice, *Lectures on the Apocalypse*, vi.
195. Stephenson, *Christology*, 1: iii.
196. Ibid., v.
197. Ibid.
198. Ibid., 1:225.
199. Ibid, 227.

reign of Christ, predicted in the Gospels, was already in operation over the world. He contended that "it was not meant when the day of Christ was termed the Last day, that it would be a day limited by time, so neither was it meant that it would not occur till time was expired, or on the point of expiring."[200] Rather, he suggested, the "last day" was an eternal period representing the complete work of Christ, which hung like a "luminary" over the entire material universe, creating the current temporal dispensation, which he termed the "mediatorial day." In other words, the current finite period of time took its substance from the eternally finished work of the mediator, Christ. This was a highly poetic and romantic vision of the interpenetration of time and eternity.[201]

Stephenson contended that Christ had received a dominion over the earth as a gift of his obedience to the Father immediately at his resurrection. "He received the heathen for his immediate inheritance, and took the uttermost parts of the habitable earth for his possession," claimed Stephenson, "he was made the head over all things; and his heralds were sent forth to proclaim the Gospel of the kingdom or joyful tidings of his inauguration."[202] This new world order was the basis of all Christian life and faith, he contended. "That the universal kingdom is actually given into the hands of Christ is the grand theme of our ministry; it is the centre round which all the doctrines of the Gospel system are suspended; it is the foundation on which all its offers of grace and glory are rested."[203]

Speaking to members of the London Missionary Society in 1822, he suggested that the fact that the world at this moment belonged to Christ was also "that which furnishes us with our justification in the employment of Missionaries; is that which authorizes the faithful servants of Christ to go to the utmost bounds of the globe."[204] There was, he argued, a great freedom in this fact. "Go wherever they will," he said of missionaries, "they cannot go beyond the extent of their commission, or travel out of the limits of their Master's authority."[205] Christians should be excited about their new status as members of Christ's kingdom, he argued. Their unwillingness to accept that the prophecies of Scripture were already

200. Ibid., 2:143.
201. Ibid., 144.
202. Stephenson, *Kingdom of God*, 6.
203. Ibid., 7.
204. Ibid.
205. Ibid.,

fulfilled derived from blindness to their new status. "We are unwilling to consider these prophecies as fulfilled," wrote Stephenson, "because we are slow to believe in the actual glory of our position as members of the body of Christ."[206]

Stephenson was hankering after greater orientation of eschatology toward the present, in which Christians recognized that their status as redeemed creatures was an already accomplished fact. This sermon was preached to the same missionary society to which Irving would two years later give his *cause célèbre* damnatory critique of the Evangelical world. Stephenson appeared at first glance to have been far more positive than Irving, but as should now be clear from this study, both Irving and Stephenson were part of the same re-appraisal of Evangelical theology. Both asserted God's authority over the physical globe; both stressed that mission was about *claiming* the reality of God's already existing sovereignty, not *creating* it through human agency.

If for Stephenson the kingdom was already established in the current historical order, as the præterist interpretation suggested, then what did the return of Christ portend? Stephenson argued that there was a difference between the "Kingdom of Christ" on the one hand, and the "Kingdom of God" on the other. He noted that Christ prayed "Our Father ... Thy Kingdom Come," and argued from this prayer that Christ himself was looking forward to a time when he would hand over his kingdom to the Father. Stephenson argued that when he returned, Christ would relinquish his claim to mediatorial government "for the exercise of which there will be no longer room" and "shall with infinite joy to himself deliver up the kingdom to the Father."[207] At this time one would find "God in all, and all in God!"[208]

In common with the other protagonists examined in this book, Stephenson was convinced that the earth would be the site of the ultimate kingdom of God, just as it was in the current era the theater of

206. Stephenson, *Christology*, 1:iv.
207. Stephenson, *Kingdom of God*, 8.
208. Ibid. This argument was also made by George Montagu. "Christ's kingdom is that for which we are to look, God's kingdom is that for which we are to pray," he argued. This position led him to reject a millennium, since he believed that Christ was *already* king of the earth and needed no future era to establish his earthly dominion. Nevertheless, he embraced the restitution of all things. He regretted that everyone who believed in the Second Advent and Christ's reign on earth had been labelled with what he thought was the misleading label of "millenarian." Montagu, *Finished Mystery*, 41, 56.

the mediatorial kingdom of Christ. "Defective indeed would be a view of the kingdom that paid no attention to the scite [sic.] of its establishment," Stephenson told the members of the London Missionary Society.[209] Acknowledging typical suspicion of "the world" within Evangelical discourse, Stephenson admitted that "one aspect indeed there is of this world, in which it is justly regarded as an object of jealous fear, and every propensity to cleave to it becomes a subject of continual mortification." Yet, he continued, "is there not another view of this God-created earth, which places it in a light attractive of our holy love and admiration?"[210]

Stephenson looked particularly to the incarnation of Christ as the evidence that God cared for and intended to redeem the material globe, although such divine involvement with the affairs of earth could be traced throughout the whole of scriptural history: "Was it not here that God inhabited the cloud—was it not here that he dwelt in human flesh?"[211] Stephenson concluded that "the earth would be delivered into the glorious liberty of the children of God" at the return of Christ. This event, he argued, would be accompanied by the resurrection of the body. "No belief may be entertained with more settled confidence than the corporeality of the risen saints," he concluded.[212] Stephenson thus placed his eschatological hope in "a risen earth adapted to a risen body."[213] The current kingdom of Christ was a dynamic era of re-conquest, the objective of which was the recovery of the world for God.

The combination of the belief in restitution of all things and the concept of a present-orientated kingdom proved highly attractive to the young man who, trying to discern his future vocation, came to live with Joseph Adam Stephenson in 1833: Frederick Denison Maurice.[214] Maurice remembered his mentor fondly, especially in relation to the connection between earth and heaven that pervaded his thought. "There was never any wide chasm between his discourse upon earthly and heavenly topics," he recalled.[215] Maurice warmed in particular to the way in which Stephenson described the incarnation of Christ as an act that displayed

---

209. Ibid., 21.
210. Ibid., 11.
211. Ibid., 11.
212. Stephenson, *Christology*, 2:163.
213. Stephenson, *Kingdom of God*, 12.
214. Morris, *F. D. Maurice*, 52.
215. J. F. Maurice, *Life of F. D. Maurice*, 1:148.

the solidarity of God with the material creation. "He never appeared to look upon the earth, as some excellent men, whose minds are continually occupied with the contemplation of moral evil, look upon it," noted Maurice. "At times he would almost forget the deformities with which six thousand years of sin had loaded it, and regard it only as the soil on which the Son of God had walked, and which he had redeemed from the curse." Maurice also enjoyed the sense of organic development that he found in Stephenson's notion of restitution, claiming that he shared with Stephenson a belief that "any future felicity which awaits the Church, can be only the full realization of that which it has, potentially, now; and cannot arise from the establishment of any new order of dynasty in the world."[216] Such thinking clearly cohered with Maurice's sense of the unfolding of a pre-existing divine order within the existing structures of the historical and material order as well as sounding much like the ideas explored in the previous chapter concerning the nature of the future life.

As well as these broad themes about the materiality of God's promise, Maurice learned from Stephenson the idea that the prophecies of Scripture were fulfilled in the coming of Christ and the years immediately following his ascension. In the preface to his *Kingdom of Christ* Maurice lauded his former teacher for this lesson:

> I can never be thankful enough for having arrived, through his teaching, at the conviction that the words, "The kingdom of heaven is at hand," were used by the Evangelists in the strictest sense; that the Apostles were not wrong in believing that the end of an age was approaching; that they had no exaggerated anticipation respecting the age that was to succeed it; that if we accepted their statements simply, we should understand far better in what state we are living; what are our responsibilities; what are our sins; what we have a right to hope for.[217]

Writing to Stephenson in 1834, Maurice explained how the idea of the complete transferal of the world into the hands of Christ had become fundamental to his thought. "I have found myself in all my private meditations, as well as in preaching," wrote Maurice, "drawn to speak of Christ as a King, and His Church as a Kingdom; and whenever I depart from

---

216. *Obituary of the Late Rev Joseph Adam Stephenson*, 4.

217. F. D. Maurice refers to his debt to Stephenson again in *Lectures on the Apocalypse*, vi–vii.

this method, I feel much less clearness and satisfaction, much less harmony between my own feelings and the Word of God."[218]

Contemporaries recognized the præterist element of Maurice's eschatology. "I think I can give you something more of Maurice's views about the Millennium and second coming of Christ," wrote his protégé, Edward Strachey (1812–1901). "He says... that Christ's reign upon earth began after the destruction of Jerusalem. All the Book of Revelation Maurice understands to refer to the dispensation that then commenced, and that is still going on."[219] Of course the notion of Christ's kingship was the central theme of his 1838 *Kingdom of Christ*, published in the same year as Stephenson's work, and the title of which was drawn from the central conviction of Stephenson that this age was that of the kingdom *of Christ* in distinction to the kingdom of God, although this was not a distinction to which Maurice drew particular attention.

Maurice combined what he had learnt from Stephenson with a range of other influences to produce this wide-ranging theological synthesis. His *Kingdom of Christ* did not, therefore, deal particularly with the prophetic basis upon which Stephenson had established his own exegesis of Scripture. Rather, the notion of the kingship appeared to have acted as a leaven to the whole of Maurice's thought. In particular, it shaped his belief that the starting point of theology must be the inviolable fact of Christ's Lordship over the world, rather than beginning with the depravity of humanity. "Christ is already king of the world," argued Maurice, "I cannot believe the devil is in any sense king of this universe. I believe Christ is its king in all senses, and that the devil is tempting us every day and hour to deny Him, and think of himself as the king."[220] This led Maurice to place eschatological emphasis on the search for the hidden existing kingdom. "I am obliged to believe," he wrote, "that we are living in a restored order; I am sure that restored order will be carried out by the full triumph of God's living will."[221]

To understand the role of præterist "millennialism" in shaping F. D. Maurice contributes to understanding more of his seemingly paradoxical theological views, particularly in helping to reconcile an emphasis in his thought upon divine initiative and revelation on the one hand, and the power of humanity to participate in building a kingdom of righteousness

218. J. F. Maurice, *Life of F. D. Maurice*, 1:167.
219. Ibid., 208.
220. Ibid., 450.
221. Ibid., 10.

upon earth on the other. A.M. Ramsey argued that "in Maurice's theological thinking we meet with two entirely different sets of ideas. On one hand he maintained that theology must start from God and the eternal world. On the other hand he pointed to the Scriptures as the record of God's saving acts in history, culminating in the incarnation, death and resurrection of Christ."[222] Jeremy Morris argues that the two elements were never resolved into a coherent whole by Maurice.[223]

It is, in fact, the broad millennial ambit of the era in which Maurice developed his theological synthesis that provides a key that unlocks at least some of these contradictions in Maurice's thought. The ideas that he learned from Stephenson allowed Maurice to claim that an historical event had inaugurated a new realm in which humans could pursue the task prescribed by Platonist philosophy. It was to him an essential premise "that men are not to gain a kingdom hereafter, but are put in possession of it now."[224] This kingdom was not a Platonic ideal, reached through reason or mystical insight. It was historically grounded in the work of Christ and in the expectation of a restitution of all things, which would be manifested upon the material globe. It was only because the union between heaven and earth had been established *by Christ in history*, that one could be confident of the renewed connection between earth and heaven, and between time and eternity in the present. Maurice felt strongly that such an interpretation of the apocalypse showed that the earliest years of the church "were nothing less than the actual manifestation of Christ's kingdom, the actual establishment of a communion between the two worlds, the creation of a new heaven and a new earth."[225] The emphasis on the historical establishment of a mediatorial kingdom cohered with the type of romantic and Neoplatonic thought that Maurice had learned from Coleridge and his cohorts at Cambridge, but his continued emphasis upon the kingdom of Christ as "that which is really and actually existing" was also a premillennialist theme transposed to a new key.[226]

---

222. Christensen, *Divine Order*, 144.
223. Morris, *F. D. Maurice*, passim.
224. F. D. Maurice, *Kingdom of Christ*, 1:377.
225. J. F. Maurice, *Life of F. D. Maurice*, 1:153.
226. F. D. Maurice, *Kingdom of Christ*, 2:143.

Reading Maurice in the light of later nineteenth-century Christian Socialism has obscured the millennialist context of his formative years.[227] Indeed, for all the present-orientation of Maurice's eschatological thought, it is important to note that he was still committed to a future dimension of God's purposes. He showed considerable interest in apocalyptic literature, arguing that restoring the book of Revelation to the regular lessons in the liturgy of the Church of England was of great benefit. Remembering his deathbed, his son, Frederick, recalled, "I constantly read parts of the Revelation to him, and he always entered into them with peculiar delight."[228] Indeed, he concluded his explanation of the constitution of the "kingdom of Christ" by pointing people to the book of Revelation, "for though we may not be able to determine which of all the chronological speculations concerning it is the least untenable, though we may not decide confidently whether it speak to us of the future or of the past, ... we shall have no doubt that it does exhibit at one period or through all periods a real kingdom of heaven upon earth."[229]

Like his premillennialist colleagues, Maurice also believed unequivocally in the second coming of Christ. He argued that "the revival of [belief in the second coming] in our day has been one great means of removing the clouds which had hindered us from looking at Christ's Church as a Kingdom and from connecting all individual blessings and rewards with its existence and its establishment in that character."[230] He also endorsed the idea of future material restitution. "Though I have no faith in man's theory of Universal Restitution," he wrote, "I am taught to expect 'a restitution of all things, which God who cannot lie has promised since the world began.'"[231] All told, his stated creed about the future was therefore one with which most historicist premillennialists would have been very content:

> So far, then, as I have at present been taught—and I must repeat again how little I feel I have been taught—respecting the future state, I would try (1st) always to connect it with the unveiling or

---

227. Jeremy Morris has called for a greater attempt to understand the formative milieu in which Maurice's thought evolved. "Reading Maurice contextually requires attention to the period in which his views were formed, and this means the late 1820s through to the early 1840s." Morris, *F. D. Maurice*, 29.

228. Maurice, *Life of F. D. Maurice*, 2:639.

229. F. D. Maurice, *Kingdom of Christ*, 1:378.

230. Ibid., 2:443.

231. J. F. Maurice, *Life of F. D. Maurice*, 2:10.

manifestation of Jesus Christ, as St. Paul and St. John do; (2nd) to connect it, as they do, with the restoration of the earth, and its deliverance from whatever hinders it from being the kingdom of God, and of His Christ; (3rd) to connect it with the manifestation of Christ in the flesh as the Lord of Man.[232]

Maurice was, in fact, well aware of his affinity with contemporary millennialism. He praised the premillennialist doctrine that God's kingdom would dawn on earth:

> I think that the Millenarians are right, and practical, and in harmony with Scripture when they bid us think more of Christ's victory over the earth and redemption of it to its true purposes, than of any new condition into which we may be brought when we go out of the earth. By doing so, they make all our feelings and interests social, they connect everything we do and feel and suffer.[233]

Maurice also believed that millennialists were right to stress God's ongoing purposes toward Israel, though he warned against any Judaizing tendency that might imply that God was only concerned with blessing small groups of elected people, rather than with establishing a universal order.[234] He also shared the premillennialist antipathy for "heavenly" hope, praising them for expunging "the wretched notion of a private selfish heaven, where compensation shall be made for troubles incurred, and prizes given for duties performed in this lower sphere."[235]

In *The Kingdom of Christ* Maurice compared his ideas with other ecclesiastical viewpoints about Christ's reign. Significantly, he was reluctant to condemn very much about the millennialist position. In fact, he found only one main flaw with millennialism: he was concerned that the contrast that some premillennialists drew between the "invisible" kingdom now in operation and the "visible" kingdom that would begin at the Second Advent made it seem either that they thought that the spiritual dimension would be occluded in the future, or that Christ was not currently the sovereign of the material world. In regard to the first option, he chided millennialists for exhibiting *too much* hope for the material world, claiming that they at times focused too much on the materiality

---

232. Ibid., 2: 248–49.
233. Ibid., 2: 244.
234. F. D. Maurice, *Kingdom of Christ*, 2:436–43.
235. Ibid., 443.

of redemption and not enough upon the spiritual aspects of future union with Christ.[236] This is an ironic critique, given that Maurice is often seen as the progenitor of world-affirming, "social Christianity," while premillennialists have been described as "world-denying"! In regard to the second issue—the fear that millennialists denied Christ's current reign over the temporal realm—it is worth quoting his critique of premillennialism at length in order to show that his vision of the kingdom of Christ differed very little from the premillennialist vision of the universality, historicity, and materiality of Christ's reign in past, present, and future that I have outlined so far in this book:

> If it be meant [by millennialists] . . . that Christ's dominion [after his second coming] will not be merely over the heart and spirit of man, over that which directly connects him with God and the unseen world, but over all his human relations his earthly associations, over the policy of rulers, over nature and over art, then, I say this is as much the truth now as it ever can be in any future period. This dominion has been asserting itself, has been making itself felt, for these eighteen centuries. The Son of Man claimed it for himself when He did not abhor the Virgin's womb, when He mingled with the ordinary transactions of men, blessing their food, their wine, and their marriage feasts. The claim may have been denied at all times; it may be denied especially at the time to which we are looking forward; but that time must assert it, not as something new, but as something old; as a government which has been actually in exercise, and the ceasing of which even for a moment would have been followed by dreariness and death throughout the universe.[237]

Few of the premillennialists examined in this book would have disagreed with Maurice on this point. Maurice did not devote his energy to attending conferences about prophetic chronology, nor did he write detailed expositions of apocalyptic scripture. However as I have attempted to prove throughout this book, the essence of the "premillennialist" theological synthesis was more than a strict notion of the millennium or the pursuit of arcane prophetic detail. Rather, it was a conviction that the kingdom of God would dawn on earth and that all Christian life and experience should by shaped by this reality. On this point, Maurice and the premillennialists were in harmony.

---

236. Ibid., 2:244–45.
237. F. D. Maurice, *Kingdom of Christ*, 2:447.

Conclusion

The alignment between F. D. Maurice and premillennialism, as well as premillennialist speculation about universal salvation and conditional immortality, their focus on the incarnation, and an emphasis on finding the eternal in and through the temporal, all underline that premillennialists were at the center of many trends in nineteenth-century church to which historians have rarely linked them. Certainly, not all premillennialists sounded these themes equally. Nevertheless, the evidence of this chapter challenges any overly-confident demarcation of Victorian religious factions. It particularly problematizes the common dichotomy between "liberal" (broad church, socially-inclined, progressive) and "conservative" (Evangelical, retributive, apocalyptic) streams of Christian thought. Premillennialism, an early-nineteenth century Evangelical creed commonly associated with pessimism, despair, and judgment was actually in the vanguard of nineteenth-century theological revisionism. Incarnational theology may have come of age after 1860, but it was born in the age of *parousia*.

6
Prophecy and Policy

> On various points, we have been misunderstood and in some cases misrepresented. It has been affirmed that . . . our theory . . . damps Christian zeal and straitens Christian liberality and that if in any case a Premillennialist is energetic and buoyant and large hearted he is so in spite of the deadening and depressing tendencies of his system,—a system which is said to lay as sure an arrest as fatalism upon all that is practical and benevolent on all that is generous and noble.
>
> —*QJP* 3 (1851), 113–14.

MILLENNIALISM HAS ALWAYS POSSESSED inherent social potential. To imagine the world as it might be if under divine control carries with it an implicit critique of the current social order. Some millennialists have stressed that one must wait for divine action to effect change; others have shaped the millennial vision into an agenda for political action.

As outlined in chapter 2, nineteenth-century premillennialism is conventionally associated with a loss of faith in the idea that human action could usher in the divine order. These Christians believed that the millennium would only occur through the personal appearance of Christ, so it seems logical to assert that they would have no interest in making the world a better place. There is, however, a problem with this interpretation: many nineteenth-century premillennialists had a *great* interest in making the world a better place. Among their number were counted some of the leading Evangelical social reformers of the generation, including Antony Ashley Cooper, who had adopted historicist premillennialist views in the early 1830s as a result of his friendship with

Edward Bickersteth.[1] Ashley thought that "there is very little seeming, and no real, hope for mankind, but in the Second Advent," and yet he was also an indefatigable social and religious reformer, campaigning for improvements in public health, factory conditions, and education.[2] Ashley's apparent eschatological pessimism was matched by a great confidence in the possibility of reform: "I assert the great improvability of urban life," he announced.[3] Most scholars recognize that Shaftesbury was both a social reformer and a premillennialist (although one recent scholar looked at his social reforming agenda and pre-emptively concluded that he was "an optimistic postmillennialist rather than a gloomy premillennialist"[4]), but he is often seen simply as the enlightened exception to the reactionary premillennialist rule.[5] In fact, as I shall show later in the chapter, he was only the most famous example of this apparent paradox of the coalescence of premillennialist eschatology and social action.[6]

This paradox is doubly taxing because the *type* of reform with which premillennialists like Shaftesbury became involved was qualitatively different to the Evangelical social agenda of the Hanoverian era. In chapter 2 I explained how the "classic" Evangelical vision for social change was typically about rescuing individuals from the power and penalty of sin in order to ensure their eternal salvation. Because this led Evangelicals to campaign against issues of immortality and ungodliness, historians have argued that Evangelicals were concerned more with social control than with social reform; more interested in changing individual behavior than with altering environmental maladies.

Boyd Hilton, for example, has argued that for Evangelicals poverty was part of the divine plan for individual behavioral change. The earth

---

1. Hodder, *Life . . . of Shaftesbury*, 1:325.

2. Shaftesbury, Personal Diary entry, 25th December 1842, University of Southampton, Shaftesbury (Broadlands) Papers, SHA/PD/2, 1838–43, 126.

3. Shaftesbury, *Speeches of the Earl of Shaftesbury*, 307.

4. V. Clark, *Allies for Armageddon*, 42.

5. Christopher Hamlin, for example, could only highlight as paradoxical that "someone like the seventh Earl of Shaftesbury, transfixed with the imminence of the last days and the world's sinfulness," worked alongside secular reformers such as Edwin Chadwick in sanitary reform. Hamlin, *Public Health*, 5.

6. Although he is the most famous premillennial social reformer, this chapter is not going to discuss Shaftesbury in depth because he is well served by existing scholarship. These treatments should be read with the context outlined in this chapter in mind. See Best, *Shaftesbury*; Lewis, *Origins of Christian Zionism*; Turnbull, *Shaftesbury: The Great Reformer*.

was seen as an arena of "moral trial" that prepared believers for their true eternal home in heaven. In such a framework Evangelical social reform tended to focus upon eliminating gross abuses and vices in order to ensure the individual a safe passage to heaven. Evangelicals eschewed formulating a long-term vision for societal renewal because it was the moral disposition of the soul *in spite* of social hardship that mattered most.[7] Other historians have concurred that this so-called "myopic" view of social change meant that Evangelicals tended to be reactionary rather than constructive in their social reforms. They campaigned ad hoc against flagrant abuses, but had little vision for the reconstruction of the social order. Their "proposals were regularly for the elimination of what was wrong, not for the achievement of some alternative goal."[8]

However, Evangelical social attitudes were changing in the era between 1820 and 1870. Only a few historians have noticed this change, mostly because this is a neglected generation in the history of Evangelicalism.[9] One of the most notable, yet overlooked, reappraisals of the changing social temperament of Evangelicalism in the mid-nineteenth century was provided by Norris Pope in a work that discussed the links between Charles Dickens' social conscience and Evangelical social reform. In *Dickens and Charity* Pope argued that, despite lampooning Evangelicals for their hypocrisy, Dickens' keen sense of social justice was

---

[7]. "The Evangelicals did not have a vision of a Christian society with mutual ties and obligations like Coleridge or Southey." Bradley, "The Politics of Godliness," 192.

[8]. Bebbington, *Evangelicalism in Modern Britain*, 135. "One would not look for advanced reformers in such a group," argued David Owen. "Their stupendous achievement in demolishing slavery atoned handsomely for the myopia with which they sometimes viewed other public issues." Owen, *English Philanthropy*, 94; Of course, the accuracy of this portrait can be questioned for the earlier period of Evangelical history too. See Hylson-Smith, *Evangelicals in the Church of England*, 91–93, for an argument that Evangelicals in the early nineteenth century were perhaps more "progressive" in certain respects than their contemporaries.

[9]. Douglas Holladay, in a brief article that also pointed to the surge of reforming activities in British society in the period 1830–50, contended that Evangelicals were an important component of these developments. He lamented that "comparatively few have sought to understood the role of evangelicalism in this period." Holladay, "Nineteenth-Century Evangelical Activism," 54. Some corrective to this neglect of the new Evangelical social agenda was offered by Donald Lewis in his *Lighten Their Darkness*. His book contains much that is relevant to the study of nineteenth-century Evangelical engagement with urban life. He also detected the link between historicist premillennialism and a revision of social attitudes, although he did not seek to explain it in great detail. This chapter offers a parallel reading of some of the issues discussed by him. D. Lewis, *Lighten Their Darkness*, esp. 29–48 and 151–78.

shared with many Evangelicals. Indeed, he often co-operated with them in ameliorative projects. Pope contends that such a unity of interest was possible because "from the 1840s onward, Evangelicals became less concerned with attacking sin in a direct and individual manner, and much more concerned with improving the physical environment.... This increased preoccupation with the social and environmental limitations on moral choice reflects a major change in Evangelical outlook."[10]

I will explore the details of this new Evangelical social vision below. The point to make here is that it was this updated attitude—more alert to the complex effects of the environment upon individual morality, more aware of the social dimensions of poverty—that was evident among those premillennialists who championed social reform. This means that not only were premillennialists involved with social reform, but also that they were actually more "modern" and even "progressive" than the older generation of Evangelicals—Christians whom they criticized for their failures in regard to articulating a vision for social justice. Historicist premillennialists therefore had a more robust view of social reform than their postmillennialist forbears!

How can this be explained? Those historians who have noticed the paradox of premillennialist social reform have argued that it was simply an accommodation of doctrine to social reality. They have suggested that "the experiences of reformers working day by day in the slums proved decisive in overriding theological scruples."[11] Expanding knowledge of urban life, garnered from the numerous public health enquiries of the 1830s and 1840s, did indeed shape Evangelical opinions, but such bare explanations have the unfortunate effect of bifurcating theology and practice and tend to relegate theological belief to a subsidiary role. Indeed, explanations that presume that theology and practice can be hermetically sealed from each other can appear somewhat comical, as in the case of the literary historian who argued that the premillennialist Charlotte Elizabeth Tonna was a forward-looking model of social compassion, despite the unfortunate fact that she was a "narrow-minded bigot possessed by religious zeal and intolerance."[12] Do we really believe that Tonna was so Janus-faced? Similarly Ivanka Kovačević and S. Barbara Kanner have argued that the social concern of Tonna was achieved *in*

---

10. Pope, *Dickens and Charity*, 28–29.
11. Ibid., 200.
12. Fryckstedt, "Charlotte Elizabeth Tonna," 88

spite of her religious beliefs: "However much Mrs Tonna took the ultra-Evangelical pose, she was not primarily concerned with the pacification of the 'dangerous class,' but with the alleviation of their sufferings; and she seems not to have been at all guilty of the class-protecting humbug ... associated with the Evangelical movement."[13] Perhaps this means that Tonna was an exceptional case; or perhaps it means that we should not so easily swallow the idea that Evangelicalism was simply a movement of class-protecting humbug in the first place.

In fact, we do not have to split theology and action artificially. In this chapter I will first explore some specific elements of the premillennialist vision that contributed toward a higher view of the social sphere as a place for Christian action predicated on the concrete life of communities as well as the moral and spiritual life of individuals, a set of values that can be described broadly as "paternalism." Second, I will make a broader argument concerning the relationship between premillennialism and the changing tone of Evangelical social reform in these decades. The emergence of a new approach to social reform and the popularity of premillennialist eschatology in the same decades of the nineteenth century can be understood as parallel aspects of an underlying shift in Evangelical theology that accorded greater attention to the temporal-spatial realm. Just as premillennialist theology rejected the idea that the body would give way to the soul or the earth would be destroyed in preference for an ethereal heaven, so the new Evangelical social agenda promoted a heightened concern for the stewardship of the temporal sphere, and a belief that one could legitimately invest effort to improve and ameliorate the physical conditions of human existence. The ethical tones of a new world-affirming Evangelicalism matched the eschatological pitch of Evangelical convictions.

It is important to note that there is no claim being made in this chapter that these premillennialists were trying to initiate or build the millennium in the way attempted by postmillennial Evangelicals, or by some seventeenth-century Puritans. Indeed, being a premillennialist did not automatically make one a strident social reformer, and the new social vision was shared by Evangelicals who were not premillennialists.[14] Rather, the new eschatology and the new social vision shared the same

---

13. Kovačević & Kanner, "Blue Book Into Novel," 159.

14. It should also be noted, of course, that "Christian Socialists" like Maurice did not necessarily think that they had a definite coherent agenda either. Hylson-Smith, *Churches in England*, 2:39.

overarching theological and cultural logic. They were both part of the growing Evangelical appreciation of the temporal-spatial sphere as a locus of authentic Christian concern. This was itself part of the development of more holistic approaches to social justice across all parts of Christian society in the Victorian era. It is this resonance that explains why premillennialists joined a growing coalition of Christian social activists, which included non-Evangelicals, literary figures, and political radicals.

Toward a Social Gospel

The previous chapter suggested some ways in which the themes of premillennialism resonated with the broader drift of nineteenth-century theological development toward a hope that the eternal could be made manifest within the temporal sphere as much as awaiting a future *dénouement*. These broad theological changes led to a revised ethical and pastoral agenda in nineteenth-century Christianity in which men and women conceived of their primary Christian duty as bringing to bear principles of justice and compassion by positive activities within the social sphere, rather than counseling individuals to await a future spiritual alleviation of their current misfortune. I also intimated that the genesis of such an approach to Christian witness, which flourished in the latter half of the century, has traditionally been located within the mid-century movement dubbed "Christian Socialism," a body of thought associated with F. D. Maurice, Charles Kingsley (1819–75), and John Malcolm Ludlow (1821–1911). Maurice's *The Kingdom of Christ* represented the central text of this movement, with its emphasis upon co-operation, solidarity, and societal harmony.[15]

Although this movement is still viewed as important, a more nuanced historiographical picture has now emerged that has identified several other distinctive Christian voices that called for a new vision of Christian social action in the mid-century period. Historians have, for example, focused on the social vision of Tractarianism, and on several influential Nonconformist leaders who wrestled with questions of Christian economics, business ethics, and the conflict between individual and

---

15. A seminal treatment of the link between F. D. Maurice and other Christian thinkers of the 1840s and the more widespread adoption of "Christian Socialism" in late-nineteenth century Britain is Jones, P. d'A, *Christian Socialist Revival*. See also Christensen, *Origin and History of Christian Socialism;* Norman, *Victorian Christian Socialists;* Phillips, *Kingdom on Earth*.

corporate responsibility. Other historians have pointed to the radical potential of popular Christian preachers like Joseph Rayner Stephens (1805–79) who combined the zeal of Methodist Evangelical field preachers with a socio-political message matched to the growing discontent of the Victorian lower classes.[16]

These studies point to a multi-dimensional mid-century discontent centered on the perceived failure of classical political economy and its expression in legislation such as the Poor Law Amendment Act (1834). A related unifying thread of these diverse movements was a growing desire to critique the spirit and consequences of industrial capitalism, particularly by suggesting that national prosperity and divine approbation could not be guaranteed by hard work alone, but rather by a proper integration of purposeful activity with times of spiritual and physical refreshment.[17] Moreover, Christians were becoming less worried about individual moral failures, and more concerned about structural socio-economic injustice.

Within this Christian social discourse there was a notable interest in the question of whether the temporal sphere of social and political relations could be a legitimate sphere for Christian endeavor toward building the kingdom of God, or whether all hopes for societal improvement must await the dawning of an "eternal" realm radically distinct from the current fallen world and unobtainable with earthly resources. For example, Thomas Binney (1798–1894), the Congregational minister of the King's Weigh House, wrote a book in 1853 entitled, *Is it Possible to Make the Best of Both Worlds?* This work attempted to reconcile the desire to enjoy the current material sphere with the promises of a blissful future life, so that "*both* parts of the performance might be expressed in sustained and harmonious verse."[18] Meanwhile, radical Christian social reformers such as Joseph Rayner Stephens framed their pleas for social reform in terms that sought to find harmony between temporal relationships and eternal principles. Stephens claimed that:

---

16. Skinner, *Tractarians and the "condition of England"*; Lyon, *Politicians in the Pulpit*; Johnson, "Between Evangelicalism and the Social Gospel"; Garnett, "Evangelicalism and Business."

17. The notion that Protestantism in general, and Evangelicalism in particular, supported a vigorous work ethic has been problematized for the eighteenth century by John Walsh in his "Bane of Industry?" On the idea that "work" was not sacrosanct and in fact meaningless without proper rest and recreation, see Garnett, "Gospel of Work."

18. Binney, *Is it Possible?* 12.

unless ... the two worlds can be brought together, unless the laws of Heaven be those of earth[,] ... unless the legislation of the Eternal be the spirit of us creatures of the day—then either there is no God, and we are in the shadowy sea of doubt and uncertainty, or we have the knowledge of God in our legislation, but deny the power.[19]

Historicist premillennialists joined this mid-century engagement with social issues, privileging statutory reforms that would ease the burdens of the poor, and calling for reforms of welfare, housing, sanitation, education, and working conditions that would mitigate the worst effects of rapid industrialization and economic modernization. I will trace this move shortly. First, it is necessary to introduce the only sustained explanation for this premillennial engagement with social reform, namely, that offered by Boyd Hilton in his *Age of Atonement*. I will briefly outline his argument, before going on to pose some problems with it, and then suggesting an alternative explanatory framework.

Boyd Hilton recognized that premillennialists struck a different note in regard to social reform than the dominant *laissez-faire* approach of Evangelicals like Thomas Chalmers and John Bird Sumner. He argued that the reason for this socially interventionist attitude was that premillennialists believed in "special providences"—direct visitations of the wrath and mercy of God to his people. This, he argued, contrasted with the more mechanistic, natural law theories of the moderate Evangelicals who believed that God worked through natural and economic cause and effect to teach and train his children. Premillennialists, he said, were thus "paternalists," who imagined an ultra-Tory God who acted to save and punish as he saw fit, calling down wrath upon specific sins and rewarding particular behaviors, rather than letting the natural consequences of general providence take their course. The premillennialist commitment to social reform, he concluded, was based on the belief that those with human power should act like their God in order to save and protect those caught in the flux of unstable and chaotic social circumstances. "Those who held an interventionist view of providence," argued Hilton, "also believed that governments on earth should take an interventionist approach to social and economic problems."[20] In other words, just as God acted in a cataclysmic or disordered way, premillennialists pursued

19. Holyoake, *Life of Joseph Rayner Stephens*, 117–18.
20. Hilton, *Age of Atonement*, 15.

ad hoc interventions in their capacity as the beneficent social superiors of those in need of occasional and specific protection.[21] Hilton did not, however, see premillennialists as progressives or in sympathy with other reforming temper of the day. Rather, he thought that they exhibited in a particularly strong way the "philistinism and morose, intolerant barrenness" of the Evangelical movement as a whole.[22]

While Hilton was correct to sense that premillennialism struck a different note from other Evangelicals in relation to social reform, it is not evident that he read very much premillennialist theology or social analysis. His analysis of premillennialism was restricted mainly to the early strand of the movement associated with Edward Irving and the Albury conferences. In fact, when challenged by Ralph Brown about some aspects of premillennialist theology that he had overlooked, Hilton dismissed the need to explore premillennialist thought any more deeply than he had done because he "was not writing the history of Evangelicalism."[23] To be fair to Hilton, the main burden of his *Age of Atonement* was to prove how one form of Evangelicalism (the classic, non-premillennialist type) had shaped British economic and social policy in the first half of the nineteenth century, and thus his reference to premillennialist ideology was only a way of highlighting that interventionist social reform was, contrary to some overly-romanticized and hagiographical views of Evangelical philanthropy, a minority interest in Victorian Evangelicalism. So Hilton did not set out to write a book about premillennialist social reform. Nevertheless, as he is the only historian to have attempted an explanation of this split within Evangelicalism—and as he did, by his own admission, want to make an argument premised on the idea that theology influenced practice—his views on this topic matter and invite critique.

Hilton believed the perfect example of the "pentecostal, pre-millenarian, adventist, and revivalist" strand of Evangelicalism—that is, the section of the movement that took a socially-interventionist stance—was the *Record* and the body of Christians ("Recordites") who rallied round the kind of themes and temperaments expressed in the pages of this journal.[24] I pointed out in chapter 2 that Hilton is not alone in viewing

21. Ibid., 94, 213.
22. Ibid., 212.
23. Hilton, "Evangelical Social Attitudes," 124.
24. Hilton, *Age of Atonement*, 10, 211. The claim that the Evangelicals associated with the *Record* were premillennialist has also been made by John Wolffe in his Oxford

the *Record* as an emblem for the kind of pessimistic turn in late 1820s Evangelicalism. As Ian Bradley has shown, the *Record* and the so-called "Recordite" Members of Parliament pursued a type of didactic interventionism. They desired to use the legislature as a tool for the inculcation of public and private godliness.[25] They were concerned particularly with issues such as Sabbath observance, national fast days, and with combating policies that seemed to concede political power to non-Anglicans. Without such statutory reforms, the *Record* feared imminent national judgment. Theirs was a dark mood. Indeed, the sense of impending judgment in the *Record* around the early 1830s meshed with the early premillennialism of Edward Irving and the Albury Conferences, which also focused upon the failures of the Establishment and the possibility of imminent judgment.

Merging the bleak tone of the Albury circle with the dark notes of the *Record* (and assuming that the *Record* was also therefore premillennialist) Hilton posited a logically plausible paradigm for explaining premillennialist social reform. Premillennialist paternalists believed in a judgmental God who loomed over the tumult of national affairs, saving only a remnant from imminent disaster. They therefore mirrored the perceived actions of their God to rescue people from social chaos.[26] But the explanation, while *looking* plausible in theory, is wrong.

The first error is that, as Donald Lewis has pointed out (although not in dialogue with Hilton: in fact, he made his point *before* Hilton wrote *Age of Atonement*), the *Record* was *not* premillennialist.[27] An editorial in 1853 stated this explicitly:

> Five and twenty years ago, when we commenced our course, we were theologians of the old school. We had not embraced the theory of the personal reign of our Lord in a state of premillenarian glory, nor did we follow on to other theological conceptions that seemed to spring more or less naturally, and in various directions, from this prolific root. Such as we were then, in all these respects, such exactly are we now.[28]

Dictionary of National Biography article, "Recordites."
25. Bradley, "Politics of Godliness," 251–98.
26. Hilton, *Age of Atonement*, 212.
27. Lewis, D., *Lighten Their Darkness*, 102.
28. *Record*, Feb 7, 1853.

The *Record* was also cool on the idea of a personal second advent. It desired to uphold what it believed to be the view of Jonathan Edwards, that the return of Christ would be a spiritual, not a physical, manifestation.[29] This anti-premillennialist stance was perhaps the result of its concern at the secessionist tendencies exhibited by some elements of radical Evangelicalism in the late 1820s and early 1830s.[30] Despite being commonly associated with the new radical and militant departures in Evangelicalism in the 1830s, then, the *Record* remained aloof from the eschatological position that is commonly seen as one of the most characteristic parts of such Evangelical "pessimism."

The second error with Hilton's explanation (again, noted by Lewis) is that the *Record* was not in favor of revising Evangelical attitudes to social reform. In fact, it campaigned against the "prevailing sickly philanthropy of the day" and rejected the idea "that the poor generally need relief only from misfortune, and not from misconduct."[31] In contrast to this "inflamed, exaggerated, and dangerous" sentiment, the *Record* wished to maintain the "intimate connexion between idleness and vice."[32] It rallied around *laissez-faire* social policy, claiming "there is no right conferred by God on any class of the population to be supported by the State."[33] It also denied that the accumulation of wealth among the industrializing classes was to blame for heightened distress among the working classes. "In short," the newspaper concluded, "we do not believe that the evils of this country, to whatever extent they exist . . . arise from any extraordinary measure of the love of riches."[34]

What is most significant about these statements made by the non-premillennialist, pro-free market *Record,* is that they suggest a more complex link between new eschatology and new social attitudes than that proposed by Hilton's elision of two groups of Evangelicals in the 1830s into just one radical and apparently gloom-laden, obscurantist wing. Non-millennialist, pro-free market, attitudes continued to exist even among radical Evangelicals who were dubious about the culture of the more moderate, urbane nature of Hanoverian Evangelicalism. But

29. *Record*, April 27, 1848.
30. Stunt, *From Awakening to Secession*, 250.
31. *Record*, Aug 29, 1844.
32. *Record*, Aug 26, 1844.
33. *Record*, Sep 2, 1844.
34. *Record*, Sep 2, 1844.

another group of Evangelicals, who were also in revisionist mood and shared some of the underlying attitudes of the Recordites in terms of their desire to re-energize the Evangelical witness, took quite a different turn, both in terms of their eschatology and their social ethics.

This becomes clear when we register that the *Record* made the claims about *laissez-faire* political economy, as transcribed above, in direct dialogue with the historicist premillennialist *Churchman's Monthly Review*. The *CMR* articulated a very different view about Evangelical attitudes toward social policy. Responding directly to the *Record*, it claimed that the views of "political economists," (and thus of the *Record*) were "in diametrical opposition to the word of God." It stated starkly that "the modern race of writers, who assume to themselves the name of 'Political Economists,' are among the most mischievous of all the unclean things that 'liberalism' has spawned."[35] The *CMR* lamented the esteem with which the Evangelical hero Thomas Chalmers' views of political economy were held by both the *Record* and the *Christian Observer*.[36] It concluded that rather than reiterating the doctrine that poverty was the result of idleness, as the *Record* and Chalmers tended to do, Christians should cultivate a sympathetic disposition toward the poor:

> Throughout the whole of God's word, there is perceptible a remarkable tone of kindness and pity toward the poor . . . their constant tone is so entirely that of kindness, pity, and compassion, that we should fill pages were we to attempt to give half the instances that offer.[37]

Where does this leave us? If we admit that the Recordites *were* believers in special providence (and I think the work of Ian Bradley and Timothy Stunt suggests there is some merit in this description), we also have to conclude that this version of providence *did not* lead to an interventionist social policy, but was in fact associated with quite the opposite socio-economic view. Hilton's argument about the tight link between social reform (and possibly his entire argument, which tries to predict Evangelical social attitudes based on prior theories of providence) therefore crumbles. This does not completely invalidate Hilton's proposal, of course, since he does mention a class a few proper premillennialists, such as Irving, Drummond, and Edward Vaughan, as examples of Evangelicals

---

35. Review of *A Plea for the Poor* by Baptist Noel, *CMR* 1 (1841), 521.
36. Review of *Notes of a Traveller*, *CMR* 2 (1842), 579.
37. Review of *Claims of Labour*, *CMR* 4 (1844), 689.

committed to an interventionist social policy, (even if he wrongly labels them "Recordites"). Hilton would probably claim that at least in these cases a commitment to special providence is still valid as an explanatory key. After all, premillennialism appeared to be grounded in the idea of a direct divine visitation (i.e., the return of Christ), so surely premillennialists were special providentialists *par excellence*?

The alert reader will guess that I wish also to close down this argument since it is based on the standard *a priori* stereotype of premillennialists that this whole book has sought to overturn. The relationship between historicist premillennialism and social reform was rooted not in any premillennialist tendency to believe in a wildly interventionist Deity, nor even in a general sense of gloom that Hilton links (perhaps with some accuracy) to the Recordites. Rather, as I argued in chapter 3, the historicist premillennialist idea of providence and history was of the slow, gradual, disclosure of the purposes of God throughout historical time. So while Hilton was correct to suspect that premillennialists rejected the idea of God as an absent law-giver—a view that they believed much of the Evangelical world had come to accept—their alternative was not a vision of a capricious deity of the kind that Hilton would have them endorse. Rather, they believed that God had established the sphere of space and time as the medium of his constant and progressive revelation.

In fact, historicist premillennialists joined the mid-century conversation about the possibility of a renewed Christian vision for society because of their robust commitment to the temporal-spatial sphere as an authentic *locus* of divine concern. In particular, they rejected the idea that salvation was only about the redemption of the individual soul. "When people say we should think more of the soul and less of the body," Shaftesbury explained to a YMCA meeting in 1851, "my answer is, that the same God who made the soul made the body also." In a significant echo of the pneumatological focus of some elements of historicist premillennialism explored in chapter 4, he added, "if the body is the temple of the Holy Ghost as St. Paul proposes it ought not to be corrupted by preventable disease, degraded by avoidable filth, and disabled for His service by unnecessary suffering."[38]

As with their eschatological revisionism, there was an underlying awareness that these individuals were deliberately reframing the Evangelical tradition of which they were a part. One of the most ardent

---

38. Shaftesbury, *Speeches of . . . Shaftesbury*, 308.

champions of Evangelical social engagement, the premillennialist publishing magnate, Robert Benton Seeley (1798–1886), thus contended:

> A great number of high professors of gospel-principles . . . like the worldly politician, or the political economist, could see nothing in the Bible but a system of theology—a solution of the question of "How shall man be justified before God?" Imbibing, (theoretically at least) sound views on this question, and rejecting the false doctrine of salvation by works, too many stopped short here; and either refused to search the Bible for any thing further, or asserted that they could find nothing else there.[39]

Seeley instead contended for a reading of scripture that would lead to the transformation of "the government, of families, societies, and kingdoms," rather than one in which the Bible was "regarded as merely a guide to heaven, and as having very little bearing upon the things of this sublunary earth."[40] The *QJP* likewise warned against those who considered "only of the truth which bears on personal salvation, comfort, and usefulness," and thereby ignored the flow of societal life through the centuries.[41] Here, of course, was the typical premillennialist endorsement of the earthiness of salvation, now transposed to a socially reforming key.

The comprehensiveness of the premillennialist eschatological settlement generated a concern to develop a vision of a Christian society. Thomas Rawson Birks linked his vision of a broad restoration in the future to the need for contemporary Christian political engagement. "If the gospel were designed merely to separate a few believers out of a fallen world, and then to leave the rest, unrebuked and uncounseled, to perish in their wickedness, it could have only a very slight connexion with the laws and policy of earthly kingdoms," he explained. However, he argued, God was a universal deity who held to account both individuals and nations for their sins. "The shadowy phantoms of vain theory, which would divorce earth, as far as possible, from heaven, are driven away by the breath of [Christ's] mouth," he contended. "He, who is the true pattern of all kingly excellence, is the same Lord whose name is the Truth, and whose great work on earth was to make temporal benefits the perpetual channel of spiritual blessings to the souls of men. . . . Religion and politics

---

39. Seeley, *Remedies Suggested*, 109.
40. Ibid., 108.
41. "Dispensations," *QJP*, 10 (1858), 47.

are blended inseparably, as light and heat in the sunshine of heaven."[42] Historicist premillennialists were moving toward a type of social gospel.

The vision that they developed can indeed be described as a version of early Victorian "paternalism," but the texture of this paternalism is different to the outlook depicted by Hilton. Paternalism was an "intricate mosaic of forces,"[43] but running through the ideology was the abrogation of *laissez-faire* social and economic individualism, and an emphasis on the duties of individuals, including the role of the governing classes, to provide for those weaker or poorer than themselves.[44] Thus, in the words of historian Kim Lawes, Victorian paternalism, "encouraged a reappraisal of the social responsibilities of government and Parliament."[45] Although eager to use the legislature for a specific religious purpose, it is not clear that the "Recordite" vision was paternalistic in this way, for its burden was for a reconstruction of the state and nation's responsibilities before God, not for the recasting of responsibilities of the ruling class toward the majority of British people.

It was not the Recordite agenda, then, but the vision of paternalism as a socially-binding system of mutual obligations—with particular focus on the duties of the rich toward the poor—that had the most resonance with the historicist premillennialist outlook. Thomas Rawson Birks sounded the resonance when he described the coherence and order of the kingdom of God, in a passage that significantly referred both to an idealized present and a hoped-for future, by claiming that "social laws are like the cohesive force which binds together the solid strata of the earth, whereby every part of the landscape retains its own place and peculiar features, from the lofty mountain-top to the lowly valley, from the elevations of royal power and grandeur, down to the quiet and peaceful homes of domestic life."[46] This premillennialist paternalism was in part shaped by the sense of corporate responsibility that inhered in members of the national church.[47] It was also formed by the belief that God had shown concern with the social order throughout history.

42. Birks. *The Christian State*, 72.
43. D. Roberts, *Paternalism in Early Victorian England*, 243.
44. Lawes, *Paternalism and Politics*, 5.
45. Ibid.
46. Birks, "Partakers of the Kingdom," 375.
47. R. Brown, "Victorian Anglican Evangelicalism," 286. My argument in this section, first written up in my doctoral thesis in late 2007, mirrors that formulated by Ralph Brown in his Oct. 2007 *Journal of Ecclesiastical History* article: "Victorian

Such sentiments reflected the growing appreciation of communal and national life within a wider historical discourse, particularly as German historical study drew attention to "the development of the larger social units within which individuals found the meaning of their lives."[48] "The sacred volume teaches true religion in all its aspects, relations, and influences. It describes nations as fully as individuals, and reveals the springs of the prosperity and health of both," pointed out John Cumming.[49] Hugh McNeile scorned the individualism of Christians who "speak of God always as the God of individuals, and seem to have no faculty to perceive Him as the God of nations."[50] Both historicist premillennialism and paternalism were therefore theories that "helped make some sense of a society that was experiencing bewildering changes," by drawing attention to some fundamental principle (be that God, social hierarchy or, increasingly the "nation") as the basis for all political, social, and—in the case of prophetically-minded Christians—eschatological, order.[51] As Henry Drummond put it in 1830:

> Religion means a system of obligations; of bindings of man to God, and of man to man: the bands which hold are the ordinances of God's appointment; and every individual is religious or otherwise, according as he sees God in the sphere in which he is moving, and fulfills to Him the purpose for which he was placed in it.[52]

Anglican Evangelicalism." I had not at this point read Brown's work (which flowed from his earlier doctoral dissertation on Thomas Rawson Birks.) Although I have subsequently sought to challenge some of his arguments in published dialog with both him and Boyd Hilton, his main assumptions concerning the breadth of premillennial eschatology, its often misleading classification as fanatical or extremist, and his call for greater alertness to the broader theological shifts that it represented are, of course, in harmony with my own. His articles (and dissertation) should be read in conjunction with this book and will offer the reader a parallel reading of the mid-century Evangelical prophetic movement that broadly comports with the underlying thesis of this book, even if clashing with some of its detail about premillennial distinctives, namely, that Brown does not account for the full eschatological vision of temporal-spatial renewal, and he also contends that, in the end, premillennialists "wanted to save souls, not bodies." R. Brown, "Evangelical Social Thought," 134.

48. Bowler, *Invention of Progress*, 49.
49. Cumming, *Destiny of Nations*, iii.
50. McNeile, *England's Protest*, 34.
51. D. Roberts, *Paternalism in Early Victorian England*, 275.
52. H. Drummond, *Social Duties*, vii.

The purpose of the work of God, Drummond argued, was the establishment of his kingdom on earth, a fact that meant that "every relationship in society shadows forth Christ."[53] Such convictions meant that premillennialists were able to go further than some other Evangelicals in trying to articulate a Christian vision for society. This focus on the life of the community and nation means that the claim made by Ian Bradley that "the Evangelicals did not have a vision of a Christian society with mutual ties and obligations like Coleridge or Southey" must therefore be highly qualified.[54]

The resonance between premillennialism and paternalism is illustrated by the most significant and clearly premillennialist-influenced Evangelical social reform group of the mid-nineteenth century, the Christian Influence Society (CIS), an Anglican Evangelical pressure group established in 1832 to encourage church-building and to sponsor literature on maintaining the established church. The group had significant premillennialist support, including Robert Benton Seeley, Charlotte Elizabeth Tonna, and Ashley. Edward Bickersteth also had connections with the group through his friendship with both Ashley and Tonna.[55] The society used the premillennialist *CMR* as its mouthpiece. The CIS attracted a good deal of Evangelical support for its campaigns for church extension during the 1830s, but its members were increasingly stung by the criticism that attending to the spiritual needs of the populace was being hindered by their material deprivation. As the *CMR* explained in 1844:

> About two years since, having set on foot, as we have seen, two great public movements, for increasing the number of churches and ministers, and for augmenting the means of the education of the poor,—the society turned its attention to the question, What degree of truth might be found in the objection often heard, "The people are starving, and you talk of new churches. They want bread, and you offer them a stone."[56]

Like many others in this era of select committees and inspectorates, the society was impressed in the late 1830s by the evidence accumulated

---

53. Ibid., 10–11.

54. Bradley, "Evangelicalism and English Public Life," 192.

55. Tonna regularly published reviews of Bickersteth's writings in *CLM*. Bickersteth wrote the introduction for her *Principalities and Powers*, ix–xii.

56. Review of *The Claims of Labour*, *CMR* 4 (1844), 672–73.

concerning the state of health, sanitation, and morality in many working-class districts of the country.[57] It was, they concluded,

> impossible to investigate this question [of whether church extension was alone a sufficient response to contemporary irreligion], without speedily perceiving that the temporal privations and sufferings of the poor were, in many cases, great, and that these sufferings often operated to hinder the entrance of the word of life.[58]

The CIS therefore turned its attention away from church extension and toward campaigning for material amelioration. Aware of the criticism that this might provoke from those who thought that missionary activity should focus upon the soul, not the body, the society defended their decision to adopt this new approach. "Without purposing for a moment to place the bodily wants of the poor before their spiritual," it argued, ". . . temporal relief must, in many cases, go hand in hand with spiritual instruction, or the latter would too often fall unheeded on the ear."[59] Or, as Robert Benton Seeley argued more bluntly against Thomas Chalmers' notion that education and moral improvement were the solution to poverty, talking to hungry people about eternity would elicit only the response of: "I have had no breakfast!"[60]

Increasingly alert to the "habitual, grinding oppression to which the labouring classes were exposed," in 1842 the CIS committee asked Charlotte Elizabeth Tonna to undertake a survey of the conditions of poverty in Britain and to suggest "on plain scriptural grounds, the inevitable consequences of such things."[61] The result was *The Perils of the Nation: An Appeal to the Legislature, the Clergy, and the Higher and Middle Classes* (1843). The book was issued under the name of its publisher, Robert Benton Seeley, in fear that little notice would be taken of a work written by a woman.[62] The book reviewed the extent of poverty in factories, mines,

---

57. Kovačević and Kanner argue that Charlotte Elizabeth Tonna's *Helen Fleetwood* was an important contribution to the "Condition of England novel" genre because of its innovative translation into fictional prose of first-hand testimonies that had originally been delivered to Parliamentary investigators. Kovačević and Kanner "Blue Book Into Novel."

58. Review of *Claims of Labour*, CMR 4 (1844), 673.

59. Ibid., 673.

60. "To the Rev. Dr. Chalmers," CMR (1844), 860.

61. Elizabeth, *Personal Recollections*, 374.

62. Ibid.

agricultural areas, commerce, and workshops. It examined the problems of public health, education, and welfare. It demanded government intervention, but also a moral reformation of "the selfish principle" of economic individualism. It called for judges, doctors, law-makers, and clergy to articulate a new vision for the social order.

In 1844, Seeley wrote a sequel to the *Perils,* entitled *Remedies suggested for some of the evils which constitute the "Perils of the Nation"* (1844). The *Perils* and the *Remedies* books were the *de facto* manifesto of the CIS. Both condemned the social conditions of industrial Britain and concluded that "the displeasure of God most undoubtedly rests upon any nation wherein the poor are systematically trodden down and oppressed."[63]

Robert Benton Seeley's solutions to "the perils of the nation" sketched in his *Remedies* included the promotion of shorter working hours, the development of a cottage allotment system, the removal of children from factories, the improvement of housing, and the reform of the Poor Law. These proposals were matched by ideas that might, from the perspective of the twenty-first century, appear to be some less progressive solutions, including the need to restrict the working opportunities of women, temperance reform, and the need for church extension. But whatever we make of the *actual* content of the reforms proposed, the real significance lay in the fact that the framework in which they were announced recognized the structural circumstances that caused poverty, and directed its ire not toward the moral culpability of the poor, but toward the "idolizing of wealth" pursued relentlessly by the new economic elite.

Indeed, in the wake of our modern global financial turmoil and the growing critique of the unmitigated effects of global capitalism, Seeley's critique sounds perceptively aware of the complexities of economic inequality. Here is Seeley inveighing with almost Marxian ire against the fictitious capital of the modern stock market:

> In one corner, we behold a whole body of men, eagerly engaged in "operations," as they are called, in Spanish, or Brazilian, or Peruvian stock. They are not working with their hands. They are not producing anything, either out of the ground, or by any skill in handiwork. Nor are they even lending the means of employment to others. All they are doing is, to shuffle about certain bits of paper, of various forms and sizes, by which shuffling as in a game of cards, some will be found, at the end of the month,

---

63. Seeley, *Remedies,* 103.

to have lost, and others to have gained, several thousands of pounds.... But it is not the less true, that while they thus swelled their already enormous hoards, the poor people who bought the stock of them at this high price, became losers of nearly all the purchase money. No dividends on the said stock have been paid for years, and many a widow and orphan has pined in hopeless poverty ever since.[64]

Seeley insisted that the "idolizing" of wealth was detrimental to social well-being. "We know that Tyre was *rich* indeed, but who ever told us that Tyre was *happy*?"[65] Moreover, he could not help but be struck—as we are still struck today when viewing the vast disparities of wealth in our allegedly successful and globally-dominant capitalist democracies—by the paradoxes of global empire and domestic social inequality. "We [are] a nation, then, of enormous wealth and unparalleled power, a nation which can cause its will to be respected and its rights to be regarded in every part of the habitable globe, still disturbed, and its very existence placed in jeopardy, by intestine evils of which oppression itself is the main cause."[66] Seeley was clear that the "haste to be rich," and the faith placed in the potential for unlimited economic accumulation, was a "cancerous spirit" that had infected both church and society.[67] "Not only does covetousness exist among us, it is honoured, worshipped, deified."[68]

In articulating this socially astute Christian paternalism, the CIS drew inspiration in particular from Michael Sadler (1780–1835), the pioneering Evangelical paternalist of the mid-nineteenth century. Sadler had identified himself with Evangelicalism as early as 1797 when he wrote *An Apology for the Methodists* in defense of local Evangelical preaching. He had also supported William Wilberforce in his election campaign of 1807. In the late 1820s and 1830s he became a vociferous opponent of the tendency in contemporary Evangelicalism to ignore domestic poverty. He particularly critiqued the alliance between Evangelical Christianity and political economy, which he believed upheld oppressive working conditions in factories.

Sadler's first major work, *Ireland: its Evils and their Remedies* (1828), was an attack on the policy of forced emigration in Ireland, and a proposal

64. Ibid., 79–80.
65. Ibid., 70.
66. Ibid., 44.
67. Ibid., 78.
68. Ibid., 84.

for a systematic reform of the Irish Poor Law. In March 1829 Sadler was elected Member of Parliament for Newark and in May 1831 was returned for Aldborough in Yorkshire. The constituency boundary changes of the Reform Act of 1832 meant that Sadler's seat disappeared. He was an unsuccessful candidate in the Borough of Leeds against Thomas Macaulay in 1832. Sadler moved to Belfast where he lived until his death in July 1835, aged 56.

During his short Parliamentary career, during which he became known for over-long parliamentary speeches, "full of matter" and statistical detail, Sadler took up the cause of factory reform.[69] He campaigned for a ten-hour day for women and children. After presiding over a famous Select Committee (1831–32) that received copious evidence of industrial abuses, he urged legislative intervention to protect those whom he saw crushed by industrial work patterns. The heart of Sadler's claim was that government intervention was essential. The state, he said, was a "universal parent"—which is probably about as direct a call for a welfare state as one could expect to hear in the Victorian age.[70] Sadler also wrote an extensive refutation of Malthusian demographics, *The Law of Population* (1830), which argued from history, agriculture, mathematics, and theology, that the supply of food would never be outstripped by the population.

There is no evidence that I have found that would help determine whether Sadler was himself a premillennialist strictly defined.[71] However, Sadler was particularly enamored of the social and economic principles established in the Old Testament. "So far did he carry his conviction," wrote Seeley, "that we believe he would scarcely have hesitated to re-enact the whole Mosaical code, for any civilized and Christian nations of the present day."[72] The comparison of Britain to Israel was a trope with its roots in the English and Scottish Reformations, and it circulated widely in the 1830s among those influenced by the historicist exegetical assumptions of sixteenth- and seventeenth-century approaches to prophecy. The conception of Britain as a chosen nation could generate an intense concern to uphold constitutional and legal religious purity. This was an

---

69. Seeley, *Memoirs of . . . Michael Thomas Sadler*, 92–93.

70. 11 Parl. Deb. (3rd ser.) (1832), 385.

71. Hilton links him to premillennialism, though this is based on Hilton's confounding of "Recordite" Evangelicalism with premillennialism. Whilst Sadler did vote with the Recordites, this was not a sure sign of his eschatological position. Hilton, *Age of Atonement*, 95.

72. Seeley, *Memoirs of . . . Michael Thomas Sadler*, 505.

approach that was indeed particularly associated with the so-called "Recordites," who had a concern to uphold national standards of Godliness, focused on the enforcement of the Sabbath and the promotion of national religious probity, such as official Fast Days, alongside a resistance to Roman Catholic civic or religious rights.[73] Such themes were certainly not opposed by Sadler and the historicist premillennialists, but Sadler's vision of how Israel should inspire British policy tended to focus more on the socio-economic provisions of the Old Testament prophets. "In the institutions of the Jewish lawgiver . . . the legal provision for the poor, holds a most conspicuous place," Sadler wrote in his treatment of Irish poverty. He recommended the principle of tithe, Sabbatical, and Jubilee act as a model for economic redistribution.[74] This was a bold claim, as Sadler himself recognized: "Only suppose that the Deity has the same merciful consideration for an Irishman as for an Israelite, and then some of the passages may, perhaps, be found striking."[75] This appeal to the socio-economic basis of the Old Testament was generally *not* endorsed by the Recordite agenda.

It was Sadler's emphasis on God's provision of a set of principles for socio-economic well-being that of course also resonated with historicist premillennialists. After all, the heart of the premillennial eschatological vision was the ongoing validity of the Old Testament with its promise of an earthly, communal salvation. The example of God's involvement with Israel underpinned their vision of the divine involvement with all dimensions of temporal life. The *CMR* explained in 1842 "that the Almighty Being, whose never-failing providence ordereth all things both in heaven and earth, is as minutely observant now of the conduct of nations and communities, as He was during the period in the history of his chosen people the Jews, when a theocracy existed among them."[76] Indeed, since premillennialists interpreted the millennium as answering the Old Testament promises for earthly restitution and renewal, Charlotte Elizabeth Tonna claimed, during a paean to Sadler, that during the age to come, Christ would reign "over a world re-modeled after the heart's longings of

---

73. Bradley, "Politics of Godliness," 251–98.
74. Sadler, *Ireland; Its Evils and Their Remedies*, 190.
75. Ibid., 191.
76. Review of *Children's Employment Commission, CMR* 2 (1842), 673.

that dear servant."⁷⁷ Here was a clear resonance between social policy and eschatological hope.

Sadler's most ardent champion was Robert Benton Seeley, who published a biographical study of Sadler's ideas in 1842. In this book, Seeley identified himself with the "paternalist" social outlook of his subject, which he described as a system designed "to foster, protect, cherish, encourage, promote: its chief means of operation, the presenting to human beings the motives of benevolence and *hope*."⁷⁸ Seeley advised the social elite of Britain to "deal paternally with your people, and they will repay your care. Feel for them; supply those wants which they cannot supply for themselves; guard them from the oppression of those who would 'make haste to be rich.'"⁷⁹

Sadlerian paternalism set its face particularly against Malthusian demographics. Malthus had argued that there were limits on agricultural production. The earth could not feed an endless number of people. Famine and disease were preventative checks designed to hold back the expansion of the population. Sadler and the premillennial paternalists rejected this idea by appealing to the goodness of the created order. Malthusian political economists, inveighed Sadler,

> would, had they it in their power, create, what they are perpetually raving about, "a vacuum!" GOD, however, has decided for a *plenum:* and the inspired voice of nature and reason, as well as of revelation, proclaims his command, "Multiply,—*replenish the earth; and subdue it:*" and the experience of thousands of years has taught the world, and ought to have instructed such, that this is the only certain road to national prosperity, as well as individual happiness.⁸⁰

Seeley took up this theme in his biography of Sadler:

> The whole tenor of that record [i.e., the Bible], is in favour of the Paternal system, and not a word about "surplus population," or of the imaginary horrors of a state in which people shall have outgrown surplus all possible supplies of food, can be found throughout its pages. It begins with a Divine command to the second father of the human race, "*Be fruitful, and multiply, and replenish the earth.*" (Gen ix. 2) And in every successive instance

---

77. "Life of M. T. Sadler," *CLM* 17 (Jan–Jun, 1842), 372.
78. Seeley, *Memoirs of . . . Michael Thomas Sadler*, 33.
79. Ibid., 621.
80. Seeley, *Memoirs of . . . Michael Thomas Sadler*, 75.

in which a blessing is conferred, *increase* seems to be the most prominent feature of benediction.[81]

This version of Evangelical paternalism was therefore premised on a highly optimistic reading of the created order. It spun its ideas for poor relief and material amelioration from a basic assumption that the natural world was created for abundant human flourishing, and that social justice was not, therefore, an abrogation of the natural laws of supply and demand, but the most authentic way to promote the universal enjoyment of the resources of the world. This foundational endorsement of the created order, all-pervasive in the Evangelical eschatology that I have introduced in this study, was the discursive link between Sadlerian paternalism and historicist premillennialism. It generated a conviction that God's central concern was not in testing individuals before dispatching them to heaven, but with the organic development of communities, living on earth, over the course of vast eons of time. Sadler believed

> it is in the order of Providence that human beings should succeed each other; that, like waves upon the shore, rolling up and breaking, and returning to the bosom of the deep, generation after generation should appear, flow up to their appointed bound, and sink again in the abyss of Eternity, in a regular and never-ceasing succession.[82]

The emphasis here on "increase, a vast and countless increase"[83] was the same theme that pervaded the premillennialist conception of historical and eschatological progress and breadth. Thomas Rawson Birks believed that it was inscribed into "the original constitution of man" that there should be "a continual multiplication" of humanity. God's promises in regard to the fertility of the human race, concluded Birks, "bear eternity stamped upon them."[84]

The premillennialist paternalist vision was rooted not, as Hilton argues, in a vision of a capricious, unpredictable deity, but rather in the central premillennial conviction that the primary site of divine concern was earthly, temporal, gradualist, communal, and holistic. In particular, these social reformers argued that Bible—and particularly the radical socioeconomic potential of the Old Testament—was applicable not only

81. Ibid, 167–68.
82. Sadler, *Law of Population*, 2:188.
83. Seeley, *Memoirs of . . . Michael Thomas Sadler*, 169.
84. Birks, *Outlines of Unfulfilled Prophecy*, 333, 350.

to issues of individual morality or even national endorsement of Protestant Christianity, but also, and most urgently, to questions of social justice. Examples of Christians turning to the Old Testament are often implied by historians to be indicative of an assumed pharisaical legalism. And yet, as was the case with Sadler (and, in our own lifetimes with initiatives such as the Jubilee 2000 anti-debt campaign) the Old Testament has a radical edge that can be mobilized for the purposes of socioeconomic critique. "The proof of their guilt," declaimed Robert Benton Seeley of Evangelicals who refused to use the Bible to critique the idolization of wealth, "is found in their systematic banishment of the word of God from their whole system of communital economy. . . . They agree to lay the Bible on the shelf, and to assert, that however necessary and supreme in its own department the concerns of God and the soul,—yet in mere sublunary matters, the management of nations &c., it is either wholly silent, or speaks without any Divine authority, or any claim to our respect."[85]

The Evangelical Social Vision of the Mid-Nineteenth Century

In what ways, then, did the premillennialist social gospel find concrete expression? In answering this question, it is necessary once again to disclaim an exact link between premillennialism and social action. Premillennialists did *not* think that they were "building" the millennium by their commitment to ameliorative social projects. Rather, they generally joined a broader coalition of Evangelicals and other Christians in projects that sought to amend the structural conditions of mid-century society. This coalition was itself a new development that manifested a shift in Evangelical social attitudes in these decades away from a focus on individual moral culpability for poverty and toward a more profound appreciation of the temporal-spatial sphere as a place of authentic Christian social concern. The attention shown by premillennialists to temporal-spatial structures represented in an eschatological key the growing attention being shown across mid-century Evangelicalism toward amelioration of the material structures that caused poverty. In one way, then, the shift I am about to outline can be seen as the broader shift of Evangelical attitudes toward the temporal-spatial sphere, of which the premillennial

---

85. Seeley, *Remedies Suggested*, 48, 51.

eschatology with which we have been concerned throughout this study was one prominent manifestation.

The neglect of mid-century Evangelical attitudes in general has already been noted. It should therefore come as little surprise that there has been very little study of changing social views of Evangelicals in these decades.[86] As Ian Shaw has argued: "The view that [nineteenth-century] Evangelicalism not only upheld the strictures of Hannah More and Wilberforce on social control and the need for the submission of the poor to their temporal condition, but also that it made little effort to ameliorate poverty needs reassessment."[87]

What was changing? In short, by the 1840s, while there was little abatement in the desire to improve the morality and spirituality of the nation, it was becoming increasingly accepted among Evangelicals that the causes of immorality and irreligion were rooted not only in the darkness of the individual's own soul but also in the depravity of the material and conditions in which she or he lived. This argument was put forward, for example, by Samuel Richard Bosanquet (1800–1882), a thinker whom Seeley quoted with approval in his *Remedies*. In his *Rights of the Poor* (1841), Bosanquet rejected as erroneous "the present disposition of writers upon charity . . . to depreciate the poor, to enumerate their crimes . . . to prove that they bring their own misfortune upon themselves by their vices."[88] Bosanquet pointed instead to the range of environmental factors that trapped people into a cycle of poverty and deprivation. A similar view was put forward by the *Christian Guardian* in 1842. Discussing the problem of the poor, it informed its readers that "it is not that they exhibit a nature more radically evil than our own, but that they are placed in circumstances which more strongly and evidently develop their corruptions, and bring out more abundantly and into stronger light before others, proofs that 'every imagination of the thoughts of man's heart is only evil continually.' . . . [A]las! ourselves infected, we go among the diseased and dying;—inmates of the same great hospital, but living in better wards."[89] Evangelicals increasingly contended that vice and

---

86. Holladay, 'Nineteenth-century Evangelical Activism," 54.

87. Shaw, *High Calvinists in Action*, 337.

88. Bosanquet, *Rights of the Poor*, 1.

89. "Our Poorer Classes," *The Christian Guardian and District Visitors' and Sunday School Teachers' Magazine* 2 (1842), 156.

profanity were greatly exacerbated, if not entirely created, by the material conditions in which many people lived.[90]

Evangelicals also began to reformulate their ideas about the *purpose* of poverty. If the sordidness of the environment promoted sin, hardened hearts, and incubated vice, then surely poverty was not a positive encouragement to spiritual reformation, as some older Evangelical thinkers had contended, but was rather a hellish sealing of the individual into a spiral of miserable degeneracy. Charlotte Elizabeth Tonna epitomized this new attitude, suggesting that the industrial mill was responsible for "murdering" the heroine of her novel *Helen Fleetwood* "and that will be declared at the judgment-seat, before all the angels of God, not only as to our Helen, but thousands and thousands more; and many a soul it has sealed up in sin, before casting the poor body into the grave."[91]

This notion that "many a soul is sealed up in sin" by the factory system implied that the environment in which people lived and worked was itself morally culpable. Evangelicals thus came to argue that not all poverty was caused, desired, or even used by God. Therefore, submission to the existing social order was not the only godly response to industrial society.[92] This was part of a broader realization that physical experience was bound to moral character, and that the soul and the body were an integrated whole. "In our pursuits, the moral and physical elements are closely, intricately, and inseparably, combined," claimed Shaftesbury.[93]

Poverty and suffering therefore began to be removed from any divine imprimatur. Historicist premillennialist John Cox stated that "it would be blasphemy to lay all the wretchedness around us at the door of sovereignty, or to say with reference to all the squalid wants and misery in our country, 'so providence ordains it.' Human legislation and political mistakes and crimes must take *their* share."[94] There was a corresponding move away from believing that individuals had sole responsibility for their material state. Robert Benton Seeley, for example, endorsed

---

90. One of the most significant proponents of this view was Charles Girdlestone (1797–1881) who took a leading role in persuading Evangelicals to become involved in sanitary reform, an attitude developed in part from the outbreak of cholera in his parish of Sedgley in 1832. See Girdlestone, *Seven Sermons* and Girdlestone, *Letters on the Unhealthy Condition*.

91. Elizabeth (Tonna), *Helen Fleetwood*, 393.

92. Gallagher, *Industrial Reformation of English Fiction*, 40–41.

93. Shaftesbury, *Speeches of . . . Shaftesbury*, 360.

94. J. Cox, *Claims of the Poor*, 10.

what he saw as the central proposition of Michael Sadler, that the poor were "'more sinned against than sinning,'" and that "though not faultless, [they] had been driven and drawn into fault by the mismanagement of their rulers."[95] Shaftesbury made a similar point in reference not so much to misrule, but to the sheer complexity of modern urban life. Referring to the traditional understanding of poverty as a consequence of individual sin, he declaimed: "Well, now, talk about its being their fault, indeed! Pray, is it their fault that they cannot improve the sewage of this great metropolis?"[96] The link between personal sin and suffering buckled under the weight of evaluating complex communal maladies such as the sanitation system of a major city. Evangelicals, among them several prominent historicist premillennialists, began to seek corporate responses to communal problems. Seeley thus argued that charity or piecemeal sentiment was inadequate. "More than mere sympathy or even alleviation is necessary. Something must be done to produce a permanent *amelioration*."[97] *Pace* Hilton, it was not a view of providence that prompted such appraisals of Evangelical social reform—it was a new alertness to the role of human agency in creating social disorder.

Thus it was that Evangelicals increasingly "put their faith in sewers and water"[98] and, indeed, in a range of other public health, education, workplace, and housing reforms in the 1840s. These new attitudes concerning poverty and the need for material reformation were not at first universally embraced among Evangelicals. Henry Drummond believed that "it is a charge brought with some justice against many of the Evangelical clergy,—that they have less sympathy for the temporal distress of the poor, than many of their clerical brethren who do not profess to be so much enlightened in spiritual truth."[99] Yet by 1850 there was a remarkable

---

95. Seeley, *Memoirs of . . . Michael Thomas Sadler*, 587.

96. *Labourer's Friend*, new ser., no. 86 (July 1851), 98–99. Norris Pope contends that by the middle of the nineteenth century Ashley was convinced that "the sty makes the pig". Pope, *Dickens and Charity*, 200.

97. Seeley, *Remedies Suggested*, 388. This phrase was repeated almost verbatim in the *CMR* in 1844, in an article criticizing district visitors who concentrated only on moral reform. The article said that district visiting "has reference to the mischiefs brought on the poor by *their own* misconduct. . . . But of the evils inflicted on the poor by *others*—this plan of relief says nothing." Review of *Report on . . . the Cottage Allotment System*, *CMR* 4 (1844), 63.

98. Hamlin, *Public Health and Social Justice*, 5.

99. Drummond, *Social Duties*, 152.

number of Evangelical-led, or Evangelical-influenced campaigns that took as their rationale the reform of the temporal-spatial sphere.

One organization that embodied some of these new trends was an off-shoot of the Christian Influence Society. The publication of *Perils of the Nation* triggered the formation of the Society for Improving the Condition of the Labouring Classes.[100] This Society was inaugurated in 1844, although it was in fact a re-foundation of the Labourer's Friend Association, which had been in existence since 1830. The original association had been established to encourage the granting of allotments to poor laborers for subsistence.[101] The association was re-founded in 1844 at the suggestion "of a number of influential gentlemen" and led by the omnipresent Ashley. The Society for Improving the Condition of the Labouring Classes gained support from several historicist premillennialists including Montagu Villiers, Emilius Bayley, Edward Auriol, Edward Bickersteth, William Pym, Robert Benton Seeley, and Hugh McNeile.[102] The threefold aim of the society was: first, to help laborers acquire portions of land (a goal inherited from the Labourer's Friend Association); second, to furnish the poor with loans; and third, to build model houses for families in London and provincial towns.[103]

The third objective became the central focus of the society's work in the later 1840s. "Model dwelling-houses" were constructed in some of London's poorest slum areas. This project was anchored by the belief that "the structure of a brother's dwelling cannot be disregarded with impunity, if on no other ground than the specific precept to that effect in the Law of God," a significant modern application of Old Testament concepts of justice that reflected the centrality of Old Testament prophecy in Evangelical eschatology in these decades.[104] The first purpose-built model dwelling house was erected in Bagnigge Wells in Thomas Dale's parish of

---

100. Elizabeth (Tonna), *Personal Recollections*, 375.

101. *Society for Improving . . . A Survey*, n.p.

102. Annual reports and other news of the society, including names of supporters and participants at meetings, can be found in *The Labourer's Friend Magazine* (1844–84.)

103. SICLC, "Thirteenth Annual Report," appended to *The Labourer's Friend Magazine*, June 1844, 4 [Page numbers refer to the bound editions held by the British Library; no volume numbers are provided]; *Society for Improving the Condition . . . A Survey*, 3–4..

104. SICLC, "Fifteenth Annual Report," appended to *The Labourer's Friend*, July 1859, 99.

St. Pancras in 1845,[105] with a further model house built in George Street, close to Montagu Villiers' church, St. George's, Bloomsbury (the home of the annual Prophecy Investigation Society lectures), during the following year.[106] This latter building, noted the society, combined

> every thing deemed essential or valuable in such an establishment—complete ventilation and drainage; an ample supply of water; separation and retirement in the sleeping apartments; with all those conveniences that, whilst conducing to the health and physical comfort of the inmates, tend to increase their self-respect, and elevate them in the scale of moral and intellectual beings.[107]

Such language was clearly indicative of the environmental concerns of the organization and reflected the growing conviction that the structural causes of poverty must be addressed if there was to be moral and spiritual improvement. As the annual report of 1859 concluded: "to attempt any material amendment of the character and habits of the poor, apart from some preliminary amelioration of their homes, is every whit as hopeless as the effort to purify the Thames without first intercepting in the sewers the normal source of its contamination."[108]

There is not space here to explore the full range of social ameliorative reforms dawning in this era that attracted Evangelical involvement. Interested readers should start with Norris Pope's work, although there is considerable scope for further research in this area. Pope identified this change of sentiment as the rise of "Evangelical environmentalism," but it might equally be called a commitment to the "reformation of space and time" because all of these new reforms focused in some way upon restructuring the temporal-spatial sphere and adjusting the material circumstances of urban Britain. These were "temporal" reforms in so far as they were concerned with ameliorating the temporal-spatial, physical environment, in contrast to what could be called the "moral" reforms of earlier Evangelicals, which attempted to prepare the believer for heaven,

---

105. SICLC, "Second Annual Report, appended to *The Labourer's Friend*, June 1846, 88.

106. Other houses were built or renovated in Portpool Lane, Hatton Garden, Charles Street, King Street and Drury Lane. SILC, *Plans for Dwelling Houses* n.d., passim.

107. Ibid.

108. SICLC, "Fifteenth Annual Report," appended to *The Labourer's Friend*, July 1859, 101.

not to improve her lot on earth. In this insistence on the authenticity of the temporal-spatial sphere as a place for Christian concern they echoed the eschatological themes that have pervaded this book.

This new social agenda may also be interpreted as the product of a new experiential sense of temporality that shaped the mindset of Victorian Britain. As I have already suggested, one reason for the greater attention toward the matrix of temporal, material, earthly structures, relationships, and experiences—whether in the eschatological or political realm—was the heightened awareness of "time" as a force that acted upon society and individuals. Dror Warhman has contended that "the realization of contemporaries that society around them was in irreversible flux made people more willing to endorse new, dynamic social views; that is to say, conceptualizations of society in which change and motion played an integral role."[109] We have seen that this was certainly the case within the eschatological realm where Evangelicals were imagining the future as essentially temporal—a realm in which time would continue to flow within a material universe. It seems also to have been shaping Evangelical social perspectives where older views of a static and even cyclical sphere were displaced with a new awareness of temporal contingency and mutability, making "reform" seem like a possibility and even a Christian obligation.

There is, in fact, a third "temporal" resonance of some of these "environmental" reforms, in that a subsection of these new initiatives explicitly attempted to reform the structures of *public time*. Such reforms were thus triply "temporal." First, they were concerned with the improvement of earthly "temporal" life; second, they sprang from an increased alertness to time itself and thus were part of a response to society that accepted the possibility of reform and change; and third, of all the social reforms of this era, their objective was most explicitly the reform of that element of "time" most narrowly defined—the counting of hours and the organization of days and weeks. As I cannot expound on all of the social reform activity of this era, it seems most fruitful to provide a brief introduction to two of these triply-temporal movements—the ten hours and early closing movements—and to suggest the ways in which they linked to the broader re-envisioning of time and eternity discussed throughout this book. These closing remarks are intended to be suggestive, rather

---

109. Wahrman, *Imagining the Middle Class*, 234. Douglas Holladay has similarly pointed to the triumph of the ideal of reform in this period that replaced more static conceptions of society. Holladay, "Nineteenth-Century Evangelical Activism," 53.

than conclusive, and to stimulate further research in the area of mid-century Christian social engagement.

The Ten Hours Movement

The ten hours movement drew some of its most prominent Evangelical support from the historicist premillennialists of the Christian Influence Society and the *CMR*. Supporters included Charlotte Elizabeth Tonna, whose novel *Mary Fleetwood* (1841) was a damning indictment of the factory system. The movement aimed throughout the 1830s and 1840s to reduce the number of working hours for women and children in factories. This objective was achieved with the passing of the 1847 Factory Act. Ashley, who led the campaign in Parliament after the death of its first champion, Michael Sadler, in 1835, stressed the need to reform the structures of public time in order to uphold the natural order of human beings created to live in relationship with God and neighbor. "We ask but a slight relaxation of toil," claimed Ashley in the House of Commons, "a time for those comforts that sweeten life, and a time for those duties that adorn it."[110]

The details of the ten hours movement have been told elsewhere, and I will not repeat them here in detail.[111] However, two points are worthy of note. First, the ten hours campaign is notable as the movement that first signaled a shift of Evangelical social attitudes. Indeed, Michael Sadler, the leading voice in factory reform until his death in 1835, offered a sharp critique of Hanoverian Evangelicalism in relation to its social responsibilities. He accused the Evangelical world of ignoring the plight of domestic wage-slaves while directing energy to ending African slavery in remote locations. Versifying the tale of the death of an overworked factory girl, Sadler imagined that the child was visited by the Evangelical daughters of the mill owner as she took her last breath. "Their tender hearts were sighing / As negro wrongs were told, / While the white slave lay dying / Who gained their father's gold!"[112] Sadler exemplified the

---

110. 123 Parl. Deb. (3rd ser.) (1844), 1101.

111. The classic treatment is Ward, *Factory Movement*. This has been supplemented by Gray, *Factory Question*. Both works were alert to the role of Evangelicalism within the factory reform movements, but their concern is with the factory movement as a whole, rather than with tracing the significance of Evangelical involvement for the history of Evangelicalism itself.

112. Sadler, "Factory Girl's Last Day," in Seeley, *Memoirs of . . . Michael Thomas*

broad changes within Evangelicalism in this era. He articulated a reforming program that focused upon the health and material well-being of the domestic poor. Ashley demonstrated a similar awareness that he was diverting from existing Evangelical social attitudes when he complained in 1841 that he had received little support from clergy for the ten hours campaign. "As a body, or even numerously though singly, they have done, are doing, and will do, nothing. And this through my whole career." The ten hours movement was at the interface between the old Evangelicalism and the new. Ashley clearly felt the tension. Interestingly he reserved a notable exception to his despair for premillennialist Edward Bickersteth, whom he called "a jewel of the first water."[113] Of course, Ashley was exaggerating somewhat. There *were* other Evangelicals supporting him. Alongside those already mentioned, Ashley clearly had his supporters. Premillennialist William Marsh for one wished that "some expression of respect for Lord Ashley's noble, humane, and Christian conduct could be given."[114] Nevertheless, the sense of struggle against inherited ideas articulated by both Sadler and Ashley suggests that the 1830s were a liminal decade for an Evangelical movement faced with the tension between a new social engagement and older ideas about political economy and its relationship with individualist conceptions of salvation.

By the mid-1840s, however, the attitudes pioneered within the ten hours movement were gaining wider purchase. Even hardened *laissez-faire* individualists began to bend to the spirit of the times. The ten hours campaigner Richard Oastler (1789–1861), who is sometimes styled as an "Evangelical" although it seems he was probably a low-church Protestant, claimed to have "converted" Thomas Chalmers to the cause of the ten hours movement in 1846. In a conversation over breakfast, Oastler told Chalmers that *laissez-faire* individualism was a product of human selfish pride, and that Christianity must support legislation that tempered such sinful greed and exploitation. Chalmers, who had initially repeated his commitment to free trade, at the end of the conversation announced: "I am a Christian. Free trade must yield to Christianity. I will give my support to the Ten Hours Bill although its principle is opposed to that of free trade."[115]

Sadler, 405.
    113. Hodder, *Life of . . . Shaftesbury*, 1:325.
    114. C. Marsh, *Life of William Marsh*, 259.
    115. Kydd, *History of the Factory Movement*, 2:250; Driver, *Richard Oastler*, 468–69.

This conversation was only recorded by Oastler, a man with a penchant for self-publicity, so its accuracy may be in doubt. It is, though, true that Chalmers endorsed the Ten Hours Bill in 1846. However, it was probably not Oastler alone who triggered the move over breakfast one morning. In fact, Oastler's dialogue captured the more complex reality that was more likely responsible for the shift in Chalmers' views in the 1840s.[116] Oastler pointed out that Chalmers had always possessed a vision for a "godly commonwealth," and that Oastler's vision for the regulation of relations between employer and worker was no different to Chalmers' vision for a well-ordered, Christian society.[117] He reminded Chalmers that modern economics valued selfish individualism, an attitude antithetical to Chalmers' concept of God. He thus hoisted Chalmers on his own civic-Calvinist petard, and asked him to understand that free trade individualism undermined the very corporate, organic, social order that Chalmers had sought to build through his experiments in Glasgow and West Port. Oastler was thus one conservative Christian talking to another, seeking to point out the inconsistencies within what was basically a shared, biblically-grounded commitment to the preservation (or creation) of a Christian society. Chalmers seemed to be listening.

Chalmers' reaction to the Irish famine in 1846 showed a similar development in his thought. He rejected the arguments of those who contended that famine relief was unnecessary because it would only encourage the vices of those who had brought misery upon themselves. While not wishing to stop private charity, he also demanded greater government aid for the victims. In May 1847 he went even further, calling for a "massive redistribution of national wealth" and offering a critique of the deification of unlimited industrial expansion.[118] In the last year of his life, Chalmers, the doyen of *laissez-faire* political economy, seemed to have absorbed the kind of critique Robert Benton Seeley had been articulating in the early 1840s.

There is a pleasing neatness to Chalmers' near-death-bed changes of heart. The man who had early embraced eschatological materialism in the 1820s, and had become increasingly enamored of premillennialist

---

116. S. J. Brown, *Thomas Chalmers*, 350–51.

117. Brown suggests that "with the collapse of his territorial church and community-building campaign, he began to acknowledge that the State was perhaps the only available regulator of social relations with sufficient power to preserve the weak from the strong." Ibid., 367.

118. Ibid. 368.

eschatology in the 1830s, was now displaying hairline cracks in his hitherto impregnable walls of *laissez-faire* political economy. His conversion to the updated Evangelicalism was, by 1847, complete. Of course, he did not miraculously turn into an advocate for the modern welfare state on the eve of his death, and the fact that he could maintain an eschatological materialism in tandem with his *laissez-faire* economics problematizes any exact or overly-schematized relationship between eschatology and social reform. Nevertheless, Chalmers exemplified the evolutionary nature of Evangelicalism in both its eschatological and social registers, a mutability missed by Hilton and others in a portrayal of an Evangelical action locked into static ideological schools of thought.

The second significant point to note about the ten hours movement is that, alongside with the early closing movement, it expressed a heightened time consciousness caused by the massive changes in industry and technology that were sweeping British society. In this way, these movements were products of the same apprehension of the pulse of time that gave rise to the prophetic sensibility of the era. The image that came to dominate the symbolic consciousness of the ten hours reformers, for example, was the little child who constantly awoke through the night and asked, with significant apocalyptic resonance, "Father, is it time?"[119] New machinery, much of it tested on children (the spinning Jenny was designed to suit the sitting posture of a child between nine and twelve)[120] had a disproportionate impact in this respect. The attempt at gaining maximum benefit from new machines created a greater awareness of time's intrusive beat and produced a sense of speed created by quickly and invariably moving metal constructions—loud, hot, fast, and dangerous; the ticking clock, the ringing bell. In Evangelical novelist Charlotte Elizabeth Tonna's *Helen Fleetwood*, Mary Fleetwood is stunned by her first experience of the factory:

> Move, move, everything moves. The wheels and the frames are always going, and the little reels twirl round as fast as ever they can; and the pulleys and chains, and great iron works over-head, are all moving; and the cotton moves so fast that it is hard to piece it quick enough; and there is a great dust, and such a noise of whirr, whirr, whirr, that at first I did not know whether I was not standing on my head.[121]

119. "The Factory Child," *Poor Man's Advocate*, 7 (1832), 54.
120. *Parl. Papers*, H.C. 1831–32(706): xv, 279, 373.
121. Elizabeth (Tonna), *Helen Fleetwood*, 110–11.

If such experiences were limited to the roughly 30 percent of people affected by mass industrialization in the cotton-producing regions, they were nevertheless disseminated much more widely and led to a set of symbols, signs, and concepts with which Evangelicals such as Charlotte Elizabeth Tonna could engage. Dror Wahrman argues that "the importance of the machine lay in its emergence as the symbol of the abruptness of current social processes entailed by industrialization and of their potential disruptive consequences. It thus came to stand for an overall uneasiness about the irreversible disjuncture effected by social change."[122]

In fact, one mechanism, the clock, was the regulator of all others, and came to stand as an icon of the factory system.[123] An illustration in *Figaro in London* in 1832, for example, depicted children being thrown to the "Factory Monster," an open-jawed beast in the shape of a clock.[124] Sitting in Parliament during the debate on his factory bill, Michael Sadler took up the theme of the young time-haunted girl and penned a poem called "The Factory Girl's Last Day," which was commonly reproduced in the ten hour literature. The poem was, it was claimed, "founded entirely on a fact given in evidence before the Committee of which he was chairman":[125] It narrates the insistent ringing of the factory bell and the repeated cry of father and foreman:"'Tis time!" The last stanza concludes:

> Again the factory's ringing
> Her last perceptions tried;
> When, from her straw-bed springing,
> "Tis time!" she shrieked, and died![126]

It is true that there were other forces at work shaping the factory reform movement, including political antipathy toward the new economic liberalism, Anglican antipathy toward Nonconformist factory owners, gender politics, and even the popular "class" conscious protest against new working methods identified by E. P. Thompson.[127] It was by no means even a majority Evangelical campaign. But it was a straw in the wind for changing Christian attempts at restructuring social relation-

---

122. Wahrman, *Imagining the Middle Class*, 229.
123. Voth, *Time and Work in England*, 49–50.
124. *Figaro in London*, no. 71, April 18, 1833, 1.
125. Seeley, *Memoirs of . . . Michael Thomas Sadler*, 403.
126. Ibid., 405.
127. E. P. Thompson, "Time, Work-Discipline & Industrial Capitalism."

ships and it was produced by the same sense of temporal momentousness that infused the prophetic movements of the era. As was the case with eschatology, Evangelicals responded to this new sense of time by imagining the reform of time, a move that led them to propose temporal reform in all senses of that term.

The Early Closing Movement

The early closing movement has received less scholarly attention than the ten hours movement. However, whereas relatively few Evangelicals participated in the ten hours campaigns, the early closing movement drew much greater support. If Ashley could somewhat legitimately complain of an absence of support from Christian ministers for his ten hours campaigns in the late 1830s, this situation had changed considerably by the late 1840s in relation to early closing. Supporters of the movement included Henry Montagu Villiers, John Cumming, Francis Close, Hugh McNeile, Hugh Stowell, Henry Hughes (1808?–52), the perpetual curate of All Saints, Gordon Square; Robert William Dibdin (1805–87), the "extremely low church" Evangelical minister of West Street Chapel, St. Giles-in-the-Fields, Thomas Dale (1797–1870), the Evangelical rector of St. Brides, Fleet Street and later vicar of St. Pancras, Richard Burgess (1796–1881), an Evangelical prebendary of St. Paul's Cathedral, Baptist Wriothesley Noel (1799–1873), the brother of Gerard Noel, and minister of John Street Baptist Chapel, Thomas Nolan (1809–82), minister of St. John's Chapel, Bedford Row; James Begg (1808–83), minister of the Free Church of Scotland in Newington, Edinburgh, Thomas Binney, William Weldon Champneys (1807–75), the pioneering "slum clergyman" of St. Mary's Whitechapel,[128] and, perhaps unsurprisingly, Ashley. Other significant supporters included F. D. Maurice,[129] the strict Baptist, Sir John Thwaites (1815–70), and Sir George Williams (1821–1905), the founder of the YMCA. The Brighton clergyman, Frederick Williamson Robertson (1816–53), was also a supporter. These individuals comprised a mixed bag of Evangelicals and non-Evangelicals, premillennialists and non-millennialists. Unlike the Christian Influence Society, the Early Closing Association was not so obviously linked to a particular vision of

---

128. Hylson-Smith, *Evangelicals in the Church of England*, 152.

129. 10th Annual Financial Statement, to June 1853, appended to *The Ninth Annual Report of the ECA* (1854), 9.

premillennial paternalism. Nevertheless, as the list makes clear, there was plenty of support from premillennialist clergy.

The early closing movement epitomized the drift of Evangelical Christian thought toward a holistic vision for societal change. Its rhetoric was oriented toward a Christian social ethic. It aimed for the promotion of harmony between employer and employed under the banner of a common humanity. The arguments of Edwin Price, a clergyman from Sheerness, were characteristic of the movement's often quite radical tone: "Overwork is a sin against the nature of man . . . and this overwork is also a sin against the Gospel of the Son of God . . . because that system of mercy consults all possible interests of our humanity, corporeal as much as spiritual—for time, as well as for eternity."[130] The movement for shorter hours coalesced around the Early Closing Association (founded 1846) and the Saturday Half-Day Holiday Association (founded 1856). The campaigns drew together a range of religious and social reformers in what was, once again, a campaign for temporal restructuring.

The attempt to abridge the hours of labor for certain sections of the working population was initiated in 1835 by John Lilwall and Samuel Carter Hall (1800–1889). The campaign was low-key, and for several years Lilwall and Hall labored almost alone and unnoticed, holding meetings such as the one later recalled by Hall that took place in a smoke-filled room in Whitechapel, "a miserable hole under a railway, the roll of trains over which necessitated frequent pauses in the proceedings."[131] In 1838 the Metropolitan Drapers Association (MDA) was formed. In 1842 its rules stated that its aim was "to obtain an abridgement of the hours of business in the drapery and other trades of the metropolis, with a view to the physical, moral, and intellectual improvement of the assistants."[132] As its name suggested, its primary concern was the women and girls who worked as dressmakers and milliners' assistants. This gave the campaign a significant gendered and socioeconomic dimension, since its main appeal was to request the women of the leisured classes to desist from placing heavy burdens upon their servants.

Despite the name, the MDA was eager to emphasize that their work was limited neither to drapers, nor to the London metropolis. It was reported that there were similar organizations in Liverpool, Manchester,

---

130. Martin, *Serpents in Hedges*, 32.
131. S. C. Hall, *Retrospect of a Long Life*, 436.
132. Metropolitan Drapers' Association, *Late-Hour System*, 4.

Edinburgh, Glasgow, Bristol, Cheltenham, Leeds, Coventry, Birmingham, Bedford, Newcastle, Nottingham, and Wolverhampton. Indeed, to reflect the broad appeal of the organization, in 1846 the name was changed to the Early Closing Association (ECA). The full story of the ECA from inception to its demise in 1961 awaits its historian and is beyond the scope of this chapter; suffice it to say that its actual achievements were piecemeal.[133]

The early closing movement in its opening stages owed much to the ten hour initiatives. Ashley noted that "I cannot dispossess my mind of the conviction that these Societies had their origin in that mighty movement first undertaken by my excellent friend, Michael Thomas Sadler."[134] Indeed, like Sadler, the movement took side-swipes at those who opposed international slavery but who did not wish to take any action toward social reform in Britain. John Cumming observed that "slavery is slavery still, disguise it as you like: if there are degrees in our sympathies, I contend that our strongest sympathy should be concentrated at home; and, when freedom has been achieved at home, then we may, with increased energy and multiplied hopes of victory, extend it to the utmost parts of the earth."[135] This argument echoed Sadler's earlier critique of Evangelical insouciance to domestic social issues.

Also, as in the ten hours movement, those involved in the early closing movement felt acutely the existential press of time. Francis Close observed:

> The fact is that we are all over-worked—we all want to go on at railroad speed.... Half the maladies we meet with, the sudden deaths—the insanity, arise from this cause—we live too fast, and want to gain too much, and do more than God has given us power and ability to do.[136]

Unlike the ten hours movement the early closing advocates at first preferred to lobby employers directly rather than seeking legislative action.[137]

---

133. For a brief overview of early closing legislation until the 1950s, see Rottenberg, "Legislated Early Shop Closing"; Whitaker, *Victorian and Edwardian Shop Workers*, 36–63.

134. Metropolitan Drapers' Association *Verbatim Report of the Fourth Annual Meeting*, 1.

135. Metropolitan Drapers' Association, *Report of the Second Annual Meeting*, 22.

136. *Late Hours of Business, Report of a Public Meeting*, 9.

137. Metropolitan Drapers' Association *Report of the Second Annual Meeting of the MDA* (1844), 7.

The tone of the meetings was therefore conciliatory. The leadership of the movement asked for sympathy with the plight of employers who were forced by pressures of the market to keep their businesses open beyond dusk. "The evil lies in the system," said Archibald Boyd (1803–83), perpetual curate of Christ Church, Gloucester, "I do not blame the masters, they are hurried on against their will, and compelled to keep pace with their neighbors, or retire into insignificance and poverty."[138] William Leask delivered a speech in which he urged reconciliation between employers and employees by appealing to their unity of interest in abridging the number of hours worked.[139] This acknowledgment of the complex *system* in which even the "oppressors" were forced to act against their will showed an increasing sophistication to Evangelical social analysis.

The challenge of the Early Closing Association was directed toward consumers: reduce the demand for goods, they argued, and employers would no longer have to keep their businesses open. This was a type of abstinence argument; indeed, several prominent temperance campaigners were present in the leadership of the Early Closing Association. "Women's Early Shopping Leagues" were formed to encourage female temperance in shopping.[140]

The early closing movement also had considerable connections with the Sunday observance movement. During the 1840s Evangelicals were increasingly arguing that Sabbath observance was not so much a religious obligation premised on the Fourth Commandment, but rather the gift of God to an overworked industrial society.[141] As William Bennett, curate of Holy Trinity and St. Mary, Guildford, concluded in 1852, "the observance of the Sabbath brings a blessing on the *body*, and a blessing for *this world*."[142] By the 1850s, Evangelicals had rebranded Sunday as God's weekly protest in support of the rights of labor. It was less the Lord's Day and more "the people's day," as the title of a popular work advocating for Sunday rest by Irish Methodist William Arthur (1819–1901) put it.[143] A short-lived journal, the *Working Man's Charter*—the charter

138. *Late Hours of Business, Report of a Public Meeting*, 11.
139. Leask, *Identity of Interests*.
140. Rottenberg, "Legislated Early Shop Closing," 121.
141. G. M. Ellis called this movement "social Sabbatarianism." Ellis, "Evangelicals and the Sunday Question."
142. Bennett, *Christian Sabbath*, 19.
143. The term was, of course, an unashamed allusion to Chartist rhetoric and a reference to the name given to the Crystal Palace (criticized by Sabbatarians for opening

in question being not the six points of the Chartists, but the freedom from tiresome labor offered by the Sabbath—combined its advocacy of Sunday closing with strong criticism of the avarice and greed of those who overworked their employees.[144] Meanwhile, numerous prize essay competitions sponsored by leading Evangelicals invited working men to write essays about what the Sabbath meant to them.[145]

Evangelical "Sabbatarianism" was therefore increasingly also becoming a "shorter hours" movement. However, even if its proponents chose to base their arguments on the benefits Sunday provided to the worker rather than moralizing about the need for workers to obey divine law, the notion of Sunday rest still had obvious scriptural resonance. The early closing movement, by contrast, did not possess even potential scriptural warrant. Where was the Bible verse that prescribed the time a business should close? The claims of the early closing movement therefore had to be constructed upon a more wide-ranging appeal to principles of Christian social justice. This helped generate a broader rationale for social action than might otherwise have existed. Thomas Nolan, for example, explained that it was essential to the very vocation of ministers of the Gospel to show solidarity with the oppressed and to enact social reforms that honored the justice of God:

> As a minister of the Gospel, next to the duties of the sanctuary, I believe it my duty to be where I can unloose the heavy burdens and let the oppressed go free. However great our duty is to expound the great truths of the Gospel, to stand between the oppressed and the oppressor; and though every other class in society were to forget what is due to the sufferer, it is ours to suffer with them rather than to forget them.[146]

This was a considerable update to Evangelical social policy, and it is particularly significant that it came from the mouth of a premillennialist. It would not have been out of place within the "Social Gospel" movement of the late Victorian era. This broadening of the meaning of Christian witness was also evident in the thought of James Begg, the Free Church of Scotland minister who married a robust defense of Presbyterian

on a Sunday), "The People's Palace." W. Arthur, *People's Day*.

144. *Working Man's Charter* (1848–49).

145. For a further discussion of the literature of this mid-century Sabbatarian movement—which tended to be highly romantic in its conception of how Sunday linked time and eternity—see Spence, "Writing the Sabbath."

146. *Proceedings . . . Salford Drapers' Association*, 24.

Calvinism (including a dose of anti-Catholicism that often got him labeled as a sectarian reactionary) with a strong sense of social justice centered on urban regeneration. He argued that social reform was integral to Christian witness. "We shall deal with the plea [for early closing] as an article of religion—a demand substantiated on the highest and holiest sanctions of the relations between man and man, and between man and his Maker."[147] He also criticized Evangelicals for giving too much attention to doctrinal purity to the neglect of Christian social action:

> There has been too much ignoring of the relative duties of our common Christianity; more jealousy among professing Christians for sound doctrine than for the social charities—in other words, more conventional adherence to the letter of the gospel than to the practical expansion of its loving, generous spirit, to the pulling down every stronghold of social prejudice, oppression, and illusion on the part of a neglected brotherhood.[148]

There was a clear broadening of gospel priorities here, rooted ultimately in the kind of conviction expressed by James Belford, the secretary to the Glasgow Milliners and Dress-makers Association and leader of the Saturday half-day holiday campaign, that "the gospel befriends the body as well as the soul."[149] Significantly, Belford rooted his demand for early closing in an eschatological vision. Citing the book of Zechariah, he observed that the eschatological future was social, holistic, and verdant:

> What a bright contrast does such a living, loving scene present to the ordinary aspect of the hurry to and fro, the crush and the crash, the cries and the curses, the prowling felons and reeling drunkards, the premature old age and precious childhood, of our great cities at the present day! . . . Zechariah contemplates the eventual establishment of the Redeemer's kingdom; beholds the ultimate realization of the symbol of Jerusalem in the view of a city brought under the influence of a triumphant Christianity. There, instead of the pallid cheek of disease, the premature decay and untimely death, anticipating in the prime years of manhood the natural destiny of age, he presents the touching picture of venerable patriarchs, and "mothers in Israel," in either sex, of longevity, cheerfully parading the public thoroughfares.

---

147. Belford, *Saturday Half-Holiday*, 1.
148. Ibid.
149. Ibid., 13.

This eschatological vision, claimed Belford, was "a teaching satire upon opposite facts" as they existed in the current age. Therefore alleviation of any characteristic that was contrary to the vision of the prophet was a Christian duty.

> If this social happiness is to form a leading feature in the most perfect and final dispensation of Christianity, any mitigation of an exactly opposite economy, and any degree of approximation to the better condition, is being in that proportion so much truer to the spirit of Christianity.

Eschatological vision, thought Belford, should be used to clarify a current program of "social regeneration."[150]

William Leask also used a millennial vision to clarify a vision of social and spiritual renewal in the present. Rich in romantic themes about the interpenetration of time and eternity, pervaded with the expectation of the return of the King Jesus, alert to the restless beat of historical time, and alive to the implications of prophecy for the temporal order, Leask's vision in many ways sums up the themes of this chapter, and indeed of the whole book. Having noted the injustices of history, Leask pondered:

> Alas! we cry in agony of spirit, is the future to be like the past? Shall succeeding historians have only to add to the frightful memorials left by their predecessors? Shall "the ages to come" resemble those that are gone? And shall our children's children plod on, groaning and foot-sore, the same dread path to eternity which our ancestors trod? No! for we look at the glorious book of PROPHECY, and a joyous change plays over our countenance; we gaze and wonder, whilst our hearts bound with the liveliest emotions, for it is a book of love and light, and as we hold converse with it, our faces shine like that of Moses. Its promises pour their glories on the coming age. Its hallowed light fills the whole field of vision, as far as the eye of strongest faith can sweep, and sheds indescribable beauty on the lot of nations yet unborn. Its voice bids the desert blossom and the wilderness rejoice, and the hills clap hands, and the valleys shout. It commands the lame to leap, and the blind to see, and the dumb to sing. It cries to the iron gate, which opens of its own accord, and the oppressed to go free. It says to the prisoners, Go forth, and to them that sit in darkness, shew yourselves. It is the poetry of the skies brought down to earth, and translated into human language that we might understand. It will continue to sing its

---

150. Ibid., 16

song of love in many an ear, until the morning of its brilliant purposes shall burst upon the gladdened earth. And its mighty power will overturn every obstacle, until the moral desert shall reveal a high way for the righteous King of men.[151]

Here was the destiny of history. The entire universe was in progress toward the liberation of humankind. And this, said Leask, is why Christian social action, such as the demand for shorter working hours, is "no utopian theory"[152] but an echo of God's universal demand for, and promise of, justice:

> Every thing pleads for man! We join the universal intercession, and plead for man! Patriot, philanthropist, Christian, minister of the gospel, we charge you to aid us, in this plea for men, that many thousand of the most interesting class of men in the most enlightened nation in the world, may be liberated from unnecessary bondage, educated, guided, enlightened, purified, SAVED![153]

For Leask, as for many other individuals who have been introduced in this book, salvation was being increasingly understood as freedom, renewal, and restitution. It was not an escape from the world so much as the world in its most authentic state. It was a plea that God's kingdom come, on earth as it is in heaven.

Conclusion

Surveying the annual Prophecy Investigation Society lecture series at St. George's, Bloomsbury, historian Stephen Orchard concluded that "in one corner of Bloomsbury the Evangelical clergy preached adventism as the only remedy for the social and national evils against which they fought. In another corner of Bloomsbury Karl Marx proposed a secular remedy, and dismissed religion as the opiate of the people."[154] It is true that socialists and premillennialists would not have recognized their shared concern for the liberation of the oppressed. Indeed, Ashley failed to recognize his allegiance even with the less radical F. D. Maurice and the Christian Socialists, a fact that perplexed fellow premillennialist John

---

151. Leask, *Identity of Interests*, 14.
152. Ibid., 4.
153. Ibid., 15
154. Orchard, "Evangelical Eschatology," 160.

McLeod Campbell. "I lately met the benevolent and practical Lord Ashley," wrote McLeod Campbell to his sister in 1845,

> and felt the light in which he sees his fellow-labourers, Mr. Maurice and Mr. Kingsley (for such, I believe, they are in purpose, and I trust also may prove to be in effect), very instructive as to our mutual ignorance of each other. He marveled to hear me mention Mr. Maurice as a man of catholic spirit; and, in the attempt to realize a Christian Socialism, he could see nothing but Democracy.[155]

As Campbell's bewilderment signifies, despite clear divergences of tone, temperament, vocabulary, and ideology, the radical social reformers and the Evangelicals of the day were actually both products of the same social-cultural forces. I do not wish to minimize their real differences, but it is also sometimes the task of the historian to observe these similarities, which were obscure to contemporaries. As C. S. Lewis noted: "Nothing strikes me more when I read the controversies of past ages than the fact that both sides . . . thought that they were as completely opposed as two sides could be, but in fact they were all the time secretly united—united with each other and against earlier and later ages—by a great mass of common assumptions."[156]

Mid-century Evangelicalism articulated a growing critique of liberal capitalism, and paid increasing attention to the reformation of the environmental structures of industrializing British society, including those issues that related to the use and abuse of time. Historicist premillennialism was on the cutting-edge of such developments because of the movement's wide-ranging revisionism concerning the relationship between God and the temporal-spatial sphere. By the 1850s, a broad coalition of socially-astute reformers had significantly re-fashioned the way in which Christians construed their task in relation to embodying the gospel within the social order. Premillennialism did not cause this re-appraisal so much as it exemplified and amplified it. The eschatology and social paternalism of specific historicist premillennialists was a powerful manifestation of a more general underlying re-assessment of the earthly, temporal sphere.

Evangelicals, alongside other Christians, were searching for a conceptual and practical integration of time and eternity that could made

---

155. Campbell, *Memoirs of John McLeod Campbell*, 1:226–7.
156. C. S. Lewis, "Introduction," 5.

sense of, and help to control, the bewildering social and economic changes that swept over British society in the mid-Victorian era. This pulled many individuals into increasingly holistic social reform projects that were concerned with the reform of time and space.

Historicist premillennialists joined this project not out of a precise desire to implement a millennial project, but rather because their entire social and theological worldview had been colored by their cultural milieu. In both its eschatological and its social register, historicist premillennialism was an important expression of the broader mid-century Evangelical rapprochement with temporality and physicality. While by the 1850s many types of Evangelical had updated their ideas about poverty and social reform, it is not coincidence that those individuals who had moved early to eschatological materialism were also some of the pioneers of a more comprehensive social agenda. Historicist premillennialism was one of the earliest indicators of the new direction of Victorian Christian attitudes toward understanding the environmental causes and remedies of injustice. It announced the characteristic late Victorian belief that the Christian gospel must find concrete expression in mundane social institutions and civic relationships.

7

The Afterlife of Mid-Nineteenth-Century Evangelical Eschatology

THE SUN STREAMED ONTO the lawn of the Church of England rectory in Beddington, Surrey, warming the three hundred guests, "both poor and rich," who had gathered on 20 July, 1864 for the annual birthday tea of William Marsh. Marsh, who was celebrating his eighty-ninth year, sat in his wheelchair and received the guests. After pleasantries, a new-fangled harmonium whirred into action, and the assembled throng sung "Lord, I Hear Showers of Blessing," a contemporary hymn written by Elizabeth Conder. Marsh addressed the crowd with an exhortatory sermon. Shaftesbury, Edward Auriol, and Charles Goodhart paid tribute to him. Marsh died five weeks later.[1]

Marsh was a generous and irenic figure. Through his rectory doors had passed the great and the good of the mid-century Evangelical world—Shaftesbury, Edward Irving, Gerard Noel, Edward Bickersteth, Charles Goodhart, Hugh McNeile, Thomas Nolan, Henry Drummond, Edward Auriol—for conference and fellowship. Many of these individuals shared with Marsh the mid-century Evangelical commitment to historicist premillennialist eschatology. Marsh had been in the vanguard of the Evangelical move toward the earthly vision of the future hope in the late 1810s. He articulated the characteristic desire for a renewal of Christian practice rooted in "primitive simplicity" in the 1820s. He became part of the Albury conferences in 1826. He then broke from Albury over its sectarianism and added his voice to the swelling establishment premillennialism of the 1830s. He helped to expand the corpus of premillennialist texts with his popular *Plain Thoughts on Prophecy* in 1840. He joined

---

1. C. Marsh, *Life of William Marsh*, 538–47.

the Prophetical Investigation Society and contributed to the St. George's Bloomsbury Lectures during the 1840s and 1850s. He gave his support to Shaftesbury's social reforms during those same decades. Throughout his life, he regularly drew people together for informal discussions of prophecy. He was the very model of a modern premillennial gentleman.

Just nine months prior to this birthday celebration, in November 1863, Marsh had convened a large conference at Beddington Park. The conference was in many ways typical of the fraternally spirited prophetic dialogue that had characterized the movement for thirty years. Yet there were also winds of spiritual and theological change blowing when the delegates gathered on a rainy November day. In the invitational material, Marsh had "made a request . . . that prayer might be offered that all who should meet on that occasion might receive 'an unction from the Holy One;'" and "that the presence of God the Holy Ghost, the Teacher, Sanctifier, and Comforter, might be felt and known amongst them."[2] His prayers were apparently answered. "Many wrote word afterwards that . . . they had never before felt so conscious of the presence of the Lord Jesus as during those meetings."[3] Marcus Rainford, who later became rector of Belgrave Chapel, Pimlico, wrote to Marsh to say that he had experienced an intense spiritual encounter. "I can truly say I had a fresh and full baptism of the Holy Spirit at your conference."[4] This focus on a desire for a personal experience of the Holy Spirit was becoming increasingly intertwined with the premillennial movement. In time, it would change the temperament of eschatological speculation, and of Evangelicalism as a whole. Its rise both signaled and precipitated the end of the historicist premillennialist project examined in this book.

The premillennialist emphasis on the Holy Spirit was not, of course, completely new. It sprang from the very convictions concerning the interpenetration of time and eternity which had undergirded the movement since the early nineteenth century. Premillennialism had emerged in the 1820s as part of a broader Evangelical emphasis on the need to rely upon the guidance and provision of the Holy Spirit; it drifted toward novel statements about the sinlessness of Christ that were rooted in the idea that the Spirit preserved his normal human flesh from sin; and it produced the kind of lyrical aspiration for glimpses of heaven on earth

2. Ibid., 506.
3. Ibid.
4. Ibid., 507.

that were discussed in chapter 5. All of these were the result of the premillennial movement's romantic hue and were the soil from which later-nineteenth century developments in Evangelical pneumatology grew.

Nevertheless, this growing emphasis on "full baptism in the Holy Ghost," with its deep desire for regular experiences of sanctifying power, was not a central theme of most of the Evangelicals discussed in this book. Most premillennialists were too convinced of the importance of Word and Sacrament as authorized by the national churches to endorse such heady individualism. While I argued in chapter 5 that there was certainly a hope that the individual might enjoy the blessings of eternity within the boundaries of time, the claim was generally made in relation to the broader Christian experience of eternal life made possible through the incarnation of Christ, rather than a hope for particular fresh infusions of divine unction through the direct and repeated visitation of the Holy Ghost. Only a handful of premillennialists, such as Edward Irving, moved toward endorsing personal charismatic experience as normative. When the Spirit was invoked in the mid-century movement, he was generally linked to corporate renewal—to the conversion of the Jews and to the restitution of all things—not to individual consolation.

From the 1860s, however, a personal doctrine of the Holy Spirit was moving center stage in the piety of the British Evangelical movement. There was an increasing sense of creating the right atmosphere, habits of mind, practices, and postures of anticipation, in order to encourage the Spirit to descend. Harmonium-led singing of sweetly phrased hymns of personal spiritual yearning were one noticeable dimension of this new development, a parallel to the guitar-led worship songs that would help Evangelicals enter into new spiritual depths almost exactly a century later. The charismatic renewal movement of the 1860s thus exhibited the increasing *application* of the speculative theologies of the mid-century concerning the interpenetration of time and eternity to the spiritual life of the individual. The new charismatic culture provided a framework in which the assertions about the individual's capacity to partake of the divine could be realized. This was the routinization of romanticism.

The hymn sung at Marsh's birthday celebration signaled the new tone, "Lord I hear showers of blessing / That thou art scattering full and free, Showers the thirsty land refreshing / Let some droppings fall on me." The unfortunate modern resonance of last line notwithstanding, the hymn spoke of the new hunger for personal spiritual unction and deeper (or "higher") Christian experience. Prophetic conferences, hitherto a time of quasi-academic fraternity based on what logical, wordy, and often closely argued and erudite papers and debates, began to shift toward providing venues for worship and spiritual encounter. The passionate yet measured expositions of the hope of the age to come were supplemented by an intense anticipation of an imminent visitation by the Spirit. As Marsh himself told those gathered at his birthday celebration, "Are we not in the habit of thinking of our Saviour as a great way off? It is not so. He is near, He is present—a refuge in temptation, under trial, and in the hour of death."[5] Marsh's statement began as if he were still writing in the 1820s against the postmillennialist school. One might have expected him to conclude his sentence by affirming the imminent bodily return of Christ. Instead, his conclusion revealed that he was less concerned about the position of Christ's coming *viz-à-viz* the millennium and more concerned with stressing Jesus' immanence in the life of the believer. Here was a discursive slippage between the cosmic vision of the second coming of Christ the King, and the personal desire for personal intimacy with Christ the consoler, as mediated by the Holy Spirit.

Marsh did not live long enough to see these developments mature, but one of the speakers at his 1863 Beddington conference, William Pennefather, helped steer premillennialism at least one decade further into its new age. Pennefather had been educated in the heady prophetic atmosphere of Trinity College Dublin in the early 1830s and it was thus no surprise that "the subject of unfulfilled prophecy, especially in connection with the second coming of the Lord, had been one of deep interest to Mr. Pennefather almost from his childhood."[6] Pennefather increasingly exemplified the new emphasis on praying for a portion of the Spirit. "No one asked so constantly to be baptized afresh with the Holy Spirit, to see again the face of the Lord Jesus, and to be again anointed with the unction that comes from the Holy One of God," noted one eulogist.[7] Pennefather established his own annual conference at Christ Church, Barnet from 1856. These annual conferences blended an interest in prophecy, the work of the Holy Spirit, personal holiness (now increasingly associated with the indwelling of the sanctifying Holy Spirit), and international mission. In 1864, Pennefather became the incumbent of St. Jude's, Mildmay Park, and his ongoing annual gatherings, which were

---

5. C. Marsh, *Life of William Marsh*, 544.
6. Braithwaite, *Life . . . of William Pennefather*, 253.
7. Ibid., 520.

a very significant venue for the promotion of this new emphasis on the Spirit in league with an ongoing interest in prophecy, became known as the Mildmay Conferences.[8]

Mildmay, in turn, was one of the streams flowing into the formation of the Keswick Conference, founded in 1875. Keswick was the main venue in which premillennialism, increasingly shorn of its complex ruminations on the age to come, blended with an emphasis on the necessity of a "second blessing" of the Holy Spirit, commonly described by speakers at this convention as a moment of surrender leading to the suppression (although not, as in the Wesleyan tradition, the entire elimination) of sin. This blessing, it came to be argued, issued in the "consecration" and the "victorious Christian life." Premillennialism was an important part of Keswick identity, the imminent return of Christ giving urgency to the quest for personal sanctity.[9]

The broad movement of which Mildmay and Keswick were a part is known as "holiness teaching," because it focused on the need for believers to be empowered by the Holy Spirit to live a "holy" life of total surrender and dedication to God. This emphasis arose from a complex web of converging emphases in the era after 1860, mixing native British with imported American teaching.[10] Although there was some variation in the exact path to holiness, believers across the late nineteenth- and early twentieth-century Evangelical world were regularly encouraged to seek the deeper or "higher" Christian life, particularly in the context of "revival" meetings of the kind pioneered by D. L. Moody (1837–99). Moody himself probably did not believe in holiness teaching strictly defined, but the revivalist culture that he helped to spawn nevertheless embodied a broader focus on the expectation of a second blessing, an experience that Moody himself had had in 1871 (he described it as "the *conscious* incoming to his Soul of a presence and power of His Spirit such as he had never known before").[11] Although ostensibly aimed at non-believers, revival events were frequently venues for (re)consecrations and for the reception of a second (or any number of subsequent) blessing(s). Accounts of revival meetings thus regularly emphasized that the spiritual renewal of the believer, rather than conversion of the penitent, was the main point

8. Bebbington, *Evangelicalism in Modern Britain*, 159–61.
9. Ibid., 152.
10. Ibid., 153–74.
11. Ibid., 163.

of the event. As one Scottish minister wrote of a period of heightened religious fervor in Motherwell in 1904–5:

> In the revival meetings ... there were happy choruses, hallelujahs, bursts of praise and wonderful prayers, but behind it all, and through it all, and sometimes in a somewhat overwhelming measure, there was that consciousness of the presence of a Higher Power that constitutes the difference between a real revival meeting and what is merely an imitation.[12]

This revivalist/holiness synthesis was broadly premillennialist, but with its new emphasis on personal empowerment and experiential unction, premillennialism shifted away from the hope of corporate, temporal-spatial renewal and became a symbol of an imminent and immediate divine visitation—whether of the Spirit or the Son. It was thus still highly romantic, but it was the romanticism of personal consolation and epiphanous vision, not the romanticism that concerned itself with the renewal of the social order and natural world. The new movement tended to emphasize rest, withdrawal, and surrender in contrast to the earlier premillennial emphases on activism, motion, and social engagement. The king was still a focus of attention, but the kingdom slipped from view.

The version of premillennialism increasingly tethered to the emerging holiness movement was the futurist version, often sounded in its dispensationalist key. Dispensationalist premillennialism had an inherent hope that the individual Christian believer would be taken to enjoy the beatific vision of heaven, while earth descended into chaos and then became a lesser eschatological resting place for Israel. It was thus a suitable partner to the new emphases on heightened spiritual experience and a kind of supra-earthly mode of existence that were sweeping across the Evangelical world. It taught believers to rest and wait for the rapture—the rescue operation of the coming king. In the words of a famous hymn sung at Moody revival meetings: "Hold the fort, for I am coming!"

By the First World War, the majority of British Evangelicals who a premillennialist eschatological position were futurist dispensationalist, at least in broad outline.[13] In alliance with the new holiness spirituality and lay missionary ethos of the late nineteenth-century Evangelical movement, premillennialism existed now not as a *doctrine* in prophetic con-

---

12. Lennie, *Glory in the Glen*, 106.
13. Bebbington, *Evangelicalism in Modern Britain*, 192.

ferences or journals, but as a *symbol* within the vibrant world of urban revivalism. It jumped from the cerebral discussions of Establishment moderates to the populist appeal of gospel hymnody and conversionist preaching. As Spurgeon put it sardonically: "A prophetical preacher enlarged so much on the 'little horn' of Daniel that one Sabbath morning he found he had but seven hearers remaining."[14] Most people therefore became familiar with the doctrine not in the types of lecture and journal issued from within the mid-nineteenth-century movement, but in the Gospel hymns of Ira D. Sankey and his imitators:

> With joy we wait our king's returning
> From His heavenly mansions fair;
> And with ten thousand saints appearing
> We shall meet Him in the air.[15]

This simplified eschatology "preached" better than the historicist version since it presented a vivid image of the return of Christ without the bother of having to wait for the last few events of prophecy that the historicist argument always claimed were still to be fulfilled. Moreover, it is from this point onward that we can claim with Bebbington that premillennialists had "their eyes . . . fixed less on the blessing of the millennium to come than on the Second Advent of Jesus Christ that would precede it."[16] In this popular premillennialism, there was really no millennium. This was at least in part because Darby's doctrine of the rapture—the removal of believers from earth—came to dominate the prophetic mind. Now, an ethereal heaven of golden gates, bells, harps, and peaceful deliverance from the world's trials were all back in vogue. A casual glance at the eschatology section of Moody's hugely popular *Sacred Songs and Solos* reveals a persistent trope of heaven described as over yonder, beyond the river, beyond the skies, on the distant shore, and so on.[17]

Populist dispensationalist premillennialism affirmed the otherworldliness of Christian salvation and thus meshed with the growing social and economic malaise in economically stagnating, imperialistically anxious late-Victorian Britain, as well as with the post-bellum, war-weary, and chaotically urbanizing United States of America. Futurist

---

14. Spurgeon, *Lectures to My Students*, 95.

15. "Rejoice! Rejoice!" *Sacred Hymns and Solos* (London: Marshall, Morgan & Scott, 1921), no. 164.

16. Bebbington, "Advent Hope in British Evangelicalism," 109.

17. The eschatological hymns are nos. 907–1046.

dispensationalist premillennialism, embedded in a spirituality that promised holiness and power amid the world's trials and temptations, attracted the attention of those who felt disillusioned with the pace of social, economic, and imperial claims, and who looked to the rescue of a king who would come and remove them from the turmoil of the world.

In 1873, the *QJP* produced its final issue. Historicist "prophetic study has not made much real progress of late years," it complained.[18] Whither historicism? Why could it not hold its own against these shifts of eschatology? Why did the previously marginal version of premillennialism become mainstream? The *QJP* blamed the rise of futurist dispensationalism, but it also noted the growing spirit of "rationalism" in the church at large. These two developments were, in fact, linked, since the latter helped accelerate the appeal of the former.

The rationalism that the *QJP* had in mind was particularly an approach to the Bible commonly labeled "higher criticism," although today simply known as "biblical criticism" or "historical criticism." This approach to the Bible, originally pioneered by biblical scholars at the University of Tübingen, viewed Scripture as a collection of literary works rather than a book of divinely inspired knowledge. It sought to understand the words of the Bible in their original cultural context. It valued the ability of reason to identify the ways in which a biblical text had been constructed. It was alert to authorial inconsistencies and textual ambiguities. It suggested that the veracity of the Bible ought to be assessed by the same criteria as applied to any text. This new sense of the mutability of biblical texts increasingly led to the opinion that the Bible was best viewed as a collection of inspiring and formative religious literature written by humans enmeshed in their cultures, not the eternally applicable and divinely inspired word of God.

This form of biblical criticism was in turn keyed into the broader attempt at reconciling theological orthodoxy with the insights of modern thought, an approach often dubbed "theological liberalism." Although the origins of this movement lay in the eighteenth century, the era after 1860 witnessed a growing acceptance of its key assertions, particularly in regard to harmonizing scripture and dogma with reason and modern life. The popularization of biological evolutionary theory by Darwin's *Origin of Species* (1859) made a technical point about animal life, but more broadly it helped disseminate the idea that all things, including religious

---

18. "Our Last," *QJP* 25 (1873), 317.

truth, are in a perpetual state of development and improvement. Theological liberalism contended that each generation should re-appraise the biblical data in the light of new discoveries about science, history, and the human condition. This comported with the higher critical attitude that claimed the Bible was a product of time and place, not a transcendent supra-historical text. This attitude was exemplified in Britain in the highly controversial collection of progressive articles published in 1860 as *Essays and Reviews*.

The effect of this liberal and critical attitude on the prophetic project was at once devastating for historicist premillennialists and, paradoxically, invigorating for futurist dispensationalist premillennialists. The new attitude made substantial challenges to any prophetic project rooted in a belief that the Bible functioned as a realistic guide to historical prophetic events. It particularly undermined historicism, which had claimed that God was the author of history: historical criticism said that history was the author of God, or, at least, of human ideas *about* God. The Bible could not be counted on as infallible prophetic disclosure because its apocalyptic symbols and visions unveiled only the human hopes and fears of the era in which the words were recorded.

At first glance, of course, historical criticism would seem equally to undermine this futurist version of prophecy, which had an equal confidence in the way that the Bible could function as a coded version of real events. And indeed, this version of premillennialism had little to recommend it in the theology faculties of Europe. But this was the point. Flourishing in an increasingly populist Evangelical movement that, with some justification, saw mainstream academic theology as a threat to classical Protestant doctrines, an academically disreputable belief had considerable attraction. Moreover, futurism had one advantage over historicism inasmuch as its claims about prophecy were all unfulfilled. It thus isolated prophecy from historical, and thus scholarly, scrutiny. It always held out the possibility that its interpretation *might* be right, and the erudite biblical critics *might* be wrong. Nothing had yet happened in history because nothing was yet *meant* to have happened and therefore when biblical critics dismissed prophecy, there was always a retort: just wait and see! If one wanted to remain premillennial, futurism offered an option that seemed to heighten faith in the supernatural in an age of skepticism without having to engage in what would be viewed as pseudo-scholarly criticism that would quickly lead to derision. The expectation of a great vindication of prophecy, without the burden of the kind of detailed work required by the historicist project, energized the revivalist sector of the Evangelical community in their general campaign against rationalism, theological revisionism, ritualism, and the secularization of public life. It was well-suited to an Evangelical movement that was increasingly receding from the dominance in British society it had once enjoyed, yet still flourishing—often ebulliently and demotically—at its margins.

The decline of historicist premillennialism was therefore not simply a matter of a set of ideas on the wrong side of history, because the florescence of alternative prophetic discourses showed (and, indeed, continues to show) that highly supernatural forms of prophetic belief succeed within the modern world of science, technology, and secular political-economic systems. Historicism decayed not only because its methodological assumptions were at odds with modern learning (although they were) but also because of the intellectual and social character of the individuals who had been its most ardent champions. As argued in this study, these individuals had prided themselves in the rationality, catholicity, erudition, and moderation of their exposition of prophetic biblical texts. As Froom reminds us:

> These men were accomplished in Biblical languages, Latin, and history, and were well acquainted with the principles of sound exegesis.... They had come to their conclusions on the basis of substantial evidence, after painstaking study consuming years and sometimes decades.[19]

In one sense, then, it was the very proximity of historicist premillennialism to the new historical-critical method—and, indeed, as I have consistently argued in this book, often to the very theological trends that, after 1860, appeared with increasing power and sophistication across the theological landscape—which paradoxically undercut the viability of the historicist project once the central plank of their eschatological synthesis had been removed.

Historicist premillennialists had always styled themselves as biblical scholars who were alert to the hermeneutical distance between reader and author (and thus denied wooden literalistic readings), alive to the lexicon of prophetic symbols, and skilled at the art of parsing and decoding. They believed they were being responsible with the text, as befitted highly educated, pastorally sensitive leaders of the national churches. Most of them denied making outlandish predictions. In other words,

19. Froom, *Prophetic Faith*, 3:750.

they possessed the tools, traits, and techniques that would become the mainstay of historical criticism. They even, of course, shared the same romantic interest in history that in the end gave purchase to the historical critical approach to the texts of Scripture.

The kind of Evangelical—equitable, erudite, and establishmentarian—who had during the mid-nineteenth century participated happily in confraternal scholastic prophetic conferences shifted naturally into historical critical methods and forms of more self-consciously liberal Christianity, and in so doing, lost the foundational rationale for the art of prophetic code breaking. As the *QJP* mourned: "Thousands who still call themselves evangelical are perhaps unconsciously leavened with these [rationalistic] principles so that prophetic truth has lost all value to them as well as all its interest."[20] It was not just the draw of "liberalism," that counted against historicism, of course: the developments within Evangelicalism itself already described in this chapter made the movement increasingly sectarian, subcultural, and, more often than not, full of the "sorry, syrupy stuff that this world calls 'pietism.'"[21] The era that was dawning saw a democratization of Evangelicalism that had moved the center of the movement away from well-educated leaders of the national churches and toward the self-consciously populist leaders of mission halls, children's clubs, and demotic revivalists. Such a culture was not conducive to the serious and sober spirit of mid-century premillennial discourse—after all, several historicist premillennialists had taken direct aim at such popular sentimentalism—nor, of course, to its implicit liberalizing tendencies inherent in the premillennialist movement itself, to which I have been concerned to draw attention throughout the book.

By the 1870s, then, Evangelical premillennialism could no longer hover between the worlds of biblical fidelity and modernizing romantic theology in the mode of the era that has been the subject of this book. On one side was the Scylla of a populist Evangelicalism that had no time for its lengthy debates and position papers, nor for its sometimes speculative theologies. On the other side was the Charybdis of liberalizing historical criticism, which, although in tune with the theological revisionism that sheltered under the wings of the historicist premillennialist movement, nevertheless denied the foundational premise of historicist interpretation, and thus denied to the movement scholarly legitimacy.

20. "Our Last," *QJP* 25 (1873), 319.
21. Bebbington, *Evangelicalism in Modern Britain*, 167.

Evangelicals who wanted to remain premillennialist therefore broke the association of millennialism with progressive, revisionist, and proto-liberal ideas. Premillennialism thus became almost exclusively the creed of Evangelicals who were consciously resisting the increasingly apparent updates (or downgrades, as they came to be called) of Nicene Christianity and, in time, itself became one of the central litmus tests of such orthodoxy—a shibboleth by which traditionalists could test whether an individual had become infected with liberal modernist apostasy, or whether they held fast to the "fundamentals" of classical Christian faith.

Those Christian leaders and thinkers who wanted to remain moderate, mainstream, and academically respectable—and to follow the paths of social justice mapped out in the 1840s and 1850s—now often moved into a more overtly progressive, non-Evangelical camp. The case of William Henry Fremantle (1831–1916) is instructive. Fremantle was the nephew of Robert William Fremantle, the Dean of Ripon and long-serving President of the Prophecy Investigation Society. His premillennial views have been quoted on several occasions throughout this book. The younger Fremantle was strongly influenced by his uncle's Evangelical spirituality, but was also decisively shaped by the growing ethical, social Christianity associated with Benjamin Jowett (1817–93) and Arthur Stanley (1815–81). Like his mentors, Fremantle increasingly suggested that Christianity was "no more (nor less) than the faithful fulfilment of common duties best expressed in terms of service to society."[22]

In 1893 Fremantle gave the Bampton Lectures at the University of Oxford. Published as *The World as the Subject of Redemption*, the lectures on the one hand sounded a theme with which his uncle, along with most other historicist premillennialists, would have been very content. He argued that

> the world, the whole of human society, is to be brought under the power of Christ, and that this is the true object of Christian endeavour. Why is the saving and training of individual souls constantly proposed as the sole object, and hardly any mention made of the larger work of saving human society, which was contemplated from the first ? Was not the original Gospel "The Gospel of the Kingdom"?[23]

---

22. Green, "Fremantle, William Henry (1831–1916)."
23. W. H. Fremantle, *The World As the Subject of Redemption*, xi.

This was pure mid-century Evangelical millennialist rhetoric. It is difficult not to imagine that Fremantle had learnt this kingdom emphasis in part from Uncle Robert and his colleagues as well as from the nascent Baliol social gospel.

On closer inspection, however, Fremantle had drained away the apocalyptic core from his vision of an earthly kingdom. While, like his premillennialist forbears, he argued that the early church had spoken not of heaven but of "a reign of Christ in this world,"[24] his lectures exhibited no eschatological expectation and no discussion of the return of Christ. He collapsed the idea of a kingdom of God into the present activity of social ethics. Taking a line of argument pioneered earlier in the century by Thomas Arnold (1795–1842), he argued that "all departments of life" were already sacred. "Each of the rings or circles of human society, the family, the communities which exist for the furtherance of science, of art, of social intercourse, of commerce, as well as for public worship, are essentially religious societies, and the Nation most of all."[25] Serving diligently and actively in each of these areas had become his eschatological hope.

Fremantle was perhaps a little troubled by his new position. "We must restore the element of hope," he argued, "But hope of what? Is the picture which has been drawn of a society universal, and Christian in all its departments, enough to kindle and sustain our hope? Are we to make little or nothing of the hopes of a life beyond the grave?"[26] His answer was essentially, yes, life beyond death was not the heart of the Christian message. His lectures concluded with a very thin vision of a future divine *dénouement*. The life to come was simply described as "a new and better state, whatever it be, beyond the chasm of death." Indeed, paradoxically, despite his robust calls for a this-worldly Christianity, he imagined life after death in somewhat old-fashioned terms, speaking about the time "when these earthly conditions fail, and when the walls of flesh fall from round about us."[27] The ethical Platonism of his Oxford mentors had certainly taught him a robust vision of holistic social Christianity but, paradoxically, had also emasculated the hope of an enduring this-worldly salvation. Fremantle focused not upon the kingdom that would dawn when Christ returned, but rather upon the contribution that each

---

24. Ibid., 321.
25. Ibid., xi.
26. Ibid., 321.
27. Ibid., 322.

generation could make to improve the world for those who came after them. Humans, not Christ, would both build and inherit the kingdom. "Let us set ourselves heartily to the bringing in of the kingdom of God on earth," he advised.[28] "It would be a noble and a Christian thing, even if there were no world to come, to devote our span of life to the benefit of those who are to come after us."[29]

Fremantle was a typical example of the waxing of a liberal social gospel movement within British Christianity. He assumed the Deanship of Ripon after his uncle's death. He turned the cathedral into a center of this kind of humane, socially astute, and ethically challenging version of liberal Protestantism. While his uncle had made his arguments for a materialist Christianity as head of a premillennialist society, Fremantle spoke for his version of earthly religion from venues such as the Churchman's Union For the Advancement of Liberal Religious Thought and the flagship liberal journal, *Modern Churchman*.[30]

William Fremantle was not, of course, simply an apostate from a previously "pure" and orthodox premillennialism. Individuals like Birks and Leask had already moved a considerable way toward typical "liberal" themes within their own careers, and Evangelicals of all kinds had modernized their views of social reform in the mid-century, an approach pioneered by a number of premillennialists. Indeed, the major theme of my argument has been the way in which premillennialism had laid the foundation for, and precipitated the development of, the type of socially engaged, this-worldly Christianity that the younger Fremantle exemplified. The demise of the historicist framework and the challenge of historical criticism after 1870 did, however, accelerate the development observable in Fremantle: an erosion of the explicitly prophetic, apocalyptic, and Adventist themes, which left the "this worldly" dimensions of the vision to stand alone as the core of a self-consciously modernist form of Christianity. Liberal social Christianity was, of course, the mirror image of the new strident populist premillennialism of the late nineteenth century, itself an emaciated version of the eschatological vision of the previous age in which the social and materialist themes were amputated. The "now" and the "not yet" of eschatology went their separate ways.

28. Ibid.,
29. Ibid., 321
30. Green, "Fremantle, William Henry (1831–1916)."

This new situation made it hard for late nineteenth-century Evangelicals to continue along the path of social reform pioneered by the mid-century generation. The authenticity and, indeed, primacy of the temporal sphere was the foundational assumption of those embracing the higher critical method and the broader liberal theological mindset with which it was interwoven. In this synthesis, historical circumstance was the decisive factor in forming human ideas of God, and religion was therefore inevitably subject to change with the times. Liberal Christianity insisted that this mutability of Christianity meant that it was right to modernize creeds and practices which were no longer in harmony with the knowledge and ethical practices of the age. Time and space were at the heart of theological liberalism, so they increasingly receded—eschatologically and socially—from "conservative" Evangelicalism. For Evangelicals concerned about the doctrinal compromises made by the new theology, it was safer to picture God as aiming to *remove* believers from the realm of space and time. Moreover, since the liberal modernization of theology often involved stressing the ethical dimensions of Christianity more than its supernatural implications, Christian social justice came to be intertwined with theological liberalism. Evangelicals therefore also moved away from social reform as a means to distance themselves from those liberal Christians who were now its most prominent advocates, an act which confirmed and heightened the ascendant eschatological dualism.

This broad conclusion about the shifts in prophetic imagination must be qualified by one observation. There remained a dedicated remnant of serious Evangelical prophetical dilettantes whose interest in decoding the complexities of prophecy could still push at times toward novel theological ideas within the grooves of Evangelicalism. The Prophecy Investigation Society, one of the central venues for eschatological debate in the period between 1840 and 1860, continued to be the home of such individuals. The minute books of the Society detail proceedings until 1862, but then have no further entries until 1890. It is unclear what occurred in these twenty-eight years, but the first note in the 1890 minute book, instructing the secretary that, under rule two of the constitution, a minute book ought to be obtained, suggests the meetings of the Society had been in abeyance for at least some of that period. The Society regained energy from the 1890s in part due to the increasingly darkening geopolitical situation, and to a growing sense of cultural decadence. As early as 1897, one of the Society's most notable members, Robert Anderson (1841–1918), who had headed the Metropolitan Police Force during the "Jack the Ripper" investigations, was giving a paper predicting that the Antichrist would be a kind of "divine Kaiser."[31]

Although far more influenced by dispensationalist futurist premillennialism than in its early days, the Society in its new incarnation still encouraged some *avant-garde* theological views. Samuel Garratt (1817–1906), who served as the President of the Society from 1900–1905, rejected the notion of eternal punishment.[32] The prominent Society member E. W. Bullinger (1837–1913) gathered around him a school of followers who advanced annihilationalism, although this was not his own explicitly stated view.[33] Conditional immortality surfaced several times as a controversial issue, in 1914 and again in 1944.[34] In 1931, it was even proposed that subscription to the premillennial advent of Christ was no longer necessary for membership of the society.[35]

This last proposal, however, was probably more a sign of imminent collapse than an expression of creative intellectual ebullience. Over the next three decades, the Society increasingly equivocated about its identity. From the 1940s it was caught between the rising tide of Evangelicals beginning to re-engage with professional biblical scholarship and the growth of a more informal, youth-oriented, and casual Evangelical subculture which had little taste for the arcane business of prophetical studies. The former might believe in the importance of eschatology, but now believed it could be (and needed to be) proved using historical-critical apparatus. The latter constituency, meanwhile, increasingly looked for the proof of Christian truth in communal experiences and contemporary worship.

The Society knew its weaknesses: in an attempt at gaining new followers it decided to abandon the practice of members giving papers at each meeting and instead asked all members to submit their views on the apocalypse in one hundred words on the back of a postcard![36] In 1946 the PIS abandoned all mention of particular prophetic schemas in its membership rules.[37] By the 1950s, it toyed with establishing an extension movement (including using American "rapture" movies) to promote interest in prophecy, but it could not reconcile this outreach either with

31. Prophecy Investigation Society, Minute Book No. 4 (1894–98), April 28, 1897.
32. E. R. Garratt, *Life . . . of Samuel Garratt*, 79–83.
33. Gribben, *Evangelical Millennialism*, 98–99.
34. Prophecy Investigation Society, Minute Book No. 7. May 5, 1914; April 9, 1924.
35. Ibid., Minute Book No. 8. Nov 5, 1931.
36. Ibid. July 19, 1945.
37. Ibid. April 11, 1946.

its finances or with the fact that its rationale was eschatological investigation, not prophetic proselytization. By the late 1950s, its finances, membership, and quality of publications were, by its own admission, in freefall. The Society ceased operations in 1962.

While it is important to note the resurgence of the prophecy movement in the first decades of the twentieth century, the movement after 1870 never enjoyed the cachet and broad appeal of its mid-nineteenth-century halcyon era, nor did it ever play host to such widespread speculative theologies as have been described in this book. Neither is there any evidence of an interest in social reform. Its dotage was marked by a faithful, yet marginal, remnant of premillennialists who were at best a special interest group within the broader church—not the urbane, erudite, socially-astute leaders of Victorian religious thought. Its Indian summer between 1900 and 1930 was triggered more by geopolitical crisis than genuine theological revival, and the flowers of its late blossoming quickly withered again in the chill winds of the mid-twentieth century.

The mid-nineteenth-century premillennialist project examined in this book was a brief and intriguing coalescence of the old and the new: a relatively old fashioned, pre-critical prophetic framework that nevertheless generated a radical, liberalizing theological and social agenda. This amalgamation of tradition and modernity broke after 1870. It would take over a century for Evangelicals to mend the breach. Yet today many Evangelicals and conservative theologians, such as N. T. Wright, have come back to the conclusions of mid-century Evangelicals about the materiality of salvation and the consequences for social justice only by deploying the very historical-critical methodology which destroyed the historicist premillennialist movement in the late nineteenth century.

That many have returned to the broad conclusions of a previous age while also abandoning the theological scaffolding that buttressed their arguments, reminds us that subsequent generations may too judge our own theological ruminations to be simultaneously daringly prescient and hopelessly compromised by our own culturally bound methodological assumptions. Those of us of faith who desire to learn something from the history of the Christian community are thus always inspired by the disputations of ancestors making audacious, iconoclastic, and prophetic challenges to the *status quo*, while also chastened by their errors to do so only with tentative humility.

Of course, there is much that is different from the past about our present interest in the future. The eschatology of the new creation in vogue in the early twenty-first century emerges not as part of the quasi-scientific study of prophecy, but because of a desire for holistic, organic, and authentic engagement with the world and its inhabitants; it emerges not so much from an intoxication with the nervous energy of industrialization, but rather with a postmodern rejection against the banality of mass consumption and against the malaise of socio-economic atomization; it takes flight not with a fierce Protestant self-confidence, but with an ecumenical hankering for ancient wisdom and monastic *shalom*; it is energized not so much with a concern for the restoration of the Jews as with an insistence that Jesus must be read in his Jewish context as the fulfillment of Jewish messianic expectations, and that those who follow him must endorse the Old Testament promises of a restoration of creation and liberation of the oppressed. Nevertheless, since our globalized, industrialized, technically rich society assumed a discernibly familiar shape during the nineteenth century, it should not be a surprise that we also find ourselves struggling to comprehend the promise and peril of our existence with some of the same hopes and fears as those Christians who first found themselves standing in the simultaneously enticing and disorienting light of our common modernity.

If the course of time sometimes leads to the rediscovery of old ideas, then similarities between contemporaries should be expected even more. Categorizing people in the past into "schools" or "parties" of ecclesiastical preference reflects both historical prejudice and our own contemporary disputes. It is not a good way to pursue historical (or, indeed, modern) truth. Evangelicals were not a different kind of Christian or an eccentric kind of Victorian: they were as shaped by their sociocultural environment as much as anyone else. The often speculative nature of eschatological debate revealed such osmosis very clearly. Premillennialists certainly spoke with a distinctive register that many then and now have viewed as eccentric, unpalatable, and misguided. Indeed, that vocabulary was slipping into obsolesce by the 1870s, thereby permanently obscuring the modernity of the early premillennialist vision to all future commentators. This book has attempted to prove that the central themes of the mid-century premillennialist movement were modern, mainstream, and widely shared. Historicist premillennialism was an important early manifestation of an increasingly prevalent nineteenth-century attitude which upheld the temporal-spatial sphere as an authentic locus of Christian concern. In expecting to see heaven on earth, they shared with diverse contemporaries an often surprising amount of common ground.

Bibliography

Primary Sources

Unpublished Manuscript Sources

Lord's Day Observance Society Archives. Lord's Day Observance Society Minute Books, vols. i–iv (1831–55). Leominster, Day One Publications, Ryelands Road, Leominster, R6 8NZ, UK.

Oxford, Bodleian Library. Additional Manuscript c.290. "The Principal Clergy of London, classified according to their opinions on the great Church questions of the day." (1844).

Shaftesbury (Broadlands) Papers. University of Southampton Library.

Prophecy Investigation Society Archives. Prophecy Investigation Society Minute Books and other ephemera (1841–1963). Prophetic Witness Movement International, P.O. Box 109 Leyland, Lancashire, PR25 1WB, UK.

Journals and Newspapers

The Christian Examiner and Church of Ireland Magazine (1833)
The Christian Guardian and District Visitors' and Sunday School Teachers' Magazine (1842)
Christian Herald (1830–35)
Christian Lady's Magazine (1834–49)
Christian Observer (1820–70)
Churchman's Monthly Review (1841–47)
Eclectic Review (1828)
Evangelical Magazine and Missionary Chronicle (sampled between 1796–1830)
Figaro in London (1833)
Free Church Magazine (1851)
Gospel Magazine, and Theological Review (1866)
Jewish Expositor (1819)
The Labourer's Friend Magazine (1831–84)
Literary Gazette (1808)
Morning Watch or Quarterly Journal on Prophecy and Theological Review (1829–33)
New Monthly Magazine and Humourist (1848)
Poor Man's Advocate (March 1832)
Quarterly Journal of Prophecy (1848–70)

Ten Hours Advocate (1846–47)
The Record (sampled between 1840 and 1855)
Working Man's Charter (1848–49)

Books, Pamphlets, Sermons, and Reports

A Catalogue of the Entire and Valuable Library of the Revd. Edward Bickersteth. London: Rayner and Hodges, 1851.

A Clergyman. *Last Vials: Being a Series of Essays Upon the Subject of the Second Advent*. n.p., 1847–56.

A Preacher in the Church of Scotland. *The Restitution of All Things in the Establishment of the Messiah's Kingdom During the Millennium*. London: A. Panton, 1829.

A Spiritual Watchman. *The Pre-Millennial Personal Advent of Christ*. London: J. Nisbett, 1832.

Aglionby, Francis Keyes. *The Life of Edward Henry Bickersteth, D.D. Bishop and Poet*. London: Longmans Green, 1907.

Alexander, William L. *Memoir of the Life and Writings of Ralph Wardlaw*. Edinburgh: A. and C. Black, 1856.

Anderson, William. *An Apology for Millennarianism*. 2nd ed. London: J. Nisbet, 1843.

———, et al. *Extracts on Prophecy, Chiefly the Approaching Advent and Kingdom of Christ*. Glasgow: J. Begg, 1835.

Auriol, Edward, ed. *Popish Darkness and Millennial Light: Being Lectures during Lent, 1851, at St. George's, Bloomsbury*. London: J. Nisbet, 1851

———. *Preaching Christ—A Sermon*. London: n.p., 1841.

———. "The Similarities and Contrast of the First and Second Advents." In Stewart, *The Priest Upon His Throne*, 26–53.

———. *Walk: A Word for the New Year*. London: Seeley, Jackson and Halliday, 1880.

Auriol, Edward, and Hugh McNeile. *Two Sermons Preached . . . the Sunday After the Death of Edward Bickersteth*. London: Seeleys, 1850.

Baillee, John. *Memoir of Rev. W. H. Hewitson: Late Minister of the Free Church of Scotland, at Dirleton*. London: J. Nisbet, 1856.

———. *Select Letters and Remains of the Late Rev. W. H. Hewitson, Dirleton*. 2 vols. London: J. Nisbet, 1853.

Bayford, John. *Messiah's Kingdom, or, A Brief Inquiry Concerning what is Revealed in Scripture Relative to the Fact, the Time, the Signs, and the Circumstances of the Second Advent of the Lord Jesus Christ*. London: Printed for the author by F. Marshall, 1820.

Bayley, Emilius, ed. *Twelve Lent Lectures on "The Signs of the Times" for the Year 1858 Delivered in St George's Church Bloomsbury*. London: J. M. Robeson, 1858.

Beaven, James. *An Account of the Life and Writings of S. Irenaeus, Bishop of Lyons and Martyr*. London: Printed for the author and sold by J. G. F. and J. Rivington, 1841.

Begg, James A. *A Connected View of some of the Scriptural Evidence of the Redeemer's Speedy Personal Return and Reign on Earth with His Glorified Saints during the Millennium*. Paisley: Alex. Gardner, 1829.

———. *The First Resurrection as Promised to the Saints*. Glasgow. Published by the author, 1844.

Belford, James. *The Saturday Half-Holiday: In its Bearing on the Due Observance of the Sabbath.* Glasgow: Hutcheson Campbell, 1867.

Bellamy, Joseph. "The Millennium." In *The Works of Joseph Bellamy D.D.* 2 vols. 1: 443–61. Boston: Doctrinal Tract and Book Society, 1853.

Bicheno, James. *Signs of the Times, or The Overthrow of the Papal Tyranny in France, the Prelude of Destruction to Popery and Despotism, but of Peace to Mankind.* Glasgow: n.p., 1794.

Bickersteth, Edward. *The Divine Warning to the Church at this Time, of our Enemies, Dangers and Duties, and as to our Future Prospects.* London: Seeley, Burnside and Seeley, 1843.

———. "Earth Yielding Its Increase." In Pym, *Good Things To Come,* 110–35.

———. "The Kingdom of Christ the Lord in Its Successive Stages and In Its Heavenly Glories." In Bickersteth, *The Second Coming,* 390–439.

———. "The Kingly Power of Our Lord Jesus Christ In Different Seasons." In Pym, *Good Things to Come,* 110–35.

———. *A Practical Guide to the Prophecies.* 7th ed. London: Seeleys, 1844.

———. *The Restoration of the Jews to Their Own Land.* 2nd ed. London: R. B. Seeley and W. Burnside, 1851.

———, ed. *The Second Coming, the Judgement, and the Kingdom of Christ: Being Lectures Delivered during Lent, 1843, at St George's, Bloomsbury.* London. J. Nisbet, 1843.

———. *The Signs of the Times in the East; A Warning to the West: Being a Practical View of Our Duties in the Light of the Prophecies which Illustrate the Present and Future State of the Church and of the World.* London: Seeley, Burnside and Seeley, 1844.

———. *A Treatise on the Lord's Supper.* 15th ed. London: Seeley, Burnside and Seeley,1823.

———. "Waiting for Christ the Fruit of the Gospel." In Birks, *The Hope of the Apostolic Church,* 1–42.

Bickersteth, Edward Henry. *Yesterday, To-day and Forever; A Poem, in Twelve Books.* 7th ed. London: Rivingtons, 1872.

Bickersteth, Robert, ed. *The Gifts of the Kingdom: Being Lectures Delivered during Lent, 1855, at St George's Church, Bloomsbury, by Twelve Clergymen of the Church of England.* London: Shaw, 1855.

Binney, Thomas. *Is It Possible to Make the Best of Both Worlds? A Book for Young Men.* London: J. Nisbet, 1851.

Birks, Thomas Rawson. *The Christian State: or, The First Principles of National Religion.* London: Seeley, Burnside, and Seeley, 1853.

———. *The First Elements of Sacred Prophecy: Including an Examination of Several Recent Expositions and of the Year-Day Theory.* London: W. Painter, 1843.

———. "The First Resurrection." In Bickersteth, *The Second Coming* 192–268.

———, ed. *The Hope of the Apostolic Church: or, the Duties and Privileges of Christians in Connexion with the Second Advent, as Unfolded in the First Epistle to the Thessalonians. Being lectures during Lent, 1845, at St. George's, Bloomsbury.* London: J. Nisbet, 1845.

———. *Memoir of the Rev. Edward Bickersteth.* 2 Vols. 2nd ed. London: Seeleys, 1852.

———. "On the Order of Christ's Kingdom." In Fremantle, *The Millennial Kingdom,* 57–88.

———. *Outlines of Unfulfilled Prophecy: Being an Inquiry into the Scripture Testimony Respecting the "Good Things to Come."* London: Seeleys, 1854.

———. "The Partakers of the Kingdom Characterized." In Dallas, *Lift Up Your Heads*, 360–403.

———. "The Resurrection to Glory." In Pym, *Good Things to Come*, 227–72.

———. "Signs of the Lord's Coming." In Cadman, *The Parables Prophetically Explained*, 213–49.

———. "The Spread of Knowledge and Scientific Discovery." In Bayley, *Twelve Lent Lectures*, 66–78.

———. *Thoughts on the Sacraments and on the Relations of Prayer and Science; Being the Substance of Three Addresses at the Islington Clerical Meeting and at Sion College*. London: Christian Book Society, 1873.

———. *Truth and Life in the Church at Home in Their Influence on the Work of Foreign Missions*. London: Seeley, Jackson and Halladay, 1855.

———. "The Unbelief of Pretended Science." In W. R. Fremantle, *Present Times*, 60–92.

———. *Village Discourses, Being the Ten Parting Sermons Preached in the Parish Church of Watton, Herts*. London: Seeley, Burnside, and Seeley. 1845.

———. *The Victory of Divine Goodness*. London: Rivingtons, 1867.

———. *The Ways of God; or, Thoughts on the Difficulties of Belief.* London: Seeley, Jackson and Halladay, 1863.

Birrell, Charles M. *The Life of William Brock, D.D.* London: J. Nisbet, 1878.

Bonar, Andrew A. *Redemption Drawing Nigh. A Defence of the Premillennial Advent.* London: J. Nisbet, 1847.

Bonar, Horatius. *The Coming and Kingdom of the Lord Jesus Christ: Being an Examination of the Work of the Rev. D. Brown, on the Second Coming of the Lord*. Kelso, UK: J. Rutherford, 1849.

———. *Prophetical Landmarks: Containing Data for Helping to Determine the Question of Christ's Pre-Millennial Advent*. London: J. Nisbet, 1847.

Bosanquet, Samuel R. *The Rights of the Poor and Christian Almsgiving, or the State and Character of the Poor and the Conduct and Duties of the Rich*. London: J. Burns, 1841.

Boys, Thomas. *God and Man, Considered in Relation to Eternity Past, Time That Is, Eternity Future, the Perfection of God in Christ*. London: Published for the author, 1860.

Braithwaite, Robert. *The Life and Letters of Rev. William Pennefather*. London: J. F. Shaw, 1878.

Bristol Drapers' Association. *A Verbatim Report of the Speeches Delivered at a Public Meeting of the Bristol Drapers' Association*. Bristol: n.p., 1844.

Brock, Mourant. *Church and the Sacraments, with an Appendix on the Christian Sabbath*. London: J. Nisbet, 1848.

———. "The City Which Hath Foundations Prepared for the Faithful and Suffering Pilgrim." In Stewart, *The Priest Upon His Throne*, 289–332.

———. *The Lord's Coming: A Great Practical Doctrine*. London: J. Nisbet, 1845.

———. "The Position of England in Relation to the Future." In Bayley, *Twelve Lent Lectures*, 103–10.

———. *The Sacrament of the Lord's Supper*. London: J. Nisbet, 1845.

Brooks, Joshua W. *The Comet Will Not Strike the Earth, Neither Burn It*. Nottingham, UK: W. Dearden, 1857.

———. *A Dictionary of Writers on Prophecies with the Titles and Occasional Description of their Works*. London: Simpkin and Marshall, 1835.

———. *Elements of Prophetical Interpretation*. London: R. B. Seeley and W. Burnside, 1836.

———. *Essays on the Advent and Kingdom of Christ and the Events Connected Therewith*. London: Simpkin and Marshall, 1843.

Brown, Abner. W. *Recollections of the Conversation Parties of the Revd. Charles Simeon*. London: Hamilton, Adams, 1863.

Brown, David. *Christ's Second Coming: Will it Be Premillennial?* 3rd ed. Edinburgh: T. & T. Clarke, 1853.

Brown, James. *An Attempt Towards a New Historical and Political Explanation of the Book of Revelation*. London: G. Cowie and Co., 1812.

———. *The Restitution of All Things: An essay on the Important Purpose of the Universal Redeemer's Destination*. London: Printed for the author, 1824.

Buxton, Charles. *Memoirs of Sir Thomas Fowell Buxton*. London: J. Murray, 1848.

Cadman, William. "The Gathering of the Saints at the Appearing of Christ." In Dallas, *Lift Up Your Heads*, 131–67.

———. "The Liberty of Christ's Kingdom." In Fremantle, *The Millennial Kingdom*, 31–56.

———, ed. *The Parables Prophetically Explained; being lectures delivered during Lent, 1853, at St. George's, Bloomsbury*. London: J. Shaw, 1853.

———. "Spread of the Knowledge of the Glory of the Lord." In Pym, *Good Things to Come*, 175–226.

———. *Wrath and Love. Remarks on the Eternity of Punishment*. London: J. Laver, 1869.

Campbell, Donald. *Memorials of John McLeod Campbell, DD, Being Selections from His Correspondence*. London: Macmillan, 1877.

Carlyle, Thomas. *Critical and Miscellaneous Essays*. 4 vols. Boston: Brown and Taggard, 1860.

———. *Sartor Resartus* (1836). Oxford World's Classics Edition. Edited by Kerry McSweeney and Peter Sabor. Oxford: Oxford University Press, 1987.

Carus, William. *Memoirs of the Life of Revd. Charles Simeon*. 3rd ed. London: J. Hatchard and Sons, 1848.

Chalmers, Thomas. "Introductory Essay." In *Serious Reflections on Time and Eternity by John Shower*, v–xxvi. Glasgow: W. Collins, 1828.

———. "The New Heavens and the New Earth." In *Sermons Preached at St. John's Church, Glasgow, by Thomas Chalmers D.D*, 191–215. Glasgow: Chalmers and Collins, 1823.

———. *Political Economy In Connexion with the Moral State and Prospects of Society*. Vol 2. London: T. Constable, 1850.

Church, R. W. *The Oxford Movement: Twelve Years 1833–1845*. London: Macmillan, 1892.

Close, Francis. *The Catholic Doctrine of the Second Advent of our Lord and Saviour Jesus Christ Considered in a Course of Four Sermons*. London: Hatchard and Son, 1846.

Cole, Henry. *A Letter to the Rev. Edward Irving, Minister of the Caledonian Chapel, Compton Street, In Refutation of the Awful Doctrines (Held by Him) of the Sinfulness, Mortality, and Corruptibility of the Body of Jesus Christ*. London: J. Eedes, 1827.

Coleridge, Samuel Taylor. *The Collected Works of Samuel Taylor Coleridge*. Vol. 9, *Aids to Reflection*. Edited by John Beer. Princeton: Princeton University Press, 1993.

———. "Notes on Irving's Ben-Ezra." In *The Complete Works of Samuel Taylor Coleridge*, edited by William G. T. Shedd, 5: 512–21. New York: Harper and Brothers, 1853.

Colvinus. *Impending Doom Foretold Respecting the Penult Dispensation: Or the Prophetic Programme of the Last Great Conflict*. Edinburgh: J. Grant, 1854.

Conybeare, William John. *Church Parties: An Essay*. London: Longman, Brown, Green and Longmans, 1854.

Cooper, Edward. *The Crisis; Or, an Attempt to Shew from Prophecy, Illustrated by the Signs of the Times, the Prospects and the Duties of the Church of Christ at the Present Period*. London: Printed for T. Cadell and W. Blackwood, 1826.

Cox, John. *The Claims of the Poor or the Duty of Christian Benevolence*. Woolwich, UK: J. Black, 1843.

———. *The Divine Order: Or, the Second Advent before the Universal Reign*. London: Ward, 1853.

———. *The Future: An Outline of Events Predicted in the Holy Scriptures*. London: Nisbet, 1862.

———. *A Millenarian's Answer of the Hope That Is In Him: Or a Brief Statement and Defence of the Doctrine of Christs' Pre-Millennial Advent and Personal Reign on Earth*. London: Published by the author, 1832.

———. *A Premillennial Manual*. London: J. Nisbet, 1851.

———. *Themes for Thought in the Prophetic Page*. London: J. Nisbet, 1860.

———. *Thoughts on the Coming and Kingdom of our Lord Jesus Christ*. London: J. Nisbet, 1835.

Croly, George. *The Apocalypse of St John*. London: C. and J. Rivington, 1827.

———. *England the Fortress of Christianity*. London: Protestant Association, 1837.

———. *The Universal Kingdom: A Sermon*. London: John Kendrick, 1848.

Cumming, John. *Apocalyptic Sketches*. London: Hall, 1849.

———. *The Christian: The Christian in his Home; the Christian in the World; A lecture*. London: Piper, Stephenson and Spence, 1859.

———. *Christ Our Passover: Or, Thoughts on the Atonement*. London: Virtue and Hall, 1854.

———. *The Church Before the Flood*. Boston: J. P. Jewett, 1854.

———. *Communion between Heaven and Earth: And the Cloud of Witnesses*. London: Kerby and Endean, 1874.

———. *The Destiny of Nations as Indicated in Prophecy*. London: Hurst and Blackett, 1864.

———. *Foreshadows: Or, Lectures on the Lord's Miracles as Shadows of the Age to Come*. London: Virtue and Hall, 1851.

———. *From Life to Life: Two Sermons on the Death of his Late Royal Highness the Prince Consort*. London: J. F. Shaw, 1861.

———. *God in History: A lecture*. London: W. Jones, 1849.

———. *God in Science: A lecture*. London: Young Men's Christian Association, 1849.

———. *The Great Tribulation: Or, The Things Coming on Earth*. London: R. Bentley, 1859.

———. *Liberty, Equality, Fraternity: Three Discourses Delivered in the Month of April, 1848, at His Own Church*. London: A. Hall, 1849.

———. *Lecture on Labour, Rest, and Recreation: Delivered at Exeter Hall.* Hobart Town, UK: Hobart Town Early Closing Association, 1885.
———. *Lectures to Young Men.* London: Virtue and Hall, 1859.
———. *Look and Live: Or, Present Salvation for All who Will Accept it.* London: J. Shaw, 1863.
———. *The Millennial Rest: Or, the World as it Will Be.* London: R. Bentley, 1862.
———. *Redemption Draweth Nigh: Or, the Great Preparation.* London: R. Bentley, 1860.
Cuninghame, William. *A Dissertation on the Seals and Trumpets of the Apocalypse.* London: J. Shaw, 1813.
———. *The Political Destiny of the Earth: As Revealed in the Bible.* Glasgow: sold by J. Smith and Son, 1834.
———. *A Summary View of the Scriptural Argument for the Second and Glorious Advent of Messiah Before the Millenium.* Glasgow: reprinted from the *Christian Observer*, 1828.
Dale, R. W. *The Atonement: The Congregational Union Lecture for 1875.* London: Hodder and Stoughton, 1875.
———. *The Old Evangelicalism and the New.* London: Hodder and Stoughton, 1889.
Dallas, Alexander. *Introduction to Prophetical Researches: Being a Brief Outline of the Divine Purpose concerning the World as It May be Gathered from Holy Scripture, Historically and Prophetically.* London: J. Nisbet, 1850.
———, ed. *Lift up Your Heads: Glimpses of Messiah's Glory: Being Lectures Delivered During Lent, 1848, at St. George's, Bloomsbury.* London: J. Nisbet, 1848.
Dallas, Anne Briscoe. *Incidents in the Life and Ministry of the Revd. Alex. R. C. Dallas.* London. J. Nisbet, 1872.
Dalton, William. "The Delay of the Second Advent, Its Causes and Practical Lessons." In Bickersteth, *The Second Coming*, 105–35.
———. *God's Dealings with Israel: Being Lectures Delivered during Lent, 1850, at St. George's, Bloomsbury.* London: J. Nisbet, 1850.
Darby, John Nelson. *The Collected Writings of J. N. Darby.* Edited by William Kelly. 34 vols. London: G. Morrish, 1867–1900.
Dialogues on Universal Restitution. London: W. Freeman, 1855.
Dobson, Austin. "The Paradox of Time." In MacLeod, *Good Words*, 16.
Drummond, Henry. *Dialogues on Prophecy.* 3 vols. London: J. Nisbet, 1827–29.
———. *Narrative of the Circumstances which Led to the Setting Up of the Church of Christ at Albury.* Printed for private circulation, 1834.
———. *The Second Advent of the Lord Jesus Christ.* Edinburgh: T. C. Jack, 1857.
———. *Social Duties on Christian Principles.* London: J. Hatchard and Sons, 1830.
Eardley, Culling Eardley. *A Brief Notice of the Life of the Rev. Edward Bickersteth.* London: Partridge and Oakey,1850.
Early Closing Association. *Annual Report, Financial Statements and Resumés of Proceedings.* London: Early Closing Association, 1855–60.
———. *For the Private Use of Members of Committees, and Other Proved Friends of the Cause. Early Closing Association. Plan of Operations.* London: Printed by W. J. and J. Sears, 1852.
———. *Oppressed Condition of the Dressmakers' and Milliners' Assistants.* London: Kent, 1856.

———. *Report of the Speeches Delivered at a Public Meeting Held at the Music Hall, Store Street, Bedford Square.* London: n.p., 1852.

Eliot, George. "Evangelical Teaching: Dr Cumming." *Westminster Review* 64 (1855) 436–62.

Elizabeth, Charlotte. (See also Tonna, Charlotte Elizabeth.)

———. *Personal Recollections.* 4th ed. London: Seeleys, 1854.

———. *Helen Fleetwood.* London: R. B. Seeley and W. Burnside, 1841.

———. *Principalities and Powers.* London: Seeley and Burnside, 1842.

Elliott, Edward Bishop. *Horæ Apocalypticæ: Or, a Commentary on the Apocalypse, Critical and Historical.* 4 vols. London: Seeley, Burnside and Seeley, 1844.

———. *Horæ Apocalypticæ* 5th. ed. London: Seeley, Burnside and Seeley, 1861.

Edinburgh Association for Promoting the Study of Prophecy. *Fourth Series of Lectures on Subjects Connected with Prophecy.* London: J. Nisbet, 1847.

———. *Lectures on Subjects Connected with Prophecy, Delivered at the Request of the Edinburgh Association for Promoting the Study of Prophecy.* Edinburgh: J. Johnstone, 1842.

"Essay I—By a Porter, Formerly a Gardener." In Bickersteth, *Prize Essays*, 3–30.

Erskine, Thomas. *The Brazen Serpent: Or, Life Coming Through Death.* Edinburgh: Waugh and Innes, 1831.

———. *The Purpose of God in the Creation of Man.* Edinburgh: Edmonston and Douglas, 1870.

———. *The Unconditional Freeness of the Gospel in Three Essays.* Edinburgh: Waugh and Innes, 1828.

Fletcher, Alexander. "Inward Religion." In *Fletcher's Sabbath Remembrance*, 289–94. London: G. Virtue, 1835.

Fremantle, W. H. *The World As the Subject of Redemption.* New York: Longman, Greens, 1901.

Fremantle, William Robert, "Christ the Heir of all Things." In Stewart, *The Priest Upon His Throne*, 1–25.

———, ed. *The Millennial Kingdom: Being Lectures Delivered during Lent, 1852, at St. George's, Bloomsbury.* London: J. Shaw, 1852.

———, ed. *Present Times and Future Prospects; Being Lectures Delivered during Lent, 1854, at St. George's, Bloomsbury.* London: J. Shaw, 1854.

———. "Unveiling of Hidden Wonders in Christ's Kingdom." In Fremantle, *The Millennial Kingdom*, 279–306.

Frere, James Hatley. *A Combined View of the Prophecies of Daniel, Esdras, and St. John.* London: F. C. and J. Rivington, 1815.

Fry, John. *Lyra Davidis: Or, a New Translation and Expostion of the Psalms; Grounded on the Principles Adopted in the Posthumous Work of the Late Bishop Horsley.* London: Ogle, Duncan, 1819.

———. *The Second Advent: Or, Glorious Epiphany of Our Lord Jesus Christ.* 2 vols. London: Ogle, Duncan, 1822.

Garratt, Evelyn R. *Life and Personal Recollections of Samuel Garratt.* London: J. Nisbet, 1908.

Geedes, Patrick. *Viri illustres: Acad. Jacob. sext. Scot. Reg anno CCCmo.* Edinburgh: Y. J. Pentland, 1884.

Girdlestone, Charles. *Seven Sermons Preached during the Prevalence of Cholera.* London: Printed for the author, 1832.

———. *The Increase of Mankind a Blessing: A Sermon.* London: J. G. F. and J. Rivington, 1842.

———. *Letters on the Unhealthy Condition of the Lower Class.* London: Longman, Brown, Green, and Longman, 1845.

Goodhart, Charles J. "The Established Holiness of the Church at the Lord's Advent." In Birks, *The Hope of the Apostolic Church*, 79–118.

———. "The Powers of the World to Come." In Stewart, *The Priest Upon His Throne.* 183–232.

Grant, James. *The End of All Things: Or, the Coming Kingdom of Christ.* London: Darton, 1866.

———. *The Metropolitan Pulpit: Or, Sketches of the Most Popular Preachers in London.* London: G. Virtue, 1839.

Grimshaw, T. S. "Introductory Lecture." In *Israel Restored: Or, the Scriptural Claims of the Jews upon the Christian Church*, edited by W. R. Fremantle, 1–40. London: J. Nisbet, 1841.

Guinness, Henry Grattan. *The Approaching End of the Age Viewed in the Light of History, Prophecy, and Science.* 2nd ed. London: Hodder and Stoughton, 1878.

Haldane, Alexander. *Memoirs of the Lives of Robert Haldane of Airthrey, and of His Brother, James Alexander Haldane.* London: Hamilton, Adams, 1852.

Hall, Samuel Carter. *Retrospect of a Long Life, from 1815 to 1883.* London. R. Bentley, 1883.

Hamilton, William. *A Defence of the Scriptural Doctrine concerning the Second Advent from the Erroneous Representations of Modern Millenarians.* Glasgow: M. Ogle, 1828.

Hanna, William. *Letters of Thomas Erskine of Linlathen.* 4 vols. Edinburgh: T. Constable, 1852.

———. *Memoirs of the Life and Writings of Thomas Chalmers.* 4 vols. Edinburgh: T. Constable, 1840–52.

———. *A Selection from the Correspondence of Thomas Chalmers.* Edinburgh: T. Constable, 1853.

Harris, Howell. *Brief Account of the Life of Howell Harris.* Trevecka, UK: n.p., 1791.

Harrison, William. "The Vastness of Christ's Kingdom." In Fremantle, *The Millennial Kingdom*, 307–38.

Henderson, Susannah. *Modern Fanaticism Unveiled.* London: Holdsworth and Ball, 1831.

Henry, Matthew. *An Exposition of the Old and New Testament.* New ed. Edited by George Burder and Joseph Hughes. Vol. 6. Philadelphia, Haswell, Barrington and Haswell, 1838.

Hiffernan, John Michael. *Sketches from Our Lord's History.* London: T. Hatchard, 1855.

Hoare, Edward H. *The Light of Prophecy: Being Lectures Delivered during Lent 1856 at St. George's, Bloomsbury.* London: John Farquhar Shaw, 1856.

———. "The Perfect Equity of Christ's Kingdom." In Fremantle, *The Millennial Kingdom*, 235–58.

———. *The Time of the End: Or, the World, the Visible Church, and the People of God at the Advent of the Lord.* London: J. Hatchard, 1846.

Hodder, Edwin. *The Life and Work of the Seventh Earl of Shaftesbury.* 3 vols. London: Cassell, 1886.

Holyoake, George Jacob. *Life of Joseph Rayner Stephens*. London: Williams and Norgate, 1881.
Horatius Bonar, D.D., a Memorial. London: J. Nisbet, 1889.
Hutton, James. *The Theory of the Earth. From the Transactions of the Royal Society of Edinburgh*. Edinburgh: n.p., 1788.
In Memoriam: The Rev. John Cumming. Printed for private distribution, 1881.
Irenaeus. "Against Heresies." In *Ante-Nicene Fathers*. Vol 1, edited by Philip Schaff. Christian Classics Ethereal Library ed. http://www.ccel.org/ccel/schaff/anf01
Irving, Edward. *Babylon and Infidelity Foredoomed of God*. Glasgow: W. Collins, 1826.
———. *For Missionaries after the Apostolical School: A Series of Orations*. London: Hamilton, Adams, 1825.
———. *The Last Days: A Discourse on the Evil Character of These Our Times*. London: R. B. Seeley and W. Burnside, 1828.
———. *The Orthodox and Catholic Doctrine of Our Lord's Human Nature*. London: Baldwin and Craddock, 1830.
———. *Preliminary Discourse to the Work of Ben Ezra*. Glasgow: n.p., 1827.
Jukes, Andrew. *The Second Death and The Restitution of All Things with some Preliminary Remarks on the Nature and Inspiration of Holy Scripture: A Letter to a Friend*. London: Longman, Green and Co, 1867.
Kydd, Samuel. *The History of the Factory Movement*. 2 vols. London: Simpkin, Marshall and Co, 1857.
Laicus, *The Second Advent Introductory to the World's Jubilee: A Letter to the Rev. Dr. Raffles on the Subject of his "Jubilee Hymn."* London: Ward, 1845.
Late Hours of Business. Report of a Public Meeting of the Inhabitants of Cheltenham. Cheltenham, UK: Rowe and Norman, 1844.
Leask, William. *Earth's Curse and Restitution*. London: Reprinted from *The Rainbow*, 1866.
———. *Identity of Interests in the Case of Employers, Employed, and the Public: Or, the Philosophy of the Early Closing Movement; A Lecture*. London, n.p., 1845.
———. *The Royal Rights of the Lord Jesus*. London: S. W. Partridge, 1866.
———. *Scriptural Doctrine of a Future Life*. London: Reprinted from *The Rainbow*. 1877.
Lee, Anna Mary. *A Scholar of a Past Generation: A Brief Memoir of Samuel Lee*. London: Seeley, 1896.
Liddon, H. P. *Life of Edward Bouverie Pusey*. 4 vols. London: Longman Green, 1893–97.
Lilwall, J. *The Half Holiday Question Considered*. London: Kent, 1856.
Lincoln, William. *Sermons on Subjects Connected with the Second Advent of our Lord Jesus Christ*. London: Partridge, 1859.
Locke, John. *An Essay Concerning Human Understanding*. London: W. Tegg, 1849.
Lord's Day Observance Society. *Annual Report of the Society for Promoting the Due Observance of the Lord's Day*. London: n.p., 1829–58.
Macaulay, Thomas Babbington. "Civil Disabilities of the Jews." In *The Works of Lord Macaulay*. Vol. 5. London: Longman Green, 1871.
Madden, Samuel. *The Nature and Time of the Second Advent of Messiah: Considered in Four Letters*. Dublin: W. Curry, 1829.
Maguire, Robert. *Time: Its Lessons and Warnings*. London: Cox and Wyman, 1860.

Maitland, Samuel Roffey. *Enquiry into the Grounds on Which the Prophetic Period of Daniel and St. John Has Been Supposed to Consist of 1260 Years*. London: Rivingtons, 1826.
Marsden, John Buxton. *Memoirs of the Life and Labours of the Rev. Hugh Stowell*. London: Hamilton, Adams, 1868.
Marsh, Catherine. *The Life of the Rev. William Marsh, D.D.* London: J. Nisbet, 1867.
Marsh, William. *A Few Plain Thoughts on Prophecy: Particularly As It Relates to the Latter Days, and Future Triumph of the Church of Christ; In Letters to a Friend*. 3rd. ed. London: Simpkin and Marshall, 1843.
———, ed. *Israel's Sins and Israel's Hope: Being Lectures Delivered during Lent, 1846, at St. George's, Bloomsbury*. London: J. Nisbet, 1846.
———. *The Right Choice: Or, the Difference between Wordly Diversions and Rational Recreations*. London: J. Nisbet, 1857.
———. *The Spirit of Primitive Christianity as Displayed in the Missions of the United Brethren Commonly Called Moravians: In the Parish Church of St. James, Bristol, on Tuesday Evening, July 12th, 1825*. London: Hatchard and Son, 1826.
Martin, Samuel. *Serpents in Hedges: A Plea for Moderation in the Hours Employed in Business*. London: Ward, 1850.
Maurice, Frederick Denison. *The Kingdom of Christ: Or, Hints to a Quaker, Respecting the Principles, Constitution, and Ordinances of the Catholic Church*. 2nd ed. 2 vols. London: Rivingtons, 1842.
———. *Theological Essays*. 2nd ed. London: Macmillan, 1853.
———. *Lectures on the Apocalypse: Or, Book of Revelation of St. John the Divine*. 2nd ed. London: Macmillan, 1885.
Maurice, John Frederick. *Life of Frederick Denison Maurice Chiefly Told in His Own Letters*. 2 vols. London: Macmillan, 1884.
M'Cree, George Wilson. *William Brock, D.D., First Pastor of Bloomsbury Chapel*. London: J. Clarke, 1876.
McNeile, Hugh. *England's Protest is England's Shield, For the Battle is the Lord's*. 2nd ed. London, J. Hatchard and Sons, 1829.
———. *EVERY EYE SHALL SEE HIM, or Prince Albert's Visit to Liverpool Used in Illustration of the Second Coming of Christ*. London: J. Hatchard, 1846.
———. *The Fourth Commandment, not Ceremonial, but Moral: A Scriptural Argument for the Religious Observance of the Lord's Day; With an Answer to Some Objections*. Liverpool: T. Kaye, 1856.
———. *Letters to a Friend Who Has Felt it His Duty to Secede from the Church of England and Who Imagines that the Miraculous Gifts of the Holy Ghost are Revived among the Seceders*. London: J. Hatchard, 1834.
———. *National Sin: What Is It? A Letter to the Right Honourable Sir George Grey, Bart., M.P., Her Majesty's Chief Secretary of State for the Home Department*. London: J. Hatchard and Son, 1849.
———. *Popular Lectures on the Prophecies Relative to the Jewish Nation*. London: J. Hatchard, 1830.
———. *Sermons on the Second Advent of Christ*. New ed. Liverpool: E. Howell, 1865.
Metropolitan Drapers' Association. *The Late-Hour System. A Full Report of the Speeches Delivered at a Meeting of the Metropolitan Drapers' Association*. London: J. Nisbet, 1844.

———. *A Report of the Proceedings at the Second Annual Meeting of the Metropolitan Drapers' Association, 1844.* London: 1844

———. *Report of the Third Annual Public Meeting of the Metropolitan Drapers' Association, Held at Exeter Hall, on Wednesday evening, March 12th, 1845.* London: 1845.

———. *Rules of the Metropolitan Drapers' Association, Established 18th October, 1842 for the Purpose of Obtaining an Abridgement of the Hours of Business in the Drapery and Other Trades of the Metropolis, etc.* London, 1845.

———. *Verbatim Report of the Fourth Annual Meeting of the Metropolitan Drapers' Association.* London: Aylott and Jones, 1846.

———. *Verbatim Report of the Morning Meeting in Aid of the £5000 Fund Being Raised by the Metropolitan Drapers' Association, to Promote an Abridgment of the Hours of Business in All Trades.* London: 1846.

Mill, John Stuart. "The Spirit of the Age." In *The Collected Works of John Stuart Mill, Volume XXIII—Newspaper Writings December 1822-July 1831 Part I*, edited by Ann P. Robson and John M. Robson, 227–34. London: Routledge and Kegan Paul, 1986. http://files.libertyfund.org/files/256/0223.22_Bk.pdf

Minton, Samuel. *The Evangelicals and "the Edinburgh": A Reply to the Article on "Church Parties."* London: Seeleys, 1851.

———. *The Glory of Christ in the Creation and Reconciliation of All Things.* 2nd ed. London: Longman Green, 1869.

———. *Our Present Position: The 1260 Years of Papal Domination Just Expiring, and "The Time of the End" Commencing; Three Sermons Preached at Eaton Chapel Square, on the Last Two Sundays of 1866.* London: Seeley, Jackson and Halladay, 1867.

Montagu, George [Viscount Mandeville, Sixth Duke of Manchester]. *The Finished Mystery: To Which is Added an Examination of Mr. Brown on the Second Advent.* London: J. Hatchard, 1847.

———. *The Intermediate State.* London: Wertheim and Macintosh, 1856.

———. *Things Hoped For: The Doctrine of the Second Advent as Embodied in the Standards of the Church of England.* London: J. Darling, 1837.

Montgomery, James. "Time—A Rhapsody." In *A Poet's Portfolio: or Minor Poems*, 140–44. London: Longman, Rees, Orme, Brown, Green, and Longman, 1835.

More, Hannah. *Thoughts on the Importance of the Manners of the Great to General Society.* London: T. Cadell and W. Davies, 1818.

Newton, John. "The Extent of Messiah's Spiritual Kingdom." In *Fifty Expository Discourses, on the Series of Scriptural Passages, Which Form the Subject of the Celebrated Oratorio of Handel: Preached in . . . 1784 and 1785, in the Parish Church of St. Mary Woolnoth.* 2 vols., 2:139–54. London: W. Young, 1803.

Noel, Gerard Thomas. *Arvendel: Or Sketches in Italy and Switzerland.* London: J. Nisbet, 1826.

———. *Brief Enquiry into the Prospects of the Church of Christ in Connexion with the Second Advent of our Lord Jesus Christ.* London: J. Hatchard, 1828.

———. *On the Merit of Works and Augmentation of Grace Thereby: A Sermon Preached at Tavistock Chapel, Drury Lane, on Tuesday, February 26, 1828; In the Course of Lectures on the Points in Controversy between Roman Catholics and Protestants.* London: J. Hatchard, 1828.

———. *Sermons: Intended Chiefly for the Use of Families*. 2 vols. London: J. Hatchard, 1826–27.
———. *Sermons Preached at Romsey*. London: Francis and John Rivington, 1853.
Nolan, Thomas. "The Saviour's Throne." In R. Bickersteth, *The Gifts of the Kingdom*, 289–334.
Obituary of the Late Rev. Joseph Adam Stephenson, M.A., Rector of Lympsham, Somerset. n.p., n.d.
Oliphant, Margaret O. W. *The Life of Edward Irving Minister of the National Scotch Church, London: Illustrated by his Journals and Correspondence*. 2 vols. London: Hurst and Blackett, 1862.
Pattison, Mark. "Learning in the Church of England." In *Essays by the Late Mark Pattison*, edited by Henry Nettleship, 2:263–308. Oxford: Clarendon, 1889.
Philpot, Benjamin. *All Travellers to Eternity*. London: J. Nisbet, 1852.
———. "Christ's Past Offering and Future Appearing In Connexion With Man's Death and Judgment." In Stewart, *The Priest Upon His Throne*, 264–88.
———. "Deliverance of the Meek in Christ's Kingdom." In Fremantle, *The Millennial Kingdom*, 161–86.
———. "The Dominion of the Second Adam Over all Creation." In Dallas, *Lift Up Your Heads*. 303–29.
———. "The Glorious Bridal of the Church." In Fremantle, *Present Times and Future Prospects*, 314–35.
———. "The Last Invitations of the Gospel." In Cadman, *The Parables Prophetically Explained*, 103–28.
Plumptre, Edward Hayes. *The Spirits in Prison: And Other Studies on the Life after Death*. London: W. Isbister, 1884.
Pratt, Josiah, and John H. Pratt. *Eclectic Notes: Or, Notes of Discussions on Religious Topics at the Meetings of the Eclectic Society, London; During the Years 1798–1814*. London: J. Nisbet, 1865.
Proceedings . . . Salford Drapers' Association. The Late Hour System. Manchester: G. and A. Falkner, 1844.
Public Tribute to Mr. John Lilwall, Honorary Secretary of the Early Closing and Saturday Half-Holiday Association. London: n.p., 1858.
Pyer, John. *The Coming Hour: Or, the Expectation of the Creation in View of the Second Advent of the Lord Christ; Thoughts Recently Expressed at Nottingham*. London: Trübner, 1860.
Pym, William Wollaston. "The Doctrine of the New Testament on the Time of the Second Advent." In Bickersteth, *The Second Coming*, 50–83.
———, ed. *Good Things to Come: Being Lectures Delivered during Lent, 1847, at St. George's, Bloomsbury*. London: J. Nisbet, 1847.
———. "Jerusalem's Glory." In Pym, *Good Things to Come*, 136–74.
———. "The Redeemer's Return: The Dawn of Zion's Glory." In Marsh, *Israel's Sins and Israel's Hopes*, 293–318.
———. *The Restitution of All Things*. London: J. Nisbet, 1843.
———. "The State of the World Before the Coming of Christ." In Fremantle, *The Millennial Kingdom*, 1–30.
Random Recollections of Exeter Hall in 1834–7 by one of the Protestant Party. London: J. Nisbet, 1838.

Report of a Conference on Conditional Immortality: Including Papers by the Revs. Samuel Minton, Dr Leask and Edward White, Held at the Cannon Street Hotel, London, Monday May 15th, 1876. London: E. Stock, 1876.

Sadler, Michael. *Ireland: Its Evils and their Remedies*. London. J. Murray, 1828.

———. *The Law of Population*. 2 Vols. London: J. Murray, 1830.

Scott, John. *The Life of the Rev. Thomas Scott, Rector of Aston Sandford, Bucks*. London: L. B. Seeley, 1822.

Scott, Thomas. *The Holy Bible . . . With Explanatory Notes*. 5th ed. Vol 5. London: L. B. Seeley, 1822.

Seeley, Robert Benton. *Essays on the Church*. London: Seeley and Burnside, 1834.

———. *Memoirs of the Life and Writings of M. T. Sadler*. London: Seeley and Burnside, 1842.

———. *Remedies Suggested for Some of the Evils Which Constitute "The Perils of the Nation"* (1844).

———. [Charlotte Elizabeth Tonna]. *Perils of the Nation*. London: Seeley and Burnside, 1843.

Seventh Day Baptists in Europe and America: A Series of Historical Papers Written in Commemoration of the One Hundredth Anniversary of the Organization of the Seventh Day Baptist General Conference; Celebrated at Ashaway, Rhode Island, August 20-25, 1902. Plainfield, NJ: Printed for the Seventh Day Baptist General Conference by the American Sabbath Tract Society, 1910.

Shaftesbury. *Speeches of the Earl of Shaftesbury: Upon Subjects Having Relation Chiefly to the Claims and Interests of the Labouring Class*. London: Chapman and Hall, 1868.

Shelford, Leonard Edmund. *A Memorial of the Rev. William Cadman*. London: Wells, Gardner, Darton, 1899.

Society for Improving the Condition of the Labouring Classes. *Plans for Dwelling Houses*. n.p., n.d.

Spicer, William Ambrose. *Our Day in the Light of Prophecy*. Nashville, TN: Review and Herald, 1917.

Spurgeon, C. H. *Lectures to My Students*. Reprint. Grand Rapids: Zondervan, 1954.

Stanley, Arthur Penrhyn. *The Life and Correspondence of Thomas Arnold*. 7th ed. London: B. Fellowes, 1852.

Steane, Edward, ed. *The Religious Condition of Christendom: Prepared at the Instance of the Evangelical Alliance, and Read Aug. 20 to Sept. 3, 1851*. London: J. Nisbet, 1852.

Stephen, James. *Essays in Ecclesiastical Biography*. 5th ed. London: Longman, Brown, Green, and Longmans, 1867.

———. *Letters: With Biographical Notes by his Daughter Caroline Emelia Stephen*. Printed for private circulation, 1906.

Stephens, Joseph Rayner. *Sketch of the Life and Opinions of Richard Oastler*. Leeds, UK: Printed by Joshua Hobson for Cobbett, 1838.

———. *The Political Pulpit: A Collection of Sermons Preached by the Rev. J. R. Stephens, in the Present Year, to Crowded Congregations in London, and Various Other Places, Principally in the Open Air*. London: W. Dugdale, 1839.

Stephenson, Joseph Adam. *The Christology of the Old and New Testaments; An Historical Development of the Predicted Occurrences of Holy Scripture*. 2 vols. London: J. G. and F. Rivington, 1838.

———. *The Kingdom of God Contemplated and the Steps of its Establishment Investigated: A Sermon, Preached before the London Missionary Society*. London: Printed for the Society, 1822.

Stewart, David Dale. *Evangelical Opinion in the Nineteenth Century*. London: Hatchards, 1879.

———. *Memoir of the Life of the Rev. James Haldane Stewart*. London: Hatchards, 1856.

Stewart, James Haldane, ed. *The Priest Upon His Throne: Being Lectures Delivered during Lent 1849, by Twelve Clergymen of the Church of England at St. George's, Bloomsbury*. London: J. Nisbet, 1849.

———. "The Recognition of the Saints." In Pym, *Good Things to Come*, 273–304.

———. *Thoughts on the Importance of Special Prayer for the General Outpouring of the Holy Spirit*. London: Religious Tract Society, 1821.

Story, Robert Herbert. *Memoirs of the Rev. Robert Story*. Cambridge: Macmillan, 1862.

Sumner, John Bird. *Christian Charity: Its Obligations and Objects with Reference to the Present State of Society in a Series of Sermons*. London: J. Hatchard, 1841.

Tate, G. Eward and Emilius Bayley. *Two Sermons Preached in the Church of St. Dunstan in the West, London, on the 22nd August, 1880, on the Occasion of the Death of the Rev. Edward Auriol*. London: Seeley, Jackson and Halliday, 1880.

Tonna, Charlotte Elizabeth. *Personal Recollections*. London: Seeley and Burnside, 1841.

Tonna, Lewis H. J. *A Memoir of Charlotte Elizabeth*. Bristol, UK: J. Wright, 1852.

Townsend, J. H. *Edward Hoare: A Record of His Life Based upon a Brief Autobiography*. London: Hodder and Stoughton, 1896.

Truths for the Last Days: Four Lectures on the Second Advent of Our Lord and Saviour Jesus Christ; By Members of the Winchester Prophetical Society. London: Wertheim and Macintosh, 1849.

Vaughan, Edward Thomas. *The Church's Expectation: A Sermon on the Second Advent*. London: Combe and Son, 1828.

———. *Expository Sermons*. London: S. Clarke, 1843.

———. *A Letter to Edward Bickersteth, Principal Secretary of the Church Missionary Society, on the Lawfulness, Expediency, Conduct and Expectation of Missions*. Leicester, UK: T. Combe, 1825.

Venn, John. *Sermons*. 2 vols. Boston: R. P. and C. Williams, 1822.

Villiers, H. Montagu. "The Advent of the Lord in Its Various Aspects and Speedy Approach." In Stewart, *The Priest Upon His Throne*, 367–98.

———. "The Glorious Majesty and Perpetuity of Christ's Kingdom." In Dallas, *Lift Up Your Heads*, 404–36.

———, ed. *The Second Coming of Christ Practically Considered: Being Lectures Delivered during Lent, 1844, at St. George's, Bloomsbury*. London: Nisbet, 1844.

———, ed. *The Titles of Christ Viewed Prophetically: Being Lectures Delivered during Lent, 1857, at St. George's, Bloomsbury; By Twelve Clergymen of the Church of England*. London: John Farquhar Shaw, 1857.

Waldegrave, Samuel. *New Testament Millennarianism*. London: Hamilton, Adams, 1854.

Wardlaw, Ralph. *Discourses on the Sabbath*. Glasgow: Archibald Fullarton, 1832.

———. *The Divine Authority and Permanent Obligation of the Sabbath*. London: Religious Tract Society, 1830

———. *Sermons*. London: A. Black, 1829.

Way, Lewis. *The Latter Rain: With Observations on the Importance of General Prayer for the Special Outpouring of the Holy Spirit*. London: John Hatchard and Son, 1821.
———. *Palingenesia: Or the World to Come*. London: M. Bosange, 1824.
———. [Basilicus, pseud.] *Thoughts on the Scriptural Expectations of the Christian Church*. London: A. Panton, 1828.
Wesley, John. "Sermon XLV: The New Birth." In *The Works of the Reverend John Wesley*. 4th ed. 6:61–72. London: J. Mason, 1840.
Wilson, Daniel. *The Divine Authority and Perpetual Obligation of the Lord's Day Asserted*. 2 vols. London: G. Wilson, 1831.
———. *The Evidences for Christianity Stated in a Popular and Practical Manner*. 2nd ed. 2 Vols. London: Stevens and Bell, 1833.
Wilson, William. *The Blessings of the Lord's Second Advent: Six Lectures Delivered during Lent, 1850 by Members of the Winchester Prophetical Investigation Society*. London: Wertheim and Macintosh, 1850.
———, ed. *Truths for the Last Days: Four Lectures on the Second Advent of Our Lord and Saviour*. London: Wertheim and Macintosh, 1849.
Wolff, Joseph. *Journal of the Rev. Joseph Wolff*. London: J. Burns, 1839.
Woodward, Henry. *Essays, Thoughts and Reflections, and Letters: With a Memoir by His Son, Thomas Woodward*. 5th ed. London: Macmillan, 1864.
———. *Essays, Thoughts and Reflections and Sermons on Various Subjects*. London: J. Duncan, 1836.

Parliamentary Papers

Hansard, 3rd Series

Secondary Works

Unpublished Theses

Acheson, Alan R. "The Evangelicals in the Church of Ireland, 1784–1859." PhD thesis, Queen's University, Belfast, 1968.
Bradley, Ian C. "The Politics of Godliness: Evangelicals in Parliament 1784–1832." DPhil thesis, University of Oxford, 1974.
Bromham, Ray G. "A More Charitable Christian Eschatology." MPhil thesis, University of Wales, 2000.
Brown, Ralph S. "Evangelicalism, Cultural Influences and Theological Change: Considered with Special Reference to the Thought of Thomas Rawson Birks." PhD thesis, Open University, 1996.
Duff, John. "'A Knot Worth Unloosing:' The Interpretation of the *New Heavens and Earth* in Seventeenth-Century England". PhD diss, Calvin College, Grand Rapids, 2014.
Garnett, E. J. "Aspects of the Relationship between Protestant Ethics and Economic Activity in Mid-Victorian England." DPhil thesis, University of Oxford, 1986.
Hodgson, John S. "The Movement for Shorter Hours, 1840–75." DPhil thesis, University of Oxford, 1940.

Holladay, J. Douglas. "'Vital Religion' In Action: The Evangelical Rationale for Some Humanitarian Reforms, circa 1823-47." MLitt thesis, University of Oxford, 1981.
Knickerbocker, Driss Richard. "The Popular Religious Tract in England, 1790-1830." DPhil thesis, University of Oxford, 1981.
Kochav, Sarah. "Britain and the Holy Land: Prophecy, the Evangelical Movement, and the Conversion and Restoration of the Jews, 1790-1845." DPhil thesis, University of Oxford, 1989.
Liechty, Joseph. "Irish Evangelicalism, Trinity College Dublin and the Mission of the Church of Ireland at the end of the eighteenth century." PhD thesis, National University of Ireland, Maynooth,1987.
Lloyd, Myfanwy J. "The Historical Work of S. T. Coleridge: The Later Prose Works." DPhil thesis, University of Oxford, 1998.
Oddy, John Arthur. "Eschatological Prophecy in the English Theological Tradition, c.1700-c.1840.' PhD thesis, King's College, London, 1982.
Orchard, Stephen C. "English Evangelical Eschatology, 1790-1850." PhD thesis, University of Cambridge, 1968.
Patterson, Mark Rayburn. "Designing the Last Days: Edward Irving, the Albury Circle, and the Theology of the Morning Watch." PhD thesis, King's College, London, 2011.
Rennie, Ian "Evangelicalism and English Public Life." PhD thesis, University of Toronto, 1962. Microfilm deposited in the Bodleian Library, Oxford.
Tolley, C. J. "The Legacy of Evangelicalism in the Lives and Writings of Certain Descendants of the Clapham Sect, with Special Reference to Biographical Literature." DPhil thesis, University of Oxford, 1980.

Unpublished Papers

Atkins, Gareth. "Time, Stasis and Stability in Anglican Evangelical Thought, 1790-1832." Paper delivered at the British Society for Eighteenth-Century Studies Annual Conference, 2006. No pages. Online: http://www.bsecsmail.org.uk/conferenceDiscussion.

Published Works

Society for Improving the Conditions of the Labouring Classes: A Survey, 1830-1939. n.p., 1939.
Allen, Peter. *Cambridge Apostles: The Early Years.* Cambridge: Cambridge University Press, 1978.
Altholz, Josef L. "Alexander Haldane, the Record and Religious Journalism." *Victorian Periodicals Review* 20 (1987) 28-31.
―――. *The Religious Periodical Press in Britain, 1760-1900.* Contributions to the Study of Religion 22. Westport, CT: Greenwood, 1989.
Annan, Noel G. "The Intellectual Aristocracy." In *Studies in Social History: A Tribute to G. M. Trevelyan,* edited by J. H. Plumb, 243-87. London: Longman Green, 1955.
Anderson, Benedict. *Imagined Communities: Reflections on the Origin and Spread of Nationalism.* London: Verso 1991.

Anderson, David R. "The Soteriological Impact of Augustine's Change from Premillennialism to Ammillennialism: Part One." *Journal of the Grace Evangelical Theological Society* 15 (2002) 25-36.

Atherstone, Andrew. "Frances Ridley Havergal's Theology of Nature." In *God's Bounty? The Churches and the Natural World*, edited by Peter Clarke and Tony Claydon, 319-22. Woodbridge, UK: Ecclesiastical History Society, 2010.

Baldacchino, Joseph. "The Value-Centered Historicism of Edmund Burke." *Modern Age* 27 (1983) 139-45.

Balleine, G. R. *A History of the Evangelical Party in the Church of England*. London: Longman Green, 1909.

Barnes, Robin. "Images of Hope and Despair: Western Apocalypticism c. 1500-1800." In McGinn et al., *The Encylopedia of Apocalpyticism*, 2:143-84.

Battiscombe, Georgina. *Shaftesbury: A Biography of the Seventh Earl*. London: Constable, 1974.

Bauckham, Richard. "Universalism: A Historical Survey." *Themelios* 4 (1979) 48-54.

Bebbington, David W. "The Advent Hope in British Evangelicalism since 1800." *Scottish Journal of Religious Studies* 9 (1988) 103-14.

———. *The Dominance of Evangelicalism: The Age of Spurgeon and Moody*. Leicester, UK: IVP, 2005.

———. "Evangelicals and the Role of Women, 1800-1930." *Christian Arena* 37 (1984) 19-23.

———. *Evangelical Conversion, 1740-1850*. North Atlantic Missiology Project, Position Paper Paper 21. Cambridge: North Atlantic Missiology Project, 1996.

———. *Evangelicalism in Modern Britain: A History from the 1730s to the 1980s*. London: Routledge, 1989.

———. *Holiness in Nineteenth-Century England*. Carlisle, UK: Paternoster, 2000.

———. "The Life of Baptist Noel." *Baptist Quarterly* 24 (1972) 389-411.

———. "Revival and Enlightenment." In *Modern Christian Revivals*, edited by Edith L. Blumhofer and Randall H. Balmer, 17-41. Urbana, IL: University of Illinois Press, 1993.

———. *Victorian Nonconformity*. Bangor, UK: Headstart History, 1992.

Beer, J. B., ed. *Questioning Romanticism*. Baltimore: Johns Hopkins University Press, 1995.

Bergmann, Werner. "The Problem of Time in Sociology." *Time and Society* 1 (1991) 81-134.

Bernstein, John Andrew. *Progress and the Quest for Meaning: A Philosophical and Historical Inquiry*. Rutherford, NJ: Fairleigh Dickinson University Press, 1993.

Binfield, Clyde. "Hebrews Hellenized? English Evangelical Nonconformity and Culture, 1840-1940." In *A History of Religion in Britain: Practice and Belief from Pre-Roman Times to the Present*, edited by Sheridan Gilley and William J. Sheils, 322-45. Oxford: Blackwell, 1994.

———. "Jews in Evangelical Dissent: The British Society, the Herschell Connection and the Pre-Millenarian Thread." In *Prophecy and Eschatology*. Studies in Church History Subsidia 10, edited by Michael Wilks, 225-70. Oxford: Blackwell, 2004.

Blomberg, Carl L. and Sung Wook Chung, eds. *A Case For Historic Premillennialism*. Grand Rapids: Baker, 2009.

Bone, Drummond. "The Question of a European Romanticism." In Beer, *Questioning Romanticism*, 123-32.

Boone, Kathleen. *The Bible Tells Them So: The Discourse of Protestant Fundamentalism.* Albany, NY: State University of New York Press, 1989.
Bowen, Desmond. *The Protestant Crusade in Ireland, 1800–1870.* Dublin: Gill and Macmillan, 1978.
Bowler, Peter J. *The Invention of Progress: Victorians and the Past.* Oxford: Blackwell, 1989.
Boyer, Paul. *When Time Shall Be No More. Prophecy Belief in Modern American Culture.* Cambridge, MA: Belknap, 1994.
Bradley, Ian. *The Call to Seriousness: The Evangelical Impact on the Victorians.* London: J. Cape, 1976.
Brandon, Samuel George Frederick. "The Deification of Time." In Fraser, *The Study of Time* 1:370–78.
Briggs, John H. Y., and Ian Sellers, eds., *Victorian Nonconformity.* London: Arnold, 1973.
Bright, Michael H. "English Literary Romanticism and the Oxford Movement." *Journal of the History of Ideas* 40 (1979) 385–404.
Brilioth, Yngve. *Three Lectures on Evangelicalism and the Oxford Movement.* London: Oxford University Press, 1934.
Brooke, John Hedley, "Science and Dissent: Some Historiographical Issues." In *Science and Dissent in England, 1688–1945,* edited by Paul Wood, 19–38. Aldershot, UK: Ashgate, 2004
Brown, Callum. *The Death of Christian Britain.* London: Routledge, 2000.
Brown, Ford K. *Fathers of the Victorians.* Cambridge: Cambridge University Press, 1961.
Brown, Ralph. "Evangelical Social Thought." *Journal of Ecclesiastical History* 60 (2009) 126–36.
———. "Victorian Anglican Evangelicalism: The Radical Legacy of Edward Irving." *Journal of Ecclesiastical History* 58 (2007) 675–704.
Brown, Stewart J. *Thomas Chalmers and the Godly Commonwealth in Scotland.* Oxford: Oxford University Press, 1982.
Buckley, Jerome Hamilton. *The Triumph of Time.* Cambridge, MA: Belknapp, 1966.
Burnham, Jonathan D. *A Story of Conflict: The Controversial Relationship between Benjamin Wills Newton and John Nelson Darby.* Carlisle, UK: Paternoster, 2004.
John Burrow, "Images of Time: From Carylylean Vulcanism to Sedimentary Gradualism." In Collini et al. *History, Religion, and Culture: British Intellectual History, 1750–1950,* 198–223.
Springer, Carolyn, ed. "History and Memory in European Romanticism." *Stanford Literature Review* 6 (1989).
Carter, Grayson. *Anglican Evangelicals: Protestant Secessions from the Via Media, c. 1800–1850.* Oxford: Oxford University Press, 2001.
Castle, Brian C. *Sing a New Song to the Lord: The Power and Potential of Hymns.* London: Darton, Longman and Todd, 1994.
Christensen, Torben. *The Divine Order: A Study in F. D. Maurice's Theology.* Leiden: Brill, 1973.
———. *Origin and History of Christian Socialism, 1848–54.* Aarhus, Denmark: Universitetsforlaget, 1962.
Clarke, Peter, and Tony Claydon. *God's Bounty? The Churches and the Natural World.* Woodbridge, UK: Ecclesiastical History Society, 2010.

Clark, G. S. R. Kitson. *Churchmen and the Condition of England, 1832–1885; A Study in the Development of Social Ideas and Practice from the Old Regime to the Modern State.* London: Methuen, 1973.

Clark, Victoria. *Allies for Armageddon: The Relentless Rise of Christian Zionism.* New Haven, CT: Yale Univeristy Press, 2007.

Coffey, John. "Puritanism, Evangelicalism and the Evangelical Protestant Tradition." In *The Advent of Evangelicalism: Exploring Historical Continuities,* edited by Michael A. G. Haykin and Kenneth J. Stewart, 252–77. Nashville, TN: B. & H. Academic, 2008.

Collini, Stefan, et al., eds. *That Noble Science of Politics: A Study in Nineteenth-Century Intellectual History.* Cambridge: Cambridge University Press, 1983.

———. *Economy, Polity and Society: British Intellectual History 1750–1950.* Cambridge: Cambridge University Press, 2000.

Connors, Richard, and Andrew Colin Gow, eds. *Anglo-American Millennialism: From Milton to the Millerites.* Leiden: Brill, 2004.

Creighton, Colin, *Richard Oastler, Evangelicalism and the Ideology of Domesticity.* Hull, UK: University of Hull. Department of Sociology and Social Anthropology, 1992.

Cross, Gary S. *A Quest for Time: The Reduction of Work in Britain and France, 1840–1940.* Berkeley: University of California Press, 1989.

Cutsinger, James S. *The Form of Transformed Vision: Coleridge and the Knowledge of God.* Macon, GA: Mercer, 1987.

Daley, Brian E. "Apocalypticism in Early Christian Theology." In McGinn et al., *Encyclopedia of Apocalypticism,* 3–47.

———. *The Hope of the Early Church: A Handbook of Patristic Eschatology.* Cambridge: Cambridge University Press, 1991.

Ditchfield, G. M. *The Evangelical Revival.* London: University College London Press, 1998.

Donaldson, Alistair W. *The Last Days of Dispensationalism: A Scholarly Critique of Popular Misconceptions.* Eugene, OR: Wipf & Stock, 2011.

Driver, Cecil. *Tory Radical: The Life of Richard Oastler.* New York: Oxford University Press, 1948.

de Lubac, Henri. *Medieval Exegesis: The Four Senses of Scripture.* 2 vols. Edinburgh: T. & T. Clark, 1998–2000.

Dzelzainis Ella. "Charlotte Elizabeth Tonna, Pre-millenarianism, and the Formation of Gender Ideology in the Ten Hours Campaign." *Victorian Literature and Culture* 31 (2003) 181–91.

Edwards, Pamela. *The Statesman's Science: History, Nature, and Law in the Political Thought of Samuel Taylor Coleridge.* New York: Columbia University Press, 2004.

Elliott-Binns, Leonard. *The Evangelical Movement in the English Church.* London: Methuen, 1928.

Ellison, Robert. H., and Carol Marie Engelhardt. "Prophecy and Anti-Popery in Victorian London: John Cumming Reconsidered." *Victorian Literature and Culture* 31 (2003) 373–89.

Eschabo, Andrew. "The Millennial Border between Tradition and Innovation: Foxe, Milton and the Idea of Historical Progress." In Connors and Gow, *Anglo-American Millennialism,* 1–42.

Fairchild, Hoxie N. "Romanticism and Religious Revival in England." *Journal of the History of Ideas* 2 (1941) 330–38.

———. "The Romantic Movement in England." *PMLA* 55 (1940) 20–26.
Ferber, Michael. *The Social Vision of William Blake*. Princeton: Princeton University Press, 1985.
Flegg, Columba Graham. *Gathered under Apostles: A Study of the Catholic Apostolic Church*. Oxford: Clarendon, 1992.
Forbes, Duncan. *The Liberal Anglican Idea of History*. Cambridge: Cambridge University Press, 1952.
Fraser, J. T., ed. *The Voices of Time: A Cooperative Survey of Man's Views of Time as Expressed by the Sciences and by the Humanities*. New York: G. Braziller Amherst, 1966.
———. "A Backward and a Forward Glance: The Uses and Problems of the Study of Time." In Fraser et al., *The Study of Time IV*, xiii–xxii.
———. "The Study of Time." In Fraser et al., *The Study of Time I*, 479–502.
Fraser, J. T., et al., eds. *The Study of Time I*. New York: Springer Verlag, 1972.
Fraser, J. T., and Nathaniel M. Lawrence, eds. *The Study of Time II*. New York: Springer Verlag 1975.
Fraser, J. T., et al., eds. *The Study of Time III*. New York: Springer Verlag, 1978.
———, eds. *The Study of Time IV*. New York: Springer Verlag, 1981.
Frederickson, Paula. "Apocalypse and Redemption in Early Christianity: From John of Patmos to Augustine of Hippo." *Vigiliae Christianae* 45 (1991), 151–83.
Froom, Leroy Edwin. *The Prophetic Faith of Our Fathers: The Historical Development of Prophetic Interpretation*. 4 vols. Washington, DC: Review and Herald, 1946–53.
———. *The Conditionalist Faith of our Fathers*. 2 vols. Washington, DC: Review and Herald, 1965–66.
Fryckstedt, Monica Correa. "Charlotte Elizabeth Tonna: A Forgotten Evangelical Writer." *Studia Neophilogica* 53 (1980) 79–102.
Fulford, Tim, ed. *Romanticism and Millenarianism*. New York: Palgrave, 2002.
Furst, Lilian R. *Romanticism*. London: Methuen, 1974.
Fyfe, Aileen. *Science and Salvation: Evangelical Popular Science Publishing in Victorian Britain*. Chicago: University of Chicago Press, 2004.
Gallagher, Catherine. *The Industrial Reformation of English Fiction*. Chicago: University of Chicago Press, 1995.
Garnett, E. J. "Evangelicalism and Business in Mid-Victorian Britain." In *Evangelical Faith and Public Zeal: Evangelicals and Society in Britain, 1780–1980*, edited by John Wolffe, 59–80. London: SPCK, 1995.
———. "The Gospel of Work and the Virgin Mary: Catholics, Protestants and Work in Nineteenth-Century Europe." In Swanson, *The Use and Abuse of Time*, 255–74.
———. "Nonconformists, Economic Ethics and the Consumer Society in Mid-Victorian Britain." In *Culture and the Nonconformist Tradition*, edited by Alan Kreider and Jane Shaw, 95–116. Cardiff: University of Wales Press, 1999.
Garrett, Clarke. *Respectable Folly: Millenarians and the French Revolution in France and England*. Baltimore: Johns Hopkins University Press, 1975.
Gell, Alfred. *The Anthropology of Time*. Oxford: Berg, 1992.
Gidney, W. T. *The History of the London Society for Promoting Christianity amongst the Jews: From 1809 to 1908*. London: London Society for Promoting Christianity Amongst the Jews, 1908.
Gill, John Clifford. *The Ten Hours Parson: Christian Social Action in the Eighteen-Thirties*. London: SPCK, 1959.

Gilley, Sheridan. "Newman and Prophecy, Evangelical and Catholic." *Journal of the United Reformed Church History Society* 3 (1985) 160–88.

———. "Edward Irving: Prophet of the Millennium." In *Revival and Religion since 1700*, edited by John Walsh et al, 95–110. London: Hambledon, 1993.

Gleadle, Kathryn. "Charlotte Elizabeth Tonna and the Mobilization of Tory Women in Early Victorian England." *Historical Journal* 50 (2007) 97–117.

González, Justo L. *Essential Theological Terms*. Louisville: Westminster John Knox Press, 2005.

Grass, Tim. *Edward Irving: The Lord's Watchman*. Milton Keynes, UK: Paternoster, 2011.

Gray, Robert Q. *The Factory Question in Industrial England*. Cambridge: Cambridge University Press, 1996.

Green, S. J. D. "Fremantle, William Henry (1831–1916)." In *Oxford Dictionary of National Biography*, edited by H. C. G. Matthew and Brian Harrison. Oxford: Oxford University Press, 2004; online ed., edited by Lawrence Goldman, May 2006, http://www.oxforddnb.com/view/article/53896 (accessed May 23, 2014).

Gribben, Crawford. *Evangelical Millennialism in the Trans-Atlantic World, 1500–2000*. London: Palgrave Macmillan, 2011.

———. *Rapture Fiction and the Evangelical Crisis*. Darlington, UK: Evangelical, 2006.

Gribben, Crawford, and Andrew R. Holmes, eds. *Protestant Millennialism, Evangelicalism and Irish Society, 1790–2005*. Basingstoke, UK: Palgrave Macmillan, 2006.

Gribben, Crawford, and Timothy C. F. Stunt, eds. *Prisoners of Hope? Aspects of Evangelical Millennialism in Britain and Ireland, 1800–1880*. Carlisle, UK: Paternoster, 2004.

Gribben, Crawford, and Mark Sweetnam. *Left Behind and the Evangelical Imagination*. Sheffield, UK: Sheffield Phoenix, 2011.

Griggs, Earl Leslie. *Collected Letters of Samuel Taylor Coleridge*. 6 vols. Oxford: Clarendon, 1956–71.

Hamlin, Christopher. *Public Health and Social Justice in the Age of Chadwick: Britain 1800–1854*. Cambridge: Cambridge University Press, 1998.

Harris, Harriet A. *Fundamentalism and Evangelicals*. Oxford: Clarendon, 1998.

Harris, Wendell V. "Interpretive Historicism: 'Signs of the Times' and *Culture and Anarchy* in their Contexts." *Nineteenth-Century Literature* 44 (1990) 441–64.

Harrison, J. F. C. *The Second Coming: Popular Millenarianism, 1780–1850*. London: Routledge and Kegan Paul, 1979.

Harrison, Mark. "The Ordering of the Urban Environment." *Past and Present* 110 (1986) 134–68.

Hart, Jennifer. "Religion and Social Control in the Mid-Nineteenth Century." In *Social Control in Nineteenth-Century Britain*, edited by A. P. Donajgrodzki, 108–37. London: Croom Helm, 1977.

Heasman, Kathleen. *Evangelicals in Action: An Appraisal of their Social Work in the Victorian Era*. London: Bles, 1962.

Helmstadter, Richard J. "The Nonconformist Conscience." In Parsons, *Religion in Victorian Britain*. Vol 4 *Interpretations*, 61–95.

Hempton, David. "Bickersteth, Bishop of Ripon: The Episcopate of a Mid-Victorian Evangelical." *Northern History* 17 (1981) 183–202.

———. "Evangelical Revival and Society: A Historiographical Review of Methodism and British Society c. 1750–1850." *Themelios* 8 (1983) 23–25.

———. "Evangelicals and Eschatology." *Journal of Ecclesiastical History* 31 (1980) 179–94.
Hempton, David, and Myrtle Hill. *Evangelical Protestantism in Ulster Society 1740–1890*. London: Routledge, 1992.
Hennell, Michael. *Sons of the Prophets: Evangelical Leaders of the Victorian Church*. London: SPCK, 1979.
Hick, John. *God and the Universe of Faiths*. London: Macmillan, 1973.
Hill, Charles E. *Regnum Caelorum: Patterns of Future Hope in Early Christianity*. Oxford: Clarendon, 1992.
Hilton, Boyd. *The Age of Atonement: The Influence of Evangelicalism on Social and Economic Thought, 1795–1865*. Oxford: Clarendon, 1988.
———. "Evangelical Social Attitudes: A Reply to Ralph Brown." *Journal of Ecclesiastical History* 60 (2009) 119–25.
———. "The Role of Providence in Evangelical Social Thought." In *History, Society and the Churches: Essays in Honour of Owen Chadwick*, edited by Derek Edward Dawson Beales and Geoffrey F. A. Best, 215–33. Cambridge: Cambridge University Press, 1985.
Hindmarsh, D. Bruce. *The Evangelical Conversion Narrative: Spiritual Autobiography in Early Modern England*. Oxford: Oxford University Press, 2005.
Holladay, J. D. "English Evangelicalism, 1820–1850: Diversity and Unity in 'Vital Religion.'" *Historical Magazine of the Protestant Episcopal Church* 51 (1982) 147–57.
———. "Nineteenth-Century Evangelical Activism: From Private Charity to State Intervention, 1830–50." *Historical Magazine of the Protestant Episcopal Church* 50 (1982) 53–79.
Horrocks, Don. *Laws of the Spiritual Order: Innovation and Reconstruction in the Soteriology of Thomas Erskine of Linlathen*. Carlisle, UK: Paternoster, 2004.
Houghton, Walter E. *The Victorian Frame of Mind, 1830–1870*. New Haven, CT: Published for Wellsley College by Yale University Press, 1957.
Hylson-Smith, Kenneth. *The Churches in England from Elizabeth I to Elizabeth II*. 3 vols. London: SCM, 1996–98.
———. *Evangelicals in the Church of England, 1734–1984*. Edinburgh: T. & T. Clark, 1988.
Iggers, Georg G. "Historicism: The History and Meaning of the Term." *Journal of the History of Ideas* 56 (1995) 129–51.
Inglis, Kenneth Stanley. *Churches and the Working Classes in England*. London: Routledge and Kegan Paul, 1963.
Itzkin, Ellisa S. "The Halévy Thesis—A Working Hypothesis? English Revivalism: Antidote for Revolution and Radicalism, 1789–1815." *Church History* 44 (1975) 47–56.
Johnson, Dale A. "Between Evangelicalism and a Social Gospel: The Case of Joseph Rayner Stephens." *Church History* 42 (1973) 229–42.
Jones, Peter d'Alroy. *The Christian Socialist Revival, 1877–1914*. Princeton: Princeton University Press, 1968.
Kidd, Thomas S. *The Great Awakening: The Roots of Evangelical Christianity in Colonial America*. New Haven, CT: Yale University Press, 2007.
Kobler, Franz. *Napoleon and the Jews*. New York: Schocken, 1976.

———. *The Vision Was There: A History of the British Movement for the Restoration of the Jews to Palestine*. London: Published for the World Jewish Congress, British Section, by Lincolns-Prager, 1956.

Knight, David. "Romanticism and the Sciences." In *Romanticism and the Sciences*, edited by Andrew Cunningham and Nicholas Jardine, 13–25. Cambridge: Cambridge University Press, 1990.

Knight, Frances. *The Nineteenth Century Church and English Society*. Cambridge: Cambridge University Press, 1995.

Kovačević, Ivanka, and S. Barbara Kanner. "Blue Book into Novel: The Forgotten Industrial Fiction of Charlotte Elizabeth Tonna." *Nineteenth Century Fiction* 25 (1970) 152–73.

Lambert, Frank. *Inventing the "Great Awakening."* Princeton: Princeton University Press, 1999.

Lambert, Frank. *Pedlar in Divinity. George Whitefield and the Transatlantic Revivals, 1737–1770*. Princeton: Princeton University Press, 1994.

Landes, David. *Revolution in Time: Clocks and the Making of the Modern World*. Cambridge: Harvard University Press, 1983.

Landes, Richard, "The Apocalyptic Year 1000." Center for Millennial Studies at Boston University. Online: http://www.mille.org/scholarship/1000/1000then_now.html.

Landes, Richard, Andrew Gow, and David C. Van Meter. *The Apocalyptic Year 1000: Religious Expectation and Social Change, 950–1050*. Oxford: Oxford University Press, 2003.

Lennie, Tom. *Glory in the Glen: A History of Evangelical Revivals in Scotland 1880–1940*. Fearn, UK: Christian Focus, 2009.

Lawes, Kim. *Paternalism and Politics: The Revival of Paternalism in Early Nineteenth-Century Britain*. Basingstoke, UK: Macmillan, 2000.

Lerner, Robert E. "The Medieval Return to the Thousand-Year Sabbath." In *The Apocalypse in the Middle Ages*, edited by Richard K. Emmerson and Bernard McGinn, 51–71. Ithaca, NY: Cornell University Press, 1992.

———. "Millennialism." In McGinn et al., *Encylopedia of Apocalypticism* 2:326–60.

———. "Refreshment of the Saints: The Time After Antichrist as a Station for Earthly Progress in Medieval Thought." *Traditio* 32 (1976) 99–144.

Lewis, C. S. "Introduction." In *On the Incarnation*, by Athanasius, 3–10. Crestwood, NY: St Vladimir's Seminary Press, 1944.

Lewis, Donald M., ed. *The Blackwell Dictionary of Evangelical Biography: 1730–1860*. 2 vols. Oxford: Blackwell, 1995.

———. *"Lighten Their Darkness": The Evangelical Mission to Working-Class London, 1828–1860*. New York: Greenwood, 1986.

———. *The Origins of Christian Zionism: Lord Shaftesbury and Evangelical Support for a Jewish Homeland*. Cambridge: Cambridge University Press, 2010.

Lindert, Peter H. "Unequal Living Standards." In *The Economic History of Britain Since 1700: Volume 1: 1700–1860*, edited by Roderick Floud and D. N. McCloskey, 357–86. 2nd ed. Cambridge: Cambridge University Press, 2004.

Livingstone, David N. "Evolution and Eschatology." *Themelios* 22 (1996–97) 26–36.

Lockley, Philip J. *Visionary Religion and Radicalism in Early Industrial England: From Southcott to Socialism*. Oxford: Oxford University Press, 2013.

Lubenow, W. C. *The Cambridge Apostles, 1820-1914: Liberalism, Imagination, and Friendship in British Intellectual and Professional Life*. Cambridge: Cambridge University Press, 1998.

Lyon, Eileen Groth. *Politicians in the Pulpit: Christian Radicalism in Britain from the Fall of the Bastille to the Disintegration of Chartism*. Aldershot, UK: Ashgate, 1999.

Macey, Samuel L. *Encyclopaedia of Time*. New York: Routledge, 1994.

Malmgreen, Gail. *Religion in the Lives of English Women*. Bloomington, IN: University of Indiana Press, 1986.

Mandelbaum, Maurice. *History, Men and Reason: A Study in Nineteenth-Century Thought*. Baltimore: Johns Hopkins Press, 1971.

Mangum, R. Todd, and Mark R. Sweetnam. *The Scofield Reference Bible: Its History and Impact on the Evangelical Church*. Colorado Springs: Paternoster, 2009.

Marsden, George M. "Defining Fundamentalism." *Christian Scholar's Review* 1 (1971) 141-51.

———. *Fundamentalism and American Culture*. New York: Oxford University Press, 2006.

———. "Introduction: The Evangelical Denomination." In *Evangelicalism in Modern America*, edited by George Marsden, xiv-xix. Grand Rapids: Eerdmans, 1984.

———. *Jonathan Edwards: A Life*. New Haven: Yale University Press, 2003.

———. *Understanding Fundamentalism and Evangelicalism*. Grand Rapids: Eerdmans, 1991.

McDannell, Colleen, and Bernhard Lang. *Heaven: A History*. New Haven, CT: Yale University Press, 1988.

McGinn, Bernard, et al., eds. *Encyclopedia of Apocalypticsm*. 3 vols. New York: Continuum, 1998.

———. *Visions of the End: Apocalyptic Traditions in the Middle Ages*. New York: Columbia University Press, 1979.

McLeod, Hugh. *Religion and the People of Western Europe 1789-1989*. Oxford: Oxford Univeristy Press, 1997.

Meacham, Jon. "Heaven Can't Wait." *Time*, April 16, 2012. Online: http://www.time.com/time/magazine/article/0,9171,2111227,00.html.

Meacham, Standish. "The Evangelical Inheritance." *Journal of British Studies* 3 (1963) 88-104.

Moore, LeRoy. "Another Look at Fundamentalism: A Response to Ernest R. Sandeen." *Church History* 37 (1968) 195-202.

Morley, John. *Death, Heaven and the Victorians*. Pittsburgh: University of Pittsburgh Press, 1971.

Morris, Jeremy N. *F. D. Maurice and the Crisis of Christian Authority*. Oxford: Oxford University Press, 2005.

Mumford, Lewis. *Technics and Civilization*. New York: Harcourt, Brace, 1946.

Munden, A. F. "The First Palmerston Bishop: Henry Montagu Villiers, Bishop of Carlisle, 1856-1860, and Bishop of Durham, 1860-1861." *Northern History* 26 (1990) 186-206.

Murray, Iain H. *The Puritan Hope: A Study in Revival and the Interpretation of Prophecy*. London: Banner of Truth, 1971.

Nebeker, Gary. "The Ecstasy of Perfected Love: The Eschatological Mysticism of J. N. Darby." In Gribben and Stunt, *Prisoners of Hope*, 69-94.

———. "John Nelson Darby and Trinity College Dublin." *Fides et Historia* 34 (2002) 87–108.
Newell, J. Philip. "Scottish Intimations of Modern Pentecostalism: A. J. Scott and the 1830 Clydeside Charismatics." *Pneuma* 4 (1982) 1–18.
Newport, Kenneth G. C. *Apocalypse and Millennium: Studies in Biblical Eisegesis.* Cambridge: Cambridge University Press, 2000.
Newsome, David. *The Parting of Friends: The Wilberforces and Henry Manning.* Cambridge, MA: Belknap, 1966.
Noll, Mark. *The Rise of Evangelicalism: The Age of Edwards, Whitefield and the Wesleys* Nottingham, UK: IVP 2004.
———, et al., eds. *Evangelicalism: Comparative Studies of Popular Protestantism in North America, the British Isles and Beyond, 1700–1990.* Oxford: Oxford University Press, 1994.
Norman, Edward R. *The Victorian Christian Socialists.* Cambridge: Cambridge University Press, 1987.
Numbers, Ronald L., and Jonathan M. Butler. *The Disappointed: Millerism and Millenarianism in the Nineteenth Century.* Bloomington, IN: Indiana University Press, 1987.
O'Brien, Susan. "Eighteenth-Century Publishing Networks in the First Years of Transatlantic Revivalism." In Noll et al., *Evangelicalism: Comparative Studies,* 38–57.
———. "A Transatlantic Community of Saints." *American Historical Review* 91 (1986), 811–32.
Oliver, W. H. *Prophets and Millennialists: The Uses of Biblical Prophecy in England from the 1790s to the 1840s.* Oxford: Oxford University Press, 1978.
Orchard, Stephen. "Evangelical Eschatology and the Missionary Awakening." *Journal of Religious History* 22 (1998) 132–51.
Owen, David E. *English Philanthropy 1660– 1960.* Cambridge, MA: Belknap, 1965.
Parry, Robin A., and Christopher H. Partridge, eds. *Universal Salvation? The Current Debate.* Carlisle, UK: Paternoster, 2003.
Parsons, Gerald, et al., eds. *Religion in Victorian Britain.* 4 vols. Manchester: Manchester University Press in association with the Open University, 1988–97.
Patterson, Mark, and Andrew Walker. "'Our Unspeakable Comfort': Irving, Albury and the Origins of the Pretribulation Rapture." *Fides et Historia* 31 (1999) 66–81.
Paz, D. G., ed. *Nineteenth Century English Religious Traditions: Retrospect and Prospect.* Westwood, CT: Greenwood, 1995.
Perry, Yaron. *British Mission to the Jews in Nineteenth-Century Palestine.* London: Cass, 2003.
Phillips, Paul T. *A Kingdom on Earth: Anglo-American Social Christianity, 1880–1940.* University Park, PA: University of Pennsylvania Press, 1996.
Pollowetzky, Michael. *Jerusalem Recovered: Victorian Intellectuals and the Birth of Modern Zionism.* Wesport, CT: Praeger, 1995.
Pope, Norris. *Dickens and Charity.* New York: Columbia University Press, 1978.
Poulett, George. "Timelessness and Romanticism." *Journal of the History of Ideas* 15 (1954) 3–22.
Powys, David K. "The Nineteenth and Twentieth-Century Debates about Hell and Universalism." In *Universalism and the Doctrine of Hell: Papers Presented at the*

Fourth Edinburgh Conference on Christian Dogmatics, 1991, edited by Nigel S. de Cameron, 93-138. Carlisle, UK: Paternoster, 1992.

Preyer, Robert O. "The Romantic Tide Reaches Trinity, Notes on Transmission of New Approaches to Traditional Studies at Cambridge, 1820-40." In *Victorian Science and Victorian Values: Literary Perspectives*, edited by James G. Paradis, and Thomas Postlewait, 39-68. New York: New York Academy of Sciences, 1981.

Prickett, Stephen R. *Romanticism and Religion: The Tradition of Coleridge and Wordsworth in the Victorian Church*. Cambridge: Cambridge University Press, 1976.

Rack, Henry D. "Evangelical Endings: Death-beds in Evangelical Biography." *Bulletin of the John Rylands University Library of Manchester* 74 (1992) 39-56.

Reardon, Bernard M. G.. *Religion in the Age of Romanticism: Studies in Early Nineteenth Century Thought*. Cambridge: Cambridge University Press, 1985.

———. *Religious Thought in the Nineteenth Century*. London: Cambridge University Press, 1966.

Reeves, Majorie. "Preface." In *Apocalyptic Spirituality: Treatises and Letters of Lactantius, Adso of Montier-en-Der, Joachim of Fiore, the Franciscan Spirituals, Savonarola*, edited by Bernard McGinn, xii-xvii. New York: Paulist, 1979.

Rennie, Ian S. "Fundamentalism and the Varieties of North Atlantic Evangelism." In Noll et al., *Evangelicalism: Comparative Studies*, 333-50.

———. "Nineteenth Century Roots of Contemporary Prophetic Interpretation." In *Dreams, Visions and Oracles*, edited by Carl Edwin Armerding and W. Ward Gasque, 41-59. Grand Rapids: Baker, 1977.

Rieder, John. "The Institutional Overdetermination of the Concept of Romanticism." *The Yale Journal of Criticism* 10 (1997) 145-63.

Roberts, David. *Paternalism in Early Victorian England*. New Brunswick: Rutgers University Press, 1979.

Rosman, Doreen M. *Evangelicals and Culture*. London: Croom Helm, 1984.

Rottenberg, Simon. "Legislated Early Shop Closing in Britain." *Journal of Law and Economics* 4 (1961) 118-30.

Rowell, Geoffrey. *Hell and the Victorians: A Study of the Nineteenth-Century Theological Controversies Concerning Eternal Punishment and the Future Life*. Oxford: Clarendon, 1974.

Rubenstein, William D., and Hilary L. Rubenstein. *Philosemitsm: Admiration and Support in the English-speaking World for Jews, 1840-1939*. New York: St Martin's Press, 1999.

Rudwick, M. J. S. *The Meaning of Fossils: Episodes in the History of Palaeontology*. New York: Science History Publications, 1976.

Ryn, Claes G. "Defining Historicism." *Humanitas* 11 (1998) 86-101.

Sandeen, Ernest R. "Defining Fundamentalism. A Reply to Prof. Marsden." *Christian Scholar's Review* 1 (1973) 227-33.

———. *The Roots of Fundamentalism: British and American Millenarianism, 1800-1930*. Chicago: University of Chicago Press, 1970.

———. "Towards a Historical Interpretation of the Origins of Fundamentalism." *Church History* 36 (1967) 66-83.

Schivelbusch, Wolfgang. *The Railway Journey: The Industrialization of Time and Space in the Nineteenth Century*. Berkeley: University of California Press, 1986.

Schwarz, Hans. *Eschatology*. Grand Rapids: Eerdmans, 2000.

Scotland, Nigel. *Evangelical Anglicans in a Revolutionary Age 1789-1901*. Carlisle, UK: Paternoster, 2004.

Scott, Patrick G. "Victorian Religious Periodicals: Fragments That Remain." In *The Materials, Sources and Methods of Ecclesiastical History*, edited by Derek Baker, 325-39. Studies in Church History 11. Oxford: Blackwell, 1975.

Shaw, Ian J. *High Calvinists in Action: Calvinism and the City; Manchester and London, c. 1810-1860*. Oxford: Oxford University Press, 2002.

Sizer, Stephen. *Christian Zionism: Road Map to Armageddon?* Leicester, UK: IVP, 2004.

Sizer, Susan S. *Gospel Hymns and Social Religion*. Philadelphia: Temple University Press, 1978.

Skinner, Simon A. *Tractarians and the "Condition of England": The Social and Political Thought of the Oxford Movement*. Oxford: Clarendon, 2004.

Smith, Mark A. "The Mountain and the Flower: The Power and Potential of Nature on the World of Victorian Evangelicalism." In Clarke and Claydon, *God's Bounty? The Churches and the Natural World*, 307-18.

Smith, Robert O. *More Desired Than Our Owne Salvation: The Roots of Christian Zionism*. Oxford: Oxford University Press, 2013.

Smyth, Charles. "The Evangelical Movement in Perspective." *Cambridge Historical Journal* 7 (1943) 160-74.

Soloway, R. A. *Prelates and People: Ecclesiastical Social Thought in England, 1783-1852*. London: Routledge and Kegan Paul, 1969.

Spence, Martin. "The Renewal of Time and Space: The Missing Element of Debate about Nineteenth-Century Premillennialism." *Journal of Ecclesiastical History* 63 (2012) 81-101.

———. "Unravelling Scottish Evangelicalism: Part One." *Scottish Bulletin of Evangelical Theology* 30 (2012) 30-50.

———. "Writing the Sabbath: The Literature of the Nineteenth-Century Sunday Observance Debate." In *The Church and Literature*, edited by Peter Clarke and Charlotte Methuen, 283-95. Woodbridge, UK: Boydell and Brewer, 2012.

Standage, Tom. *The Victorian Internet: The Remarkable Story of the Telegraph and the Nineteenth Century's Online Pioneers*. London: Weidenfeld and Nicolson, 1998.

Stevenson, Peter K. *God In Our Nature: The Incarnational Theology of John McLeod Campbell*. Carlisle, UK: Paternoster, 2005.

Strachan, C. Gordon. *The Pentecostal Theology of Edward Irving*. London: Dartman, Longman and Todd, 1973.

Stunt, Timothy C. F. *From Awakening to Secession: Radical Evangelicals in Switzerland and Britain, 1815-35*. Edinburgh T. & T. Clark, 2000.

———. "Geneva and British Evangelicals in the Early Nineteenth Century." *Journal of Ecclesiastical History* 32 (1982) 35-46.

———. "Influences in the Early Development of J. N. Darby." In Gribben and Stunt, *Prisoners of Hope*, 44-68.

———. "John Nelson Darby: The Scholarly Enigma." *Brethren Archivists and Historians Network Review* 2 (2003) 70-4.

Swanson, Robert N. *The Use and Abuse of Time in Christian History: Papers Read at the 1999 Summer Meeting and the 2000 Winter Meeting of the Ecclesiastical History Society*. Studies in Church History 37. Woodbridge, UK: Boydell and Brewer, 2002.

Sweeney, Douglas A. *The American Evangelical Story: The History of the Movement*. Grand Rapids: Baker, 2005.

Sweetnam, Mark. Lecture given at Darby Day, Trinity College, Dublin, 17th September 2009. MP3 audio. Online: http://homepage.eircom.net/~sweetnam/Mark%20Sweetnam%20-%20Darbys%20Differential%20Hermeneutic.mp3

Thompson, E. P. *The Making of the English Working Class*. Harmondsworth, UK: Penguin, 1963.

———. "Time, Work-Discipline and Industrial Capitalism." *Past and Present* 38 (1967) 56–97.

Time and Society. 9 vols. Thousand Oaks, CA: Sage, 1992–2000.

Tolley, Christopher. *Domestic Biography: The Legacy of Evangelicalism in Four Nineteenth-Century Families*. Oxford: Clarendon, 1997.

Toon, Peter. *Evangelical Theology, 1833–1856: A Response to Tractarianism*. London: Marshall, Morgan and Scott, 1979.

Tuchman, Barbara Wertheim. *Bible and Sword: England and Palestine from the Bronze Age to Balfour*. New York: Funk and Wagnels, 1986.

Turnbull, Richard. "Eschatology and the Social Order: A Historical Perspective." *Whitefield Briefing* 3 (1998) 1–4.

———. *Shaftesbury: The Great Reformer*. Oxford: Lion, 2010.

Whitaker, Wilfred B. *Victorian and Edwardian Shop Workers*. Newton Abbot, UK: David and Charles, 1973.

Vidler, Alexander R. *The Church in an Age of Revolution*. Harmondsworth, UK: Penguin, 1990.

Voth, Hans-Joachim. *Time and Work in England 1750–1830*. Oxford: Clarendon, 2000.

Walker, David P. *The Decline of Hell: Seventeenth-Century Discussions of Eternal Torment*. Chicago: University of Chicago Press, 1964.

Walsh, John D. "The Bane of Industry? Popular Evangelicalism and Work in the Eighteenth Century." In Swanson, *The Use and Abuse of Time*, 223–41.

———. "Joseph Milner's Evangelical Church History." *Journal of Ecclesiastical History* 10 (1959) 174–87.

———. "Origins of the Evangelical Revival." In *Essays in Modern Church History in Memory of Norman Skyes*, edited by G. V. Bennet and John D. Walsh, 132–62. London: Black, 1996.

Ward, J. T. *The Factory Movement, 1830–1855*. London: Macmillan, 1962.

Ward, W. Reginald. *Early Evangelicalism: A Global Intellectual History 1670–1789*. Cambridge: Cambridge University Press, 2006.

———. *The Protestant Evangelical Awakening*. Cambridge: Cambridge University Press, 1992.

Warhman, Dror. *Imagining the Middle Class: The Political Representation of Class in Britain c. 1780–1840*. Cambridge: Cambridge University Press, 1995.

Waterman, Anthony M. C. "The Ideological Alliance of Political Economy and Christian Theology 1798–1833." *Journal of Ecclesiastical History* 34 (1982) 231–44.

Watts, Michael R. *The Dissenters*. 2 vols. Oxford: Clarendon, 1978–95.

Weber, Timothy P. *Living in the Shadow of the Second Coming: American Premillennialism, 1875–1925*. New York: Oxford University Press, 1979.

Wheeler, Michael. *Death and the Future Life in Victorian Literature and Theology*. Cambridge: Cambridge University Press, 1990.

Whitrow, G. J. "Reflections on the History of the Concept of Time." In Fraser et al., *The Study of Time* I:1–11.

Wittmer, Michael E. *Heaven Is A Place on Earth: Why Everything You Do Matters to God.* Grand Rapids: Zondervan, 2004.

Wolffe, John. *The Expansion of Evangelicalism: The Age of Wilberforce, More, Chalmers and Finney.* Nottingham, UK: IVP, 2006.

———. *God and Greater Britain: Religion and National Life in Britain and Ireland 1843–1945.* London: Routledge 1994.

———. *The Protestant Crusade in Great Britain, 1829–1860.* Oxford: Clarendon, 1991.

———. "Recordites (*act.* 1828–c.1860)." In *Oxford Dictionary of National Biography*, online edn., edited by Lawrence Goldman. Oxford: OUP, January 2013. http://www.oxforddnb.com/view/theme/93815 (accessed July 27, 2013).

Wood, A. Skevington. "The Eschatology of Irenaeus." *Evangelical Quarterly* 41 (1969) 30–41.

Index

Adso of Montier-en-Der, 34
Albert Edward, Prince of Wales (King Edward VII), 164n67
Albury Conferences, 54, 55, 56, 61, 212, 213, 250
Alexander I (Tsar of Russia), 116
Alexandra, Princess, 164n67
allegorical interpretation of Scripture, 109–11, 120
Anabaptists, 35
Anderson, Robert, 264
Anderson, William, 111
Anglo-Catholicism, 27. *See also* Oxford Movement
Annan, Noel, 27
annihilationism. *See* conditional immortality
Antichrist, 33–34, 49, 265
apocalypticism, 7, 32–36, 190. *See also* catastrophism
apokatastasis, 103, 124, 154
Arnold, Thomas, 41, 72, 262
Arthur, William, 243
Ashley Cooper, Anthony. *See* Shaftesbury, 7th Earl of
Ashley, Lord. *See* Shaftesbury, 7th Earl of
atonement, 6, 172
Augustine of Hippo, Saint 32–33, 35
Auriol, Edward, 143, 167, 232, 250

Baconian inductivism, 82
Bampton Lectures, 156, 261
Basilicus. *See* Way, Lewis
Bayford, John, 47, 53
Bayley, Emilius, 60, 232

Bebbington, David W., 47n64, 51n79, 65, 256
Beddington Park conference, 251–3
Bede, the Venerable, 34
Begg, James, 122n85, 240, 244
Begg, James A., 122, 128, 134, 167, 170
Belford, James, 245–46
Bell, Rob, 8
Ben Ezra, Juan Josafat, 53, 57
Bengel, Albrecht, 36
Bennett, William, 243
Benson, A.C., 144
Beza, Theodore, 133
Bickersteth, Edward, 5, 56, 60, 77, 95, 109, 114, 117, 122, 123, 125, 132, 133, 138, 140, 144, 163, 165, 191, 205, 220, 232, 236, 250
Bickersteth, Edward Henry, 163–5
Binney, Thomas, 210, 240
Birks, Thomas Rawson, 6, 57, 58, 76n9, 79, 80, 85, 89, 90, 92, 93, 95, 96, 99, 108, 123, 126, 130, 135, 139–40, 143, 149, 150, 157, 162–65, 167, 169, 190, 217, 218, 218–19, 227, 263
Blake, William, 67, 179, 180
bodily resurrection: *see* resurrection of the body
Bogue, David, 63, 126
Bonar, Horatius, 57n102, 59, 60, 94, 142, 167
Bonnet, Charles, 125
Bosanquet, Samuel Richard, 229
Boyd, Archibald, 243
Boys, Thomas, 126, 136, 144, 155
Brethren, 11, 43, 49, 50, 51, 61, 120
Bridges, Charles, 132

299

INDEX

British empire, 15, 76, 95–97, 144, 191, 223
broad church, 7, 27, 40, 41, 147, 152, 203
Brock, Mourant, 57, 96, 141, 150
Brooks, Joshua W., 60, 103, 104, 122, 137, 143
Brown, David, ix, 29
Brown, Ford K., 26
Brown, James, 91, 161, 168
Brown, Ralph, 122, 123, 212, 218n47
Bucer, Martin, 113
Buckley, Jerome, 3
Bullinger, E.W., 265
Burder, George, 133
Burgess, Richard, 240
Burgh, William, 49, 84
Burns, James Drummond, 24
Burrow, John, 86
Buxton, Thomas Fowell, 14–15

cable telegraph, 69, 94, 96
Cadman, William, 130, 135, 141, 142
Chambers, Robert, 91
California gold rush, 93
Calvin, John, 112
Calvinism, 44–45, 123n89, 152, 155, 172, 237, 245
Campbell, John McLeod, 171–73, 175, 248
Carlyle, Thomas, 3, 72, 125
Catastrophism
    geological theory, 69–70, 87;
    metaphor for end of time, 56, 60, 72, 85, 87, 99 144;
    providence and, 69.
    See also apocalypticism
Catholic Apostolic Church, 42—3, 56n95
Chalmers, Thomas, 16, 20, 22, 38, 42, 131–33, 211, 215, 221, 236–38
Champneys, William Weldon, 240
Charles, Thomas, 37
chiliasm. *See* millennium
Christian Herald, 60, 106, 137, 175
Christian Influence Society, 220–24, 232, 235, 240

Christian Lady's Magazine, 60, 121, 126, 135, 170, 175, 220n55
Christian Observer, 16, 19, 21, 23, 24, 25, 31, 38, 40, 42, 54, 102, 183, 185, 215
Christian socialism, 179, 200, 209, 248
Church Missionary Society, 15, 56
Church, R.W., 27
Churchman's Monthly Review, 60, 76–79, 84, 86, 88–89, 91, 94–95, 105, 127, 156, 180, 215, 220–21, 225, 231n97, 235
cities, 7, 94, 142 205–7, 231, 233
Clapham Sect, 13, 18, 27, 41, 56
Clayton, John, 39
Close, Francis, 47, 240, 242
Coleridge, Samuel Taylor, 125, 179, 180, 199, 206n7, 220
common sense philosophy, 10, 107–12
Comte, Augustus, 71
conditional immortality, 157–61.
    See also death; post-mortem salvation
Congress of Vienna, 116
Continental Society, 44–45
Conversazione Society, 179
Conybeare, J. W., 41
Cooper, Edward, 55
Cooper, Robert Bransby, 52
Cornerstone University, 1n3
Corpus Christi College, Oxford, 2, 184
Cowper, William, 94
Cox, John, 46, 141, 166, 191, 230
creation, the, 21–22, 25, 46, 64, 77, 81, 90–92, 99, 123, 127–29, 131–32, 168, 171, 178, 190, 197. *See also* new creation; palingenesia; restitution of all things
Croly, George, 94, 142
Crystal Palace, 243n143
Cumming, John, 6, 74, 96, 97, 128, 134, 136, 141, 142, 143, 154, 219, 240, 242
Cunninghame, William, 53
curse, 102, 106, 127–28, 150, 159, 173, 197
Cuvier, George, 69n140

Dale, Robert W., 22, 166
Dale, Thomas, 232, 240
Dallas, Alexander, 84, 150, 168, 184
Dalton, William, 141
Daly, Robert, 49, 58, 184
Darby, John Nelson, x, 43, 46, 49–51, 55, 58–59, 61, 63, 118–124, 138, 184, 256
Darwin, Charles, 257
de Alcazar, Luis, 192
de Saussure, Henri, 69n140
death:
 as entry into eternal life, 1, 5, 16–17, 23–24, 62, 87n53, 111, 262;
 as evangelistic tool, 16
 premillennialist attitude toward 136–40, 145, 160, 161n58, 163, 176, 188.
 See also conditional immortality; post-mortem salvation
deep time, 69–70, 92. *See also* geology
Devil, 32, 103, 157, 148, 160, 164, 166, 168, 177, 198
Dibdin, William, 240
Dickens, Charles, 41, 206
dispensationalist premillennialism, x, 49–51, 55, 59n110, 61, 87, 97, 118–23, 138, 255–58, 265.
dispensations, 54, 76, 98, 118, 150, 162, 194, 198, 246
Drummond, Henry, 54, 56, 83, 88, 219, 231, 250
dualism, 23, 29, 120, 138, 264. *See also* Platonism

Early Closing Association, 3, 234, 238, 240–47
earthliness, 15, 33, 39–40, 119–20
earthly kingdom, 32, 104, 113, 118, 191, 220, 262. *See also* kingdom of Christ; kingdom of God; millennium
Eclectic Review, 12, 107
Edinburgh Association for Promoting the Study of Prophecy, 59
Edinburgh Review, 41
Edward, Jonathan, 37, 214
Eichhorn, Johann Gottfried, 192

Elizabeth, Charlotte. *See* Tonna, Charlotte Elizabeth
Elliot, George, 41, 75
Elliott, Edward B, 57, 61, 77–79, 84, 103
Erskine, Thomas, 152–54, 189–90
eschatology (definition), 22–23, 28–29
Essays and Reviews, 149, 258
established church, 43, 51, 59, 122–23, 220
eternal punishment, 147–49, 155, 157–65, 181, 182–83, 265. *See also* conditional immortality, eternity; hell; post-mortem salvation; universalism
eternity:
 as opposite of time, 3, 5, 6, 14–25, 85;
 as quality of existence, 28, 51, 62, 65, 72–73, 90, 92, 111, 129, 136, 146, 149, 168–69, 177 80, 199, 244,n145, 246, 251–52;
 as synonym of heaven, 5, 22–25;
 relationship to duration , 181–83, 185–88
Eusebius, 32, 192n192
Evangelical Alliance, 11, 164, 182

Faber, George Stanley, 53
factory reform, 3, 224, 235–40
Fairchild, Hoxie, 125
Fichte, Johann Gottlieb, 70, 71, 124
fifth monarchists, 35, 47n69
Finch, Henry, 133
first resurrection, 134. *See also* resurrection of the body
Fletcher, Alexander, 10
Francke, Augustus, 10n3
Fraser, Julius Thomas, 4
Freemantle, William Henry, 261–63
Freemantle, William Robert, 76, 134, 261
French revolution, 19, 55, 114–5
Frere, James Hatley, 47, 53, 54, 58, 59n112, 81
Frey, Friedrich, 116
Froom, Edwin Leroy, 57, 61, 259
Fry, John, 47, 53
fundamentalism, 51, 80–3

futurism, x, 47–51, 53, 58, 59, 60n117, 61, 75, 82, 84–86, 97, 102n11, 107, 110, 111, 121, 123, 184, 192, 255–56, 258–59, 265. *See also* dispensationalist premillennialism

Garnett, E. J., 3, 210n17
Garratt, Samuel, 265
Gell, Alfred 4
Genevan *réveil*, 44, 45
geology, 69–70, 78, 87, 90–92, 146, 153. *See also* catastrophism: geological theory; deep time
Gibbon, Edward, 77–78
Girdlestone, Charles, 230n90
Gladstone, William, 12
glossolalia, 174–75
God-man, 169, 191
Goodhart, Charles, 97, 130, 134, 141, 142, 170, 180, 250
Grant, James, 58
Gregory of Nysa, 164n74
Gribben, Crawford, 109–10
Grotius, Hugo, 192
Guinness, Henry Grattan, 48

Haldane, Alexander, 44
Haldane, Robert, 44
Halévy Thesis, 19n43
Hall, Samuel Carter, 241
Hammond, Henry, 192
Hare, Julius, 179
Harris, Howell, 10
Harris, Wendell V., 93
Harrison, Brian, 2
Harrison, William, 144, 162
Hartley, David, 161n58
Hawtrey, Charles, 54, 116
heaven, 1, 5–6, 14, 20, 21–26, 28, 33, 39, 40, 63, 64, 65, 67, 74, 80, 99, 100–102, 105, 106–7, 111–13, 118–21, 126–38, 140, 141, 145, 146, 150, 157, 160, 169, 170, 178, 180, 186–90, 196, 199–201, 206, 208, 211, 217, 225, 227, 233, 247, 251, 255–56, 262, 267
Hegel, Georg, 70, 71

Helen Fleetwood (Charlotte Elizabeth Tonna), 221n57, 230, 238
hell, 6, 14, 147–49, 157, 159, 162–65, 182, 188. *See also* eternal punishment
Helmstadter, Richard J., 23
Henderson, Susannah, 63
Henry, Matthew, 112
Herder, Johann Gottfried, 192
Herrenschneider, Johan Samuel, 192
Hewitson, William Hepburn, 29
Hiffernan, John Michael, 183–90
higher criticism, 257–60, 264
Hilton, Boyd, 6, 20, 22, 61, 88–90, 131, 132, 143, 147, 148n4, 149n9, 205–6, 211–18, 224n71, 227, 231, 238
historic premillennialism, 121n82
historical criticism. *See* higher criticism
historicism (cultural disposition), 70–3
historicism (interpretation of apocalyptic Scripture), 47–54. *See also* historicist premillennialism
historicist premillennialism: adoption in the nineteenth century, 53–61;
compared with other forms of premillennialism, 47–52, 117–23, 256–60;
decline of, 257–63;
definition of, ix, 6;
misconceptions of, 29–30, 55, 61, 211–6, 218n47
Hoare, Edward, 95, 169
Hoare, Edward Newenham, 60, 95n89, 106
holiness movement, 253–4
Holy Spirit, 35, 42, 46, 63, 171–78, 251–54
Houghton, Walter, 71n147
Hughes, Henry, 240
Hughes, Joseph, 113
Hus, Jan, 11
Hutton, James, 69

incarnation, x, 22, 52, 65, 131, 147, 165–78, 180, 191, 196, 199, 203, 252

industrial revolution *see* industrialization
industrialization, 7, 43, 210–11, 214, 222, 224, 230, 235–40, 243, 248, 267
intermediate state, 137, 149, 161n58. *See also* post-mortem salvation
Ireneaus, 32, 38, 120, 150
Irving, Edward, 58, 60, 61, 63, 125, 138, 152, 161n58, 173–76, 195, 212, 215, 250, 252
Israel:
as a model for social reform, 225–26;
relationship to the church, 49n74, 112–14, 118–24, 201, 226, 267;
restoration of, 105, 111, 112–17, 145, 155–56

Jerome, Saint, 34n10
Joachim of Fiore, 34, 52
Jowett, Benjamin, 261
Justin Martyr, 32, 38

Kanner, S. Barbara, 207
Keble, John, 27
Keswick Convention, 254
Kingdom of Christ, 45, 47, 57, 66–67, 98, 101, 103–5, 112–13, 117–21, 129, 133, 144, 145, 162, 166, 178–79, 190–202, 245, 255, 261–63. *See also* Kingdom of God; Maurice, F. D.; mediatorial kingdom; millennium
Kingdom of God, 7, 35, 45, 50, 52, 64, 76, 93, 94, 96–97, 98, 101, 117, 125, 129, 135, 146, 162, 167, 186, 210, 218, 247
Kingsley, Charles, 179, 209
Kovačević, Ivanka, 207

Labourer's Friend Association, 232
Lactantius, 32
Lacunza Y Diaz, Manuel, 53
laissez-faire, 211–16, 236–38
Leask, William, 98, 110, 158–61, 168, 243, 246–47, 263
Lee, Samuel, 192n192

Lewis, C.S., 248
Lewis, Donald, 60n115, 123n89, 206n9, 213–14
liberalism:
economic 214, 239, 248;
political 18–19, 71, 115, 144, 215;
theological, x, 6, 40, 51, 107, 146–47, 152, 156, 203, 257–64.
See also laissez-faire
Lilwall, John, 241
literalism, 47, 81–86, 107–24, 126, 158–59, 259
Livingstone, David, 22
Locke, John, 10, 181–83
London Missionary Society, 42, 194, 196
London Society for Promoting Christianity Amongst the Jews, 166
Lord's Day Observance Society, 243
Ludlow, John Malcolm, 179, 209
Luther, Martin, 112
Lyell, Charles, 69

Macaulay, Thomas Babington, 47, 71, 89, 224
Madden, Samuel, 108
Maguire, Robert, 69
Maitland, Samuel Roffey, 49
Malthus, Thomas, 22, 141, 224–27
Manchester, 7th Duke of (George Montagu), 46, 54, 137, 195n208
Marsden, George, 82–83, 86
Marsh, William, 117, 150, 236, 250–53
Marx, Karl, 222, 247
Maude, William, 158
Maurice, Frederick Denison, 27, 65, 66, 148, 164–65, 178–203, 208n14, 209, 240, 247–48
McGinn, Bernard, 28
McNeile, Hugh, 54, 56, 117, 128, 141, 155n40, 158, 219, 232, 240, 250
Mede, Joseph, 52–54, 61
mediatorial kingdom, 194–99. *See also* kingdom of Christ
Metropolitan Drapers' Association, 241–42
Mildmay conferences, 253–54
Mill, John Stuart, 70, 93

millennium, ix, 32–40, 45–47, 50–54, 62–63, 91n71, 104–7, 121, 124n92, 125–26, 149–51, 156, 163, 192, 195n208, 198, 204–5, 225–26, 228, 255–56. *See also* dispensationalist premillennialism; historicist premillennialism
Miller, Hugh, 153n31
Minton, Samuel, 157–58
Minton-Steinhouse, Samuel. *See* Minton, Samuel
Montagu, George. *See* Manchester, 7th Duke of
Moody, Dwight L., 50, 254
Moravians, 11
More, Hannah, 14, 26, 229
Morris, Jeremy, 199, 200n227

Napoleonic Wars, 12
Nebeker, Gary L., 120
new creation, 1–2, 8, 91n71, 102–7, 126–33, 148, 150, 153n31, 165, 201, 225, 266. *See also* creation, the; restitution of all things
Newman, John Henry, 27
Newport, Kenneth, 29, 30
Newsome, David, 72
Newton, Isaac, 52
Newton, John, 38, 193
Niebuhr, Barthold, 70, 78
Noel, Baptist W., 240
Noel, Caroline, 154
Noel, Gerald T., 5, 50, 75, 88, 100–101, 105, 109, 116–17, 128, 130, 151, 153–54, 167–70, 175, 180, 240, 250
Nolan, Frederick, 81
Nolan, Thomas, 105, 240, 244, 250

Oastler, Richard, 236–37
Oetinger, Friedrich Christoph, 124, 125n93
Oliver, W.H., 54, 55n93, 104n19
Orchard, Stephen, 247
Origen, 64n74, 103, 110–11, 120
Origenism. *See* Origen
Ottoman Empire, 76, 115, 152

Owen, Robert, 18
Oxford Movement, 27, 43n46, 120n78, 209

palingenesia, 124–25. *See also* restitution of all things
paternalism, 208, 211–13, 218–28
Pattinson, Mark, 27
Pennefather, William, 59, 183, 253–54
pessimism, 6, 29–30, 39, 61, 72, 115, 120, 142–44, 203, 205, 213–14
Peterson, Johan Wilhelm, 36
Philip Spenner, 10n3
Philpot, Benjamin, 135, 167, 168
pietism, 1 9, 11
Platonism, 33, 159, 179, 199, 262. *See also* dualism
Plumptre, Edward H., 164, 190
Plymouth Brethren. *See* Brethren
political economy, 210–17, 223, 226, 236–38, 259. *See also* laissez-faire; liberalism: economic
poor laws, 19, 20, 222, 224
Pope, Norris, 231n96, 233
postmillennialism, ix, 31, 34–35, 37–40, 46, 47, 52–3, 55, 57n102, 62–64, 107, 205, 207
post-mortem salvation, 148–49. *See also* conditional immortality; intermediate state; universalism
Poulett, George, 68
poverty, 6, 20, 22, 203–5, 249
Powerscourt conferences, 49, 58, 184
Powerscourt, Theodosia, 49
Powys, David, 148
Praeterism, 191–93, 195, 198–99
premillennialism. *See* dispensationalist premillennialism; historicist premillennialism; millennium
Prickett, Stephen, 66
Priestly, Joseph, 161n58
progress. *See* time: progress and
Prophecy Investigation Society, 59–60, 76, 233, 247, 261, 264–66
Prophetical Alliance, 59
providence, 52, 71, 79, 211–16, 225–27, 230–31
Puritans, 35–36, 113–14, 208

INDEX

Pusey, Edward, 27
Pyer, John, 127
Pym, William, 90, 102–3, 105, 121, 137, 169, 232

quadriga, 110
Quarterly Journal of Prophecy, 41n39, 60, 75, 77, 79n22, 80, 84, 86, 87, 88, 89, 90, 91, 93, 95, 98, 106, 109, 110, 111, 127, 133, 135, 141, 144, 150, 156, 170, 204, 217, 257, 260

railways, 69, 95
Rainbow, 158
Ramsey, A. M., 199
Ranke, Leopold von, 70, 78
rapture, 1, 50, 59, 74, 120–21, 123, 255–56, 265
Reardon, Bernard, 66, 67
Record, 19, 44, 60–61, 212–16, 218, 224–25
Recordites, 212–16. See also *Record*
refrigerium sanctorum, 34
religious census (1851), 13
renewal of creation. See *new creation*
Rennie, Ian, 44
restitution of all things, 67, 91n71, 98, 102–33, 139–40, 153, 156–65, 170, 195n208, 196–97, 200, 225–26, 247, 252. See also new creation; palingenesia
resurrection of the body, 6, 23–25, 64, 87n53, 134–40, 160–61, 170, 196
resurrection of the dead: see resurrection of the body
return of Christ. See second advent
Revelation (Biblical book), 32, 48, 61, 75, 77, 80, 92, 104, 134, 192–93, 198, 200
Robertson, Frederick William, 240
romanticism, ix, 7, 21n48, 43, 65–73, 252, 255;
    history and, 77–86, 260;
    restitution of all things and, 107, 124–33; 135–36, 145;
    sabbatarianism and, 3, 244n145;

theological revisionism and, 165, 179–99, 260
Roquetaillade, John of, 34
Rosman, Doreen, 18n38, 21, 22
Rowell, Geoffrey, 148, 164

sabbatarianism, 2–3, 243–44. See also sabbath
sabbath, 2, 13, 34, 44, 213, 225, 243–44. See also sabbatarianism
Sadler, Michael, 223–27, 231, 235–36, 239, 242
salvation, 1, 39, 57, 86, 104–7, 113, 118–24, 125, 130, 132–33, 145, 191–202, 225, 250, 262. See also conditional immortality, eternity, heaven; kingdom of Christ; kingdom of God; post-mortem salvation; universalism
Sandeen, Ernest H., 50–51, 59n110, 60n115, 80–84
Sankey, Ira D., 256
Satan. See *Devil*
Saturday Half-Day Holiday Association, 241, 245
Schelling, Friedrich, 71, 124
Schlegel, Friederick von, 79
Schleiermacher, Friedrich, 67, 124
Scofield Reference Bible, 50
Scott, Alexander John, 43, 175
Scott, Thomas, 14, 37, 38, 39, 62
second advent, ix, 1, 6, 33–34, 38, 45–47, 50–54, 56, 62–63, 66, 87n53, 91n71, 95, 97, 101, 104–6, 112, 116–17, 132, 137–38, 153n31, 165–71, 192–95, 198, 200–201, 205, 214, 246, 253, 256, 265
second coming. See second advent
Seeley, Robert Benton, 217, 220, 221–24, 226–28, 229, 230–31, 232, 237
Shaftesbury, 7th Earl of (Anthony Ashley Cooper), x, 6n11, 69, 204–5, 220, 231n96, 216, 230–32, 235, 236, 240, 242, 247, 248, 250, 251
Shaw, Ian, 229
Simeon, Charles, 27, 39n29, 46, 117

Sizer, Susan, 30
social gospel, x, 33, 166, 209–28, 244, 262–63
Society for Improving the Condition of the Labouring Classes, 232–33
Society for the Investigation of Prophecy, 58, 59n110
Society for the Suppression of Vice, 18
soul, 5–6, 14, 17, 22, 23, 25, 63, 64, 111–12, 129, 134–40, 145, 159–61, 206, 216, 218n47, 221, 228–30, 245. See also conditional immortality
Spurgeon, Charles Haddon, 256
Stanley, Arthur, 261
steamships, 96–96
Stephen, James, 13
Stephens, Joseph Rayner, 210–11
Stephenson, Joseph Adam, 132, 191–99
Stewart, James Haldane, 42, 54, 59n112, 104, 127, 135–36
Stunt, Timothy, 215
Sumner, John Bird, 20, 211
Sunday observance. See sabbatarianism

Taborites, 35
telegraph. See cable telegraph
Ten Hours Movement, 3, 224, 235–40
Tennyson, Alfred, 3, 70, 97
Thompson, E. P., 55, 239
Thwaites, John, 240
time:
  as a metaphor for life, 14–26, 68, 94–95;
  God and, x, 7, 33, 52, 73–74;
  historical, 74–80, 86–92;
  industrialization and, 69, 92, 94–95, 238–40;
  nineteenth-century experience of, 3–4, 68–72, progress and, 20, 86–92, 97–99, 140–45, 147–54;
  scholarship of, 4–5;
  social reform and, 233–49.
  See also eternity; geology
Todd, James, 49
Tolley, Christopher, 14n24
tongues, speaking in. See *glossolalia*

Tonna, Charlotte Elizabeth, 6, 60, 75, 117, 121, 207–8, 220, 221–22, 225–26, 230, 235, 238–39
Townsend, George, 127
tractarianism. See Oxford Movement
Trinity College, Cambridge, 179, 190n186
Trinity College, Dublin, 49
Trollope, Anthony, 41
Tübingen, University of, 257
Turkish Empire . See Ottoman Empire

Unitarianism, 36, 161n58
universalism, 103, 147–57, 159–60, 162–65
urbanization. See cities
utopianism, 18

Vaughan, Edward Thomas, 45, 54, 169, 171, 176–78
Venn, John, 15, 16, 17, 18, 21, 23
Victoria, Queen, 13
Villiers, Henry Montagu, 59, 60, 232, 233, 240

Waldegrave, Samuel, 156
Walker, David, 148n5
Wahrman, Dror, 239
Ward, W.R., 21, 38
Wardlaw, Ralph, 28
Wars of Religion, 36, 192
Watts, Isaac, 9
Way, Lewis, 45, 47, 53, 58, 103n14, 111, 116, 124, 134, 137, 149
Weber, Timothy, 55n92
Werner, Gottlieb, 69n140
Wesley, Charles, 37n23
Wesley, John, 10, 11, 18, 39
Whiston, William, 52
Whitby, Daniel, 36
Wilberforce, William, 13, 26, 27, 44, 223, 229
Wilks, Samuel C., 185
Williams, George, 240
Wilson, Daniel, 10
Wilson, H.B., 149
Wolffe, John, 83, 212n24
Woodward, Henry, 183–90

Woodward, Richard, 183
Wordsworth, William, 129, 136
Working Man's Charter, 243–44
worldliness, 17–18, 21, 63–4, 120n78
Wright, N. T., 1, 100, 266
Wright, Richard, 161n58

year-day theory, 48, 52, 86–86. *See also* futurism; historicism (interpretation of apocalyptic Scripture)

Zionism, 114. *See also* Israel: restoration of

www.ingramcontent.com/pod-product-compliance
Lightning Source LLC
Chambersburg PA
CBHW050621300426
44112CB00012B/1594